THE COMPLETE WORKS OF SAMUEL TAYLOR COLERIDGE.

WITH AN INTRODUCTORY ESSAY

UPON HIS

PHILOSOPHICAL AND THEOLOGICAL OPINIONS.

EDITED BY

PROFESSOR SHEDD.

IN SEVEN VOLUMFS.

VOL. IV.

NEW YORK:
HARPER & BROTHERS, PUBLISHERS,
Nos. 329 AND 331 PEARL STREET,
FRANKLIN SQUARE.
1853.

THE

COMPLETE WORKS

OF

SAMUEL TAYLOR COLERIDGE.

VOL. IV.

LECTURES UPON SHAKSPEARE

AND OTHER DRAMATISTS.

NEW YORK:
HARPER & BROTHERS.
1853.

NOTES AND LECTURES

UPON

SHAKSPEARE,

AND

SOME OF THE OLD POETS AND DRAMATISTS,

WITH OTHER LITERARY REMAINS

OF S. T. COLERIDGE.

EDITED BY MRS. H. N. COLERIDGE.

NEW YORK:
HARPER & BROTHERS.
1853.

TO

JOSEPH HENRY GREEN, ESQ.,

MEMBER OF THE ROYAL COLLEGE OF SURGEONS,

THE APPROVED FRIEND OF COLERIDGE,

This Volume

IS GRATEFULLY INSCRIBED.

ADVERTISEMENT.

THE present publication is for the most part a re-print of volumes i. and ii. of the Literary Remains, first published by my late husband in 1836. It consists in great measure of notes on poetry and dramatic literature, either written by my father's own hand, or taken down by others from his lectures. Of matter relating to the drama, and to poetry, however, there was not quite enough to fill a second volume; I have therefore added to the remarks on Shakspeare and contemporary dramatists, Dante, Milton, and other poets, some miscellaneous pieces, which, as being critical or on literary subjects, agree generally with the main contents of the volumes. Some of the lectures themselves, though purporting to be on the drama, appear miscellaneous. An old reviewer of the Literary Remains inquired how Asiatic and Greek Mythology, the Kabeiri, and the Samothracian Mysteries came to be treated of in the same discourse with Robinson Crusoe?—a question which would not have been asked by one who had been acquainted with the author's excursive habits of thought and of speech. His practice in this respect has been several times explained and, in some respects, vindicated by intelligent disciples, who had perceived the subtle logic of his "exhaustive and cyclical mode of discoursing."

The "Selections from Mr. Coleridge's Literary Correspondence," with the "Historie and Gestes of Maxilian," are republished by permission of the Messrs. Blackwood, to whose Magazine they were contributed on their first appearance. Notes of the late Editor are signed Ed., those of the present S. C. The Preface of the original Editor of the Literary Remains is re-printed, with the exception of a passage not applicable to the present publication.

PREFACE.

Mr. Coleridge by his will, dated in September, 1829, authorized his executor, if he should think it expedient, to publish any of the notes or writing made by him (Mr. C.) in his books, or any other of his manuscripts or writings, or any letters which should thereafter be collected from, or supplied by, his friends or correspondents. Agreeably to this authority, an arrangement was made, under the superintendence of Mr. Green, for the collection of Coleridge's literary remains; and at the same time the preparation for the press of such part of the materials as should consist of criticism and general literature, was intrusted to the care of the present Editor. The volume now offered to the public is the first result of that arrangement. It must in any case stand in need of much indulgence from the ingenuous reader;—*multa sunt condonanda in opere postumo;* but a short statement of the difficulties attending the compilation may serve to explain some apparent anomalies, and to preclude some unnecessary censure.

The materials were fragmentary in the extreme—Sibylline leaves;—notes of the lecturer, memoranda of the investigator, outpourings of the solitary and self-communing student. The fear of the press was not in them. Numerous as they were too, they came to light, or were communicated, at different times, before and after the printing was commenced; and the dates, the occasions, and the references, in most instances remained to be discovered or conjectured. To give to such materials method and continuity, as far as might be—to set them forth in the least disadvantageous manner which the circumstances would permit—was a delicate and perplexing task; and the Editor is painfully sensible that he could bring few qualifications for the undertaking, but such as were involved in a many years' intercourse with the author himself, a patient study of his writings, a reverential admiration of his genius, and an affectionate desire to help in extending its beneficial influence.

The contents of this volume are drawn from a portion only of the manuscripts intrusted to the Editor: the remainder of the collection, which, under favorable circumstances, he hopes may hereafter see the light, is at least of equal value with what is now presented to the reader as a sample. In perusing the following pages, the reader will, in a few instances, meet with disquisitions of a transcendental character, which, as a general rule, have been avoided: the truth is, that they were sometimes found so indissolubly intertwined with the more popular matter which preceded and followed, as to make separation impracticable. There are very many to whom no apology will be necessary in this respect; and the Editor only adverts to it for the purpose of obviating, as far as may be, the possible complaint of the more general reader. But there is another point to which, taught by past experience, he attaches more importance, and as to which, therefore, he ventures to put in a more express and particular caution. In many of the books and papers, which have been used in the compilation of these volumes, passages from other writers, noted down by Mr. Coleridge as in some way remarkable, were mixed up with his own comments on such passages, or with his reflections on other subjects, in a manner very embarrassing to the eye of a third person undertaking to select the original matter, after the lapse of several years. The Editor need not say that he has not knowingly admitted any thing that was not genuine. It is possible that some cases of mistake in this respect may have occurred. There may be one or two passages—they can not well be more—printed in this volume which belong to other writers; and if such there be, the Editor can only plead in excuse, that the work has been prepared by him amidst many distractions, and hope that, in this instance at least, no ungenerous use will be made of such a circumstance to the disadvantage of the author, and that persons of greater reading or more retentive memories than the Editor, who may discover any such passages, will do him the favor to communicate the fact.

To those who have been kind enough to communicate books

and manuscripts for the purpose of the present publication, the Editor and, through him, Mr. Coleridge's executor return their grateful thanks. In most cases a specific acknowledgment has been made. But, above and independently of all others, it is to Mr. and Mrs. Gillman, and to Mr. Green himself, that the public are indebted for the preservation and use of the principal part of the contents of this volume. The claims of those respected individuals on the gratitude of the friends and admirers of Coleridge and his works are already well known, and in due season those claims will receive additional confirmation.

With these remarks, sincerely conscious of his own inadequate execution of the task assigned to him, yet confident withal of the general worth of the contents of the following pages—the Editor commits the reliques of a great man to the indulgent consideration of the Public.

Lincoln's Inn,
August 11, 1836.

L'ENVOY.

He was one who with long and large arm still collected precious armfuls in whatever direction he pressed forward, yet still took up so much more than he could keep together, that those who followed him gleaned more from his continual droppings than he himself brought home;—nay, made stately corn-ricks therewith, while the reaper himself was still seen only with a strutting armful of newly-cut sheaves. But I should misinform you grossly if I left you to infer that his collections were a heap of incoherent *miscellanea*. No! the very contrary. Their variety, conjoined with the too great coherency, the too great both desire and power of referring them in systematic, nay, genetic subordination, was that which rendered his schemes gigantic and impracticable, as an author, and his conversation less instructive as a man. *Auditorem inopem ipsa copia fecit.*—Too much was given, all so weighty and brilliant as to preclude a chance of its being all received—so that it not seldom passed over the hearer's mind like a roar of many waters.

CONTENTS.

LITERARY REMAINS.

Extract from a Letter written by Mr. Coleridge, in February, 1818, *to a gentleman who attended the course of Lectures given in the spring of that year. See the Canterbury Magazine, September,* 1834.—Ed.

My next Friday's lecture will, if I do not grossly flatter-blind myself, be interesting, and the points of view not only original, but new to the audience. I make this distinction, because sixteen or rather seventeen years ago, (*a*)* I delivered eighteen lectures on Shakspeare at the Royal Institution; three fourths of which appeared at that time startling paradoxes, although they have since been adopted even by men, who then made use of them as proofs of my flighty and paradoxical turn of mind; all to prove that Shakspeare's judgment was, if possible, still more wonderful than his genius; or rather that the contradistinction itself between judgment and genius rested on an utterly false theory. This, and its proofs and grounds have been—I should not have said adopted, but produced as their own legitimate children by some, and by others the merit of them attributed to a foreign writer, whose lectures were not given orally till two years after mine, rather than to their countryman; though I dare appeal to the most adequate judges, as Sir George Beaumont, the Bishop of Durham, Mr. Sotheby, and afterwards to Mr. Rogers and Lord Byron, whether there is one single principle in Schlegel's work (which is not an admitted drawback from its merits), that was not established and applied in detail by me. Plutarch tells

* The letters refer to Notes at the end of the Volume by the present editor.

us, that egotism is a venial fault in the unfortunate, and justifiable in the calumniated, &c.

* * * * * * *

Extract from a Letter to J. Briton, Esq.

28th Feb., 1819, Highgate.

Dear Sir,—First permit me to remove a very natural, indeed almost inevitable, mistake, relative to my lectures: namely, that I *have* them, or that the lectures of one place or season are in any way repeated in another. So far from it, that on any point that I had ever studied (and on no other should I dare discourse —I mean, that I would not lecture on any subject for which I had to *acquire* the main knowledge, even though a month's or three months' previous time were allowed me; on no subject that had not employed my thoughts for a large portion of my life since earliest manhood, free of all outward and particular purpose)—on any point within my habit of thought, I should greatly prefer a subject I had never lectured on, to one which I had repeatedly given; and those who have attended me for any two seasons successively will bear witness, that the lecture given at the London Philosophical Society, on the *Romeo and Juliet*, for instance, was as different from that given at the Crown and Anchor, as if they had been by two individuals who, without any communication with each other, had only mastered the same principles of philosophic criticism. This was most strikingly evidenced in the coincidence between my lectures and those of Schlegel; such, and so close, that it was fortunate for my moral reputation that I had not only from five to seven hundred ear-witnesses that the passages had been given by me at the Royal Institution two years before Schlegel commenced his lectures at Vienna, but that notes had been taken of these by several men and ladies of high rank.(*b*) The fact is this; during a course of lectures, I faithfully employ all the intervening days in collecting and digesting the materials, whether I have or have not lectured on the same subject before, making no difference. The day of the lecture, till the hour of commencement, I devote to the consideration, what of the mass before me is best fitted to answer the purposes of a lecture, that is, to keep the audience awake and interested during the delivery, and to leave a sting behind, that is, a disposition to study the subject anew, under the light of a new principle. Several times, however, partly from apprehension respecting my health and animal spirits, partly from the wish to possess copies that might afterwards be marketable among the publishers, I have previously written the lecture; but before I had proceeded twenty minutes, I have been obliged to push the MS. away, and give the subject a new turn. Nay, this was so notorious, that many of my auditors used to threaten me, when they saw any number of written papers upon my desk, to steal them away; declaring they never felt so secure of a good lecture as when they perceived that I had not a single scrap of writing before me. I take far, far more pains than would go to the set composition of a lecture, both by varied reading and by meditation; but for the words, illustrations, &c., I know almost as little as any one of the audience (that is, those of any thing like the same education with myself) what they will be five minutes before the lecture begins. Such is my way, for such is my nature; and in attempting any other, I should only torment myself in order to disappoint my auditors—torment myself during the delivery, I mean; for in all other respects it would be a much shorter and easier task to deliver them from writing. I am anxious to preclude any semblance of affectation; and have therefore troubled you with this lengthy preface before I have the hardihood to assure you, that you might as well ask me what my dreams were in the year 1814, as what my course of lectures was at the Surrey Institution. *Fuimus Troes.*

SHAKSPEARE,

WITH INTRODUCTORY MATTER ON POETRY, THE DRAMA, AND THE STAGE.

DEFINITION OF POETRY.

POETRY is not the proper antithesis to prose, but to science. Poetry is opposed to science, and prose to metre. The proper and immediate object of science is the acquirement, or communication, of truth; the proper and immediate object of poetry is the communication of immediate pleasure. This definition is useful; but as it would include novels and other works of fiction, which yet we do not call poems, there must be some additional character by which poetry is not only divided from opposites, but likewise distinguished from disparate, though similar, modes of composition. Now how is this to be effected? In animated prose, the beauties of nature, and the passions and accidents of human nature, are often expressed in that natural language which the contemplation of them would suggest to a pure and benevolent mind; yet still neither we nor the writers call such a work a poem, though no work could deserve that name which did not include all this, together with something else. What is this? It is that pleasurable emotion, that peculiar state and degree of excitement, which arises in the poet himself in the act of composition;—and in order to understand this, we must combine a more than ordinary sympathy with the objects, emotions, or incidents contemplated by the poet, consequent on a more than common sensibility, with a more than ordinary activity of the mind in respect of the fancy and the imagination. Hence is produced a more vivid reflection of the truths of nature and of the human heart, united with a constant activity modifying and correcting these truths by that sort of pleasurable emotion, which the exertion of all our faculties gives in a certain degree; but which can only be felt in perfection under the full play of those powers of mind, which are spontaneous rather than voluntary, and in which the effort required bears no proportion to the activity enjoyed. This is the state which permits the production of a highly pleasurable whole, of which each part shall also communicate for itself a distinct and conscious pleasure; and hence arises the definition, which I trust is now intelligible, that poetry, or rather a poem, is a species of composition, opposed to science, as having intellectual pleasure for its object, and as attaining its end by the use of language natural to us in a state of excitement,—but distinguished from other species of composition, not excluded by the former criterion, by permitting a pleasure from the whole consistent with a consciousness of pleasure from the component parts;—and the perfection of which is, to communicate from each part the greatest immediate pleasure compatible with the largest sum of pleasure on the whole. This, of course, will vary with the different modes of poetry;—and that splendor of particular lines, which would be worthy of admiration in an impassioned elegy, or a short indignant satire, would be a blemish and proof of vile taste in a tragedy or an epic poem.

It is remarkable, by the way, that Milton in three incidental words has implied all which for the purposes of more distinct apprehension, which at first must be slow-paced in order to be distinct, I have endeavored to develop in a precise and strictly adequate definition. Speaking of poetry, he says, as in a parenthesis, "which is simple, sensuous, passionate." How awful is the power of words!—fearful often in their consequences when merely felt, not understood; but most awful when both felt and understood!—Had these three words only been properly understood by, and present in the minds of, general readers, not only almost a library of false poetry would have been either precluded or still-born, but, what is of more consequence, works truly excellent and capable of enlarging the understanding, warming and purifying the heart, and placing in the centre of the whole being the germs of noble and manlike actions, would have been the common diet of the intellect instead. For the first condition, simplicity,—while, on the one hand, it distinguishes poetry from the arduous processes of science, laboring towards an end not yet arrived at, and supposes a smooth and finished road, on which the reader is to walk onward easily, with streams murmuring by his side, and trees and flowers and human dwellings to make his journey as delightful as the object of it is desirable, instead of having to toil with the pioneers, and painfully make the road on which others are to travel,—precludes, on the other hand, every affectation and morbid peculiarity;—the second condition, sensuousness, insures that framework of objectivity, that definiteness and articulation of imagery, and that modification of the images themselves, without which poetry becomes flattened into mere didactics of practice, or evaporated into a hazy, unthoughtful day-dreaming; and the third condition, passion, provides that neither thought nor imagery shall be simply objective, but that the *passio vera* of humanity shall warm and animate both.

To return, however, to the previous definition, this most general and distinctive character of a poem originates in the poetic genius itself; and though it comprises whatever can with any propriety be called a poem (unless that word be a mere lazy synonyme for a composition in metre), it yet becomes a just, and not merely discriminative, but full and adequate, definition of poetry in its highest and most peculiar sense, only so far as the distinction still results from the poetic genius, which sustains and modifies the emotions, thoughts, and vivid representations of the poem by the energy without effort of the poet's own mind,—by the spontaneous activity of his imagination and fancy, and by whatever else with these reveals itself in the balancing and reconciling of opposite or discordant qualities, sameness with difference, a sense of novelty and freshness with old or customary objects, a more than usual state of emotion with more than usual order, self-possession and judgment with enthusiasm and vehement feeling,—and which, while it blends and harmonizes the natural and the artificial, still subordinates art to nature, the manner to the matter, and our admiration of the poet to our sympathy with the images, passions, characters, and incidents of the poem :—

Doubtless, this could not be, but that she turns
Bodies to *spirit* by sublimation strange,
As fire converts to fire the things it burns—
As we our food into our nature change !

From their gross matter she abstracts *their* forms,
And draws a kind of quintessence from things,
Which to her proper nature she transforms
To bear them light on her celestial wings !

Thus doth she, when from *individual states*
She doth abstract the universal kinds,
Which then reclothed in divers names and fates
*Steal access thro' our senses to our minds.**

GREEK DRAMA. (*c*) †

It is truly singular that Plato,—whose philosophy and religion were but exotic at home, and a mere opposition to the finite in

* Sir John Davies on the Immortality of the Soul, sect. iv. The words and lines in italics are substituted to apply these verses to the poetic genius. The greater part of this latter paragraph may be found adopted, with some alterations, in the *Biographia Literaria*, III. p. 374; but I have thought it better in this instance and some others, to run the chance of bringing a few passages twice over to the recollection of the reader, than to weaken the force of the original argument by breaking the connection.—*Ed.*

† The Notes to this Essay, to which the numbers refer, are placed at the end of the volume.

all things, genuine prophet and anticipator as he was of the Protestant Christian æra,—should have given in his Dialogue of the Banquet, a justification of our Shakspeare. (1) For he relates that, when all the other guests had either dispersed or fallen asleep, Socrates only, together with Aristophanes and Agathon, remained awake, and that, while he continued to drink with them out of a large goblet, he compelled them, though most reluctantly, to admit that it was the business of one and the same genius to excel in tragic and comic poetry, or that the tragic poet ought, at the same time, to contain within himself the powers of comedy.* Now, as this was directly repugnant to the entire theory of the ancient critics, and contrary to all their experience, it is evident that Plato must have fixed the eye of his contemplation on the innermost essentials of the drama, abstracted from the forms of age or country. In another passage he even adds the reason, namely, that opposites illustrate each other's nature, and in their struggle draw forth the strength of the combatants, and display the conqueror as sovereign even on the territories of the rival power.

Nothing can more forcibly exemplify the separative spirit of the Greek arts than their comedy as opposed to their tragedy. But as the immediate struggle of contraries supposes an arena common to both, so both were alike ideal; that is, the comedy of Aristophanes rose to as great a distance above the ludicrous of real life, as the tragedy of Sophocles above its tragic events and passions, (2)—and it is in this one point, of absolute ideality, that the comedy of Shakspeare and the old comedy of Athens coincide. In this also alone did the Greek tragedy and comedy unite; in every thing else they were exactly opposed to each other. (3) Tragedy is poetry in its deepest earnest; comedy is poetry in unlimited jest. Earnestness consists in the direction and convergence of all the powers of the soul to one aim, and in the volun-

* —— *ἐξεγρόμενος δὲ ἰδεῖν τοὺς μὲν ἄλλους καθεύδοντας καὶ οἰχομένους, Αγάθωνα δὲ καὶ 'Αριστοφάνην καὶ Σωκράτη ἔτι μόνους ἐγρηγορέναι, καὶ πίνειν ἐκ φιάλης μεγάλης ἐπὶδεξιά. τὸν οὖν Σωκράτη αὐτοῖς διαλέγεσθαι· καὶ τὰ μὲν ἄλλα ὁ 'Αριστόδημος οὐκ ἔφη μεμνῆσθαι τὸν λόγον· (οὔτε γὰρ ἐξ ἀρχῆς παραγενέσθαι, ὑπονυστάζειν τε) τὸ μέντοι κεφάλαιον ἔφη, προσαναγκάζειν τὸν Σωκράτη ὁμολογεῖν αὐτοὺς τοῦ αὐτοῦ ἀνδρὸς εἶναι κωμῳδίαν καὶ τραγωδίαν ἐπίστασθαι ποιεῖν, καὶ τὸν τέχνῃ τραγῳδοποιὸν ὄντα, καὶ κωμῳδοποιὸν εἶναι.*

Symp. sub fine.

tary restraint of its activity in consequence; the opposite, therefore, lies in the apparent abandonment of all definite aim or end, and in the removal of all bounds in the exercise of the mind,—attaining its real end, as an entire contrast, most perfectly, the greater the display is of intellectual wealth squandered in the wantonness of sport without an object, and the more abundant the life and vivacity in the creations of the arbitrary will.

The later comedy, even where it was really comic, was doubtless likewise more comic, the more free it appeared from any fixed aim. Misunderstandings of intention, fruitless struggles of absurd passion, contradictions of temper, and laughable situations there were; but still the form of the representation itself was serious; it proceeded as much according to settled laws, and used as much the same means of art, though to a different purpose, as the regular tragedy itself. But in the old comedy the very form itself is whimsical; the whole work is one great jest, comprehending a world of jests within it, among which each maintains its own place without seeming to concern itself as to the relation in which it may stand to its fellows. In short, in Sophocles, the constitution of tragedy is monarchical, but such as it existed in elder Greece, limited by laws, and therefore the more venerable,—all the parts adapting and submitting themselves to the majesty of the heroic sceptre:—in Aristophanes, comedy, on the contrary, is poetry in its most democratic form, and it is a fundamental principle with it, rather to risk all the confusion of anarchy, than to destroy the independence and privileges of its individual constituents,—place, verse, characters, even single thoughts, conceits, and allusions, each turning on the pivot of its own free will.

The tragic poet idealizes his characters by giving to the spiritual part of our nature a more decided preponderance over the animal cravings and impulses, than is met with in real life: the comic poet idealizes his characters by making the animal the governing power, and the intellectual the mere instrument. But as tragedy is not a collection of virtues and perfections, but takes care only that the vices and imperfections shall spring from the passions, errors, and prejudices which arise out of the soul;—so neither is comedy a mere crowd of vices and follies, but whatever qualities it represents, even though they are in a certain sense amiable, it still displays them as having their origin in some dependence on our lower nature, accompanied with a defect in true freedom of spirit and self-subsistence, and subject to that unconnection by contradictions of the inward being, to which all folly is owing.

The ideal of earnest poetry consists in the union and harmonious melting down, and fusion of the sensual into the spiritual,—of man as an animal into man as a power of reason and self-government. And this we have represented to us most clearly in the plastic art, or statuary; where the perfection of outward form is a symbol of the perfection of an inward idea; where the body is wholly penetrated by the soul, and spiritualized even to a state of glory, and like a transparent substance, the matter, in its own nature darkness, becomes altogether a vehicle and fixure of light, a mean of developing its beauties, and unfolding its wealth of various colors without disturbing its unity, or causing a division of the parts. The sportive ideal, on the contrary, consists in the perfect harmony and concord of the higher nature with the animal, as with its ruling principle and its acknowledged regent. The understanding and practical reason are represented as the willing slaves of the senses and appetites, and of the passions arising out of them. Hence we may admit the appropriateness to the old comedy, as a work of defined art, of allusions and descriptions, which morality can never justify, and, only with reference to the author himself, and only as being the effect or rather the cause of the circumstances in which he wrote, can consent even to palliate. (4)

The old comedy rose to its perfection in Aristophanes, and in him also it died with the freedom of Greece. Then arose a species of drama, more fitly called, dramatic entertainment than comedy, but of which, nevertheless, our modern comedy (Shakspeare's altogether excepted) is the genuine descendant. Euripides had already brought tragedy lower down and by many steps nearer to the real world than his predecessors had ever done, and the passionate admiration which Menander and Philemon expressed for him, and their open avowals that he was their great master, entitle us to consider their dramas as of a middle species, between tragedy and comedy,—not the tragi-comedy, or thing of heterogeneous parts, but a complete whole, founded on principles of its own. Throughout we find the drama of Menander distinguishing itself from tragedy, but not, as the genuine old comedy, contrasting with, and opposing it. Tragedy, indeed, carried the thoughts into the mythologic world, in order to raise the emotions, the fears, and the hopes, which convince the inmost heart that their final cause is not to be discovered in the limits of mere mortal life, and force us into a presentiment, however dim, of a state in which those struggles of inward free will with outward necessity, which form the true subject of the tragedian, shall be reconciled and solved ;—the entertainment or new comedy, on the other hand, remained within the circle of experience. Instead of the tragic destiny, it introduced the power of chance ; even in the few fragments of Menander and Philemon now remaining to us, we find many exclamations and reflections concerning chance and fortune, as in the tragic poets concerning destiny. In tragedy, the moral law, either as obeyed or violated, above all consequences—its own maintenance or violation constituting the most important of all consequences—forms the ground ; the new comedy, and our modern comedy in general (Shakspeare excepted as before), lies in prudence or imprudence, enlightened or misled self-love. The whole moral system of the entertainment exactly like that of fable, consists in rules of prudence, with an exquisite conciseness, and at the same time an exhaustive fulness of sense. An old critic said that tragedy was the flight or elevation of life, comedy (that of Menander) its arrangement or ordonnance. (5)

Add to these features a portrait-like truth of character,—not so far indeed as that a *bona fide* individual should be described or imagined, but yet so that the features which give interest and permanence to the class should be individualized. The old tragedy moved in an ideal world,—the old comedy in a fantastic world. As the entertainment, or new comedy, restrained the creative activity both of the fancy and the imagination, it indemnified the understanding in appealing to the judgment for the probability of the scenes represented. The ancients themselves acknowledged the new comedy as an exact copy of real life. The grammarian, Aristophanes, somewhat affectedly exclaimed : "O Life and Menander, which of you two imitated the other ?" In short, the form of this species of drama was poetry, the stuff or matter was prose. It was prose rendered delightful by the blandishments and measured motions of the muse. Yet even this was not universal. The mimes of Sophron, so passionately admired by Plato, were written in prose, and were scenes out of real life conducted in dialogue. The exquisite Feast of Adonis (Συρακούσιαι ἢ Ἀδωνιάζουσαι) in Theocritus, we are told, with some others of his eclogues, were close imitations of certain mimes of Sophron—free translations of the prose into hexameters. (6)

It will not be improper, in this place, to make a few remarks on the remarkable character and functions of the chorus in the Greek tragic drama.

The chorus entered from below, close by the orchestra, and there, pacing to and fro during the choral odes, performed their solemn measured dance. In the centre of the *orchestra*, directly over against the middle of the *scene*, there stood an elevation with steps in the shape of a large altar, as high as the boards of the *logeion* or movable stage. This elevation was named the *thymele* (θυμέλη), and served to recall the origin and original purpose of the chorus, as an altar-song in honor of the presiding deity. Here, and on these steps, the persons of the chorus sate collectively, when they were not singing; attending to the dialogue as spectators, and acting as (what in truth they were) the ideal representatives of the real audience, and of the poet himself in his own character, assuming the supposed impressions made by the drama, in order to direct and rule them. But when the chorus itself formed part of the dialogue, then the leader of the band, the foreman or *coryphæus*, ascended, as some think, the level summit of the *thymele*, in order to command the stage, or, perhaps, the whole chorus advanced to the front of the orchestra, and thus put themselves in ideal connection, as it were, with the *dramatis personæ* there acting. This *thymele* was in the centre of the whole edifice, all the measurements were calculated, and the semicircle of the amphitheatre was drawn, from this point. It had a double use, a two-fold purpose; it constantly reminded the spectators of the origin of tragedy as a religious service, and declared itself as the ideal representative of the audience by having its place exactly in the point, to which all the radii from the different seats or benches converged. (7)

In this double character, as constituent parts, and yet at the same time as spectators, of the drama, the chorus could not but tend to enforce the unity of place;—not on the score of any supposed improbability, which the understanding or common sense might detect in a change of place ;—but because the senses themselves put it out of the power of any imagination to conceive a place coming to and going away from the persons, instead of the persons changing their place. Yet there are instances in which, during the silence of the chorus, the poets have hazarded this by a change in that part of the scenery which represented the more distant objects to the eye of the spectator—a demonstrative proof, that this alternately extolled and ridiculed unity (as ignorantly ridiculed as extolled) was grounded on no essential principle of reason, but arose out of circumstances which the poet could not remove, and therefore took up into the form of the drama, and co-organized it with all the other parts into a living whole. (8)

The Greek tragedy may rather be compared to our serious opera than to the tragedies of Shakspeare ; nevertheless, the difference is far greater than the likeness. In the opera all is subordinated to the music, the dresses and the scenery ;—the poetry is a mere vehicle for articulation, and as little pleasure is lost by ignorance of the Italian language, so is little gained by the knowledge of it. But in the Greek drama all was but as instruments and accessories to the poetry ; and hence we should form a better notion of the choral music from the solemn hymns and psalms of austere church music than from any species of theatrical singing. A single flute or pipe was the ordinary accompaniment ; and it is not to be supposed, that any display of musical power was allowed to obscure the distinct hearing of the words. On the contrary, the evident purpose was to render the words more audible, and to secure by the elevations and pauses greater facility of understanding the poetry. For the choral songs are, and ever must have been, the most difficult part of the tragedy ; there occur in them the most involved verbal compounds, the newest expressions, the boldest images, the most recondite allusions. Is it credible that the poets would, one and all, have been thus prodigal of the stores of art and genius, if they had known that in the representation the whole must have been lost to the audience,—at a time too when the means of after-publication were so difficult and expensive, and the copies of their works so slowly and narrowly circulated ? (9)

The masks also must be considered—their vast variety and admirable workmanship. Of this we retain proof by the marble masks which represented them ; but to this in the real mask we must add the thinness of the substance and the exquisite fitting on to the head of the actor; so that not only were the very eyes painted with a single opening left for the pupil of the actor's eye, but in some instances, even the iris itself was painted, when the color was a known characteristic of the divine or heroic personage represented. (10)

Finally, I will note down those fundamental characteristics which contra-distinguish the ancient literature from the modern generally, but which more especially appear in prominence in the tragic drama. The ancient was allied to statuary, the modern refers to painting. In the first there is a predominance of rhythm and melody, in the second of harmony and counterpoint. The Greeks idolized the finite, and therefore were the masters of all grace, elegance, proportion, fancy, dignity, majesty—of whatever, in short, is capable of being definitely conveyed by defined forms or thoughts: the moderns revere the infinite, and affect the indefinite as a vehicle of the infinite;—hence their passions, their obscure hopes and fears, their wandering through the unknown, their grander moral feelings, their more august conception of man as man, their future rather than their past—in a word, their sublimity. (11)

PROGRESS OF THE DRAMA.

Let two persons join in the same scheme to ridicule a third, and either take advantage of, or invent, some story for that purpose, and mimicry will have already produced a sort of rude comedy. It becomes an inviting treat to the populace, and gains an additional zest and burlesque by following the already established plan of tragedy; and the first man of genius who seizes the idea, and reduces it into form,—into a work of art,—by metre and music, is the Aristophanes of the country.

How just this account is will appear from the fact that in the first or old comedy of the Athenians, most of the *dramatis personæ* were living characters introduced under their own names; and no doubt, their ordinary dress, manner, person and voice were closely mimicked. In less favorable states of society, as that of England in the middle ages, the beginnings of comedy would be constantly taking place from the mimics and satirical minstrels; but from want of fixed abode, popular government, and the successive attendance of the same auditors, it would still remain in embryo. I shall, perhaps, have occasion to observe that this remark is not without importance in explaining the essential differences of the modern and ancient theatres.

Phenomena, similar to those which accompanied the origin of tragedy and comedy among the Greeks, would take place among the Romans much more slowly, and the drama would, in any case, have much longer remained in its first irregular form from the character of the people, their continual engagements in wars of conquest, the nature of their government, and their rapidly increasing empire. But, however this might have been, the conquest of Greece precluded both the process and the necessity of it; and the Roman stage at once presented imitations or translations of the Greek drama. This continued till the perfect establishment of Christianity. Some attempts, indeed, were made to adapt the persons of Scriptural or ecclesiastical history to the drama; and sacred plays, it is probable, were not unknown in Constantinople under the emperors of the East. The first of the kind is, I believe, the only one preserved,—namely, the *Χριστὸς Πάσχων*, or "Christ in his sufferings," by Gregory Nazianzen,—possibly written in consequence of the prohibition of profane literature to the Christians by the apostate Julian.* In the West, however, the enslaved and debauched Roman world became too barbarous for any theatrical exhibitions more refined than those of pageants and chariot-races; while the spirit of Christianity, which in its most corrupt form still breathed general humanity, whenever controversies of faith were not concerned, had done away the cruel combats of the gladiators, and the loss of the distant provinces prevented the possibility of exhibiting the engagements of wild beasts.

I pass, therefore, at once to the feudal ages which soon succeeded, confining my observation to this country; though, indeed, the same remark with very few alterations will apply to all the other states, into which the great empire was broken. Ages of darkness succeeded;—not, indeed, the darkness of Russia or of the barbarous lands unconquered by Rome; for from the time of Honorius to the destruction of Constantinople and the consequent introduction of ancient literature into Europe, there was a contin-

* A.D. 363. But I believe the prevailing opinion amongst scholars now is, that the Χριστὸς Πάσχων is not genuine.—*Ed.*

ued succession of individual intellects;—the golden chain was never wholly broken, though the connecting links were often of baser metal. A dark cloud, like another sky, covered the entire cope of heaven,—but in this place it thinned away, and white stains of light showed a half-eclipsed star behind it,—in that place it was rent asunder, and a star passed across the opening in all its brightness, and then vanished. Such stars exhibited themselves only; surrounding objects did not partake of their light. There were deep wells of knowledge, but no fertilizing rills and rivulets. For the drama, society was altogether a state of chaos, out of which it was, for a while at least, to proceed anew, as if there had been none before it. And yet it is not undelightful to contemplate the eduction of good from evil. The ignorance of the great mass of our countrymen was the efficient cause of the reproduction of the drama; and the preceding darkness and the returning light were alike necessary in order to the creation of a Shakspeare.

The drama recommenced in England, as it first began in Greece, in religion. The people were not able to read,—the priesthood were unwilling that they should read; and yet their own interest compelled them not to leave the people wholly ignorant of the great events of sacred history. They did that, therefore, by scenic representations, which in after-ages it has been attempted to do in Roman Catholic countries by pictures. They presented Mysteries, and often at great expense; and reliques of this system still remain in the south of Europe, and indeed throughout Italy, where at Christmas the convents and the great nobles rival each other in the scenic representation of the birth of Christ and its circumstances. I heard two instances mentioned to me at different times, one in Sicily and the other in Rome, of noble devotees, the ruin of whose fortunes was said to have commenced in the extravagant expense which had been incurred in presenting the *præsepe* or manger. But these Mysteries, in order to answer their design, must not only be instructive, but entertaining; and as, when they became so, the people began to take pleasure in acting them themselves—in interloping,—(against which the priests seem to have fought hard and yet in vain) the most ludicrous images were mixed with the most awful personations; and whatever the subject might be, however sublime, however pathetic, yet the Vice and the Devil, who are the genuine antecessors of Harlequin and the Clown, were necessary component parts. I have myself a piece of this kind which I transcribed a few years ago at Helmstadt, in Germany, on the education of Eve's children, in which after the fall and repentance of Adam, the offended Maker, as in proof of his reconciliation, condescends to visit them, and to catechize the children,—who with a noble contempt of chronology are all brought together from Abel to Noah. The good children say the ten Commandments, the Belief and the Lord's Prayer; but Cain and his rout, after he had received a box on the ear for not taking off his hat, and afterwards offering his left hand, is prompted by the devil so to blunder in the Lord's Prayer as to reverse the petitions and say it backward!*

Unaffectedly I declare I feel pain at repetitions like these, however innocent. As historical documents they are valuable; but I am sensible that what I can read with my eye with perfect innocence, I can not without inward fear and misgivings pronounce with my tongue.

Let me, however, be acquitted of presumption if I say that I can not agree with Mr. Malone, that our ancestors did not perceive the ludicrous in these things, or that they paid no separate attention to the serious and comic parts. Indeed his own statement contradicts it. For what purpose should the Vice leap upon the Devil's back and belabor him, but to produce this separate attention? The people laughed heartily, no doubt. Nor can I conceive any meaning attached to the words "separate attention," that is not fully answered by one part of an exhibition exciting seriousness or pity, and the other raising mirth and loud laughter. That they felt no impiety in the affair is most true. For it is the very essence of that system of Christian polytheism, which in all its essentials is now fully as gross in Spain, in Sicily and the south of Italy, as it ever was in England in the days of Henry VI.—(nay, more so, for a Wicliffe had not then appeared only, but scattered the good seed widely), it is an essential part, I say, of that system to draw the mind wholly from its own inward whispers and quiet discriminations, and to habituate the conscience to pronounce sentence in every case according to the established verdicts of the church and the casuists. I have looked

* See pp. 238, 239, where this is told more at length and attributed to Hans Sachs.—*Ed.*

through volume after volume of the most approved casuists,—and still I find disquisitions whether this or that act is right, and under what circumstances, to a minuteness that makes reasoning ridiculous, and of a callous and unnatural immodesty, to which none but a monk could harden himself, who has been stripped of all the tender charities of life, yet is goaded on to make war against them by the unsubdued hauntings of our meaner nature, even as dogs are said to get the *hydrophobia* from excessive thirst. I fully believe that our ancestors laughed as heartily, as their posterity do at Grimaldi;—and not having been told that they would be punished for laughing, they thought it very innocent; and if their priests had left out murder in the catalogue of their prohibitions (as indeed they did under certain circumstances of heresy), the greater part of them,—the moral instincts common to all men having been smothered and kept from development,—would have thought as little of murder.

However this may be, the necessity of at once instructing and gratifying the people produced the great distinction between the Greek and the English theatres;—for to this we must attribute the origin of tragi-comedy, or a representation of human events more lively, nearer the truth, and permitting a larger field of moral instruction, a more ample exhibition of the recesses of the human heart, under all the trials and circumstances that most concern us, than was known or guessed at by Æschylus, Sophocles, or Euripides;—and at the same time we learn to account for, and—relatively to the author—perceive the necessity of, the Fool or Clown, or both, as the substitutes of the Vice and the Devil, which our ancestors had been so accustomed to see in every exhibition of the stage, that they could not feel any performance perfect without them. Even to this day in Italy, every opera—(even Metastasio obeyed the claim throughout)—must have six characters, generally two pairs of cross lovers, a tyrant and a confidant, or a father and two confidants, themselves lovers;—and when a new opera appears, it is the universal fashion to ask—which is the tyrant, which the lover? &c.

It is the especial honor of Christianity, that in its worst and most corrupted form it can not wholly separate itself from morality;—whereas the other religions in their best form (I do not include Mohammedanism, which is only an anomalous corruption of Christianity, like Swedenborgianism), have no connection with it. The very impersonation of moral evil under the name of Vice, facilitated all other impersonations; and hence we see that the Mysteries were succeeded by Moralities, or dialogues and plots of allegorical personages. Again, some character in real history had become so famous, so proverbial, as Nero for instance, that they were introduced instead of the moral quality, for which they were so noted;—and in this manner the stage was moving on to the absolute production of heroic and comic real characters, when the restoration of literature, followed by the ever-blessed Reformation, let in upon the kingdom not only new knowledge, but new motive. A useful rivalry commenced between the metropolis on the one hand, the residence, independently of the court and nobles, of the most active and stirring spirits who had not been regularly educated, or who, from mischance or otherwise, had forsaken the beaten track of preferment,—and the universities on the other. The latter prided themselves on their closer approximation to the ancient rules and ancient regularity—taking the theatre of Greece, or rather its dim reflection, the rhetorical tragedies of the poet Seneca, as a perfect ideal, without any critical collation of the times, origin, or circumstances;—whilst, in the meantime, the popular writers, who could not, and would not abandon what they had found to delight their countrymen sincerely, and not merely from inquiries first put to the recollection of rules, and answered in the affirmative, as if it had been an arithmetical sum, did yet borrow from the scholars whatever they advantageously could, consistently with their own peculiar means of pleasing.

And here let me pause for a moment's contemplation of this interesting subject.

We call, for we see and feel, the swan and the dove both transcendently beautiful. As absurd as it would be to institute a comparison between their separate claims to beauty from any abstract rule common to both, without reference to the life and being of the animals themselves,—or as if, having first seen the dove, we abstracted its outlines, gave them a false generalization, called them the principles or ideal of bird-beauty, and then proceeded to criticize the swan or the eagle;—not less absurd is it to pass judgment on the works of a poet on the mere ground that they have been called by the same class-name with the works of other poets in other times and circumstances, or on any ground, indeed, save that of their inappropriateness to their own end and being, their want of significance, as symbols or physiognomy.

O! few have there been among critics, who have followed with the eye of the imagination the imperishable yet ever wandering spirit of poetry through its various metempsychoses, and consequent metamorphoses; or who have rejoiced in the light of clear perception at beholding with each new birth, with each rare *avatar*, the human race frame to itself a new body, by assimilating materials of nourishment out of its new circumstances, and work for itself new organs of power appropriate to the new sphere of its motion and activity! (*d*)

I have before spoken of the Romance, or the language formed out of the decayed Roman and the Northern tongues; and comparing it with the Latin, we find it less perfect in simplicity and relation—the privileges of a language formed by the mere attraction of homogeneous parts;—but yet more rich, more expressive and various, as one formed by more obscure affinities out of a chaos of apparently heterogeneous atoms. As more than a metaphor,—as an analogy of this, I have named the true genuine modern poetry the romantic; and the works of Shakspeare are romantic poetry revealing itself in the drama. If the tragedies of Sophocles are in the strict sense of the word tragedies, and the comedies of Aristophanes comedies, we must emancipate ourselves from a false association arising from misapplied names, and find a new word for the plays of Shakspeare. For they are, in the ancient sense, neither tragedies nor comedies, nor both in one,—but a different *genus*, diverse in kind, and not merely different in degree. They may be called romantic dramas, or dramatic romances. (*e*)

A deviation from the simple forms and unities of the ancient stage is an essential principle, and, of course, an appropriate excellence, of the romantic drama. For these unities were to a great extent the natural form of that which in its elements was homogeneous, and the representation of which was addressed preeminently to the outward senses;—and though the fable, the language and the characters appealed to the reason rather than to the mere understanding, inasmuch as they supposed an ideal state rather than referred to an existing reality—yet it was a reason which was obliged to accommodate itself to the senses, and so far became a sort of more elevated understanding. On the other hand, the romantic poetry—the Shaksperian drama—appealed to the imagination rather than to the senses, and to the reason as contemplating our inward nature, and the workings of the passions in their most retired recesses. But the reason, as reason, is independent of time and space; it has nothing to do with them: and hence the certainties of reason have been called eternal truths. As for example—the endless properties of the circle;—what connection have they with this or that age, with this or that country?—The reason is aloof from time and space; the imagination is an arbitrary controller over both;—and if only the poet have such power of exciting our internal emotions as to make us present to the scene in imagination chiefly, he acquires the right and privilege of using time and space as they exist in imagination, and obedient only to the laws by which the imagination itself acts (*f*). These laws it will be my object and aim to point out as the examples occur, which illustrate them. But here let me remark what can never be too often reflected on by all who would intelligently study the works either of the Athenian dramatists, or of Shakspeare, that the very essence of the former consists in the sternest separation of the diverse in kind and the disparate in the degree, whilst the latter delights in interlacing, by a rainbow-like transfusion of hues, the one with the other.

And here it will be necessary to say a few words on the stage and on stage-illusion.

A theatre, in the widest sense of the word, is the general term for all places of amusement through the ear or eye, in which men assemble in order to be amused by some entertainment presented to all at the same time and in common. Thus, an old Puritan divine says:—"Those who attend public worship and sermons only to amuse themselves, make a theatre of the church, and turn God's house into the devil's. *Theatra ædes diabololatricæ.*" The most important and dignified species of this *genus* is, doubtless, the stage (*res theatralis histrionica*), which, in addition to the generic definition above given, may be characterized in its idea, or according to what it does, or ought to, aim at, as a combination of several or of all the fine arts in an harmonious whole, having a distinct end of its own, to which the peculiar end of each of the component arts, taken separately, is made subordinate and subservient—that, namely, of imitating reality—whether external things, actions, or passions—under a semblance of reality. Thus, Claude imitates a landscape at sunset, but only as a picture; while a forest-scene is not presented to the spectators as a picture, but as a forest; and though, in the full sense of the word, we are no more deceived by the one than by the other, yet are our feelings very differently affected; and the pleasure derived from the one is not composed of the same elements as that afforded by the other, even on the supposition that the *quantum* of both were equal. In the former, a picture, it is a condition of all genuine delight that we should not be deceived; in the latter, stage-scenery (inasmuch as its principal end is not in or for itself, as is the case in a picture, but to be an assistance and means to an end out of itself), its very purpose is to produce as much illusion as its nature permits. These, and all other stage presentations, are to produce a sort of temporary half-faith, which the spectator encourages in himself and supports by a voluntary contribution on his own part, because he knows that it is at all times in his power to see the thing as it really is. I have often observed that little children are actually deceived by stage-scenery, never by pictures; though even these produce an effect on their impressible minds, which they do not on the minds of adults. The child, if strongly impressed, does not indeed positively think the picture to be the reality; but yet he does not think the contrary. As Sir George Beaumont was showing me a very fine engraving from Rubens, representing a storm at sea without any vessel or boat introduced, my little boy, then about five years old, came dancing and singing into the room, and all at once (if I may so say) *tumbled in* upon the print. He instantly started, stood silent and motionless, with the strongest expression, first of wonder and then of grief in his eyes and countenance, and at length said, "And where is the ship? But that is sunk, and the men are all drowned!" still keeping his eyes fixed on the print Now what pictures are to little children, stage illusion is to men, provided they retain any part of the child's sensibility; except, that in the latter instance, the suspension of the act of comparison, which permits this sort of negative belief, is somewhat more assisted by the will, than in that of a child respecting a picture.

The true stage-illusion in this and in all other things consists—not in the mind's judging it to be a forest, but, in its remission of the judgment that it is not a forest. And this subject of stage-illusion is so important, and so many practical errors and false criticisms may arise, and indeed have arisen, either from reasoning on it as actual delusion (the strange notion, on which the French critics built up their theory, and on which the French poets justify the construction of their tragedies), or from denying it altogether (which seems the end of Dr. Johnson's reasoning, and which, as extremes meet, would lead to the very same consequences, by excluding whatever would not be judged probable by us in our coolest state of feeling, with all our faculties in even balance), that these few remarks will, I hope, be pardoned, if they should serve either to explain or to illustrate the point. For not only are we never absolutely deluded—or any thing like it, but the attempt to cause the highest delusion possible to beings in their senses sitting in a theatre, is a gross fault, incident only to low minds, which, feeling that they can not affect the heart or head permanently, endeavor to call forth the momentary affections. There ought never to be more pain than is compatible with co-existing pleasure, and to be amply repaid by thought.

Shakspeare found the infant stage demanding an intermixture of ludicrous character as imperiously as that of Greece did the chorus, and high language accordant. And there are many advantages in this;—a greater assimilation to nature, a greater scope of power, more truths, and more feelings;—the effects of contrast, as in Lear and the Fool; and especially this, that the true language of passion becomes sufficiently elevated by your having previously heard, in the same piece, the lighter conversation of men under no strong emotion. The very nakedness of the stage, too, was advantageous—for the drama thence became something between a recitation and a re-presentation; and the absence or paucity of scenes allowed a freedom from the laws of unity of place and unity of time, the observance of which must either confine the drama to as few subjects as may be counted on the fingers, or involve gross improbabilities, far more striking than the violation would have caused. Thence, also, was precluded the danger of a false ideal—of aiming at more than what is possible on the whole. What play of the ancients, with reference to their ideal, does not hold out more glaring absurdities than any in Shakspeare? On the Greek plan a man could more easily be a poet than a dramatist; upon our plan more easily a dramatist than a poet.

THE DRAMA GENERALLY, AND PUBLIC TASTE.

Unaccustomed to address such an audience, and having lost by a long interval of confinement the advantages of my former short schooling, I had miscalculated in my last Lecture the proportion of my matter to my time, and by bad economy and unskilful management, the several heads of my discourse failed in making the entire performance correspond with the promise publicly circulated in the weekly annunciation of the subjects, to be treated. It would indeed have been wiser in me, and perhaps better on the whole, if I had caused my Lectures to be announced only as continuations of the main subject. But if I be, as perforce I must be, gratified by the recollection of whatever has appeared to give you pleasure, I am conscious of something better, though less flattering, a sense of unfeigned gratitude for your forbearance with my defects. Like affectionate guardians, you see without disgust the awkwardness, and witness with sympathy the growing pains, of a youthful endeavor, and look forward with a hope, which is its own reward, to the contingent results of practice—to its intellectual maturity.

In my last address I defined poetry to be the art, or whatever better term our language may afford, of representing external nature and human thoughts, both relatively to human affections, so as to cause the production of as great immediate pleasure in each part as is compatible with the largest possible sum of pleasure on the whole. Now this definition applies equally to painting and music as to poetry ; and in truth the term poetry is alike applicable to all three. The vehicle alone constitutes the difference ; and the term 'poetry' is rightly applied by eminence to measured words, only because the sphere of their action is far wider, the power of giving permanence to them much more certain, and incomparably greater the facility, by which men, not defective by nature or disease, may be enabled to derive habitual pleasure and instruction from them. On my mentioning these considerations to a painter of great genius, who had been, from a most honorable enthusiasm, extolling his own art, he was so struck with their truth, that he exclaimed, "I want no other arguments ;—poetry, that is, verbal poetry, must be the greatest ; all that proves final causes in the world, proves this ; it would be shocking to think otherwise !"—And in truth, deeply, O! far more than words can express, as I venerate the Last Judgment and the Prophets of Michel Angelo Buonaroti,—yet the very pain which I repeatedly felt as I lost myself in gazing upon them, the painful consideration that their having been painted in *fresco* was the sole cause that they had not been abandoned to all the accidents of a dangerous transportation to a distant capital, and that the same caprice which made the Neapolitan soldiery destroy all the exquisite masterpieces on the walls of the church of the *Trinitado Monte*, after the retreat of their antagonist barbarians, might as easily have made vanish the rooms and open gallery of Raffael, and the yet more unapproachable wonders of the sublime Florentine in the Sixtine Chapel, forced upon my mind the reflection: How grateful the human race ought to be that the works of Euclid, Newton, Plato, Milton, Shakspeare, are not subjected to similar contingencies,—that they and their fellows, and the great, though inferior, peerage of undying intellect, are secured;—secured even from a second irruption of Goths and Vandals, in addition to many other safeguards, by the vast empire of English language, laws, and religion founded in America, through the overflow of the power and the virtue of my country;—and that now the great and certain works of genuine fame can only cease to act for mankind, when men themselves cease to be men, or when the planet on which they exist, shall have altered its relations, or have ceased to be. Lord Bacon, in the language of the gods, if I may use an Homeric phrase, has expressed a similar thought:—

Lastly, leaving the vulgar arguments, that by learning man excelleth man in that wherein man excelleth beasts; that by learning man ascendeth to the heavens and their motions, where in body he can not come, and the like; let us conclude with the dignity and excellency of knowledge and learning in that whereunto man's nature doth most aspire, which is, immortality or continuance: for to this tendeth generation, and raising houses and families; to this tend buildings, foundations, and monuments; to this tendeth the desire of memory, fame, and celebration, and in effect the strength of all other human desires. We see then how far the monuments of wit and learning are more durable than the monuments of power, or of the hands. For have not the verses of Homer continued twenty-five hundred years, or more, without the loss of a syllable or letter; during which time, infinite palaces, temples, castles, cities, have been decayed and demolished? It is not possible to have the true pictures or statues of Cyrus, Alexander, Cæsar; no, nor of the kings or great personages of much later years; for the originals can not last, and the copies can not but lose of the life and truth. But the images of men's wits and knowledges remain in books, exempted from the wrong of time, and capable of perpetual renovation. Neither are they fitly to be called images, because they generate still, and cast their seeds in the minds of others, provoking and causing infinite actions and opinions in succeeding ages: so that, if the invention of the ship was thought so noble, which carrieth riches and commodities from place to place, and consociateth the most remote regions in participation of their fruits; how much more are letters to be magnified, which, as ships, pass through the vast seas of time, and make ages so distant to participate of the wisdom, illuminations, and inventions, the one of the other?*

But let us now consider what the drama should be. And first, it is not a copy, but an imitation, of nature. This is the universal principle of the fine arts. In all well laid out grounds what delight do we feel from that balance and antithesis of feelings and thoughts! How natural! we say;—but the very wonder which caused the exclamation, implies that we perceived art at the same moment. We catch the hint from nature itself. Whenever in mountains or cataracts we discover a likeness to any thing artificial which yet we know is not artificial—what pleasure! And so it is in appearances known to be artificial, which appear to be natural. This applies in due degrees, regulated by steady good sense, from a clump of trees to the Paradise Lost or Othello. It would be easy to apply it to painting, and even, though with greater abstraction of thought, and by more subtle yet equally just analogies—to music. But this belongs to others; suffice it that one great principle is common to all the fine arts, a principle which probably is the condition of all consciousness, without which we should feel and imagine only by discontinuous moments, and be plants or brute animals instead of men;—I mean that ever-varying balance, or balancing, of images, notions, or feelings, conceived as in opposition to each other;—in short, the perception of identity and contrariety; the least degree of which constitutes likeness, the greatest absolute difference; but the infinite gradations between these two form all the play and all the interest of our intellectual and moral being, till it leads us to a feeling and an object more awful than it seems to me compatible with even the present subject to utter aloud; though I am most desirous to suggest it. For there alone are all things at once different and the same; there alone, as the prin-

* Advancement of Learning, book 1. *sub fine.*

ciple of all things, does distinction exist unaided by division; there are will and reason, succession of time and unmoving eternity, infinite change and ineffable rest!—

Return, Alpheus! the dread voice is past
Which shrunk thy streams!

——— Thou honor'd flood,
Smooth-*flowing* Avon, crown'd with vocal reeds,
That strain I heard was of a higher mood!—
But now my *voice* proceeds.

We may divide a dramatic poet's characteristics before we enter into the component merits of any one work, and with reference only to those things which are to be the materials of all, into language, passion, and character; always bearing in mind that these must act and react on each other,—the language inspired by the passion, and the language and the passion modified and differenced by the character. To the production of the highest excellences in these three, there are requisite in the mind of the author;—good sense; talent; sensibility; imagination;—and to the perfection of a work we should add two faculties of lesser importance, yet necessary for the ornaments and foliage of the column and the roof—fancy and a quick sense of beauty.

As to language;—it can not be supposed that the poet should make his characters say all that they would, or that, his whole drama considered, each scene, or paragraph should be such as, on cool examination, we can conceive it likely that men in such situations would say, in that order, or with that perfection. And yet, according to my feelings, it is a very inferior kind of poetry, in which, as in the French tragedies, men are made to talk in a style which few indeed even of the wittiest can be supposed to converse in, and which both is, and on a moment's reflection appears to be, the natural produce of the hot-bed of vanity, namely, the closet of an author, who is actuated originally by a desire to excite surprise and wonderment at his own superiority to other men,—instead of having felt so deeply on certain subjects, or in consequence of certain imaginations, as to make it almost a necessity of his nature to seek for sympathy,—no doubt, with that honorable desire of permanent action which distinguishes genius.—Where then is the difference?—In this, that each part should be proportionate, though the whole may be perhaps impossible. At all events, it should be compatible with sound sense and logic in the mind of the poet himself.

It is to be lamented that we judge of books by books, instead of referring what we read to our own experience. One great use of books is to make their contents a motive for observation. The German tragedies have in some respects been justly ridiculed. In them the dramatist often becomes a novelist in his directions to the actors, and thus degrades tragedy into pantomime. Yet still the consciousness of the poet's mind must be diffused over that of the reader or spectator ; but he himself, according to his genius, elevates us, and by being always in keeping, prevents us from perceiving any strangeness, though we feel great exultation. Many different kinds of style may be admirable, both in different men, and in different parts of the same poem.

See the different language which strong feelings may justify in Shylock, and learn from Shakspeare's conduct of that character the terrible force of every plain and calm diction, when known to proceed from a resolved and impassioned man.

It is especially with reference to the drama, and its characteristics in any given nation, or at any particular period, that the dependence of genius on the public taste becomes a matter of the deepest importance. I do not mean that taste which springs merely from caprice or fashionable imitation, and which, in fact, genius can and by degrees will, create for itself; but that which arises out of wide-grasping and heart-enrooted causes, which is epidemic, and in the very air that all breathe. This it is which kills, or withers, or corrupts. Socrates, indeed, might walk arm and arm with Hygeia, whilst pestilence, with a thousand furies running to and fro, and clashing against each other in a complexity and agglomeration of horrors, was shooting her darts of fire and venom all around him. Even such was Milton ; yea, and such, in spite of all that has been babbled by his critics in pretended excuse for his damning, because for them too profound excellences,—such was Shakspeare. But alas ! the exceptions prove the rule. For who will dare to force his way out of the crowd,—not of the mere vulgar,—but of the vain and banded aristocracy of intellect, and presume to join the almost supernatural beings that stand by themselves aloof?

Of this diseased epidemic influence there are two forms especially preclusive of tragic worth. The first is the necessary growth of a sense and love of the ludicrous, and a morbid sensibility of the assimilative power,—an inflammation produced by cold and weakness,—which in the boldest burst of passion will lie in wait for a jeer at any phrase, that may have an accidental coincidence in the mere words with something base or trivial. For instance,—to express woods, not on a plain, but clothing a hill, which overlooks a valley, or dell, or river, or the sea,—the trees rising one above another, as the spectators in an ancient theatre, —I know no other word in our language (bookish and pedantic terms out of the question) but *hanging* woods, the *sylvæ superimpendentes* of Catullus ;* yet let some wit call out in a slang tone,—" the gallows !" and a peal of laughter would damn the play. Hence it is that so many dull pieces have had a decent run, only because nothing unusual above, or absurd below, mediocrity furnished an occasion,—a spark for the explosive materials collected behind the orchestra. But it would take a volume of no ordinary size, however laconically the sense were expressed, if it were meant to instance the effects, and unfold all the causes, of this disposition upon the moral, intellectual, and even physical character of a people, with its influences on domestic life and individual deportment. A good document upon this subject would be the history of Paris society and of French, that is, Parisian, literature from the commencement of the latter half of the reign of Louis XIV. to that of Bonaparte, compared with the preceding philosophy and poetry even of Frenchmen themselves.

The second form, or more properly, perhaps, another distinct cause, of this diseased disposition is matter of exultation to the philanthropist and philosopher, and of regret to the poet, the painter, and the statuary alone, and to them only as poets, painters, and statuaries ;—namely, the security, the comparative equability, and ever increasing sameness of human life. Men are now so seldom thrown into wild circumstances, and violences of excitement, that the language of such states, the laws of association of feeling with thought, the starts and strange far-flights of the assimilative power on the slightest and least obvious likeness presented by thoughts, words, or objects,—these are all judged of by authority, not by actual experience,—by what men have

* Confestim Peneos adest, viridantia Tempe,
Tempæ, quæ cingunt sylvæ superimpendentes.
Epith. Pel. et Th. 286.

been accustomed to regard as symbols of these states, and not the natural symbols, or self-manifestations of them.

Even so it is in the language of man, and in that of nature. The sound *sun*, or the figures *s*, *u*, *n*, are purely arbitrary modes of recalling the object, and for visual mere objects they are not only sufficient, but have infinite advantages from their very nothingness *per se*. But the language of nature is a subordinate *Logos*, that was in the beginning, and was with the thing it represented, and was the thing it represented.

Now the language of Shakspeare, in his Lear for instance, is a something intermediate between these two ; or rather it is the former blended with the latter,—the arbitrary, not merely recalling the cold notion of the thing, but expressing the reality of it, and, as arbitrary language is an heirloom of the human race, being itself a part of that which it manifests. What shall I deduce from the preceding positions ? Even this,—the appropriate, the never to be too much valued advantage of the theatre, if only the actors were what we know they have been,—a delightful, yet most effectual remedy for this dead palsy of the public mind. What would appear mad or ludicrous in a book, when presented to the senses under the form of reality, and with the truth of nature, supplies a species of actual experience. This is indeed the special privilege of a great actor over a great poet. No part was ever played in perfection, but nature justified herself in the hearts of all her children, in what state soever they were, short of absolute moral exhaustion, or downright stupidity. There is no time given to ask questions, or to pass judgments ; we are taken by storm, and, though in the histrionic art many a clumsy counterfeit, by caricature of one or two features, may gain applause as a fine likeness, yet never was the very thing rejected as a counterfeit. O ! when I think of the inexhaustible mine of virgin treasure in our Shakspeare, that I have been almost daily reading him since I was ten years old,—that the thirty intervening years have been unintermittingly and not fruitlessly employed in the study of the Greek, Latin, English, Italian, Spanish and German *belle lettrists*, and the last fifteen years in addition, far more intensely in the analysis of the laws of life and reason as they exist in man, —and that upon every step I have made forward in taste, in acquisition of facts from history or my own observation, and in knowledge of the different laws of being and their apparent exceptions, from accidental collision of disturbing forces,—that at every new accession of information, after every successful exercise of meditation, and every fresh presentation of experience, I have unfailingly discovered a proportionate increase of wisdom and intuition in Shakspeare;—when I know this, and know too, that by a conceivable and possible, though hardly to be expected, arrangement of the British theatres, not all, indeed, but a large, a very large, proportion of this indefinite all—(round which no comprehension has yet drawn the line of circumscription, so as to say to itself, 'I have seen the whole')—might be sent into the heads and hearts—into the very souls of the mass of mankind, to whom, except by this living comment and interpretation, it must remain forever a sealed volume, a deep well without a wheel or a windlass;—it seems to me a pardonable enthusiasm to steal away from sober likelihood, and share in so rich a feast in the fairy world of possibility! Yet even in the grave cheerfulness of a circumspect hope, much, very much, might be done; enough, assuredly, to furnish a kind and strenuous nature with ample motives for the attempt to effect what may be effected.

SHAKSPEARE, A POET GENERALLY.

Clothed in radiant armor, and authorized by titles sure and manifold, as a poet, Shakspeare came forward to demand the throne of fame, as the dramatic poet of England. His excellences compelled even his contemporaries to seat him on that throne, although there were giants in those days contending for the same honor. Hereafter I would fain endeavor to make out the title of the English drama as created by, and existing in, Shakspeare, and its right to the supremacy of dramatic excellence. But he had shown himself a poet, previously to his appearance as a dramatic poet; and had no Lear, no Othello, no Henry IV., no Twelfth Night ever appeared, we must have admitted that Shakspeare possessed the chief, if not every, requisite of a poet,—deep feeling and exquisite sense of beauty, both as exhibited to the eye in the combinations of form, and to the ear in sweet and appropriate melody; that these feelings were under the command of his own will; that in his very first productions he projected his mind out of his own particular being, and felt, and made others feel, on subjects no way connected with himself, except by force of contemplation and that sublime faculty by which a great mind becomes that, on which it meditates. To this must be added that affectionate love of nature and natural objects, without which no man could have observed so steadily, or painted so truly and passionately, the very minutest beauties of the external world :—

And when thou hast on foot the purblind hare,
Mark the poor wretch; to overshoot his troubles,
How he outruns the wind, and with what care,
He cranks and crosses with a thousand doubles;
The many musits through the which he goes
Are like a labyrinth to amaze his foes.

Sometimes he runs among the flock of sheep,
To make the cunning hounds mistake their smell;
And sometime where earth-delving conies keep,
To stop the loud pursuers in their yell;
And sometime sorteth with a herd of deer:
Danger deviseth shifts, wit waits on fear.

For there his smell with others' being mingled,
The hot scent-snuffing hounds are driven to doubt,
Ceasing their clamorous cry, till they have singled,
With much ado, the cold fault cleanly out,
Then do they spend their mouths; echo replies,
As if another chase were in the skies.

By this poor Wat far off, upon a hill,
Stands on his hinder legs with listening ear,
To hearken if his foes pursue him still:
Anon their loud alarums he doth hear,
And now his grief may be compared well
To one sore-sick, that hears the passing bell.

Then shalt thou see the dew-bedabbled wretch
Turn, and return, indenting with the way:
Each envious brier his weary legs doth scratch,
Each shadow makes him stop, each murmur stay.
For misery is trodden on by many,
And being low, never relieved by any.

Venus and Adonis.

And the preceding description :—

But lo! from forth a copse that neighbors by,
A breeding jennet, lusty, young and proud, &c.

is much more admirable, but in parts less fitted for quotation.

Moreover Shakspeare had shown that he possessed fancy, considered as the faculty of bringing together images dissimilar in the main by some one point or more of likeness, as in such a passage as this:—

> Full gently now she takes him by the hand,
> A lily prisoned in a jail of snow,
> Or ivory in an alabaster band:
> So white a friend ingirts so white a foe!—*Ib.*

And still mounting the intellectual ladder, he had as unequivocally proved the indwelling in his mind of imagination, or the power by which one image or feeling is made to modify many others, and by a sort of fusion to force many into one;—that which afterwards showed itself in such might and energy in Lear, where the deep anguish of a father spreads the feeling of ingratitude and cruelty over the very elements of heaven;—and which, combining many circumstances into one moment of consciousness, tends to produce that ultimate end of all human thought and human feeling, unity, and thereby the reduction of the spirit to its principle and fountain, who is alone truly one. Various are the workings of this the greatest faculty of the human mind, both passionate and tranquil. In its tranquil and purely pleasurable operation, it acts chiefly by creating out of many things, as they would have appeared in the description of an ordinary mind, detailed in unimpassioned succession, a oneness, even as nature, the greatest of poets, acts upon us, when we open our eyes upon an extended prospect. Thus the flight of Adonis in the dusk of the evening:—

> Look! how a bright star shooteth from the sky;
> So glides he in the night from Venus' eye!

How many images and feelings are here brought together without effort and without discord, in the beauty of Adonis, the rapidity of his flight, the yearning, yet hopelessness, of the enamored gazer, while a shadowy ideal character is thrown over the whole! Or this power acts by impressing the stamp of humanity, and of human feelings, on inanimate or mere natural objects:—

> Lo! here the gentle lark, weary of rest,
> From his moist cabinet mounts up on high,
> And wakes the morning, from whose silver breast
> The sun ariseth in his majesty.

Who doth the world so gloriously behold,
The cedar-tops and hills seem burnish'd gold.

Or again, it acts by so carrying on the eye of the reader as to make him almost lose the consciousness of words,—to make him see every thing flashed, as Wordsworth has grandly and appropriately said,—

Flashed upon that inward eye
Which is the bliss of solitude;—

and this without exciting any painful or laborious attention, without any anatomy of description (a fault not uncommon in descriptive poetry)—but with the sweetness and easy movement of nature. This energy is an absolute essential of poetry, and of itself would constitute a poet, though not one of the highest class;—it is, however, a most hopeful symptom, and the Venus and Adonis is one continued specimen of it.

In this beautiful poem there is an endless activity of thought in all the possible associations of thought with thought, thought with feeling, or with words, of feelings with feelings, and of words with words.

Even as the sun, with purple-color'd face,
Had ta'en his last leave of the weeping morn,
Rose-cheek'd Adonis hied him to the chase:
Hunting he loved, but love he laughed to scorn.
Sick-thoughted Venus makes amain unto him,
And like a bold-faced suitor 'gins to woo him.

Remark the humanizing imagery and circumstances of the first two lines, and the activity of thought in the play of words in the fourth line. The whole stanza presents at once the time, the appearance of the morning, and the two persons distinctly characterized, and in six simple verses puts the reader in possession of the whole argument of the poem.

Over one arm the lusty courser's rein,
Under the other was the tender boy,
Who blush'd and pouted in a dull disdain,
With leaden appetite, unapt to toy,
She red and hot, as coals of glowing fire,
He red for shame, but frosty to desire:—

This stanza and the two following afford good instances of that poetic power, which I mentioned above, of making every thing present to the imagination—both the forms, and the passions which modify those forms, either actually, as in the representations of love, or anger, or other human affections; or imaginatively, by the different manner in which inanimate objects, or objects unimpassioned themselves, are caused to be seen by the mind in moments of strong excitement, and according to the kind of the excitement,—whether of jealousy, or rage, or love, in the only appropriate sense of the word, or of the lower impulses of our nature, or finally of the poetic feeling itself. It is, perhaps, chiefly in the power of producing and reproducing the latter that the poet stands distinct.

The subject of the Venus and Adonis is unpleasing; but the poem itself is for that very reason the more illustrative of Shakspeare. There are men who can write passages of deepest pathos and even sublimity, on circumstances personal to themselves, and stimulative of their own passions; but they are not, therefore, on this account poets. Read that magnificent burst of woman's patriotism and exultation, Deborah's song of victory; it is glorious, but nature is the poet there. It is quite another matter to become all things and yet remain the same,—to make the changeful god be felt in the river, the lion and the flame;—this it is, that is the true imagination. Shakspeare writes in this poem, as if he were of another planet, charming you to gaze on the movements of Venus and Adonis, as you would on the twinkling dances of two vernal butterflies.

Finally, in this poem and the Rape of Lucrece, Shakspeare gave ample proof of his possession of a most profound, energetic, and philosophical mind, without which he might have pleased, but could not have been a great dramatic poet. Chance and the necessity of his genius combined to lead him to the drama his proper province: in his conquest of which we should consider both the difficulties which opposed him, and the advantages by which he was assisted.

SHAKSPEARE'S JUDGMENT EQUAL TO HIS GENIUS.

Thus then Shakspeare appears, from his Venus and Adonis and Rape of Lucrece alone, apart from all his great works, to have possessed all the conditions of the true poet. Let me now proceed to destroy, as far as may be in my power, the popular notion that he was a great dramatist by mere instinct, that he grew immortal in his own despite, and sank below men of second or third-rate power, when he attempted aught beside the drama—even as bees construct their cells and manufacture their honey to admirable perfection; but would in vain attempt to build a nest. Now this mode of reconciling a compelled sense of inferiority with a feeling of pride, began in a few pedants, who having read that Sophocles was the great model of tragedy, and Aristotle the infallible dictator of its rules, and finding that the Lear, Hamlet, Othello, and other master-pieces were neither in imitation of Sophocles, nor in obedience to Aristotle,—and not having (with one or two exceptions) the courage to affirm, that the delight which their country received from generation to generation, in defiance of the alterations of circumstances and habits, was wholly groundless,—took upon them, as a happy medium and refuge, to talk of Shakspeare as a sort of beautiful *lusus naturæ*, a delightful monster,—wild, indeed, and without taste or judgment, but like the inspired idiots so much venerated in the East, uttering, amid the strangest follies, the sublimest truths. In nine places out of ten in which I find his awful name mentioned, it is with some epithet of "wild," "irregular," "pure child of nature," &c. If all this be true, we must submit to it; though to a thinking mind it can not but be painful to find any excellence, merely human, thrown out of all human analogy, and thereby leaving us neither rules for imitation, nor motives to imitate;—but if false, it is a dangerous falsehood;—for it affords a refuge to secret self-conceit,—enables a vain man at once to escape his reader's indignation by general swoln panegyrics, and merely by his *ipse dixit* to treat, as contemptible, what he has not intellect enough to comprehend, or soul to feel, without assigning any reason, or referring his opinion to any demonstrative principle; thus leaving Shakspeare as a sort of grand Lama, adored indeed, and his very excrements prized as relics, but with no authority or real influence. I grieve that every late voluminous edition of his works would enable me to substantiate the present charge with a variety of facts, one tenth of which would of themselves exhaust the time allotted to me. Every critic, who has or has not made a collection of black-letter books—in itself a useful and respectable amusement,—puts on the seven-league boots of self-opinion, and strides at once from an illustrator into a supreme judge, and blind and deaf, fills his three-ounce phial at the waters of Niagara; and determines positively the greatness of the cataract to be neither more nor less than his three-ounce phial has been able to receive.

I think this a very serious subject. It is my earnest desire—my passionate endeavor,—to enforce at various times, and by various arguments and instances, the close and reciprocal connection of just taste with pure morality. Without that acquaintance with the heart of man, or that docility and childlike gladness to be made acquainted with it, which those only can have, who dare look at their own hearts—and that with a steadiness which religion only has the power of reconciling with sincere humility;—without this, and the modesty produced by it, I am deeply convinced that no man, however wide his erudition, however patient his antiquarian researches, can possibly understand, or be worthy of understanding, the writings of Shakspeare.

Assuredly that criticism of Shakspeare will alone be genial which is reverential. The Englishman, who, without reverence, a proud and affectionate reverence, can utter the name of William Shakspeare, stands disqualified for the office of critic. He wants one at least of the very senses, the language of which he is to employ, and will discourse at best, but as a blind man, while the whole harmonious creation of light and shade with all its subtle interchange of deepening and dissolving colors rises in silence to the silent *fiat* of the uprising Apollo. However inferior in ability I may be to some who have followed me, I own I am proud that I was the first in time who publicly demonstrated to the full extent of the position, that the supposed irregularity and extravagances of Shakspeare were the mere dreams of a pedantry that arraigned the eagle because it had not the dimensions of the swan. In all the successive courses of lectures delivered by me, since my first attempt at the Royal Institution, it has been, and it still remains, my object, to prove that in all points from the most important to the most minute, the judgment of Shakspeare is commensurate with his genius—nay, that his genius reveals itself in his judgment, as in its most exalted form. And the more gladly do I recur to this subject from the clear conviction, that to judge aright, and with distinct consciousness of the grounds of our judgment, concerning the works of Shakspeare, implies the power and the means of judging rightly of all other works of intellect, those of abstract science alone excepted.

It is a painful truth that not only individuals, but even whole nations, are ofttimes so enslaved to the habits of their education and immediate circumstances, as not to judge disinterestedly even on those subjects, the very pleasure arising from which consists in its disinterestedness, namely, on subjects of taste and polite literature. Instead of deciding concerning their own modes and customs by any rule of reason, nothing appears rational, becoming, or beautiful to them, but what coincides with the peculiarities of their education. In this narrow circle, individuals may attain to exquisite discrimination, as the French critics have done in their own literature; but a true critic can no more be such without placing himself on some central point, from which he may command the whole, that is, some general rule, which, founded in reason, or the faculties common to all men, must therefore apply to each—than an astronomer can explain the movements of the solar system without taking his stand in the sun. And let me remark, that this will not tend to produce despotism, but, on the contrary, true tolerance, in the critic. He will, indeed, require, as the spirit and substance of a work, something true in human nature itself, and independent of all circumstances; but in the mode of applying it, he will estimate genius and judgment according to the felicity with which the imperishable soul of intellect, shall have adapted itself to the age, the place, and the existing manners. The error he will expose, lies in reversing this, and holding up the mere circumstances as perpetual to the utter neglect of the power which can alone animate them. For art can not exist without, or apart from, nature; and what has man of his own to give to his fellow-man, but his own thoughts and feelings, and his observations, so far as they are modified by his own thoughts or feelings?

Let me, then, once more submit this question to minds emancipated alike from national, or party, or sectarian prejudice:—Are the plays of Shakspeare works of rude uncultivated genius, in which the splendor of the parts compensates, if aught can compensate, for the barbarous shapelessness and irregularity of the whole? Or is the form equally admirable with the matter, and the judgment of the great poet, not less deserving our wonder than his genius?—Or, again, to repeat the question in other words:—

Is Shakspeare a great dramatic poet on account only of those beauties and excellences which he possesses in common with the ancients, but with diminished claims to our love and honor to the full extent of his differences from them?—Or are these very differences additional proofs of poetic wisdom, at once results and symbols of living power as contrasted with lifeless mechanism—of free and rival originality as contra-distinguished from servile imitation, or, more accurately, a blind copying of effects, instead of a true imitation of the essential principles?—Imagine not that I am about to oppose genius to rules. No! the comparative value of these rules is the very cause to be tried. The spirit of poetry, like all other living powers, must of necessity circumscribe itself by rules, were it only to unite power with beauty. It must embody in order to reveal itself; but a living body is of necessity an organized one; and what is organization but the connection of parts in and for a whole, so that each part is at once end and means?—This is no discovery of criticism;—it is a necessity of the human mind; and all nations have felt and obeyed it, in the invention of metre, and measured sounds, as the vehicle and *involucrum* of poetry—itself a fellow-growth from the same life—even as the bark is to the tree!

(*g*) No work of true genius dares want its appropriate form, neither indeed is there any danger of this. As it must not, so genius can not, be lawless; for it is even this that constitutes it genius—the power of acting creatively under laws of its own origination. How then comes it that not only single *Zoili*, but whole nations have combined in unhesitating condemnation of our great dramatist, as a sort of African nature, rich in beautiful monsters—as a wild heath where islands of fertility look the greener from the surrounding waste, where the loveliest plants now shine out among unsightly weeds, and now are choked by their parasitic growth, so intertwined that we can not disentangle the weed without snapping the flower?—In this statement I have had no reference to the vulgar abuse of Voltaire,* save as far as

* Take a slight specimen of it.

Je suis bien loin assurément de justifier en tout la tragédie d'Hamlet: *c'est une pièce grossière et barbare, qui ne serait pas supportée par la plus vile populace de la France et de l'Italie.* Hamlet y devient fou au second acte, et sa maîtresse fole au troisième; le prince tue le père de sa maîtresse, feignant de tuer un rat, et l'heröine se jette dans la rivière. On fait sa fosse sur le théâtre; des fossoyeurs disent des *quolibets* dignes d'eux, en

his charges are coincident with the decisions of Shakspeare's own commentators and (so they would tell you) almost idolatrous admirers. The true ground of the mistake lies in the confounding mechanical regularity with organic form. The form is mechanic, when on any given material we impress a pre-determined form, not necessarily arising out of the properties of the material;—as when to a mass of wet clay we give whatever shape we wish it to retain when hardened. The organic form, on the other hand, is innate; it shapes, as it develops, itself from within, and the fulness of its development is one and the same with the perfection of its outward form. Such as the life is, such is the form. Nature, the prime genial artist, inexhaustible in diverse powers, is equally inexhaustible in forms;—each exterior is the physiognomy of the being within—its true image reflected and thrown out from the concave mirror;—and even such is the appropriate excellence of her chosen poet, of our own Shakspeare—himself a nature humanized, a genial understanding directing self-consciously a power and an implicit wisdom deeper even than our consciousness.

I greatly dislike beauties and selections in general; but as proof positive of his unrivalled excellence, I should like to try Shakspeare by this criterion. Make out your amplest catalogue of all the human faculties, as reason or the moral law, the will, the feeling of the coincidence of the two (a feeling *sui generis et demonstratio demonstrationum*) called the conscience, the understanding or prudence, wit, fancy, imagination, judgment—and then of the objects on which these are to be employed, as the beauties, the terrors, and the seeming caprices of nature, the realities and the capabilities, that is, the actual and the ideal, of the human mind, conceived as an individual or as a social being, as in innocence or in guilt, in a play-paradise, or in a war-field of temptation;—and then compare with Shakspeare under each of these heads all or any of the writers in prose and verse that have

tenant dans leurs mains des têtes de morts; le prince Hamlet répond à leurs *grossièretés abominables par des folies non moins dégoûtantes.* Pendant ce temps-là, un des acteurs fait la conquête de la Pologne. *Hamlet, sa mère, et son beau-père boivent ensemble sur le théâtre; on chante à table, on s'y querelle, on se bat, on se tue: on croirait que cet ouvrage est le fruit de l'imagination d'un sauvage ivre.* Dissertation before Semiramis.

This is not, perhaps, very like Hamlet; but nothing can be more like Voltaire.—*Ed.*

ever lived! Who, that is competent to judge, doubts the result? —And ask your own hearts—ask your own common-sense—to conceive the possibility of this man being—I say not, the drunken savage of that wretched socialist, whom Frenchmen, to their shame, have honored before their elder and better worthies—but the anomalous, the wild, the irregular, genius of our daily criticism! What! are we to have miracles in sport?—Or, I speak reverently, does God choose idiots by whom to convey divine truths to man? (*h*)

RECAPITULATION AND SUMMARY

OF THE CHARACTERISTICS OF SHAKSPEARE'S DRAMAS.*

In lectures, of which amusement forms a large part of the object, there are some peculiar difficulties. The architect places his foundation out of sight, and the musician tunes his instrument before he makes his appearance; but the lecturer has to try his chords in the presence of the assembly; an operation not likely, indeed, to produce much pleasure, but yet indispensably necessary to a right understanding of the subject to be developed.

Poetry in essence is as familiar to barbarous as to civilized nations. The Laplander and the savage Indian are cheered by it as well as the inhabitants of London and Paris;—its spirit takes up and incorporates surrounding materials, as a plant clothes itself with soil and climate, whilst it exhibits the working of a vital principle within independent of all accidental circumstances. And to judge with fairness of an author's works, we ought to distinguish what is inward and essential from what is outward and circumstantial. It is essential to poetry that it be simple, and appeal to the elements and primary laws of our nature; that it be sensuous, and by its imagery elicit truth at a flash; that it be impassioned, and be able to move our feelings and awaken our affections. In comparing different poets with each other, we should inquire which have brought into the fullest play our imagination and our reason, or have created the greatest excitement and produced the completest harmony. If we consider great exquisiteness of language and sweetness of metre alone, it is impossible to deny to Pope the character of a delight-

* For the most part communicated by Mr. Justice Coleridge.—*Ed.*

ful writer; but whether he be a poet, must depend upon our definition of the word; and, doubtless, if every thing that pleases be poetry, Pope's satires and epistles must be poetry. This, I must say, that poetry, as distinguished from other modes of composition, does not rest in metre, and that it is not poetry, if it make no appeal to our passions or our imagination. One character belongs to all true poets, that they write from a principle within, not originating in any thing without; and that the true poet's work in its form, its shapings, and its modifications, is distinguished from all other works that assume to belong to the class of poetry, as a natural from an artificial flower, or as the mimic garden of a child from an enamelled meadow. In the former the flowers are broken from their stems and stuck into the ground; they are beautiful to the eye and fragrant to the sense, but their colors soon fade, and their odor is transient as the smile of the planter;—while the meadow may be visited again and again with renewed delight; its beauty is innate in the soil, and its bloom is of the freshness of nature. (*i*)

The next ground of critical judgment, and point of comparison, will be as to how far a given poet has been influenced by accidental circumstances. As a living poet must surely write, not for the ages past, but for that in which he lives, and those which are to follow, it is, on the one hand, natural that he should not violate, and on the other, necessary that he should not depend on, the mere manners and modes of his day. See how little does Shakspeare leave us to regret that he was born in his particular age! The great æra in modern times was what is called the Restoration of Letters;—the ages preceding it are called the dark ages; but it would be more wise, perhaps, to call them the ages in which we were in the dark. It is usually overlooked that the supposed dark period was not universal, but partial and successive, or alternate; that the dark age of England was not the dark age of Italy, but that one country was in its light and vigor, whilst another was in its gloom and bondage. But no sooner had the Reformation sounded through Europe like the blast of an archangel's trumpet, than from king to peasant there arose an enthusiasm for knowledge; the discovery of a manuscript became the subject of an embassy; Erasmus read by moonlight, because he could not afford a torch, and begged a penny, not for the love of charity, but for the love of learning. The three great points of attention were religion, morals, and taste ; men of genius as well as men of learning, who in this age need to be so widely distinguished, then alike became copyists of the ancients ; and this, indeed, was the only way by which the taste of mankind could be improved, or their understandings informed. Whilst Dante imagined himself a humble follower of Virgil, and Ariosto of Homer, they were both unconscious of that greater power working within them, which in many points carried them beyond their supposed originals. All great discoveries bear the stamp of the age in which they are made ;—hence we perceive the effects of the purer religion of the moderns, visible for the most part in their lives ; and in reading their works we should not content ourselves with the mere narratives of events long since passed, but should learn to apply their maxims and conduct to ourselves.

Having intimated that times and manners lend their form and pressure to genius, let me once more draw a slight parallel between the ancient and modern stage, the stages of Greece and of England. The Greeks were polytheists ; their religion was local ; almost the only object of all their knowledge, art, and taste, was their gods ; and, accordingly, their productions were, if the expression may be allowed, statuesque, whilst those of the moderns are picturesque. (*j*) The Greeks reared a structure, which in its parts, and as a whole, filled the mind with the calm and elevated impression of perfect beauty, and symmetrical proportion. The moderns also produced a whole, a more striking whole ; but it was by blending materials and fusing the parts together. And as the Pantheon is to York Minster or Westminster Abbey, so is Sophocles compared with Shakspeare ; (*k*) in the one a completeness, a satisfaction, an excellence, on which the mind rests with complacency ; in the other a multitude of interlaced materials, great and little, magnificent and mean, accompanied, indeed, with the sense of a falling short of perfection, and yet, at the same time, so promising of our social and individual progression, that we would not, if we could, exchange it for that repose of the mind which dwells on the forms of symmetry in the acquiescent admiration of grace. This general characteristic of the ancient and modern drama might be illustrated by a parallel of the ancient and modern music ;—the one consisting of melody arising from a succession only of pleasing sounds,—the modern embracing harmony also, the result of combination and the effect of a whole. (*l*)

I have said, and I say it again, that great as was the genius of Shakspeare, his judgment was at least equal to it. Of this any one will be convinced, who attentively considers those points in which the dramas of Greece and England differ, from the dissimilitude of circumstances by which each was modified and influenced. The Greek stage had its origin in the ceremonies of a sacrifice, such as of the goat to Bacchus, whom we most erroneously regard as merely the jolly god of wine;—for among the ancients he was venerable, as the symbol of that power which acts without our consciousness in the vital energies of nature,—the *vinum mundi*,—as Apollo was that of the conscious agency of our intellectual being. (*m*) The heroes of old under the influences of this Bacchic enthusiasm, performed more than human actions;—hence tales of the favorite champions soon passed into dialogue. On the Greek stage the chorus was always before the audience; the curtain was never dropped, as we should say; and change of place being therefore, in general, impossible, the absurd notion of condemning it merely as improbable in itself was never entertained by any one. If we can believe ourselves at Thebes in one act, we may believe ourselves at Athens in the next. If a story lasts twenty-four hours or twenty-four years, it is equally improbable. There seems to be no just boundary but what the feelings prescribe. But on the Greek stage where the same persons were perpetually before the audience, great judgment was necessary in venturing on any such change. The poets never, therefore, attempted to impose on the senses by bringing places to men, but they did bring men to places, as in the well-known instance in the Eumenides, where during an evident retirement of the chorus from the orchestra, the scene is changed to Athens, and Orestes is first introduced in the temple of Minerva, and the chorus of Furies come in afterwards in pursuit of him.*

In the Greek drama there were no formal divisions into scenes

* Æsch. Eumen. v. 230–239. *Notandum est, scenam jam Athenas translatam sic institui, ut primo Orestes solus conspiciatur in templo Minervæ supplex ejus simulacrum venerans; paulo post autem eum consequantur Eumenides, &c.* Schütz's note. The recessions of the chorus were termed μεταναστάσεις. There is another instance in the Ajax, v. 814.—*Ed.*

and acts ; there were no means, therefore, of allowing for the necessary lapse of time between one part of the dialogue and another, and unity of time in a strict sense was, of course, impossible. To overcome that difficulty of accounting for time, which is effected on the modern stage by dropping a curtain, the judgment and great genius of the ancients supplied music and measured motion, and with the lyric ode filled up the vacuity. In the story of the Agamemnon of Æschylus, the capture of Troy is supposed to be announced by a fire lighted on the Asiatic shore, and the transmission of the signal by successive beacons to Mycenæ. The signal is first seen at the 21st line, and the herald from Troy itself enters at the 486th, and Agamemnon himself at the7 83d line. But the practical absurdity of this was not felt by the audience, who, in imagination, stretched minutes into hours, while they listened to the lofty narrative odes of the chorus which almost entirely filled up the interspace. Another fact deserves attention here, namely, that regularly on the Greek stage a drama, or acted story, consisted in reality of three dramas, called together a trilogy, and performed consecutively in the course of one day. Now you may conceive a tragedy of Shakspeare's as a trilogy connected in one single representation. Divide Lear into three parts, and each would be a play with the ancients ; or take the three Æschylean dramas of Agamemnon, and divide them into, or call them, as many acts, and they together would be one play. (*n*) The first act would comprise the usurpation of Ægisthus, and the murder of Agamemnon ; the second, the revenge of Orestes, and the murder of his mother ; and the third, the penance and absolution of Orestes ;—occupying a period of twenty-two years.

The stage in Shakspeare's time was a naked room with a blanket for a curtain ; but he made it a field for monarchs. That law of unity, which has its foundations, not in the factitious necessity of custom, but in nature itself, the unity of feeling, is everywhere and at all times observed by Shakspeare in his plays. Read Romeo and Juliet ;—all is youth and spring ; —youth with its follies, its virtues, its precipitancies ;—spring with its odors, its flowers, and its transiency ; it is one and the same feeling that commences, goes through, and ends the play. The old men, the Capulets and the Montagues, are not common old men ; they have an eagerness, a heartiness, a vehemence, the effect of spring; with Romeo, his change of passion, his sudden marriage, and his rash death, are all the effects of youth;—whilst in Juliet love has all that is tender and melancholy in the nightingale, all that is voluptuous in the rose, with whatever is sweet in the freshness of spring; but it ends with a long deep sigh like the last breeze of the Italian evening. (*o*) This unity of feeling and character pervades every drama of Shakspeare.

It seems to me that his plays are distinguished from those of all other dramatic poets by the following characteristics:

1. Expectation in preference to surprise. It is like the true reading of the passage—'God said, Let there be light, and there was *light*;'—not there *was* light. As the feeling with which we startle at a shooting star compared with that of watching the sunrise at the pre-established moment, such and so low is surprise compared with expectation.

2. Signal adherence to the great law of nature, that all opposites tend to attract and temper each other. Passion in Shakspeare generally displays libertinism, but involves morality; and if there are exceptions to this, they are, independently of their intrinsic value, all of them indicative of individual character, and, like the farewell admonitions of the parent, have an end beyond the parental relation. Thus the Countess's beautiful precepts to Bertram, by elevating her character, raise that of Helena her favorite, and soften down the point in her which Shakspeare does not mean us not to see, but to see and to forgive, and at length to justify. And so it is in Polonius, who is the personified memory of wisdom no longer actually possessed. This admirable character is always misrepresented on the stage. Shakspeare never intended to exhibit him as a buffoon; for although it was natural that Hamlet,—a young man of fire and genius, detesting formality, and disliking Polonius on political grounds, as imagining that he had assisted his uncle in his usurpation,—should express himself satirically,—yet this must not be taken as exactly the poet's conception of him. In Polonius a certain induration of character had arisen from long habits of business; but take his advice to Laertes, and Ophelia's reverence for his memory, and we shall see that he was meant to be represented as a statesman somewhat past his faculties—his recollections of life all full of wisdom, and showing a knowledge of human nature, whilst

what immediately takes place before him, and escapes from him, is indicative of weakness.

But as in Homer all the deities are in armor, even Venus ; so in Shakspeare all the characters are strong. Hence real folly and dulness are made by him the vehicles of wisdom. There is no difficulty for one being a fool to imitate a fool ; but to be, remain, and speak like a wise man and a great wit, and yet so as to give a vivid representation of a veritable fool,—*hic labor, hoc opus est.* A drunken constable is not uncommon, nor hard to draw ; but see and examine what goes to make up a Dogberry.

3. Keeping at all times in the high road of life. Shakspeare has no innocent adulteries, no interesting incests, no virtuous vice ;—he never renders that amiable which religion and reason alike teach us to detest, or clothes impurity in the garb of virtue, like Beaumont and Fletcher, the Kotzebues of the day. Shakspeare's fathers are roused by ingratitude, his husbands stung by unfaithfulness ; in him, in short, the affections are wounded in those points in which all may, nay, must, feel. Let the morality of Shakspeare be contrasted with that of the writers of his own, or the succeeding age, or of those of the present day, who boast their superiority in this respect. No one can dispute that the result of such a comparison is altogether in favor of Shakspeare ; —even the letters of women of high rank in his age were often coarser than his writings. If he occasionally disgusts a keen sense of delicacy, he never injures the mind ; he neither excites, nor flatters passion, in order to degrade the subject of it ; he does not use the faulty thing for a faulty purpose, nor carries on warfare against virtue, by causing wickedness to appear as no wickedness, through the medium of a morbid sympathy with the unfortunate. In Shakspeare vice never walks as in twilight ; nothing is purposely out of its place ;—he inverts not the order of nature and propriety,—does not make every magistrate a drunkard or glutton, nor every poor man meek, humane, and temperate ; he has no benevolent butchers, nor any sentimental ratcatchers.

4. Independence of the dramatic interest on the plot. The interest in the plot is always in fact on account of the characters, not *vice versa*, as in almost all other writers ; the plot is a mere canvass and no more. Hence arises the true justification of the same stratagem being used in regard to Benedict and Beatrice,—

the vanity in each being alike. Take away from the Much Ado About Nothing all that which is not indispensable to the plot, either as having little to do with it, or, at best, like Dogberry and his comrades, forced into the service, when any other less ingeniously absurd watchmen and night-constables would have answered the mere necessities of the action ;—take away Benedict, Beatrice, Dogberry, and the reaction of the former on the character of Hero,—and what will remain ? In other writers the main agent of the plot is always the prominent character ; in Shakspeare it is so, or is not so, as the character is in itself calculated, or not calculated, to form the plot. Don John is the mainspring of the plot of this play; but he is merely shown and then withdrawn.

5. Independence of the interest on the story as the groundwork of the plot. Hence Shakspeare never took the trouble of inventing stories. It was enough for him to select from those that had been already invented or recorded such as had one or other, or both, of two recommendations, namely, suitableness to his particular purpose, and their being parts of popular tradition,—names of which we had often heard, and of their fortunes, and as to which all we wanted was, to see the man himself. So it is just the man himself, the Lear, the Shylock, the Richard, that Shakspeare makes us for the first time acquainted with. Omit the first scene in Lear, and yet every thing will remain ; so the first and second scenes in the Merchant of Venice. Indeed it is universally true.

6. Interfusion of the lyrical—that which in its very essence is poetical—not only with the dramatic, as in the plays of Metastasio, where at the end of the scene comes the *aria* as the *exit* speech of the character,—but also in and through the dramatic. Songs in Shakspeare are introduced as songs only, just as songs are in real life, beautifully as some of them are characteristic of the person who has sung or called for them, as Desdemona's 'Willow,' and Ophelia's wild snatches, and the sweet carollings in As You Like It. But the whole of the Midsummer Night's Dream is one continued specimen of the dramatized lyrical. And observe how exquisitely the dramatic of Hotspur ;—

> Marry, and I'm glad on't with all my heart;
> I'd rather be a kitten and cry—mew, &c.

melts away into the lyric of Mortimer ;—

I understand thy looks: that pretty Welsh
Which thou pourest down from these swelling heavens,
I am too perfect in, &c.

Henry IV. part i. act iii. sc. i.

7. The characters of the *dramatis personæ*, like those in real life, are to be inferred by the reader;—they are not told to him. And it is well worth remarking that Shakspeare's characters, like those in real life, are very commonly misunderstood, and almost always understood by different persons in different ways. The causes are the same in either case. If you take only what the friends of the character say, you may be deceived, and still more so, if that which his enemies say; nay, even the character himself sees himself through the medium of his character, and not exactly as he is. Take all together, not omitting a shrewd hint from the clown or the fool, and perhaps your impression will be right; and you may know whether you have in fact discovered the poet's own idea, by all the speeches receiving light from it, and attesting its reality by reflecting it.

Lastly, in Shakspeare the heterogeneous is united, as it is in nature. You must not suppose a pressure or passion always acting on or in the character!—passion in Shakspeare is that by which the individual is distinguished from others, not that which makes a different kind of him. Shakspeare followed the main march of the human affections. He entered into no analysis of the passions or faiths of men, but assured himself that such and such passions and faiths were grounded in our common nature, and not in the mere accidents of ignorance or disease. This is an important consideration and constitutes our Shakspeare the morning star, the guide and the pioneer, of true philosophy.

OUTLINE OF AN INTRODUCTORY LECTURE UPON SHAKSPEARE.

Of that species of writing termed tragi-comedy, much has been produced and doomed to the shelf. Shakspeare's comic are continually re-acting upon his tragic characters. Lear, wandering amidst the tempest, has all his feelings of distress increased by the overflowings of the wild wit of the Fool, as vinegar poured upon wounds exacerbates their pain. Thus even his comic humor tends to the development of tragic passion.

The next characteristic of Shakspeare is his keeping at all times in the high road of life, &c.* Another evidence of his exquisite judgment is, that he seizes hold of popular tales; Lear and the Merchant of Venice were popular tales, but are so excellently managed, that both are the representations of men in all countries and of all times.

His dramas do not arise absolutely out of some one extraordinary circumstance, the scenes may stand independently of any such one connecting incident, as faithful representations of men and manners. In his mode of drawing characters there are no pompous descriptions of a man by himself; his character is to be drawn, as in real life, from the whole course of the play, or out of the mouths of his enemies or friends. This may be exemplified in Polonius, whose character has been often misrepresented. Shakspeare never intended him for a buffoon, &c.†

Another excellence of Shakspeare in which no writer equals him, is in the language of nature. So correct is it, that we can see ourselves in every page. The style and manner have also that felicity, that not a sentence can be read, without its being discovered if it is Shaksperian. In observation of living characters—of landlords and postilions Fielding has great excellence; but in drawing from his own heart, and depicting that species of character, which no observation could teach, he failed in comparison with Richardson, who perpetually places himself, as it were, in a day-dream. Shakspeare excels in both. Witness the accuracy of character in Juliet's Nurse; while for the great characters of Iago, Othello, Hamlet, Richard III., to which he could never have seen any thing similar, he seems invariably to have asked himself, How should I act or speak in such circumstances? His comic characters are also peculiar. A drunken constable was not uncommon; but he makes folly a vehicle for wit, as in Dogberry: every thing is a *sub-stratum* on which his genius can erect the mightiest superstructure.

To distinguish that which is legitimate in Shakspeare from

* See the foregoing Essay.—S. C.

† See the Notes on Hamlet, which contain the same general view of the character of Polonius. As there are a few additional hints in the present report, I have thought it worth printing.—S. C.

what does not belong to him, we must observe his varied images symbolical of novel truth, thrusting by, and seeming to trip up each other, from an impetuosity of thought, producing a flowing metre and seldom closing with the line. In Pericles, a play written fifty years before, but altered by Shakspeare, his additions may be recognized to half a line, from the metre, which has the same perfection in the flowing continuity of interchangeable metrical pauses in his earliest plays, as in Love's Labor's Lost.*

Lastly contrast his *morality* with the writers of his own or of the succeeding age, &c.† If a man speak injuriously of our friend, our vindication of him is naturally warm. Shakspeare has been accused of profaneness. I for my part have acquired from perusal of him, a habit of looking into my own heart, and am confident that Shakspeare is an author of all others the most calculated to make his readers better as well as wiser.

Shakspeare, possessed of wit, humor, fancy and imagination, built up an outward world from the stores within his mind, as the bee finds a hive‡ from a thousand sweets gathered from a thousand flowers. He was not only a great poet, but a great philosopher. Richard III., Iago, and Falstaff are men who reverse the order of things, who place intellect at the head, whereas it ought to follow, like Geometry, to prove and to confirm. No man, either hero or saint, ever acted from an unmixed motive; for let him do what he will rightly, still Conscience whispers "it is your duty." Richard, laughing at conscience and sneering at religion, felt a confidence in his intellect, which urged him to commit the most horrid crimes, because he felt himself, although inferior in form and shape, superior to those around him; he felt

* Lamb comparing Fletcher with Shakspeare, writes thus: "Fletcher's ideas moved slow; his versification, though sweet, is tedious, it stops at every turn; he lays line upon line, making up one after the other, adding image to image so deliberately, that we see their junctures. Shakspeare mingles every thing, runs line into line, embarrasses sentences and metaphors; before one idea has burst its shell, another is hatched and clamorous for disclosure." *Characters of Dram. Writers, contemp. with Shakspeare.*

† See the foregoing Essay.

‡ There must have been some mistake in the report of this sentence, unless there was a momentary lapse of mind on the part of the lecturer.

he possessed a power, which they had not. Iago, on the same principle, conscious of superior intellect, gave scope to his envy, and hesitated not to ruin a gallant, open and generous friend in the moment of felicity, because he was not promoted as he expected. Othello was superior in place, but Iago felt him to be inferior in intellect, and unrestrained by conscience, trampled upon him.—Falstaff, not a degraded man of genius, like Burns, but a man of degraded genius, with the same consciousness of superiority to his companions, fastened himself on a young Prince, to prove how much his influence on an heir-apparent would exceed that of a statesman. With this view he hesitated not to adopt the most contemptible of all characters, that of an open and professed liar: even his sensuality was subservient to his intellect; for he appeared to drink sack, that he might have occasion to show off his wit. One thing, however, worthy of observation, is the perpetual contrast of labor in Falstaff to produce wit, with the ease with which Prince Henry parries his shafts; and the final contempt which such a character deserves and receives from the young king, when Falstaff exhibits the struggle of inward determination with an outward show of humility.

ORDER OF SHAKSPEARE'S PLAYS.

Various attempts have been made to arrange the plays of Shakspeare, each according to its priority in time, by proofs derived from external documents. How unsuccessful these attempts have been might easily be shown, not only from the widely different results arrived at by men, all deeply versed in the black-letter books, old plays, pamphlets, manuscript records and catalogues of that age, but also from the fallacious and unsatisfactory nature of the facts and assumptions on which the evidence rests. In that age, when the press was chiefly occupied with controversial or practical divinity,—when the law, the church and the state engrossed all honor and respectability,—when a degree of disgrace, *levior quædam infamiæ macula*, was attached to the publication of poetry, and even to have sported with the Muse, as a private relaxation, was supposed to be—a venial fault, indeed, yet—something beneath the gravity of a wise man,—when the professed poets were so poor, that the very expenses of the press demanded the liberality of some wealthy individual, so that two thirds of Spenser's poetic works, and those most highly praised by his learned admirers and friends, remained for many years in manuscript, and in manuscript perished,—when the amateurs of the stage were comparatively few, and therefore for the greater part more or less known to each other,—when we know that the plays of Shakspeare, both during and after his life, were the property of the stage, and published by the players, doubtless according to their notions of acceptability with the visitants of the theatre,—in such an age, and under such circumstances, can an allusion or reference to any drama or poem in the publication of a contemporary be received as conclusive evidence, that such drama or poem had at that time been published? Or, further, can the priority of publication itself prove any thing in favor of actually prior composition.

We are tolerably certain, indeed, that the Venus and Adonis, and the Rape of Lucrece, were his two earliest poems, and though not printed until 1593, in the twenty-ninth year of his age, yet there can be little doubt that they had remained by him in manuscript many years. For Mr. Malone has made it highly probable, that he had commenced a writer for the stage in 1591, when he was twenty-seven years old, and Shakspeare himself assures us that the Venus and Adonis was the first heir of his invention.*

Baffled, then, in the attempt to derive any satisfaction from outward documents, we may easily stand excused if we turn our researches towards the internal evidences furnished by the writings themselves, with no other positive *data* than the known facts, that the Venus and Adonis was printed in 1593, the Rape of Lucrece in 1594, and that the Romeo and Juliet had appeared in 1595,—and with no other presumptions than that the poems, his very first productions, were written many years earlier,—(for who can believe that Shakspeare could have remained to his twenty-ninth or thirtieth year without attempting poetic composition of any kind?)—and that between these and Romeo and Juliet there had intervened one or two other dramas, or the chief materials, at least, of them, although they may very possi-

* But if the first heir of my invention prove deformed, I shall be sorry it had so noble a godfather, &c.

Dedication of the V. and A. to Lord Southampton.

bly have appeared after the success of the Romeo and Juliet and some other circumstances had given the poet an authority with the proprietors, and created a prepossession in his favor with the theatrical audiences.

CLASSIFICATION ATTEMPTED, 1802.

First Epoch.

The London Prodigal.
Cromwell.
Henry VI., three parts, first edition.
The old King John.
Edward III.
The old Taming of the Shrew.
Pericles.

All these are transition-works, *Uebergangswerke;* not his, yet of him.

Second Epoch.

All's Well That Ends Well :—but afterwards worked up afresh (*umgearbeitet*), especially Parolles.
The Two Gentlemen of Verona; a sketch.
Romeo and Juliet; first draft of it.

Third Epoch

rises into the full, although youthful Shakspeare; it was the negative period of his perfection.

Love's Labor's Lost.
Twelfth Night.
As You Like It.
Midsummer Night's Dream.
Richard II.
Henry IV. and V.
Henry VIII.; *Gelegenheitsgedicht.*
Romeo and Juliet, as at present.
Merchant of Venice.

Fourth Epoch.

Much Ado About Nothing.
Merry Wives of Windsor; first edition.
Henry VI.; *rifacimento.*

Fifth Epoch.

The period of beauty was now past; and that of δεινότης and grandeur succeeds.

Lear.
Macbeth.
Hamlet.
Timon of Athens; an after-vibration of Hamlet.
Troilus and Cressida; *Uebergang in die Ironie.*
The Roman Plays.
King John, as at present.
Merry Wives of Windsor. } *umgearbeitet.*
Taming of the Shrew. }
Measure for Measure.
Othello.
Tempest.
Winter's Tale.
Cymbeline.

CLASSIFICATION ATTEMPTED, 1810.

Shakspeare's earliest dramas I take to be,

Love's Labor's Lost.
All's Well That Ends Well.
Comedy of Errors.
Romeo and Juliet.

In the second class I reckon

Midsummer Night's Dream.
As You Like It.
Tempest.
Twelfth Night.

In the third, as indicating a greater energy—not merely of poetry, but—of all the world of thought, yet still with some of the growing pains, and the awkwardness of growth, I place

Troilus and Cressida.
Cymbeline.
Merchant of Venice.
Much Ado About Nothing.
Taming of the Shrew.

In the fourth, I place the plays containing the greatest characters :

Macbeth.
Lear.
Hamlet.
Othello.

And lastly, the historic dramas, in order to be able to show my reasons for rejecting some whole plays, and very many scenes in others.

CLASSIFICATION ATTEMPTED, 1819.

I think Shakspeare's earliest dramatic attempt—perhaps even prior in conception to the Venus and Adonis, and planned before he left Stratford—was Love's Labor's Lost. Shortly afterwards I suppose Pericles and certain scenes in Jeronymo to have been produced ; and in the same epoch, I place the Winter's Tale and Cymbeline, differing from the Pericles by the entire *rifacimento* of it, when Shakspeare's celebrity as poet, and his interest, no less than his influence as a manager, enabled him to bring forward the laid-by labors of his youth. The example of Titus Andronicus, which, as well as Jeronymo, was most popular in Shakspeare's first epoch, had led the young dramatist to the lawless mixture of dates and manners. In this same epoch I should place the Comedy of Errors, remarkable as being the only specimen of poetical farce in our language, that is, intentionally such ; so that all the distinct kinds of drama, which might be educed *à priori*, have their representatives in Shakspeare's works. I say intentionally such ; for many of Beaumont and Fletcher's plays, and the greater part of Ben Jonson's comedies are farce-plots. I add All's Well That Ends Well, originally intended as the counterpart of Love's Labor's Lost, Taming of the Shrew, Midsummer Night's Dream, Much Ado About Nothing, and Romeo and Juliet.

Second Epoch.

Richard II.
King John.
Henry VI.,—*rifacimento* only.
Richard III.

Third Epoch.

Henry IV.

Henry V.
Merry Wives of Windsor.
Henry VIII.,—a sort of historical masque, or show play.

Fourth Epoch

gives all the graces and facilities of a genius in full possession and habitual exercise of power, and peculiarly of the feminine, the *lady's* character.

Tempest.
As You Like It.
Merchant of Venice.
Twelfth Night,

and, finally, at its very point of culmination,—

Lear.
Hamlet.
Macbeth.
Othello.

Last Epoch,

when the energies of intellect in the cycle of genius were, though in a rich and more potentiated form, becoming predominant over passion and creative self-manifestation.

Measure for Measure.
Timon of Athens.
Coriolanus.
Julius Cæsar.
Antony and Cleopatra.
Troilus and Cressida.

Merciful, wonder-making Heaven ! what a man was this Shakspeare ! Myriad-minded, indeed, he was.

NOTES ON THE TEMPEST.

THERE is a sort of improbability with which we are shocked in dramatic representation, not less than in a narrative of real life. Consequently, there must be rules respecting it ; and as rules are nothing but means to an end previously ascertained—(inattention to which simple truth has been the occasion of all the pedantry of the French school),—we must first determine what the immediate end or object of the drama is. And here, as I have previously remarked, I find two extremes of critical decision;—the French, which evidently presupposes that a perfect delusion is to be aimed at,—an opinion which needs no fresh confutation; and the exact opposite to it, brought forward by Dr. Johnson, who supposes the auditors throughout in the full reflective knowledge of the contrary. In evincing the impossibility of delusion, he makes no sufficient allowance for an intermediate state, which I have before distinguished by the term, illusion, and have attempted to illustrate its quality and character by reference to our mental state, when dreaming. In both cases we simply do not judge the imagery to be unreal; there is a negative reality, and no more. Whatever, therefore, tends to prevent the mind from placing itself, or being placed, gradually in that state in which the images have such negative reality for the auditor, destroys this illusion, and is dramatically improbable.

Now the production of this effect—a sense of improbability—will depend on the degree of excitement in which the mind is supposed to be. Many things would be intolerable in the first scene of a play, that would not at all interrupt our enjoyment in the height of the interest, when the narrow cockpit may be made to hold

> The vasty field of France, or we may cram
> Within its wooden O, the very casques
> That did affright the air at Agincourt.

Again, on the other hand, many obvious improbabilities will be endured, as belonging to the groundwork of the story rather than to the drama itself, in the first scenes, which would disturb or disentrance us from all illusion in the acme of our excitement; as for instance, Lear's division of his kingdom, and the banishment of Cordelia.

But, although the other excellences of the drama besides this dramatic probability, as unity of interest, with distinctness and subordination of the characters, and appropriateness of style, are all, so far as they tend to increase the inward excitement, means towards accomplishing the chief end, that of producing and supporting this willing illusion,—yet they do not on that account cease to be ends themselves; and we must remember that, as such, they carry their own justification with them, as long as they do not contravene or interrupt the total illusion. It is not even always, or of necessity, an objection to them, that they prevent the illusion from rising to as great a height as it might otherwise have attained;—it is enough that they are simply compatible with as high a degree of it as is requisite for the purpose. Nay, upon particular occasions, a palpable improbability may be hazarded by a great genius for the express purpose of keeping down the interest of a merely instrumental scene, which would otherwise make too great an impression for the harmony of the entire illusion. Had the panorama been invented in the time of Pope Leo X., Raffael would still, I doubt not, have smiled in contempt at the regret, that the broom-twigs and scrubby bushes at the back of some of his grand pictures were not as probable trees as those in the exhibition.

The Tempest is a specimen of the purely romantic drama, in which the interest is not historical, or dependent upon fidelity of portraiture, or the natural connection of events,—but is a birth of the imagination, and rests only on the coaptation and union of the elements granted to, or assumed by, the poet. It is a species of drama which owes no allegiance to time or space, and in which, therefore, errors of chronology and geography—no mortal sins in any species—are venial faults, and count for nothing. It addresses itself entirely to the imaginative faculty; and although the illusion may be assisted by the effect on the senses of the complicated scenery and decorations of modern times, yet this sort of assistance is dangerous. For the principal and only genuine excitement ought to come from within,—from the moved and sympathetic imagination; whereas, where so much is addressed to the mere external senses of seeing and hearing, the spiritual vision is apt to languish, and the attraction from without will withdraw the mind from the proper and only legitimate interest which is intended to spring from within.

The romance opens with a busy scene admirably appropriate to the kind of drama, and giving, as it were, the key-note to the whole harmony. It prepares and initiates the excitement required for the entire piece, and yet does not demand any thing from the spectators, which their previous habits had not fitted them to understand. It is the bustle of a tempest, from which the real horrors are abstracted;—therefore it is poetical, though not in strictness natural—(the distinction to which I have so often alluded)—and is purposely restrained from concentering the interest on itself, but used merely as an induction or tuning for what is to follow.

In the second scene, Prospero's speeches, till the entrance of Ariel, contain the finest example, I remember, of retrospective narration for the purpose of exciting immediate interest, and putting the audience in possession of all the information necessary for the understanding of the plot.* Observe, too, the perfect probability of the moment chosen by Prospero (the very Shakspeare himself, as it were, of the tempest) to open out the truth to his daughter, his own romantic bearing, and how completely any thing that might have been disagreeable to us in the magician, is reconciled and shaded in the humanity and natural feelings of the father. In the very first speech of Miranda the simplicity and tenderness of her character are at once laid open; —it would have been lost in direct contact with the agitation of the first scene. The opinion once prevailed, but, happily, is now abandoned, that Fletcher alone wrote for women;—the truth is, that with very few, and those partial exceptions, the female characters in the plays of Beaumont and Flether are, when of the light kind, not decent; when heroic, complete viragos. But in Shakspeare all the elements of womanhood are holy, and there is the sweet, yet dignified feeling of all that *continuates* society, as sense of ancestry and of sex, with a purity unassailable by sophistry, because it rests not in the analytic processes, but in that sane equipoise of the faculties, during which the feelings are representative of all past experience,—not of the individual only,

* *Pro.* Mark his condition, and th' event; then tell me,
If this might be a brother.
Mira. I should sin,
To think but nobly of my grandmother;
Good wombs have bore bad sons.
Pro. Now the condition, &c.

Theobald has a note upon this passage, and suggests that Shakspeare placed it thus:—

Pro. Good wombs have bore bad sons,—
Now the condition.

Mr. Coleridge writes in the margin: "I can not but believe that Theobald is quite right."—*Ed.*

but of all those by whom she has been educated, and their predecessors even up to the first mother that lived. Shakspeare saw that the want of prominence, which Pope notices for sarcasm, was the blessed beauty of the woman's character, and knew that it arose not from any deficiency, but from the more exquisite harmony of all the parts of the moral being constituting one living total of head and heart. He has drawn it, indeed, in all its distinctive energies of faith, patience, constancy, fortitude,—shown in all of them as following the heart, which gives its results by a nice tact and happy intuition, without the intervention of the discursive faculty, sees all things in and by the light of the affections, and errs, if it ever err, in the exaggerations of love alone. In all the Shaksperian women there is essentially the same foundation and principle ; the distinct individuality and variety are merely the result of the modification of circumstances, whether in Miranda the maiden, in Imogen the wife, or in Katherine the queen.

But to return. The appearance and characters of the super or ultra-natural servants are finely contrasted. Ariel has in every thing the airy tint which gives the name ; and it is worthy of remark that Miranda is never directly brought into comparison with Ariel, lest the natural and human of the one and the supernatural of the other should tend to neutralize each other ; Caliban, on the other hand, is all earth, all condensed and gross in feelings and images ; (*p*) he has the dawnings of understanding without reason or the moral sense, and in him, as in some brute animals, this advance to the intellectual faculties, without the moral sense, is marked by the appearance of vice. For it is in the primacy of the moral being only that man is truly human ; in his intellectual powers he is certainly approached by the brutes, and, man's whole system duly considered, those powers can not be considered other than means to an end, that is, to morality.

In this scene, as it proceeds, is displayed the impression made by Ferdinand and Miranda on each other ; it is love at first sight :

> At the first sight
> They have chang'd eyes :—

and it appears to me, that in all cases of real love, it is at one moment that it takes place. That moment may have been prepared by previous esteem, admiration, or even affection,—yet love seems to require a momentary act of volition, by which a tacit bond of devotion is imposed,—a bond not to be thereafter broken without violating what should be sacred in our nature. How finely is the true Shaksperian scene contrasted with Dryden's vulgar alteration of it, in which a mere ludicrous psychological experiment, as it were, is tried—displaying nothing but indelicacy without passion. Prospero's interruption of the courtship has often seemed to me to have no sufficient motive; still his alleged reason—

lest too light winning
Make the prize light—

is enough for the ethereal connections of the romantic imagination, although it would not be so for the historical.* The whole courting scene, indeed, in the beginning of the third act, between the lovers, is a masterpiece; and the first dawn of disobedience in the mind of Miranda to the command of her father is very finely drawn, so as to seem the working of the Scriptural command, *Thou shalt leave father and mother*, &c. O! with what exquisite purity this scene is conceived and executed! Shakspeare may sometimes be gross, but I boldly say that he is always moral and modest. Alas! in this our day decency of manners is preserved at the expense of morality of heart, and delicacies for vice are allowed, whilst grossness against it is hypocritically, or at least morbidly, condemned.

In this play are admirably sketched the vices generally accompanying a low degree of civilization; and in the first scene of the second act Shakspeare has, as in many other places, shown the tendency in bad men to indulge in scorn and contemptuous expressions, as a mode of getting rid of their own uneasy feelings of inferiority to the good, and also, by making the good ridiculous, of rendering the transition of others to wickedness easy. Shakspeare never puts habitual scorn into the mouths of other than bad men, as here in the instances of Antonio and Sebastian. The scene of the intended assassination of Alonzo and Gonzalo is

* *Fer.* Yes, faith, and all his Lords, the Duke of Milan,
And his brave son, being twain.

Theobald remarks that nobody was lost in the wreck; and yet that no such character is introduced in the fable, as the Duke of Milan's son. Mr. C. notes: "Must not Ferdinand have believed he was lost in the fleet that the tempest scattered?"—*Ed.*

an exact counterpart of the scene between Macbeth and his lady, only pitched in a lower key throughout, as designed to be frustrated and concealed, and exhibiting the same profound management in the manner of familiarizing a mind, not immediately recipient, to the suggestion of guilt, by associating the proposed crime with something ludicrous or out of place,—something not habitually matter of reverence. By this kind of sophistry the imagination and fancy are first bribed to contemplate the suggested act, and at length to become acquainted with it. Observe how the effect of this scene is heightened by another counterpart of it in low life,—that between the conspirators Stephano, Caliban, and Trinculo in the second scene of the third act, in which there are the same essential characteristics.

In this play and in this scene of it are also shown the springs of the vulgar in politics,—of that kind of politics which is inwoven with human nature. In his treatment of this subject, wherever it occurs, Shakspeare is quite peculiar. In other writers we find the particular opinions of the individual; in Massinger it is rank republicanism; in Beaumont and Fletcher even *jure divino* principles are carried to excess;—but Shakspeare never promulgates any party tenets. He is always the philosopher and the moralist, but at the same time with a profound veneration for all the established institutions of society, and for those classes which form the permanent elements of the state—especially never introducing a professional character, as such, otherwise than as respectable. If he must have any name, he should be styled a philosophical aristocrat, delighting in those hereditary institutions which have a tendency to bind one age to another, and in that distinction of ranks, of which, although few may be in possession, all enjoy the advantages. Hence, again, you will observe the good nature with which he seems always to make sport with the passions and follies of a mob, as with an irrational animal. He is never angry with it, but hugely content with holding up its absurdities to its face; and sometimes you may trace a tone of almost affectionate superiority, something like that in which a father speaks of the rogueries of a child. See the good-humored way in which he describes Stephano passing from the most licentious freedom to absolute despotism over Trinculo and Caliban. The truth is, Shakspeare's characters are all *genera* intensely individualized; the results of meditation, of which observation supplied the drapery and the colors necessary to combine them with each other. He had virtually surveyed all the great component powers and impulses of human nature,—had seen that their different combinations and subordinations were in fact the individualizers of men, and showed how their harmony was produced by reciprocal disproportions of excess or deficiency. The language in which these truths are expressed was not drawn from any set fashion, but from the profoundest depths of his moral being, and is therefore for all ages.

LOVE'S LABOR'S LOST.

The characters in this play are either impersonated out of Shakspeare's own multiformity by imaginative self-position, or out of such as a country town and school-boy's observation might supply,—the curate, the schoolmaster, the Armado (who even in my time was not extinct in the cheaper inns of North Wales), and so on. The satire is chiefly on follies of words. Biron and Rosaline are evidently the pre-existent state of Benedict and Beatrice, and so, perhaps, is Boyet of Lafeu, and Costard of the Tapster in Measure for Measure; and the frequency of the rhymes, the sweetness as well as the smoothness of the metre, and the number of acute and fancifully illustrated aphorisms, are all as they ought to be in a poet's youth. True genius begins by generalizing and condensing; it ends in realizing and expanding. It first collects the seeds.

Yet if this juvenile drama had been the only one extant of our Shakspeare, and we possessed the tradition only of his riper works, or accounts of them in writers who had not even mentioned this play,—how many of Shakspeare's characteristic features might we not still have discovered in Love's Labor's Lost, though as in a portrait taken of him in his boyhood.

I can never sufficiently admire the wonderful activity of thought throughout the whole of the first scene of the play, rendered natural, as it is, by the choice of the characters, and the whimsical determination on which the drama is founded. A whimsical determination certainly;—yet not altogether so very improbable to those who are conversant in the history of the middle ages, with their Courts of Love, and all that lighter drapery of chivalry, which engaged even mighty kings with a sort of serio-comic interest, and may well be supposed to have occupied more completely the smaller princes, at a time when the noble's or prince's court contained the only theatre of the domain or principality. This sort of story, too, was admirably suited to Shakspeare's times, when the English court was still the foster-mother of the state and the muses; and when, in consequence, the courtiers, and men of rank and fashion, affected a display of wit, point, and sententious observation, that would be deemed intolerable at present,—but in which a hundred years of controversy, involving every great political, and every dear domestic, interest, had trained all but the lowest classes to participate. Add to this the very style of the sermons of the time, and the eagerness of the Protestants to distinguish themselves by long and frequent preaching, it will be found that, from the reign of Henry VIII. to the abdication of James II., no country ever received such a national education as England.

Hence the comic matter chosen in the first instance is a ridiculous imitation or apery of this constant striving after logical precision, and subtle opposition of thoughts, together with a making the most of every conception or image, by expressing it under the least expected property belonging to it, and this, again, rendered specially absurd by being applied to the most current subjects and occurrences. The phrases and modes of combination in argument were caught by the most ignorant from the custom of the age, and their ridiculous misapplication of them is most amusingly exhibited in Costard; whilst examples suited only to the gravest propositions and impersonations, or apostrophes to abstract thoughts impersonated, which are in fact the natural language only of the most vehement agitations of the mind, are adopted by the coxcombry of Armado as mere artifices of ornament.

The same kind of intellectual action is exhibited in a more serious and elevated strain in many other parts of this play. Biron's speech at the end of the fourth act is an excellent specimen of it. It is logic clothed in rhetoric;—but observe how Shakspeare, in his two-fold being of poet and philosopher, avails himself of it to convey profound truths in the most lively images,—the whole remaining faithful to the character supposed to utter the lines, and the expressions themselves constituting a further development of that character:—

Other slow arts entirely keep the brain:
And therefore finding barren practisers,
Scarce show a harvest of their heavy toil:
But love, first learned in a lady's eyes,
Lives not alone immured in the brain;
But, with the motion of all elements,
Courses as swift as thought in every power;
And gives to every power a double power,
Above their functions and their offices.
It adds a precious seeing to the eye,
A lover's eyes will gaze an eagle blind;
A lover's ear will hear the lowest sound,
When the suspicious tread of theft is stopp'd:
Love's feeling is more soft and sensible,
Than are the tender horns of cockled snails;
Love's tongue proves dainty Bacchus gross in taste;
For valor, is not love a Hercules,
Still climbing trees in the Hesperides?
Subtle as Sphinx; as sweet and musical,
As bright Apollo's lute, strung with his hair;
And when love speaks, the voice of all the gods
Makes heaven drowsy with the harmony.
Never durst poet touch a pen to write,
Until his ink were temper'd with love's sighs;
O, then his lines would ravish savage ears,
And plant in tyrants mild humility.
From women's eyes this doctrine I derive:
They sparkle still the right Promethean fire;
They are the books, the arts, the academes,
That show, contain, and nourish all the world;
Else, none at all in aught proves excellent;
Then fools you were these women to forswear;
Or, keeping what is sworn, you will prove fools.
For wisdom's sake, a word that all men love;
Or for love's sake, a word that loves all men;
Or for men's sake, the authors of these women;
Or women's sake, by whom we men are men;
Let us once lose our oaths, to find ourselves,
Or else we lose ourselves to keep our oaths:
It is religion, to be thus forsworn:
For charity itself fulfils the law:
And who can sever love from charity?—

This is quite a study;—sometimes you see this youthful god of poetry connecting disparate thoughts purely by means of resemblances in the words expressing them—a thing in character in lighter comedy, especially of that kind in which Shakspeare delights, namely, the purposed display of wit, though, sometimes, too, disfiguring his graver scenes;—but more often you may see him doubling the natural connection or order of logical consequence in the thoughts by the introduction of an artificial and sought for resemblance in the words, as, for instance, in the third line of the play—

> And then grace us in the disgrace of death;—

this being a figure often having its force and propriety, as justified by the law of passion, which, inducing in the mind an unusual activity, seeks for means to waste its superfluity—when in the highest degree—in lyric repetitions and sublime tautology—(*at her feet he bowed, he fell, he lay down; at her feet he bowed, he fell; where he bowed, there he fell down dead*)—and, in lower degrees, in making the words themselves the subjects and materials of that surplus action, and for the same cause that agitates our limbs, and forces our very gestures into a tempest in states of high excitement.

The mere style of narration in Love's Labor's Lost, like that of Ægeon in the first scene of the Comedy of Errors, and of the Captain in the second scene of Macbeth, seems imitated with its defects and its beauties from Sir Philip Sidney; whose Arcadia, though not then published, was already well known in manuscript copies, and could hardly have escaped the notice and admiration of Shakspeare as the friend and client of the Earl of Southampton. The chief defect consists in the parentheses and parenthetic thoughts and descriptions, suited neither to the passion of the speaker, nor the purpose of the person to whom the information is to be given, but manifestly betraying the author himself—not by way of continuous under-song, but—palpably, and so as to show themselves addressed to the general reader. However, it is not unimportant to notice how strong a presumption the diction and allusions of this play afford, that, though Shakspeare's acquirements in the dead languages might not be such as we suppose in a learned education, his habits had, nevertheless, been scholastic, and those of a student. For a young author's first work almost always bespeaks his recent pursuits, and his first observations of life are either drawn from the immediate employments of his youth, and from the characters and images most deeply impressed on his mind in the situations in which those employments had placed him;—or else they are fixed on such objects and occurrences in the world, as are easily connected with, and seem to bear upon, his studies and the hitherto exclusive subjects of his meditation. Just as Ben Jonson, who applied himself to the drama after having served in Flanders, fills his earliest plays with true or pretended soldiers, the wrongs and neglects of the former, and the absurd boasts and knavery of their counterfeits. So Lessing's first comedies are placed in the universities, and consist of events and characters conceivable in an academic life.

I will only further remark the sweet and tempered gravity, with which Shakspeare in the end draws the only fitting moral which such a drama afforded. Here Rosaline rises up to the full height of Beatrice:—

Ros. Oft have I heard of you, my lord Biron,
Before I saw you, and the world's large tongue
Proclaims you for a man replete with mocks;
Full of comparisons, and wounding flouts,
Which you on all estates will execute
That lie within the mercy of your wit:
To weed this wormwood from your fruitful brain,
And therewithal, to win me, if you please,
(Without the which I am not to be won,)
You shall this twelvemonth term from day to day
Visit the speechless sick, and still converse
With groaning wretches; and your talk shall be,
With all the fierce endeavor of your wit,
To enforce the pained impotent to smile.
Biron. To move wild laughter in the throat of death?
It can not be; it is impossible;
Mirth can not move a soul in agony.
Ros. Why, that's the way to choke a gibing spirit,
Whose influence is begot of that loose grace,
Which shallow laughing hearers give to fools:
A jest's prosperity lies in the ear
Of him that hears it, never in the tongue
Of him that makes it: then, if sickly ears,
Deaf'd with the clamors of their own dear groans,
Will hear your idle scorns, continue then,
And I will have you, and that fault withal;
But, if they will not, throw away that spirit,
And I shall find you empty of that fault,
Right joyful of your reformation.

Act v. sc. 2. In Biron's speech to the Princess:

— and, therefore, like the eye,
Full of *straying* shapes, of habits, and of forms—

Either read *stray*, which I prefer; or throw *full* back to the preceding lines—

like the eye, full
Of straying shapes, &c.

In the same scene:

Biron. And what to me, my love? and what to me?
Ros. You must be purged too, your sins are rank;
You are attaint with fault and perjury:
Therefore, if you my favor mean to get,
A twelvemonth shall you spend, and never rest,
But seek the weary beds of people sick.

There can be no doubt, indeed, about the propriety of expunging this speech of Rosaline's; it soils the very page that retains it. But I do not agree with Warburton and others in striking out the preceding line also. It is quite in Biron's character; and Rosaline not answering it immediately, Dumain takes up the question for him, and, after he and Longaville are answered, Biron, with evident propriety, says:—

Studies my mistress? &c.

MIDSUMMER NIGHT'S DREAM.

Act i. sc. 1.

Her. O cross! too high to be enthrall'd to low—
Lys. Or else misgrafted, in respect of years;
Her. O spite! too old to be engag'd to young—
Lys. Or else it stood upon the choice of friends.
Her. O hell! to chuse love by another's eye!

THERE is no authority for any alteration;—but I never can help feeling how great an improvement it would be, if the two former of Hermia's exclamations were omitted;—the third and only appropriate one would then become a beauty, and most natural.

Ib. Helena's speech:—

I will go tell him of fair Hermia's flight, &c.

I am convinced that Shakspeare availed himself of the title of this play in his own mind, and worked upon it as a dream throughout, but especially, and, perhaps, unpleasingly, in this broad determination of ungrateful treachery in Helena, so undisguisedly avowed to herself, and this, too, after the witty cool philosophizing that precedes. The act itself is natural, and the resolve so to act is, I fear, likewise too true a picture of the lax hold which principles have on a woman's heart, when opposed to, or even separated from, passion and inclination. For women are less hypocrites to their own minds than men are, because in general they feel less proportionate abhorrence of moral evil in and for itself, and more of its outward consequences, as detection, and loss of character than men—their natures being almost wholly extroitive. Still, however just in itself, the representation of this is not poetical; we shrink from it, and can not harmonize it with the ideal.

Act ii. sc. 1. Theobald's edition.

Through bush, *through* brier—
* * * * *
Through flood, *through* fire—

What a noble pair of ears this worthy Theobald must have had! The eight amphimacers or cretics,—

Ovĕr hīll, ōvĕr dāle,
Thōrŏ' būsh, thōrŏ' brīer,
Ovĕr pārk, ōvĕr pāle,
Thōrŏ' flōōd, thōrŏ fīre—

have a delightful effect on the ear in their sweet transition to the trochaic,—

I dŏ wāndĕr ēv'ry whērĕ
Swīftĕr thān thĕ mōōnĕs sphērĕ, &c.

The last words as sustaining the rhyme, must be considered, as in fact they are, trochees in time.

It may be worth while to give some correct examples in English of the principal metrical feet:

Pyrrhic or Dibrach, ◡ ◡ = *bŏdў, spĭrĭt.*
Tribrach, ◡ ◡ ◡ = *nŏbŏdў*, hastily pronounced.
Iambus ◡ — = *dĕlīght.*
Trochee, — ◡ = *līghtlў.*
Spondee, — — = *Gōd spāke.*

The paucity of spondees in single words in English and, indeed, in the modern languages in general, makes, perhaps, the greatest distinction, metrically considered, between them and the Greek and Latin.

Dactyl, — ᴗ ᴗ = *mĕrrĭlў.*
Anapæst, ᴗ ᴗ — = *ă prŏpōs*, or the first three syllables of *cĕrĕmōny.**
Amphibrachys, ᴗ — ᴗ = *dĕlīghtfŭl.*
Amphimacer, — ᴗ — = *ōvĕr hīll.*
Antibacchius, ᴗ — — = *thĕ Lōrd Gōd.*
Bacchius, — — ᴗ = *Hēlvēllўn.*
Molossus, — — — = *John James Jones.*

These simple feet may suffice for understanding the metres of Shakspeare, for the greater part at least :—but Milton can not be made harmoniously intelligible without the composite feet, the Ionics, Pæons, and Epitrites.

Ib. sc. 2 Titania's speech :—(Theobald adopting Warburton's reading.)

> Which she, with pretty and with swimming gate
> *Follying* (her womb then rich with my young squire)
> Would imitate, &c.

Oh ! oh ! Heaven have mercy on poor Shakspeare, and also on Mr. Warburton's mind's eye !

Act v. sc. 1. Theseus' speech :—(Theobald.)

> And what poor [*willing*] duty can not do,
> Noble respect takes it in might, not merit.

To my ears it would read far more Shaksperian thus :

> And what poor duty can not do, *yet would*
> Noble respect, &c.

Ib. sc. 2.

> *Puck.* Now the hungry lion roars,
> And the wolf behowls the moon;
> Whilst the heavy ploughman snores
> All with weary task foredone, &c.

Very Anacreon in perfectness, proportion, grace, and spontaneity ! So far it is Greek ;—but then add, O ! what wealth, what wild ranging, and yet what compression and condensation of,

* Written probably by mistake for "cĕrĕmōnious."

English fancy! In truth, there is nothing in Anacreon more perfect than these thirty lines, or half so rich and imaginative. They form a speckless diamond.

COMEDY OF ERRORS.

THE myriad-minded man, our, and all men's, Shakspeare, has in this piece presented us with a legitimate farce in exactest consonance with the philosophical principles and character of farce, as distinguished from comedy and from entertainments. A proper farce is mainly distinguished from comedy by the license allowed, and even required, in the fable, in order to produce strange and laughable situations. The story need not be probable, it is enough that it is possible. A comedy would scarcely allow even the two Antipholuses; because, although there have been instances of almost indistinguishable likeness in two persons, yet these are mere individual accidents, *casus ludentis naturæ,* and the *verum* will not excuse the *inverisimile.* But farce dares add the two Dromios, and is justified in so doing by the laws of its end and constitution. In a word, farces commence in a postulate, which must be granted.

AS YOU LIKE IT.

Act i. sc. 1.

> *Oli.* What, boy!
> *Orla.* Come, come, elder brother, you are too young in this.
> *Oli.* Wilt thou lay hands on me, villain?

THERE is a beauty here. The word 'boy' naturally provokes and awakens in Orlando the sense of his manly powers; and with the retort of 'elder brother,' he grasps him with firm hands, and makes him feel he is no boy.

Ib. *Oli.* Farewell, good Charles.—Now will I stir this gamester: I hope, I shall see an end of him; for my soul, yet I know not why, hates nothing more than him. Yet he's gentle; never school'd, and yet learn'd; full of noble device; of all sorts enchantingly beloved! and, indeed, so much in the heart of the world, and especially of my own people, who best know him, that I am altogether misprized: but it shall not be so long; this wrestler shall clear all.

This has always appeared to me one of the most un-Shakspeerian speeches in all the genuine works of our poet; yet I should be nothing surprised, and greatly pleased, to find it hereafter a fresh beauty, as has so often happened to me with other supposed defects of great men. 1810.

It is too venturous to charge a passage in Shakspeare with want of truth to nature; and yet at first sight this speech of Oliver's expresses truths, which it seems almost impossible that any mind should so distinctly, so livelily, and so voluntarily, have presented to itself in connection with feelings and intentions so malignant, and so contrary to those which the qualities expressed would naturally have called forth. But I dare not say that this seeming unnaturalness is not in the nature of an abused wilfulness, when united with a strong intellect. In such characters there is sometimes a gloomy self-gratification in making the absoluteness of the will (*sit pro ratione voluntas!*) evident to themselves by setting the reason and the conscience in full array against it. 1818.

Ib. sc. 2.

Celia. If you saw yourself with *your* eyes, or knew yourself with *your* judgment, the fear of your adventure would counsel you to a more equal enterprise.

Surely it should be '*our* eyes' and '*our* judgment.'

Ib. sc. 3.

> *Cel.* But is all this for your father?
> *Ros.* No, some of it is for *my child's father.*

Theobald restores this as the reading of the older editions. It may be so: but who can doubt that it is a mistake for 'my father's child,' meaning herself? According to Theobald's note, a most indelicate anticipation is put into the mouth of Rosalind without reason;—and besides what a strange thought, and how out of place, and unintelligible!

Act iv. sc. 2.

> Take thou no scorn
> To wear the horn, the lusty horn;
> It was a crest ere thou wast born.

I question whether there exists a parallel instance of a phrase, that like this of 'horns' is universal in all languages, and yet for which no one has discovered even a plausible origin.

TWELFTH NIGHT.

Act i. sc. 1. Duke's speech :—

> — so full of shapes is fancy,
> That it alone is high fantastical.

WARBURTON's alteration of *is* into *in* is needless. 'Fancy' may very well be interpreted 'exclusive affection,' or 'passionate preference.' Thus, bird-fanciers, gentlemen of the fancy, that is, amateurs of boxing, &c. The play of assimilation,—the meaning one sense chiefly, and yet keeping both senses in view, is perfectly Shaksperian.

Act ii. sc. 3. Sir Andrew's speech :—

An explanatory note on *Pigrogromitus* would have been more acceptable than Theobald's grand discovery that 'lemon' ought to be 'leman.'

Ib. Sir Toby's speech : (Warburton's note on the Peripatetic philosophy.)

> Shall we rouse the night-owl in a catch, that will draw three souls out of one weaver ?

O genuine, and inimitable (at least I hope so) Warburton ! This note of thine, if but one in five millions, would be half a one too much.

Ib. sc. 4.

> *Duke.* My life upon't, young though thou art, thine eye
> Hath stay'd upon some favor that it loves ;
> Hath it not, boy ?
> *Vio.* A little, by your favor.
> *Duke.* What kind of woman is't ?

And yet Viola was to have been presented to Orsino as a eunuch! —Act i. sc. 2. Viola's speech. Either she forgot this, or else she had altered her plan.

Ib.

> *Vio.* A blank, my lord ; she never told her love !—
> But let concealment, &c.

After the first line (of which the last five words should be spoken with, and drop down in, a deep sigh), the actress ought to make a pause ; and then start afresh, from the activity of thought, born of suppressed feelings, and which thought had accumulated during the brief interval, as vital heat under the skin during a dip in cold water.

Ib. sc. 5.

Fabian. Though our silence be drawn from us by *cars*, yet peace.

Perhaps, 'cables.'

Act iii. sc. 1.

Clown. A sentence is but a *cheveril* glove to a good wit. (Theobald's note.)

Theobald's etymology of 'cheveril' is, of course, quite right ; —but he is mistaken in supposing that there were no such things as gloves of chicken-skin. They were at one time a main article in chirocosmetics.

Act v. sc. 1. Clown's speech :—

So that, *conclusions to be as kisses,* if your four negatives make your two affirmatives, why, then, the worse for my friends, and the better for my foes.

(Warburton reads 'conclusion to be asked, is.')

Surely Warburton could never have wooed by kisses and won, or he would not have flounder-flatted so just and humorous, nor less pleasing than humorous, an image into so profound a nihility. In the name of love and wonder, do not four kisses make a double affirmative ? The humor lies in the whispered 'No !' and the inviting 'Don't !' with which the maiden's kisses are accompanied, and thence compared to negatives, which by repetition constitute an affirmative.

ALL'S WELL THAT ENDS WELL.

Act i. sc. 1.

Count. If the living be enemy to the grief, the excess makes it soon mortal.
Bert. Madam, I desire your holy wishes.
Laf. How understand we that ?

Bertram and Lafeu, I imagine, both speak together,—Lafeu referring to the Countess's rather obscure remark.

Act ii. sc. 1. (Warburton's note.)

> *King.* —let *higher* Italy
> (Those *'bated*, that inherit but the fall
> Of the last monarchy) see, that you come
> Not to woo honor, but to wed it.

It would be, I own, an audacious and unjustifiable change of the text; but yet, as a mere conjecture, I venture to suggest 'bastards,' for ''bated.' As it stands, in spite of Warburton's note, I can make little or nothing of it. Why should the king except the then most illustrious states, which, as being republics, were the more truly inheritors of the Roman grandeur?—With my conjecture, the sense would be;—'let higher, or the more northern part of Italy—(unless 'higher' be a corruption for 'hir'd,' —the metre seeming to demand a monosyllable) (those bastards that inherit the infamy only of their fathers) see, &c.' The following 'woo' and 'wed' are so far confirmative as they indicate Shakspeare's manner of connection by unmarked influences of association from some preceding metaphor. This it is which makes his style so peculiarly vital and organic. Likewise 'those girls of Italy' strengthen the guess. The absurdity of Warburton's gloss, which represents the king calling Italy superior, and then excepting the only part the lords were going to visit, must strike every one.

Ib. sc. 3.

> *Laf.* They say, miracles are past; and we have our philosophical persons to make modern and familiar, things supernatural and *causeless.*

Shakspeare, inspired, as it might seem, with all knowledge, here uses the word 'causeless' in its strict philosophical sense;—cause being truly predicable only of *phenomena*, that is, things natural, and not of *noumena*, or things supernatural.

Act iii. sc. 5.

> *Dia.* The Count Rousillon:—know you such a one?
> *Hel.* But by the ear that hears most nobly of him;
> His face I know not.

Shall we say here, that Shakspeare has unnecessarily made his loveliest character utter a lie?—Or shall we dare think that, where to deceive was necessary, he thought a pretended verbal verity a double crime, equally with the other a lie to the hearer, and at the same time an attempt to lie to one's own conscience?

MERRY WIVES OF WINDSOR.

Act i. sc. 1.

> *Shal.* The luce is the fresh fish, the salt fish is an old coat.

I CAN not understand this. Perhaps there is a corruption both of words and speakers. Shallow no sooner corrects one mistake of Sir Hugh's, namely 'louse' for 'luce,' a pike, but the honest Welchman falls into another, namely, 'cod' (*baccalà*) *Cambrice* 'cot' for coat.

> *Shal.* The luce is the fresh fish—
> *Evans.* The salt fish is an old cot.

'Luce is a fresh fish, and not a louse,' says Shallow. 'Aye, aye,' quoth Sir Hugh; 'the *fresh* fish is the luce; it is an old cod that is the salt fish.' At all events, as the text stands, there is no sense at all in the words.

Ib. sc. 3.

> *Fal.* Now, the report goes, she has all the rule of her husband's purse; she hath a legion of angels.
> *Pist.* As many devils entertain; and *To her, boy,* say I.

Perhaps it is—

> As many devils enter (or enter'd) swine; and *to her, boy,* say I:—

a somewhat profane, but not un-Shaksperian, allusion to the 'legion' in St. Luke's 'gospel.'

MEASURE FOR MEASURE.

THIS play, which is Shakspeare's throughout, is to me the most painful—say rather, the only painful—part of his genuine works. The comic and tragic parts equally border on the μισητὸν,—the one being disgusting, the other horrible; and the pardon and marriage of Angelo not merely baffles the strong indignant claim of justice—(for cruelty, with lust and damnable baseness, can not be forgiven, because we can not conceive them as being morally repented of)—but it is likewise degrading to the character of woman. Beaumont and Fletcher, who can follow Shakspeare in his errors only, have presented a still worse, because more loathsome and contradictory, instance of the same kind in the Night-Walker, in the marriage of Alathe to Algripe. Of the counterbalancing beauties of Measure for Measure, I need say nothing; for I have already remarked that the play is Shakspeare's throughout.

Act iii. sc. 1.

Ay, but to die, and go we know not where, &c.

This natural fear of Claudio, from the antipathy we have to death, seems very little varied from that infamous wish of Mæcenas, recorded in the 101st epistle of Seneca:

Debilem facito manu
Debilem pede, coxa, &c.—Warburton's note.

I can not but think this rather an heroic resolve, than an infamous wish. It appears to me to be the grandest symptom of an immortal spirit, when even that bedimmed and overwhelmed spirit recked not of its own immortality, still to seek to be,—to be a mind, a will.

As fame is to reputation, so heaven is to an estate, or immediate advantage. The difference is, that the self-love of the former can not exist but by a complete suppression and habitual supplantation of immediate selfishness. In one point of view, the miser is more estimable than the spendthrift;—only that the miser's present feelings are as much of the present as the spendthrift's. But *cæteris paribus*, that is, upon the supposition that whatever is good or lovely in the one coexists equally in the other, then, doubtless, the master of the present is less a selfish being, an animal, than he who lives for the moment with no inheritance in the future. Whatever can degrade man, is supposed in the latter case, whatever can elevate him, in the former. And as to self;—strange and generous self! that can only be such a self by a complete divestment of all that men call self,—of all that can make it either practically to others, or consciously to the individual himself, different from the human race in its ideal. Such self is but a perpetual religion, an inalienable acknowledgment of God, the sole basis and ground of being. In this sense, how can I love God, and not love myself as far as it is of God?

Ib. sc. 2.

> Pattern in himself to know,
> Grace to stand, and virtue go.

Worse metre, indeed, but better English would be,—

> Grace to stand, virtue to go.

CYMBELINE.

Act i. sc. 1.

> You do not meet a man, but frowns: our bloods
> No more obey the heavens, than our courtiers'
> Still seem, as does the king's.

THERE can be little doubt of Mr. Tyrwhitt's emendations of 'courtiers' and 'king,' as to the sense;—only it is not impossible that Shakspeare's dramatic language may allow of the word, 'brows' or 'faces' being understood after the word 'courtiers,' which might then remain in the genitive case plural. But the nominative plural makes excellent sense, and is sufficiently elegant, and sounds to my ear Shaksperian. What, however, is meant by 'our bloods no more obey the heavens?' Dr. Johnson's assertion, that 'bloods' signify 'countenances,' is, I think, mistaken both in the thought conveyed—(for it was never a popular belief that the stars governed men's countenances)—and in the usage, which requires an antithesis of the blood,—or the temperament of the four humors, choler, melancholy, phlegm, and the red globules, or the sanguine portion, which was supposed not to be in our own power, but, to be dependent on the influences of the heavenly bodies,—and the countenances which are in our power really, though from flattery we bring them into a no less apparent dependence on the sovereign, than the former are in actual dependence on the constellations.

I have sometimes thought that the word 'courtiers' was a misprint for 'countenances,' arising from an anticipation, by foreglance of the compositor's eye, of the word 'courtier' a few lines below. The written *r* is easily and often confounded with the written *n*. The compositor read the first syllable *court*, and —his eye at the same time catching the word courtier lower down—he completed the word without reconsulting the copy. It is not unlikely that Shakspeare intended first to express, generally, the same thought, which a little afterwards he repeats with a particular application to the persons meant;—a common usage of the pronominal 'our,' where the speaker does not really mean to include himself; and the word 'you' is an additional confirmation of the 'our,' being used in this place, for 'men' generally and indefinitely, just as 'you do not meet' is the same as 'one does not meet.'

Act i. sc. 2. Imogen's speech :—

—My dearest husband,
I something fear my father s wrath; but nothing
(Always reserv'd my holy duty) what
His rage can do on me.

Place the emphasis on 'me;' for 'rage' is a mere repetition of 'wrath.'

Cym. O disloyal thing
That should'st repair my youth, thou heapest
A year's age on me!

How is it that the commentators take no notice of the un-Shaksperian defect in the metre of the second line, and what in Shakspeare is the same, in the harmony with the sense and feeling? Some word or words must have slipped out after 'youth,' —probably 'and see:'—

That should'st repair my youth!—and see, thou heap'st, &c.

Ib. sc. 4. Pisanio's speech :—

—For so long
As he could make me with *this* eye or ear
Distinguish him from others, &c.

But '*this* eye,' in spite of the supposition of its being used δεικτικῶς, is very awkward. I should think that either 'or'—or 'the' was Shakspeare's word :—

As he could make me or with eye or ear.

Ib. sc. 7. Iachimo's speech :—

Hath nature given them eyes
To see this vaulted arch, and the rich crop
Of sea and land, which can distinguish 'twixt
The fiery orbs above, and the twinn'd stones
Upon the number'd beach.

I would suggest 'cope' for 'crop.' As to 'twinn'd stones'—may it not be a bold *catachresis* for muscles, cockles, and other empty shells with hinges, which are truly twinned? I would take Dr. Farmer's 'umber'd,' which I had proposed before I ever heard of its having been already offered by him: but I do not adopt his interpretation of the word, which I think is not derived from *umbra*, a shade, but from *umber*, a dingy yellow-brown soil, which most commonly forms the mass of the sludge on the sea-shore, and on the banks of tide rivers at low water. One other possible interpretation of this sentence has occurred to me, just barely worth mentioning—that the 'twinn'd stones' are the *augrim* stones upon the numbered beech, that is, the astronomical tables of beech-wood.

Act v. sc. 5.

Sooth. When as a lion's whelp, &c.

It is not easy to conjecture why Shakspeare should have introduced this ludicrous scroll, which answers no one purpose, either propulsive or explicatory, unless as a joke on etymology. (*q*)

TITUS ANDRONICUS.

Act i. sc. 1. Theobald's note.

I never heard it so much as intimated, that he (Shakspeare) turned his genius to stage-writing, before he associated with the players, and became one of their body.

THAT Shakspeare never 'turned his genius to stage-writing,' as Theobald most *Theobaldice* phrases it, before he became an actor, is an assertion of about as much authority as the precious story that he left Stratford for deer-stealing, and that he lived by holding gentlemen's horses at the doors of the theatre, and other trash of that arch-gossip, old Aubrey. The metre is an argument against Titus Andronicus being Shakspeare's, worth a score such chronological surmises. Yet I incline to think that both in this play and in Jeronymo, Shakspeare wrote some passages, and that they are the earliest of his compositions.

Act v. sc. 2.

I think it not improbable that the lines from—

I am not mad; I know thee well enough —;
* * * * * * *
So thou destroy Rapine, and Murder there.

were written by Shakspeare in his earliest period. But instead of the text—

Revenge, *which makes the foul offender quake*,
Tit. Art thou Revenge? and art thou sent to me?—

the words in italics ought to be omitted.

TROILUS AND CRESSIDA.

Mr. Pope (after Dryden) informs us, that the story of Troilus and Cressida was originally the work of one Lollius, a Lombard: but Dryden goes yet further; he declares it to have been written in Latin verse, and that Chaucer translated it.—*Lollius was a historiographer of Urbino in Italy.* Note in Stockdale's edition, 1807.

'Lollius was a historiographer of Urbino in Italy.' So affirms the notary, to whom the Sieur Stockdale committed the *disfacimento* of Ayscough's excellent edition of Shakspeare. Pity that the researchful notary has not either told us in what century, and of what history, he was a writer, or been simply content to depose, that Lollius, if a writer of that name existed at all, was a somewhat somewhere. The notary speaks of the *Troy Boke* of Lydgate, printed in 1513. I have never seen it; but I deeply regret that Chalmers did not substitute the whole of Lydgate's works from the MSS. extant, for the almost worthless Gower.

The Troilus and Cressida of Shakspeare can scarcely be classed with his dramas of Greek and Roman history; but it forms an intermediate link between the fictitious Greek and Roman histories, which we may call legendary dramas, and the proper ancient histories; that is, between the Pericles or Titus Andronicus, and the Coriolanus, or Julius Cæsar. Cymbeline is a *congener* with Pericles, and distinguished from Lear by not having any declared prominent object. But where shall we class the Timon of Athens? Perhaps immediately below Lear. It is a Lear of the satirical drama; a Lear of domestic or ordinary life;—a local eddy of passion on the high road of society, while all around is the week-day goings on of wind and weather; a Lear, therefore, without its soul-searching flashes, its ear-cleaving thunder-claps, its meteoric splendors,—without the contagion and the fearful sympathies of nature, the fates, the furies, the frenzied elements, dancing in and out, now breaking through, and scattering,—now hand in hand with,—the fierce or fantastic group of human passions, crimes, and anguishes, reeling on the unsteady ground, in a wild harmony to the shock and the swell of an earthquake. But my present subject was Troilus and Cressida; and I suppose that, scarcely knowing what to say of it, I by a cunning of instinct ran off to subjects on which I should find it difficult not to say too much, though certain after all that I should still leave the better part unsaid, and the gleaning for others richer than my own harvest.

Indeed, there is no one of Shakspeare's plays harder to characterize. The name and the remembrances connected with it, prepare us for the representation of attachment no less faithful than fervent on the side of the youth, and of sudden and shameless inconstancy on the part of the lady. And this is, indeed, as the gold thread on which the scenes are strung, though often kept out of sight, and out of mind by gems of greater value than itself. But as Shakspeare calls forth nothing from the mausoleum of history, or the catacombs of tradition, without giving, or eliciting, some permanent and general interest, and brings forward no subject which he does not moralize or intellectualize,—so here he has drawn in Cressida the portrait of a vehement passion, that, having its true origin and proper cause in warmth of temperament, fastens on, rather than fixes to, some one object by liking and temporary preference.

> There's language in her eye, her cheek, her lip,
> Nay, her foot speaks; her wanton spirits look out
> At every joint and motive of her body.

This Shakspeare has contrasted with the profound affection represented in Troilus, and alone worthy the name of love;—affection, passionate indeed,—swoln with the confluence of youthful instincts and youthful fancy, and growing in the radiance of hope newly risen, in short enlarged by the collective sympathies of nature;—but still having a depth of calmer element in a will stronger than desire, more entire than choice, and which gives permanence to its own act by converting it into faith and duty. Hence with excellent judgment, and with an excellence higher than mere judgment can give, at the close of the play, when Cressida has sunk into infamy below retrieval and beneath hope, the same will, which had been the substance and the basis of his love, while the restless pleasures and passionate longings, like sea-waves, had tossed but on its surface,—this same moral energy is represented as snatching him aloof from all neighborhood with her dishonor, from all lingering fondness and languishing regrets, whilst it rushes with him into other and nobler duties, and deepens the channel, which his heroic brother's death had left empty for its collected flood. Yet another secondary and subordinate purpose Shakspeare has inwoven with his delineation of these two characters,—that of opposing the inferior civilization, but purer morals, of the Trojans to the refinements, deep policy, but duplicity and sensual corruptions of the Greeks.

To all this, however, so little comparative projection is given,—nay, the masterly group of Agamemnon, Nestor, and Ulysses, and, still more in advance, that of Achilles, Ajax, and Thersites, so manifestly occupy the fore-ground, that the subservience and vassalage of strength and animal courage to intellect and policy seems to be the lesson most often in our poet's view, and which he has taken little pains to connect with the former more interesting moral impersonated in the titular hero and heroine of the drama. But I am half inclined to believe, that Shakspeare's main object, or shall I rather say, his ruling impulse, was to translate the poetic heroes of paganism into the not less rude, but more intellectually vigorous, and more *featurely*, warriors of Christian chivalry,—and to substantiate the distinct and graceful profiles or outlines of the Homeric epic into the flesh and blood of the romantic drama,—in short, to give a grand history-piece in the robust style of Albert Durer.

The character of Thersites, in particular, well deserves a more careful examination, as the Caliban of demagogic life ;—the admirable portrait of intellectual power deserted by all grace, all moral principle, all not momentary impulse ;—just wise enough to detect the weak head, and fool enough to provoke the armed fist of his betters ;—one whom malcontent Achilles can inveigle from malcontent Ajax, under the one condition, that he shall be called on to do nothing but abuse and slander, and that he shall be allowed to abuse as much and as purulently as he likes, that is, as he can ;—in short, a mule,—quarrelsome by the original discord of his nature,—a slave by tenure of his own baseness,—made to bray and be brayed at, to despise and be despicable. 'Aye, Sir, but say what you will, he is a very clever fellow, though the best friends will fall out. There was a time when Ajax thought he deserved to have a statue of gold erected to him, and handsome Achilles, at the head of the Myrmidons, gave no little credit to his *friend Thersites!*'

Act iv. sc. 5. Speech of Ulysses:

> O, these encounterers, so glib of tongue,
> That give a *coasting* welcome ere it comes—

Should it be 'accosting?' 'Accost her, knight, accost!' in the Twelfth Night. Yet there sounds a something so Shaksperian in the phrase—'give a coasting welcome,' ('coasting' being taken as the epithet and adjective of 'welcome,') that had the following words been, 'ere *they land*,' instead of 'ere it comes,' I should have preferred the interpretation. The sense now is, 'that give welcome to a salute ere it comes.'

CORIOLANUS.

THIS play illustrates the wonderfully philosophic impartiality of Shakspeare's politics. His own country's history furnished him with no matter, but what was too recent to be devoted to patriotism. Besides, he knew that the instruction of ancient history would seem more dispassionate. In Coriolanus and Julius Cæsar, you see Shakspeare's good-natured laugh at mobs. Compare this with Sir Thomas Brown's aristocracy of spirit.

Act i. sc. 1. Coriolanus' speech:—

> He that depends
> Upon your favors, swims with fins of lead,
> And hews down oaks with rushes. Hang ye! Trust ye?

I suspect that Shakspeare wrote it transposed;

> Trust ye? Hang ye!

Ib. sc. 10. Speech of Aufidius:—

> Mine emulation
> Hath not that honor in't, it had; for where

I thought to crush him in an equal force,
True sword to sword; I'll potch at him some way,
Or wrath, or craft may get him.—
My valor (poison'd
With only suffering stain by him) for him
Shall fly out of itself: nor sleep, nor sanctuary,
Being naked, sick, nor fane, nor capitol,
The prayers of priests, nor times of sacrifices,
Embankments all of fury, shall lift up
Their rotten privilege and custom 'gainst
My hate to Marcius.

I have such deep faith in Shakspeare's heart-lore, that I take for granted that this is in nature, and not as a mere anomaly; although I can not in myself discover any germ of possible feeling, which could wax and unfold itself into such sentiment as this. However, I perceive that in this speech is meant to be contained a prevention of shock at the after-change in Aufidius' character.

Act ii. sc. 1. Speech of Menenius:—

The most sovereign prescription in *Galen*, &c.

Was it without, or in contempt of, historical information that Shakspeare made the contemporaries of Coriolanus quote Cato and Galen? I can not decide to my own satisfaction.

Ib. sc. 3. Speech of Coriolanus:—

Why in this wolvish gown should I stand here—

That the gown of the candidate was of whitened wool, we know. Does 'wolvish' or 'woolvish' mean 'made of wool?' If it means 'wolfish,' what is the sense?

Act iv. sc. 7. Speech of Aufidius:—

All places yield to him ere he sits down, &c.

I have always thought this, in itself so beautiful speech, the least explicable from the mood and full intention of the speaker of any in the whole works of Shakspeare. I cherish the hope that I am mistaken, and that, becoming wiser, I shall discover some profound excellence in that, in which I now appear to detect an imperfection.

JULIUS CÆSAR.

Act i. sc. 1.

> *Mar.* What meanest *thou* by that? Mend me, thou saucy fellow!

THE speeches of Flavius and Marullus are in blank verse. Wherever regular metre can be rendered truly imitative of character, passion, or personal rank, Shakspeare seldom, if ever, neglects it. Hence this line should be read:—

> What mean'st by that? mend me, thou saucy fellow!

I say regular metre: for even the prose has in the highest and lowest dramatic personage, a Cobbler or a Hamlet, a rhythm so felicitous and so severally appropriate, as to be a virtual metre.

Ib. sc. 2.

> *Bru.* A soothsayer bids you beware the Ides of March.

If my ear does not deceive me, the metre of this line was meant to express that sort of mild philosophic contempt, characterizing Brutus even in his first casual speech. The line is a trimeter,—each *dipodia* containing two accented and two unaccented syllables, but variously arranged, as thus:—

∪ — — ∪	— ∪ ∪ —	∪ — ∪ —
A soothsayer	bids you beware	the Ides of March.

Ib. Speech of Brutus:—

> Set honor in one eye, and death i' the other,
> And I will look on *both* indifferently.

Warburton would read 'death' for 'both;' but I prefer the old text. There are here three things, the public good, the individual Brutus' honor, and his death. The latter two so balanced each other, that he could decide for the first by equipoise; nay—the thought growing—that honor had more weight than death. That Cassius understood it as Warburton, is the beauty of Cassius as contrasted with Brutus.

Ib. Cæsar's speech:—

> He loves no plays,
> As thou dost, Antony; he hears no music, &c.

This is not a trivial observation, nor does our poet mean barely by it, that Cassius was not a merry, sprightly man; but that he had not a due temperament of harmony in his disposition. Theobald's Note.

O Theobald! what a commentator wast thou, when thou wouldst affect to understand Shakspeare, instead of contenting thyself with collating the text! The meaning here is too deep for a line ten-fold the length of thine to fathom.

Ib. sc. 3. Cæsar's speech:

> Be *factious* for redress of all these griefs;
> And I will set this foot of mine as far,
> As who goes farthest.

I understand it thus: 'You have spoken as a conspirator; be so in *fact*, and I will join you. Act on your principles, and realize them in a fact.'

Act ii. sc. 1. Speech of Brutus:—

> It must be by his death; and, for my part,
> I know no personal cause to spurn at him,
> But for the general. He would be crown'd:
> How that might change his nature, there's the question.
> ——— And, to speak truth of Cæsar,
> I have not known when his affections sway'd
> More than his reason.
> ——— So Cæsar may;
> Then, lest he may, prevent.

This speech is singular;—at least, I do not at present see into Shakspeare's motive, his *rationale*, or in what point of view he meant Brutus' character to appear. For surely—(this, I mean, is what I say to myself, with my present *quantum* of insight, only modified by my experience in how many instances I have ripened into a perception of beauties, where I had before descried faults)—surely, nothing can seem more discordant with our historical preconceptions of Brutus, or more lowering to the intellect of the Stoico-Platonic tyrannicide, than the tenets here attributed to him—to him, the stern Roman republican; namely,—that he would have no objection to a king, or to Cæsar, a monarch in Rome, would Cæsar but be as good a monarch as he now seems disposed to be! How, too, could Brutus say that he found no personal cause—none in Cæsar's past conduct as a man? Had he not passed the Rubicon? Had he not entered Rome as a conqueror? Had he not placed his Gauls in the Senate?—Shakspeare, it may be said, has not brought these things forward—True;—and this is just the ground of my perplexity. What character did Shakspeare mean his Brutus to be?

Ib. Speech of Brutus :—

For if thou *path* thy native semblance on—

Surely, there need be no scruple in treating this 'path' as a mere misprint or mis-script for 'put.' In what place does Shakspeare,—where does any other writer of the same age—use 'path' as a verb for 'walk?' (*r*)

Ib. sc. 2. Cæsar's speech :—

She dreamt last night she saw my *statue*—

No doubt, it should be *statua*, as in the same age, they more often pronounced 'heroes' as a trisyllable than dissyllable. A modern tragic poet would have written,—

Last night she dreamt, that she my statue saw—

But Shakspeare never avails himself of the supposed license of transposition, merely for the metre. There is always some logic either of thought or passion to justify it.

Act iii. sc. 1. Antony's speech :—

Pardon me, Julius—here wast thou bay'd, brave hart;
Here didst thou fall; and here thy hunters stand
Sign'd in thy spoil, and crimson'd in thy death.
O world! thou wast the forest to this hart,
And this, indeed, O world! the heart of thee.

I doubt the genuineness of the last two lines ;—not because they are vile ; but first, on account of the rhythm, which is not Shaksperian, but just the very tune of some old play, from which the actor might have interpolated them ; and secondly, because they interrupt, not only the sense and connection, but likewise the flow both of the passion, and (what is with me still more decisive) of the Shaksperian link of association. As with many another parenthesis or gloss slipt into the text, we have only to read the passage without it, to see that it never was in it. I venture to say there is no instance in Shakspeare fairly like this. Conceits he has ; but they not only rise out of some word in the lines before, but also lead to the thought in the lines following. Here the conceit is a mere alien : Antony forgets an image, when he is even touching it, and then recollects it, when the thought last in his mind must have led him away from it.

Act iv. sc. 3. Speech of Brutus :—

—— What, shall one of us,
That struck the foremost man of all this world,
But for *supporting robbers.*

This seemingly strange assertion of Brutus is unhappily verified in the present day. What is an immense army, in which the lust of plunder has quenched all the duties of the citizen, other than a horde of robbers, or differenced only as fiends are from ordinarily reprobate men? Cæsar supported, and was supported by, such as these; and even so Bonaparte in our days.

I know no part of Shakspeare that more impresses on me the belief of his genius being superhuman, than this scene between Brutus and Cassius. In the Gnostic heresy it might have been credited with less absurdity than most of their dogmas, that the Supreme had employed him to create, previously to his function of representing, characters.

ANTONY AND CLEOPATRA.

Shakspeare can be complimented only by comparison with himself: all other eulogies are either heterogeneous, as when they are in reference to Spenser or Milton; or they are flat truisms, as when he is gravely preferred to Corneille, Racine, or even his own immediate successors, Beaumont and Fletcher, Massinger and the rest. The highest praise, or rather form of praise, of this play, which I can offer in my own mind, is the doubt which the perusal always occasions in me, whether the Antony and Cleopatra is not, in all exhibitions of a giant power in its strength and vigor of maturity, a formidable rival of Macbeth, Lear, Hamlet, and Othello. *Feliciter audax* is the motto for its style comparatively with that of Shakspeare's other works, even as it is the general motto of all his works compared with those of other poets. Be it remembered, too, that this happy valiancy of style is but the representative and result of all the material excellences so expressed.

This play should be perused in mental contrast with Romeo and Juliet;—as the love of passion and appetite opposed to the love of affection and instinct. But the art displayed in the character of Cleopatra is profound ; in this, especially, that the sense of criminality in her passion is lessened by our insight into its depth and energy, at the very moment that we can not but perceive that the passion itself springs out of the habitual craving of a licentious nature, and that it is supported and reinforced by voluntary stimulus and sought-for associations, instead of blossoming out of spontaneous emotion.

Of all Shakspeare's historical plays, Antony and Cleopatra is by far the most wonderful. There is not one in which he has followed history so minutely, and yet there are few in which he impresses the notion of angelic strength so much ;—perhaps none in which he impresses it more strongly. This is greatly owing to the manner in which the fiery force is sustained throughout, and to the numerous momentary flashes of nature counteracting the historic abstraction. As a wonderful specimen of the way in which Shakspeare lives up to the very end of this play, read the last part of the concluding scene. And if you would feel the judgment as well as the genius of Shakspeare in your heart's core, compare this astonishing drama with Dryden's All For Love.

Act i. sc. 1. Philo's speech :

His captain's heart
Which in the scuffles of great fights hath burst
The buckles on his breast, *reneges* all temper—

It should be ' reneagues,' or ' reniegues,' as ' fatigues,' &c.

Ib.

Take but good note, and you shall see in him
The triple pillar of the world transform'd
Into a strumpet's *fool.*

Warburton's conjecture of ' stool' is ingenious, and would be a probable reading, if the scene opening had discovered Antony with Cleopatra on his lap. But, represented as he is walking and jesting with her, ' fool' must be the word. Warburton's objection is shallow, and implies that he confounded the dramatic with the epic style. The ' pillar' of a state is so common a metaphor, as to have lost the image in the thing meant to be imaged.

Ib. sc. 2.

Much is breeding ;
Which, like the courser's hair, hath yet but life,
And not a serpent's poison.

This is so far true to appearance, that a horse-hair, 'laid,' as Hollinshed says, 'in a pail of water,' will become the supporter of seemingly one worm, though probably of an immense number of small slimy water-lice. The hair will twirl round a finger, and sensibly compress it. It is a common experiment with school-boys in Cumberland and Westmoreland.

Act ii. sc. 2. Speech of Enobarbus :—

> Her gentlewomen, like the Nereids,
> So many *mermaids*, tended her i' th' eyes,
> And made their bends adornings. At the helm
> A seeming mermaid steers.

I have the greatest difficulty in believing that Shakspeare wrote the first 'mermaids.' He never, I think, would have so weakened by useless anticipation the fine image immediately following. The epithet 'seeming' becomes so extremely improper after the whole number had been positively called 'so many mermaids.'

TIMON OF ATHENS.

Act i. sc. 1.

> *Tim.* The man is honest.
> *Old Ath.* *Therefore he will be,* Timon.
> His honesty rewards him in itself.

WARBURTON's comment—'If the man be honest, for that reason he will be so in this, and not endeavor at the injustice of gaining my daughter without my consent'—is, like almost all his comments, ingenious in blunder ; he can never see any other writer's thoughts for the mist-working swarm of his own. The meaning of the first line the poet himself explains, or rather unfolds, in the second. 'The man is honest !'—True ;—and for that very cause, and with no additional or extrinsic motive, he will be so. No man can be justly called honest, who is not so for honesty's sake, itself including its own reward. Note, that 'honesty' in Shakspeare's age retained much of its old dignity, and that contradistinction of the *honestum* from the *utile*, in which its very essence and definition consist. If it be *honestum*, it can not depend on the *utile*.

Ib. Speech of Apemantus, printed as prose in Theobald's edition :—

> So, so! aches contract, and starve your supple joints!

I may remark here the fineness of Shakspeare's sense of musical period, which would almost by itself have suggested (if the hundred positive proofs had not been extant) that the word 'aches' was then *ad libitum*, a dissyllable—*aitches*. For read it, 'aches,' in this sentence, and I would challenge you to find any period in Shakspeare's writings with the same musical, or rather dissonant, notation. Try the one, and then the other, by your ear, reading the sentence aloud, first with the word as a dissyllable and then as a monosyllable, and you will feel what I mean.*

Ib. sc. 2. Cupid's speech : Warburton's correction of—

> There taste, touch, all pleas'd from thy table rise—

> Th' ear, taste, touch, smell, &c.

This is indeed an excellent emendation.

Act ii. sc. 1. Senator's speech :—

> —nor then silenc'd with
> "Commend me to your master"—*and the cap*
> *Plays in the right hand, thus* :—

Either, methinks, 'plays' should be 'play'd,' or 'and' should be changed to 'while.' I can certainly understand it as a parenthesis, an interadditive of scorn ; but it does not sound to my ear as in Shakspeare's manner.

Ib. sc. 2. Timon's speech (Theobald) :

> And that unaptness made *you* minister,
> Thus to excuse yourself.

Read *your* ;—at least I can not otherwise understand the line. You made my chance indisposition and occasional unaptness your minister—that is, the ground on which you now excuse your-

* It is, of course, a verse,—

> Achès contract, and starve your supple joints,—

and is so printed in all later editions. But Mr. C. was reading it in prose in Theobald ; and it is curious to see how his ear detected the rhythmical necessity for pronouncing "aches" as a dissyllable, although the metrical necessity seems for the moment to have escaped him.—*Ed.*

self. Or, perhaps, no correction is necessary, if we construe 'made you' as 'did you make;' 'and that unaptness did you make help you thus to excuse yourself.' But the former seems more in Shakspeare's manner, and is less liable to be misunderstood.*

Act iii. sc. 3. Servant's speech :—

> How fairly this lord strives to appear foul!—takes virtuous copies to be wicked; *like those that under hot, ardent zeal would set whole realms on fire. Of such a nature is his politic love.*

This latter clause I grievously suspect to have been an addition of the players, which had hit, and, being constantly applauded, procured a settled occupancy in the prompter's copy. Not that Shakspeare does not elsewhere sneer at the Puritans; but here it is introduced so *nolenter volenter* (excuse the phrase) by the head and shoulders!—and is besides so much more likely to have been conceived in the age of Charles I.

Act iv. sc. 2. Timon's speech :—

> Raise me this beggar, and *deny't* that lord.—

Warburton reads 'denude.'

I can not see the necessity of this alteration. The editors and commentators are, all of them, ready enough to cry out against Shakspeare's laxities and licenses of style, forgetting that he is not merely a poet, but a dramatic poet; that, when the head and the heart are swelling with fulness, a man does not ask himself whether he has grammatically arranged, but only whether (the context taken in) he has conveyed, his meaning. 'Deny' is here clearly equal to 'withhold;' and the 'it,' quite in the genius of vehement conversation, which a syntaxist explains by ellipses and *subauditurs* in a Greek or Latin classic, yet triumphs over as ignorances in a contemporary, refers to accidental and artificial rank or elevation, implied in the verb 'raise.' Besides, does the word 'denude' occur in any writer before, or of, Shakspeare's age?

* 'Your' is the received reading now.—*Ed.*

ROMEO AND JULIET.

I HAVE previously had occasion to speak at large on the subject of the three unities of time, place, and action, as applied to the drama in the abstract, and to the particular stage for which Shakspeare wrote, as far as he can be said to have written for any stage but that of the universal mind. I hope I have in some measure succeeded in demonstrating that the former two, instead of being rules, were mere inconveniences attached to the local peculiarities of the Athenian drama; that the last alone deserved the name of a principle, and that in the preservation of this unity Shakspeare stood pre-eminent. Yet, instead of unity of action, I should greatly prefer the more appropriate, though scholastic and uncouth, words homogeneity, proportionateness, and totality of interest,—expressions, which involve the distinction, or rather the essential difference, betwixt the shaping skill of mechanical talent, and the creative, productive, life-power of inspired genius. In the former each part is separately conceived, and then by a succeeding act put together;—not as watches are made for wholesale—(for there each part supposes a pre-conception of the whole in some mind),—but more like pictures on a motley screen. Whence arises the harmony that strikes us in the wildest natural landscapes,—in the relative shapes of rocks, the harmony of colors in the heaths, ferns, and lichens, the leaves of the beech and the oak, the stems and rich brown branches of the birch and other mountain trees, varying from verging autumn to returning spring,—compared with the visual effect from the greater number of artificial plantations?—From this, that the natural landscape is effected, as it were, by a single energy modified *ab intra* in each component part. And as this is the particular excellence of the Shaksperian drama generally, so is it especially characteristic of the Romeo and Juliet.

The groundwork of the tale is altogether in family life, and the events of the play have their first origin in family feuds. Filmy as are the eyes of party-spirit, at once dim and truculent, still there is commonly some real or supposed object in view, or principle to be maintained; and though but the twisted wires on the plate of rosin in the preparation for electrical pictures, it is still a guide in some degree, an assimilation to an outline. But in family quarrels, which have proved scarcely less injurious to states, wilfulness, and precipitancy, and passion from mere habit and custom, can alone be expected. With his accustomed judgment, Shakspeare has begun by placing before us a lively picture of all the impulses of the play; and, as nature ever presents two sides, one for Heraclitus, and one for Democritus, he has, by way of prelude, shown the laughable absurdity of the evil by the contagion of it reaching the servants, who have so little to do with it, but who are under the necessity of letting the superfluity of sensorial power fly off through the escape-valve of wit-combats, and of quarrelling with weapons of sharper edge, all in humble imitation of their masters. Yet there is a sort of unhired fidelity, an *ourishness* about all this that makes it rest pleasant on one's feelings. All the first scene, down to the conclusion of the Prince's speech, is a motley dance of all ranks and ages to one tune, as if the horn of Huon had been playing behind the scenes.

Benvolio's speech—

> Madam, an hour before the worshipp'd sun
> Peer'd forth the golden window of the east—

and, far more strikingly, the following speech of old Montague—

> Many a morning hath he there been seen
> With tears augmenting the fresh morning dew—

prove that Shakspeare meant the Romeo and Juliet to approach to a poem, which, and indeed its early date, may be also inferred from the multitude of rhyming couplets throughout. And if we are right, from the internal evidence, in pronouncing this one of Shakspeare's early dramas, it affords a strong instance of the fineness of his insight into the nature of the passions, that Romeo is introduced already love-bewildered. The necessity of loving creates an object for itself in man and woman; and yet there is a difference in this respect between the sexes, though only to be known by a perception of it. It would have displeased us if Juliet had been represented as already in love, or as fancying herself so;—but no one, I believe, ever experiences any shock at Romeo's forgetting his Rosaline, who had been a mere name for the yearning of his youthful imagination, and rushing into his passion for Juliet. Rosaline was a mere creation of his fancy; and we should remark the boastful positiveness of Romeo in a love of his own making, which is never shown where love is really near the heart.

> When the devout religion of mine eye
> Maintains such falsehood, then turn tears to fires!
> * * * * *
> One fairer than my love! the all-seeing sun
> Ne'er saw her match, since first the world begun.

The character of the Nurse is the nearest of any thing in Shakspeare to a direct borrowing from mere observation; and the reason is, that as in infancy and childhood the individual in nature is a representative of a class,—just as in describing one larch-tree, you generalize a grove of them,—so it is nearly as much so in old age. The generalization is done to the poet's hand. Here you have the garrulity of age strengthened by the feelings of a long-trusted servant, whose sympathy with the mother's affections gives her privileges and rank in the household; and observe the mode of connection by accidents of time and place, and the child-like fondness of repetition in a second childhood, and also that happy, humble, ducking under, yet constant resurgence against, the check of her superiors!—

> Yes, madam!—Yet I can not choose but laugh, &c.

In the fourth scene we have Mercutio introduced to us. O! how shall I describe that exquisite ebullience and overflow of youthful life, wafted on over the laughing waves of pleasure and prosperity, as a wanton beauty that distorts the face on which she knows her lover is gazing enraptured, and wrinkles her forehead in the triumph of its smoothness! Wit ever wakeful, fancy busy and procreative as an insect, courage, an easy mind that, without cares of its own, is at once disposed to laugh away those of others, and yet to be interested in them,—these and all congenial qualities, melting into the common *copula* of them all, the man of rank and the gentleman, with all its excellences and all its weaknesses, constitute the character of Mercutio!

Act i. sc. 5.

> *Tyb.* It fits when such a villain is a guest;
> I'll not endure him.
> *Cap.* He shall be endur'd.
> What, goodman boy!—I say, he shall:—Go to;—
> Am I the master here, or you?—Go to.

> You'll not endure him!—God shall mend my soul—
> You'll make a mutiny among my guests!
> You will set cock-a-hoop! you'll be the man!
> *Tyb.* Why, uncle, 'tis a shame.
> *Cap.* Go to, go to,
> You are a saucy boy! &c.—

How admirable is the old man's impetuosity at once contrasting, yet harmonized, with young Tybalt's quarrelsome violence! But it would be endless to repeat observations of this sort. Every leaf is different on an oak-tree; but still we can only say—our tongues defrauding our eyes—'This is another oak-leaf!'

Act ii. sc. 2. The garden scene:

Take notice in this enchanting scene of the contrast of Romeo's love with his former fancy; and weigh the skill shown in justifying him from his inconstancy by making us feel the difference of his passion. Yet this, too, is a love in, although not merely of, the imagination.

Ib.

> *Jul.* Well, do not swear; although I joy in thee,
> I have no joy in this contract to-night:
> It is too rash, too unadvis'd, too sudden, &c.

With love, pure love, there is always an anxiety for the safety of the object, a disinterestedness, by which it is distinguished from the counterfeits of its name. Compare this scene with act iii. sc. 1, of the Tempest. I do not know a more wonderful instance of Shakspeare's mastery in playing a distinctly rememberable variety on the same remembered air, than in the transporting love confessions of Romeo and Juliet and Ferdinand and Miranda. There seems more passion in the one, and more dignity in the other; yet you feel that the sweet girlish lingering and busy movement of Juliet, and the calmer and more maidenly fondness of Miranda, might easily pass into each other.

Ib. sc. 3. The Friar's speech:—

The reverend character of the Friar, like all Shakspeare's representations of the great professions, is very delightful and tranquillizing, yet it is no digression, but immediately necessary to the carrying on of the plot.

Ib. sc. 4.

> *Rom.* Good-morrow to you both. What counterfeit did I give you? &c.

Compare again, Romeo's half-exerted, and half real, ease of mind with his first manner when in love with Rosaline! His will had come to the clenching point.

Ib. sc. 6.

> *Rom.* Do thou but close our hands with holy words,
> Then love-devouring death do what he dare,
> It is enough I may but call her mine.

The precipitancy, which is the character of the play, is well marked in this short scene of waiting for Juliet's arrival.

Act iii. sc. 1.

> *Mer.* No, 'tis not so deep as a well, nor so wide as a church-door; but 'tis enough: 'twill serve: ask for me to-morrow, and you shall find me a grave man, &c.

How fine an effect the wit and raillery habitual to Mercutio, even struggling with his pain, give to Romeo's following speech, and at the same time so completely justifying his passionate revenge on Tybalt!

Ib. Benvolio's speech:

> But that he tilts
> With piercing steel at bold Mercutio's breast.

This small portion of untruth in Benvolio's narrative is finely conceived.

Ib. sc. 2. Juliet's speech:

> For thou wilt lie upon the wings of night
> Whiter than new snow on a raven's back.—

Indeed the whole of this speech is imagination strained to the highest; and observe the blessed effect on the purity of the mind. What would Dryden have made of it?—

Ib.

> *Nurse.* Shame come to Romeo.
> *Jul.* Blister'd be thy tongue
> For such a wish!

Note the Nurse's mistake of the mind's audible struggles with itself for its decision *in toto*.

Ib. sc. 3. Romeo's speech:—

> 'Tis torture, and not mercy: heaven's here,
> Where Juliet lives, &c.

All deep passions are a sort of atheists, that believe no future.

Ib. sc. 5.

> *Cap.* Soft, take me with you, take me with you, wife—
> How! will she none? &c.

A noble scene! Don't I see it with my own eyes?—Yes! but not with Juliet's. And observe in Capulet's last speech in this scene his mistake, as if love's causes were capable of being generalized.

Act iv. sc. 3. Juliet's speech:—

> O, look! methinks I see my cousin's ghost
> Seeking out Romeo, that did spit his body
> Upon a rapier's point:—Stay, Tybalt, stay!—
> Romeo, I come! this do I drink to thee.

Shakspeare provides for the finest decencies. It would have been too bold a thing for a girl of fifteen;—but she swallows the draught in a fit of fright. (s.)

Ib. sc. 5.

As the audience know that Juliet is not dead, this scene is, perhaps, excusable. But it is a strong warning to minor dramatists not to introduce at one time many separate characters agitated by one and the same circumstance. It is difficult to understand what effect, whether that of pity or of laughter, Shakspeare meant to produce;—the occasion and the characteristic speeches are so little in harmony! For example, what the Nurse says is excellently suited to the Nurse's character, but grotesquely unsuited to the occasion.

Act v. sc. 1. Romeo's speech:—

> O mischief! thou art swift
> To enter in the thoughts of desperate men!
> I do remember an apothecary, &c.

This famous passage is so beautiful as to be self-justified; yet, in addition, what a fine preparation it is for the tomb scene!

Ib. sc. 3. Romeo's speech:—

> Good gentle youth, tempt not a desperate man,
> Fly hence and leave me.

The gentleness of Romeo was shown before, as softened by

love; and now it is doubled by love and sorrow and awe of the place where he is.

Ib. Romeo's speech :—

How oft when men are at the point of death
Have they been merry! which their keepers call
A lightning before death. O, how may I
Call this a lightning?—O, my love, my wife! &c.

Here, here, is the master example how beauty can at once increase and modify passion!

Ib. Last scene.

How beautiful is the close! The spring and the winter meet; winter assumes the character of spring, and spring the sadness of winter.

SHAKSPEARE'S ENGLISH HISTORICAL PLAYS.

THE first form of poetry is the epic, the essence of which may be stated as the successive in events and characters. This must be distinguished from narration, in which there must always be a narrator, from whom the objects represented receive a coloring and a manner;—whereas in the epic, as in the so-called poems of Homer, the whole is completely objective, and the representation is a pure reflection. The next form into which poetry passed was the dramatic;—both forms having a common basis with a certain difference, and that difference not consisting in the dialogue alone. Both are founded on the relation of providence to the human will; and this relation is the universal element, expressed under different points of view according to the difference of religion, and the moral and intellectual cultivation of different nations. In the epic poem fate is represented as overruling the will, and making it instrumental to the accomplishment of its designs :—

——— Διὸς δὲ τελείετο βουλή.

In the drama, the will is exhibited as struggling with fate, a great and beautiful instance and illustration of which is the Prometheus of Æschylus; and the deepest effect is produced, when the fate is represented as a higher and intelligent will, and the opposition of the individual as springing from a defect.

In order that a drama may be properly historical, it is necessary that it should be the history of the people to whom it is addressed. In the composition, care must be taken that there appear no dramatic improbability, as the reality is taken for granted. It must, likewise, be poetical;—that only, I mean, must be taken which is the permanent in our nature, which is common, and therefore deeply interesting to all ages. The events themselves are immaterial, otherwise than as the clothing and manifestation of the spirit that is working within. In this mode, the unity resulting from succession is destroyed, but is supplied by a unity of a higher order, which connects the events by reference to the workers, gives a reason for them in the motives, and presents men in their causative character. It takes, therefore, that part of real history which is the least known, and infuses a principle of life and organization into the naked facts, and makes them all the framework of an animated whole.

In my happier days, while I had yet hope and onward-looking thoughts, I planned an historical drama of King Stephen, in the manner of Shakspeare. Indeed it would be desirable that some man of dramatic genius should dramatize all those omitted by Shakspeare, as far down as Henry VII. Perkin Warbeck would make a most interesting drama. A few scenes of Marlow's Edward II. might be preserved. After Henry VIII., the events are too well and distinctly known, to be, without plump inverisimilitude, crowded together in one night's exhibition. Whereas, the history of our ancient kings,—the events of their reigns, I mean, —are like stars in the sky;—whatever the real interspaces may be, and however great, they seem close to each other. The stars —the events—strike us and remain in our eye, little modified by the difference of dates. An historic drama is, therefore, a collection of events borrowed from history, but connected together in respect of cause and time, poetically and by dramatic fiction. It would be a fine national custom to act such a series of dramatic histories in orderly succession, in the yearly Christmas holidays, and could not but tend to counteract that mock cosmopolitism, which under a positive term really implies nothing but a negation of, or indifference to, the particular love of our country. By its nationality must every nation retain its independence;—I mean a nationality *quoad* the nation. Better thus;—nationality in each individual, *quoad* his country, is equal to the sense of individuality *quoad* himself; but himself as subsensuous, and central. Patriotism is equal to the sense of individuality reflected from every other individual. There may come a higher virtue in both—just cosmopolitism. But this latter is not possible but by antecedence of the former.

Shakspeare has included the most important part of nine reigns in his historical dramas—namely—King John, Richard II.—Henry IV. (two)—Henry V.—Henry VI. (three) including Edward V. and Henry VIII., in all ten plays. There remain, therefore, to be done, with the exception of a single scene or two that should be adopted from Marlow, eleven reigns—of which the first two appear the only unpromising subjects;—and those two dramas must be formed wholly or mainly of invented private stories, which, however, could not have happened except in consequence of the events and measures of these reigns, and which should furnish opportunity both of exhibiting the manners and oppressions of the times, and of narrating dramatically the great events;—if possible, the death of the two sovereigns, at least of the latter, should be made to have some influence on the finale of the story. All the rest are glorious subjects; especially Henry I. (being the struggle between the men of arms and of letters, in the persons of Henry and Becket), Stephen, Richard I., Edward II., and Henry VII.

KING JOHN.

Act i. sc. 1.

> *Bast.* James Gurney, wilt thou give us leave awhile?
> *Gur.* Good leave, good Philip.
> *Bast.* Philip? *sparrow!* James, &c.

THEOBALD adopts Warburton's conjecture of '*spare me.*'

O true Warburton! and the *sancta simplicitas* of honest dull Theobald's faith in him! Nothing can be more lively or characteristic than 'Philip? Sparrow!' Had Warburton read old Skelton's 'Philip Sparrow,' an exquisite and original poem, and, no doubt, popular in Shakspeare's time, even Warburton would scarcely have made so deep a plunge into the *bathetic* as to have deathified 'sparrow' into 'spare me!'

Act iii. sc. 2. Speech of Faulconbridge:—

> Now, by my life, this day grows wondrous hot;
> Some *airy* devil hovers in the sky, &c.

Theobald adopts Warburton's conjecture of 'fiery.'

I prefer the old text: the word 'devil' implies 'fiery.' You need only read the line, laying a full and strong emphasis on 'devil,' to perceive the uselessness and tastelessness of Warburton's alteration.

RICHARD II.

I HAVE stated that the transitional link between the epic poem and the drama is the historic drama; that in the epic poem a pre-announced fate gradually adjusts and employs the will and the events as its instruments, whilst the drama, on the other hand, places fate and will in opposition to each other, and is then most perfect, when the victory of fate is obtained in consequence of imperfections in the opposing will, so as to leave a final impression that the fate itself is but a higher and a more intelligent will.

From the length of the speeches, and the circumstance that, with one exception, the events are all historical, and presented in their results, not produced by acts seen by, or taking place before, the audience, this tragedy is ill suited to our present large theatres. But in itself, and for the closet, I feel no hesitation in placing it as the first and most admirable of all Shakspeare's purely historical plays. For the two parts of Henry IV. form a species of themselves, which may be named the mixed drama. The distinction does not depend on the mere quantity of historical events in the play compared with the fictions; for there is as much history in Macbeth as in Richard, but in the relation of the history to the plot. In the purely historical plays, the history forms the plot; in the mixed, it directs it; in the rest, as Macbeth, Hamlet, Cymbeline, Lear, it subserves it. But, however unsuited to the stage this drama may be, God forbid that even there it should fall dead on the hearts of jacobinized Englishmen! Then, indeed, we might say—*præteriit gloria mundi!* For the spirit of patriotic reminiscence is the all-permeating soul of this noble work. It is, perhaps, the most purely historical of Shakspeare's dramas. There are not in it, as in the others, characters introduced merely for the purpose of giving a greater individuality and realness, as in the comic parts of Henry IV., by presenting, as it were, our very selves. Shakspeare avails himself of every opportunity to effect the great object of the historic drama, that, namely, of familiarizing the people to the great names of their country, and thereby of exciting a steady patriotism, a love of just liberty, and a respect for all those fundamental institutions of social life, which bind men together:—

This royal throne of kings, this scepter'd isle,
This earth of majesty, this seat of Mars,
This other Eden, demi-paradise;
This fortress, built by nature for herself,
Against infection, and the hand of war;
This happy breed of men, this little world;
This precious stone set in the silver sea,
Which serves it in the office of a wall,
Or as a moat defensive to a home,
Against the envy of less happier lands;
This blessed plot, this earth, this realm, this England,
This nurse, this teeming womb of royal kings,
Fear'd by their breed, and famous by their birth, &c.

Add the famous passage in King John:—

This England never did, nor ever shall,
Lie at the proud foot of a conqueror,
But when it first did help to wound itself.
Now these her princes are come home again,
Come the three corners of the world in arms,
And we shall shock them: naught shall make us rue,
If England to itself do rest but true.

And it certainly seems that Shakspeare's historic dramas produced a very deep effect on the minds of the English people, and in earlier times they were familiar even to the least informed of all ranks, according to the relation of Bishop Corbett. Marlborough, we know, was not ashamed to confess that his principal acquaintance with English history was derived from them; and I believe that a large part of the information as to our old names and achievements even now abroad is due, directly or indirectly, to Shakspeare.

Admirable is the judgment with which Shakspeare always in the first scene prepares, yet how naturally, and with what concealment of art, for the catastrophe. Observe how he here presents the germ of all the after-events in Richard's insincerity, partiality, arbitrariness, and favoritism, and in the proud, tempestuous temperament of his barons. In the very beginning, also, is displayed that feature in Richard's character, which is never forgotten throughout the play—his attention to decorum, and high feeling of the kingly dignity. These anticipations show with what judgment Shakspeare wrote, and illustrate his care to connect the past and future, and unify them with the present by forecast and reminiscence.

It is interesting to a critical ear to compare the six opening lines of the play—

> Old John of Gaunt, time-honored Lancaster,
> Hast thou, according to thy oath and band, &c.

each closing at the tenth syllable, with the rhythmless metre of the verse in Henry VI. and Titus Andronicus, in order that the difference, indeed, the heterogeneity, of the two may be felt *etiam in simillimis prima superficie.* Here the weight of the single words supplies all the relief afforded by intercurrent verse, while the whole represents the mood. And compare the apparently defective metre of Bolingbroke's first line,—

> Many years of happy days befall—

with Prospero's,

> Twelve years since, Miranda! twelve years since—

The actor should supply the time by emphasis, and pause on the first syllable of each of these verses.

Act i. sc. 1. Bolingbroke's speech :—

> First (heaven be the record to my speech!)
> In the devotion of a subject's love, &c.

I remember in the Sophoclean drama no more striking example of the τὸ πρέπον καὶ σεμνὸν than this speech ; and the rhymes in the last six lines well express the preconcertedness of Bolingbroke's scheme so beautifully contrasted with the vehemence and sincere irritation of Mowbray.

Ib. Bolingbroke's speech :—

> Which blood, like sacrificing Abel's, cries,

Even from the tongueless caverns of the earth,
To *me*, for justice and rough chastisement.

Note the δεινὸν of this 'to me,' which is evidently felt by Richard :—

How high a pitch his resolution soars!

and the affected depreciation afterwards ;—

As he is but my father's brother's son.

Ib. Mowbray's speech :—

In haste whereof, most heartily I pray
Your highness to assign our trial day.

The occasional interspersion of rhymes, and the more frequent winding up of a speech therewith—what purpose was this designed to answer ? In the earnest drama, I mean. Deliberateness ? An attempt, as in Mowbray, to collect himself and be cool at the close ?—I can see that in the following speeches the rhyme answers the end of the Greek chorus, and distinguishes the general truths from the passions of the dialogue ; but this does not exactly justify the practice, which is unfrequent in proportion to the excellence of Shakspeare's plays. One thing, however, is to be observed,—that the speakers are historical, known, and so far formal, characters, and their reality is already a fact. This should be borne in mind. The whole of this scene of the quarrel between Mowbray and Bolingbroke seems introduced for the purpose of showing by anticipation the characters of Richard and Bolingbroke. In the latter there is observable a decorous and courtly checking of his anger in subservience to a predetermined plan, especially in his calm speech after receiving sentence of banishment compared with Mowbray's unaffected lamentation. In the one, all is ambitious hope of something yet to come ; in the other it is desolation and a looking backward of the heart.

Ib. sc. 2.

Gaunt. Heaven's is the quarrel; for heaven's substitute,
His deputy anointed in his right,
Hath caus'd his death : the which, if wrongfully,
Let heaven revenge; for I may never lift
An angry arm against his minister.

Without the hollow extravagance of Beaumont and Fletcher's

ultra-royalism, how carefully does Shakspeare acknowledge and reverence the eternal distinction between the mere individual, and the symbolic or representative, on which all genial law, no less than patriotism, depends. The whole of this second scene commences, and is anticipative of, the tone and character of the play at large.

Ib. sc. 3. In none of Shakspeare's fictitious dramas, or in those founded on a history as unknown to his auditors generally as fiction, is this violent rupture of the succession of time found :—a proof, I think, that the pure historic drama, like Richard II. and King John, had its own laws.

Ib. Mowbray's speech :—

> A dearer *merit*
> Have I deserved at your highness' hand.

O, the instinctive propriety of Shakspeare in the choice of words !

Ib. Richard's speech :—

> Nor never by advised purpose meet,
> To plot, contrive, or complot any ill
> 'Gainst us, our state, our subjects, or our land.

Already the selfish weakness of Richard's character opens. Nothing will such minds so readily embrace, as indirect ways softened down to their *quasi*-consciences by policy, expedience, &c.

Ib. Mowbray's speech :—

> . . . . . All the world's my way.
> 'The world was all before him.'—*Milt.*

Ib.

> *Boling.* How long a time lies in our little word !
> Four lagging winters, and four wanton springs,
> End in a word : such is the breath of kings.

Admirable anticipation !

Ib. sc. 4. This is a striking conclusion of a first act,—letting the reader into the secret ;—having before impressed us with the dignified and kingly manners of Richard, yet by well-managed anticipations leading us on to the full gratification of pleasure in our own penetration. In this scene a new light is thrown on Richard's character. Until now he has appeared in all the beauty of royalty ; but here, as soon as he is left to himself, the inherent weakness of his character is immediately shown. It is a weakness, however, of a peculiar kind, not arising from want of personal courage, or any specific defect of faculty, but rather an intellectual feminineness, which feels a necessity of ever leaning on the breasts of others, and of reclining on those who are all the while known to be inferiors. To this must be attributed as its consequences all Richard's vices, his tendency to concealment, and his cunning, the whole operation of which is directed to the getting rid of present difficulties. Richard is not meant to be a debauchee; but we see in him that sophistry which is common to man, by which we can deceive our own hearts, and at one and the same time apologize for, and yet commit the error. Shakspeare has represented this character in a very peculiar manner. He has not made him amiable with counterbalancing faults; but has openly and broadly drawn those faults without reserve, relying on Richard's disproportionate sufferings and gradually emergent good qualities for our sympathy; and this was possible, because his faults are not positive vices, but spring entirely from defect of character.

Act ii. sc. 1.

K. Rich. Can sick men play so nicely with their names?

Yes! on a death-bed there is a feeling which may make all things appear but as puns and equivocations. And a passion there is that carries off its own excess by plays on words as naturally, and, therefore, as appropriately to drama, as by gesticulations, looks, or tones. This belongs to human nature as such, independently of associations and habits from any particular rank of life or mode of employment; and in this consists Shakspeare's vulgarisms, as in Macbeth's—

The devil damn thee black, thou cream-fac'd loon! &c.

This is (to equivocate on Dante's words) in truth the *nobile volgare eloquenza*. Indeed it is profoundly true that there is a natural, an almost irresistible, tendency in the mind, when immersed in one strong feeling, to connect that feeling with every sight and object around it; especially if there be opposition, and the words addressed to it are in any way repugnant to the feeling itself, as here in the instance of Richard's unkind language:

Misery makes sport to mock itself.

No doubt, something of Shakspeare's punning must be attributed to his age, in which direct and formal combats of wit were a favorite pastime of the courtly and accomplished. It was an age more favorable, upon the whole, to vigor of intellect than the present, in which a dread of being thought pedantic dispirits and flattens the energies of original minds. But independently of this, I have no hesitation in saying that a pun, if it be congruous with the feeling of the scene, is not only allowable in the dramatic dialogue, but oftentimes one of the most effectual intensives of passion.

Ib.

> *K. Rich.* Right; you say true: as Hereford's love, so his;
> As theirs, so mine; and all be as it is.

The depth of this compared with the first scene :—

> How high a pitch, &c.

There is scarcely any thing in Shakspeare in its degree, more admirably drawn than York's character; his religious loyalty struggling with a deep grief and indignation at the king's follies; his adherence to his word and faith, once given in spite of all, even the most natural, feelings. You see in him the weakness of old age, and the overwhelmingness of circumstances, for a time surmounting his sense of duty—the junction of both exhibited in his boldness in words and feebleness in immediate act; and then again his effort to retrieve himself in abstract loyalty, even at the heavy price of the loss of his son. This species of accidental and adventitious weakness is brought into parallel with Richard's continually increasing energy of thought, and as constantly diminishing power of acting;—and thus it is Richard that breathes a harmony and a relation into all the characters of the play.

> *Queen.* To please the king I did; to please myself
> I can not do it; yet I know no cause
> Why I should welcome such a guest as grief,
> Save bidding farewell to so sweet a guest
> As my sweet Richard: yet again, methinks,
> Some unborn sorrow, ripe in sorrow's womb,
> Is coming toward me; and my inward soul
> With nothing trembles: at something it grieves,
> More than with parting from my lord the king.

It is clear that Shakspeare never meant to represent Richard as a vulgar debauchee, but a man with a wantonness of spirit in external show, a feminine *friendism*, an intensity of woman-like love of those immediately about him, and a mistaking of the delight of being loved by him for a love of him. And mark in this scene Shakspeare's gentleness in touching the tender superstitions, the *terræ incognitæ* of presentiments, in the human mind; and how sharp a line of distinction he commonly draws between these obscure forecastings of general experience in each individual, and the vulgar errors of mere tradition. Indeed, it may be taken once for all as the truth, that Shakspeare, in the absolute universality of his genius, always reverences whatever arises out of our moral nature; he never profanes his muse with a contemptuous reasoning away of the genuine and general, however unaccountable, feelings of mankind.

The amiable part of Richard's character is brought full upon us by his queen's few words—

> . . . . so sweet a guest
> As my sweet Richard;—

and Shakspeare has carefully shown in him an intense love of his country, well knowing how that feeling would, in a pure historic drama, redeem him in the hearts of the audience. Yet even in this love there is something feminine and personal:—

> Dear earth, I do salute thee with my hand,—
> As a long parted mother with her child
> Plays fondly with her tears, and smiles in meeting;
> So weeping, smiling, greet I thee, my earth,
> And do thee favor with my royal hands.

With this is combined a constant overflow of emotions from a total incapability of controlling them, and thence a waste of that energy, which should have been reserved for actions, in the passion and effort of mere resolves and menaces. The consequence is moral exhaustion, and rapid alternations of unmanly despair and ungrounded hope—every feeling being abandoned for its direct opposite upon the pressure of external accident. And yet when Richard's inward weakness appears to seek refuge in his despair, and his exhaustion counterfeits repose, the old habit of kingliness, the effect of flatterers from his infancy, is ever and anon producing in him a sort of wordy courage which only serves to betray more clearly his internal impotence. The second and third scenes of the third act combine and illustrate all this :—

Aumerle. He means, my lord, that we are too remiss;
Whilst Bolingbroke, through our security,
Grows strong and great, in substance, and in friends.
K. Rich. Discomfortable cousin! know'st thou not,
That when the searching eye of heaven is hid
Behind the globe, and lights the lower world,
Then thieves and robbers range abroad unseen,
In murders and in outrage, bloody here;
But when, from under this terrestrial ball,
He fires the proud tops of the eastern pines,
And darts his light through every guilty hole,
Then murders, treasons, and detested sins,
The cloke of night being pluckt from off their backs,
Stand bare and naked, trembling at themselves?
So when this thief, this traitor, Bolingbroke, &c.
* * * * *
Aumerle. Where is the Duke my father with his power?
K. Rich. No matter where; of comfort no man speak:
Let's talk of graves, of worms, and epitaphs,
Make dust our paper, and with rainy eyes
Write sorrow on the bosom of the earth, &c.
* * * * *
Aumerle. My father hath a power, inquire of him;
And learn to make a body of a limb.
K. Rich. Thou chid'st me well: proud Bolingbroke, I come
To change blows with thee for our day of doom.
This ague-fit of fear is over-blown;
An easy task it is to win our own.
* * * * *
Scroop. Your uncle York hath join'd with Bolingbroke.—
* * * * *
K. Rich. Thou hast said enough,
Beshrew thee, cousin, which didst lead me forth
Of that sweet way I was in to despair!
What say you now? what comfort have we now?
By heaven, I'll hate him everlastingly,
That bids me be of comfort any more.
* * * * *

Act iii. sc. 3. Bolingbroke's speech:

Noble lord,
Go to the rude ribs of that ancient castle, &c.

Observe the fine struggle of a haughty sense of power and ambition in Bolingbroke with the necessity for dissimulation.

Ib. sc. 4. See here the skill and judgment of our poet in giving reality and individual life, by the introduction of accidents in his historic plays, and thereby making them dramas, and not histories. How beautiful an islet of repose—a melancholy repose, indeed—is this scene with the Gardener and his Servant. And how truly affecting and realizing is the incident of the very horse Barbary, in the scene with the Groom in the last act!—

Groom. I was a poor groom of thy stable, King,
When thou wert King; who, travelling towards York,
With much ado, at length have gotten leave
To look upon my sometime master's face.
O, how it yearn'd my heart, when I beheld,
In London streets, that coronation day,
When Bolingbroke rode on roan Barbary!
That horse, that thou so often hast bestrid;
That horse, that I so carefully have dress'd!
K. Rich. Rode he on Barbary?

Bolingbroke's character, in general, is an instance how Shakspeare makes one play introductory to another; for it is evidently a preparation for Henry IV., as Gloster in the third part of Henry VI. is for Richard III.

I would once more remark upon the exalted idea of the only true loyalty developed in this noble and impressive play. We have neither the rants of Beaumont and Fletcher, nor the sneers of Massinger;—the vast importance of the personal character of the sovereign is distinctly enounced, whilst, at the same time, the genuine sanctity which surrounds him is attributed to, and grounded on, the position in which he stands as the convergence and exponent of the life and power of the state.

The great end of the body politic appears to be to humanize, and assist in the progressiveness of, the animal man;—but the problem is so complicated with contingencies as to render it nearly impossible to lay down rules for the formation of a state. And should we be able to form a system of government, which should so balance its different powers as to form a check upon each, and so continually remedy and correct itself, it would, nevertheless, defeat its own aim;—for man is destined to be guided by higher principles, by universal views, which can never be fulfilled in this state of existence,—by a spirit of progressiveness which can never be accomplished, for then it would cease to be. Plato's Republic is like Bunyan's Town of Man-Soul,—a description of an individual, all of whose faculties are in their proper subordination and inter-dependence; and this it is assumed may be the prototype of the state as one great individual. But there is this sophism in it, that it is forgotten that the human faculties, indeed, are parts and not separate things; but that you could never get chiefs who were wholly reason, ministers who were wholly understanding, soldiers all wrath, laborers all concupiscence, and so on through the rest. Each of these partakes of, and interferes with, all the others.

HENRY IV. PART I.

Act i. sc. 1. King Henry's speech :—

> No more the thirsty entrance of this soil
> Shall daub her lips with her own children's blood.

A most obscure passage: but I think Theobald's interpretation right, namely, that 'thirsty entrance' means the dry penetrability, or bibulous drought, of the soil. The obscurity of this passage is of the Shaksperian sort.

Ib. sc. 2. In this, the first introduction of Falstaff, observe the consciousness and the intentionality of his wit, so that when it does not flow of its own accord, its absence is felt, and an effort visibly made to recall it. Note also throughout how Falstaff's pride is gratified in the power of influencing a prince of the blood, the heir-apparent, by means of it. Hence his dislike to Prince John of Lancaster, and his mortification when he finds his wit fail on him:—

> *P. John.* Fare you well, Falstaff: I, in my condition,
> Shall better speak of you than you deserve.
> *Fal.* I would you had but the wit; 'twere better than your dukedom.—Good faith, this same young sober-blooded boy doth not love me;—nor a man can not make him laugh.

Act ii. sc. 1. Second Carrier's speech :—

> . . . . breeds fleas like a *loach*.

Perhaps it is a misprint, or a provincial pronunciation, for 'leach,' that is, blood-suckers. Had it been gnats, instead of fleas, there might have been some sense, though small probability, in Warburton's suggestion of the Scottish 'loch.' Possibly 'loach,' or 'lutch,' may be some lost word for dovecote, or poultry-lodge, notorious for breeding fleas. In Stevens's or my reading, it should properly be 'loaches,' or 'leeches,' in the plural; except that I think I have heard anglers speak of trouts like *a* salmon.

Act iii. sc. 1.

> *Glend. Nay*, if you melt, then will she run mad.

This 'nay' so to be dwelt on in speaking, as to be equivalent to a dissyllable–υ, is characteristic of the solemn Glendower; but the imperfect line

> *She bids you*
> Upon the wanton rushes lay you down, &c.

is one of those fine hair-strokes of exquisite judgment peculiar to Shakspeare;—thus detaching the Lady's speech, and giving it the individuality and entireness of a little poem, while he draws attention to it.

HENRY IV. PART II.

Act ii. sc. 2.

> *P. Hen.* Sup any women with him?
> *Page.* None, my lord, but old mistress Quickly, and mistress Doll Tear-sheet.
> * * * * * * * *
> *P. Hen.* This Doll Tear-sheet should be some road.

I AM sometimes disposed to think that this respectable young lady's name is a very old corruption for Tear-street—street-walker, *terere stratam* (*viam*). Does not the Prince's question rather show this?—

> 'This Doll Tear-street should be some road?'

Act iii. sc. 1. King Henry's speech: —

> . . . . . Then, *happy low, lie down;*
> Uneasy lies the head that wears a crown.

I know no argument by which to persuade any one to be of my opinion, or rather of my feeling; but yet I can not help feeling that 'Happy low-lie-down!' is either a proverbial expression, or the burthen of some old song, and means, 'Happy the man, who lays himself down on his straw bed or chaff pallet on the ground or floor!'

Ib. sc. 2. Shallow's speech :—

> *Rah, tah, tah,* would 'a say; *bounce,* would 'a say, &c.

That Beaumont and Fletcher have more than once been guilty of sneering at their great master, can not, I fear, be denied; but the passage quoted by Theobald from the Knight of the Burning Pestle is an imitation. If it be chargeable with any fault, it is with plagiarism, not with sarcasm.

HENRY V.

Act i. sc. 2. Westmoreland's speech :—

> They know your *grace* hath cause, and means, and might;
> So hath your *highness;* never King of England
> Had nobles richer, &c.

Does 'grace' mean the king's own peculiar domains and legal revenue, and 'highness' his feudal rights in the military service of his nobles?—I have sometimes thought it possible that the words 'grace' and 'cause' may have been transposed in the copying or printing;—

> They know your cause hath grace, &c.

What Theobald meant, I can not guess. To me his pointing makes the passage still more obscure. Perhaps the lines ought to be recited dramatically thus :—

> They know your Grace hath cause, and means, and might:—
> So *hath* your Highness—never King of England
> *Had* nobles richer, &c.

He breaks off from the grammar and natural order from earnestness, and in order to give the meaning more passionately.

Ib. Exeter's speech :—

> Yet that is but a *crush'd* necessity.

Perhaps it may be 'crash' for 'crass' from *crassus*, clumsy; or it may be 'curt,' defective, imperfect; any thing would be better than Warburton's ''scus'd,' which honest Theobald, of course, adopts. By the by, it seems clear to me that this speech of Exeter's properly belongs to Canterbury, and was altered by the actors for convenience.

Act iv. sc. 3. K. Henry's speech:—

> We would not *die* in that man's company
> That fears his fellowship to die with us.

Should it not be 'live' in the first line?

Ib. sc. 5.

> *Const. O diable!*
> *Orl. O seigneur! le jour est perdu, tout est perdu!*
> *Dan. Mort de ma vie!* all is confounded, all!
> Reproach and everlasting shame
> Sit mocking in our plumes!—*O meschante fortune!*
> Do not run away!

Ludicrous as these introductory scraps of French appear, so instantly followed by good, nervous mother-English, yet they are judicious, and produce the impression which Shakspeare intended,—a sudden feeling struck at once on the ears, as well as the eyes, of the audience, that 'here come the French, the baffled French braggards!'—And this will appear still more judicious, when we reflect on the scanty apparatus of distinguishing dresses in Shakspeare's tiring-room.

HENRY VI. PART I.

Act i. sc. 1. Bedford's speech:—

> Hung be the heavens with black, yield day to night;
> Comets, importing change of times and states,
> Brandish your crystal tresses in the sky;
> And with them scourge the bad revolting stars
> That have consented unto Henry's death!
> Henry the fifth, too famous to live long!
> England ne'er lost a king of so much worth.

READ aloud any two or three passages in blank verse even from Shakspeare's earliest dramas, as Love's Labor's Lost, or Romeo and Juliet; and then read in the same way this speech, with especial attention to the metre; and if you do not feel the impossibility of the latter having been written by Shakspeare, all I dare suggest is, that you may have ears,—for so has another animal,—but an ear you can not have, *me judice.*

RICHARD III.

This play should be contrasted with Richard II. Pride of intellect is the characteristic of Richard, carried to the extent of even boasting to his own mind of his villany, whilst others are present to feed his pride of superiority; as in his first speech, act ii. sc. 1. Shakspeare here, as in all his great parts, develops in a tone of sublime morality the dreadful consequences of placing the moral, in subordination to the mere intellectual, being. In Richard there is a predominance of irony, accompanied with apparently blunt manners to those immediately about him, but formalized into a more set hypocrisy towards the people as represented by their magistrates.

LEAR.

Of all Shakspeare's plays Macbeth is the most rapid, Hamlet the slowest, in movement, Lear combines length with rapidity,—like the hurricane and the whirlpool, absorbing while it advances. It begins as a stormy day in summer, with brightness; but that brightness is lurid, and anticipates the tempest. (*t*)

It was not without forethought, nor is it without its due significance, that the division of Lear's kingdom is in the first six lines of the play stated as a thing already determined in all its particulars, previously to the trial of professions, as the relative rewards of which the daughters were to be made to consider their several portions. The strange, yet by no means unnatural, mixture of selfishness, sensibility, and habit of feeling derived from, and fostered by, the particular rank and usages of the individual;—the intense desire of being intensely beloved,—selfish, and yet characteristic of the selfishness of a loving and kindly nature alone;—the self-supportless leaning for all pleasure on another's breast;—the craving after sympathy with a prodigal disinterestedness, frustrated by its own ostentation, and the mode and nature of its claims ;—the anxiety, the distrust, the jealousy, which more or less accompany all selfish affections, and are amongst the surest contradistinctions of mere fondness from true love, and which originate Lear's eager wish to enjoy his daughter's violent professions, whilst the inveterate habits of sovereignty convert the wish into claim and positive right, and an incompliance with it into crime and treason ;—these facts, these passions, these moral verities, on which the whole tragedy is founded, are all prepared for, and will to the retrospect be found implied, in these first four or five lines of the play. They let us know that the trial is but a trick ; and that the grossness of the old king's rage is in part the natural result of a silly trick suddenly and most unexpectedly baffled and disappointed.

It may here be worthy of notice, that Lear is the only serious performance of Shakspeare, the interest and situations of which are derived from the assumption of a gross improbability ; whereas Beaumont and Fletcher's tragedies are, almost all of them, founded on some out of the way accident or exception to the general experience of mankind. But observe the matchless judgment of our Shakspeare. First, improbable as the conduct of Lear is in the first scene, yet it was an old story rooted in the popular faith,—a thing taken for granted already, and consequently without any of the effects of improbability. Secondly, it is merely the canvass for the characters and passions,—a mere occasion for,—and not, in the manner of Beaumont and Fletcher, perpetually recurring as the cause, and *sine qua non* of,—the incidents and emotions. Let the first scene of this play have been lost, and let it only be understood that a fond father had been duped by hypocritical professions of love and duty on the part of two daughters to disinherit the third, previously, and deservedly, more dear to him ;—and all the rest of the tragedy would retain its interest undiminished, and be perfectly intelligible. The accidental is nowhere the groundwork of the passions, but that which is catholic, which in all ages has been and ever will be, close and native to the heart of man,—parental anguish from filial ingratitude, the genuineness of worth, though coffined in bluntness, and the execrable vileness of a smooth iniquity. Perhaps I ought to have added the Merchant of Venice ; but here too the same remarks apply. It was an old tale ; and substitute any other danger than that of the pound of flesh (the circumstance in which the improbability lies), yet all the situations and the emotions appertaining to them remain equally excellent and appropriate. Whereas take away from the Mad Lover of Beaumont and Fletcher the fantastic hypothesis of his engagement to cut out his own heart, and have it presented to his mistress, and all the main scenes must go with it.

Kotzebue is the German Beaumont and Fletcher, without their poetic powers, and without their *vis comica*. But, like them, he always deduces his situations and passions from marvellous accidents, and the trick of bringing one part of our moral nature to counteract another ; as our pity for misfortune and admiration of generosity and courage to combat our condemnation of guilt, as in adultery, robbery, and other heinous crimes ;—and, like them too, he excels in his mode of telling a story clearly and interestingly, in a series of dramatic dialogues. Only the trick of making tragedy-heroes and heroines out of shopkeepers and barmaids was too low for the age, and too unpoetic for the genius, of Beaumont and Fletcher, inferior in every respect as they are to their great predecessor and contemporary. How inferior would they have appeared, had not Shakspeare existed for them to imitate ;—which in every play, more or less, they do, and in their tragedies most glaringly :—and yet—(O shame ! shame !)—they miss no opportunity of sneering at the divine man, and subidetracting from his merits ! (*u*)

To return to Lear. Having thus in the fewest words, and in a natural reply to as natural a question,—which yet answers the secondary purpose of attracting our attention to the difference or diversity between the characters of Cornwall and Albany,—provided the premisses and *data*, as it were, for our after-insight into the mind and mood of the person, whose character, passions, and sufferings are the main subject-matter of the play ;—from Lear, the *persona patiens* of his drama, Shakspeare passes without delay to the second in importance, the chief agent and prime mover, and introduces Edmund to our acquaintance, preparing us with the same felicity of judgment, and in the same easy and natural way, for his character in the seemingly casual communication of its origin and occasion. From the first drawing up of the curtain Edmund has stood before us in the united strength and beauty of earliest manhood. Our eyes have been questioning him. Gifted as he is with high advantages of person, and further endowed by nature with a powerful intellect and a strong energetic will, even without any concurrence of circumstances and accident, pride will necessarily be the sin that most easily besets him. But Edmund is also the known and acknowledged son of the princely Gloster: he, therefore, has both the germ of pride, and the conditions best fitted to evolve and ripen it into a predominant feeling. Yet hitherto no reason appears why it should be other than the not unusual pride of person, talent, and birth,—a pride auxiliary, if not akin, to many virtues, and the natural ally of honorable impulses. But alas! in his own presence his own father takes shame to himself for the frank avowal that he is his father,—he has "blushed so often to acknowledge him that he is now brazed to it!" Edmund hears the circumstances of his birth spoken of with a most degrading and licentious levity,—his mother described as a wanton by her own paramour, and the remembrance of the animal sting, the low criminal gratifications connected with her wantonness and prostituted beauty, assigned as the reason, why "the whoreson must be acknowledged!" This, and the consciousness of its notoriety; the gnawing conviction that every show of respect is an effort of courtesy, which recalls, while it represses, a contrary feeling;—this is the ever trickling flow of wormwood and gall into the wounds of pride,—the corrosive *virus* which inoculates pride with a venom not its own, with envy, hatred, and a lust for that power which in its blaze of radiance would hide the dark spots on his disc,—with pangs of shame personally undeserved, and therefore felt as wrongs, and with a blind ferment of vindictive working towards the occasions and causes, especially towards a brother, whose stainless birth and lawful honors were the constant remembrancers of his own debasement, and were ever in the way to prevent all chance of its being unknown, or overlooked and forgotten. Add to this, that with excellent judgment, and provident for the claims of the moral sense,—for that which, relatively to the drama, is called poetic justice, and as the fittest means for reconciling the feelings of the spectators to the horrors of Gloster's after-sufferings,—at least, of rendering them somewhat less unendurable—(for I will not disguise my conviction, that in this one point the tragic in this play has been urged beyond the outermost mark and *ne plus ultra* of the dramatic)—Shakspeare has precluded all excuse and palliation of the guilt incurred by both the parents of the base-born Edmund, by Gloster's confession that he was at the time a married man, and already blest with a lawful heir of his fortunes. The mournful alienation of brotherly love, occasioned by the law of primogeniture in noble families, or rather by the unnecessary distinctions engrafted thereon, and this in children of the same stock, is still almost proverbial on the continent,—especially, as I know from my own observation, in the south of Europe,—and appears to have been scarcely less common in our own island before the Revolution of 1688, if we may judge from the characters and sentiments so frequent in our elder comedies. There is the younger brother, for instance, in Beaumont and Fletcher's play of the Scornful Lady, on the one side, and Oliver in Shakspeare's As You Like It, on the other. Need it be said how heavy an aggravation, in such a case, the stain of bastardy must have been, were it only that the younger brother was liable to hear his own dishonor and his mother's infamy related by his father with an excusing shrug of the shoulders, and in a tone betwixt waggery and shame!

By the circumstances here enumerated as so many predisposing causes, Edmund's character might well be deemed already sufficiently explained; and our minds prepared for it. But in this tragedy the story or fable constrained Shakspeare to introduce wickedness in an outrageous form in the persons of Regan and Goneril. He had read nature too heedfully not to know, that courage, intellect, and strength of character are the most impressive forms of power, and that to power in itself, without reference to any moral end, an inevitable admiration and complacency appertains, whether it be displayed in the conquests of a Bonaparte or Tamerlane, or in the form and the thunder of a cataract. But in the exhibition of such a character it was of the highest importance to prevent the guilt from passing into utter monstrosity,—which again depends on the presence or absence of causes and temptations sufficient to account for the wickedness, without the necessity of recurring to a thorough fiendishness of nature for its origination. For such are the appointed relations of intellectual power to truth, and of truth to goodness, that it becomes both morally and poetically unsafe to present what is admirable,—what our nature compels us to admire—in the mind, and what is most detestable in the heart, as co-existing in the same individual without any apparent connection, or any modification of the one by the other. That Shakspeare has in one instance, that of Iago, approached to this, and that he has done it successfully, is, perhaps, the most astonishing proof of his genius, and the opulence of its resources. But in the present tragedy, in which he was compelled to present a Goneril and a Regan, it was most carefully to be avoided ;—and therefore the only one conceivable addition to the inauspicious influences on the preformation of Edmund's character is given, in the information that all the kindly counteractions to the mischievous feelings of shame, which might have been derived from co-domestication with Edgar and their common father, had been cut off by his absence from home, and foreign education from boyhood to the present time, and a prospect of its continuance, as if to preclude all risk of his interference with the father's views for the elder and legitimate son :—

> He hath been out nine years, and away he shall again.

Act i. sc. 1.

> *Cor.* Nothing, my lord.
> *Lear.* Nothing?
> *Cor.* Nothing.
> *Lear.* Nothing can come of nothing: speak again.
> *Cor.* Unhappy that I am, I can not heave
> My heart into my mouth: I love your majesty
> According to my bond; nor more, nor less.

There is something of disgust at the ruthless hypocrisy of her sisters, and some little faulty admixture of pride and sullenness in Cordelia's 'Nothing ;' and her tone is well contrived, indeed, to lessen the glaring absurdity of Lear's conduct, but answers the yet more important purpose of forcing away the attention from the nursery-tale, the moment it has served its end, that of supplying the canvass for the picture. This is also materially furthered by Kent's opposition, which displays Lear's moral incapability of resigning the sovereign power in the very act of disposing of it. Kent is, perhaps, the nearest to perfect goodness in all Shakspeare's characters, and yet the most individualized. There is an extraordinary charm in his bluntness, which is that only of a nobleman arising from a contempt of overstrained courtesy, and combined with easy placability where goodness of heart is apparent. His passionate affection for, and fidelity to Lear, act on our feelings in Lear's own favor : virtue itself seems to be in company with him.

Ib. sc. 2. Edmund's Speech :—

> Who, in the lusty stealth of nature, take
> More composition and fierce quality
> Than doth, &c.

Warburton's note upon a quotation from Vanini.

Poor Vanini !—Any one but Warburton would have thought this precious passage more characteristic of Mr. Shandy than of atheism. If the fact really were so (which it is not, but almost the contrary), I do not see why the most confirmed theist might not very naturally utter the same wish. But it is proverbial that the youngest son in a large family is commonly the man of the greatest talents in it; and as good an authority as Vanini has said—*incalescere in venerem ardentius, spei sobolis injuriosum esse.*

In this speech of Edmund you see, as soon as a man can not reconcile himself to reason, how his conscience flies off by way of appeal to nature, who is sure upon such occasions never to find fault, and also how shame sharpens a predisposition in the heart to evil. For it is a profound moral, that shame will naturally generate guilt; the oppressed will be vindictive, like Shylock, and in the anguish of undeserved ignominy the delusion secretly springs up, of getting over the moral quality of an action by fixing the mind on the mere physical act alone.

Ib. Edmund's speech :—

> This is the excellent foppery of the world! that, when we are sick in fortune (often the surfeit of our own behavior), we make guilty of our disasters, the sun, the moon, and the stars, &c.

Thus scorn and misanthropy are often the anticipations and mouth-pieces of wisdom in the detection of superstitions. Both individuals and nations may be free from such prejudices by being below them, as well as by rising above them.

Ib. sc. 3. The Steward should be placed in exact antithesis to Kent, as the only character of utter irredeemable baseness in Shakspeare. Even in this the judgment and invention of the poet are very observable ;—for what else could the willing tool of a Goneril be ? Not a vice but this of baseness was left open to him.

Ib. sc. 4. In Lear old age is itself a character,—its natural imperfections being increased by life-long habits of receiving a prompt obedience. Any addition of individuality would have been unnecessary and painful; for the relations of others to him, of wondrous fidelity and of frightful ingratitude, alone sufficiently distinguish him. Thus Lear becomes the open and ample play-room of nature's passions.

Ib.

Knight. Since my young lady's going into France, Sir; the fool hath much pin'd away.

The Fool is no comic buffoon to make the groundlings laugh,—no forced condescension of Shakspeare's genius to the taste of his audience. Accordingly the poet prepares for his introduction, which he never does with any of his common clowns and fools, by bringing him into living connection with the pathos of the play. He is as wonderful a creation as Caliban;—his wild babblings, and inspired idiocy, articulate and gauge the horrors of the scene.

The monster Goneril prepares what is necessary, while the character of Albany renders a still more maddening grievance possible, namely, Regan and Cornwall in perfect sympathy of monstrosity. Not a sentiment, not an image, which can give pleasure on its own account, is admitted; whenever these creatures are introduced, and they are brought forward as little as possible, pure horror reigns throughout. In this scene, and in all the early speeches of Lear, the one general sentiment of filial ingratitude prevails as the main-spring of the feelings;—in this early stage the outward object causing the pressure on the mind, which is not yet sufficiently familiarized with the anguish for the imagination to work upon it.

Ib.

Gon. Do you mark that, my lord?
Alb. I can not be so partial, Goneril,
To the great love I bear you.
Gon. Pray you content, &c.

Observe the baffled endeavor of Goneril to act on the fears of Albany, and yet his passiveness, his *inertia;* he is not convinced, and yet he is afraid of looking into the thing. Such characters always yield to those who will take the trouble of governing them, or for them. Perhaps, the influence of a princess, whose choice of him had royalized his state, may be some little excuse for Albany's weakness.

Ib. sc. 5.

> *Lear.* O let me not be mad, not mad, sweet heaven!
> Keep me in temper! I would not be mad!—

The mind's own anticipation of madness! The deepest tragic notes are often struck by a half sense of an impending blow. The Fool's conclusion of this act by a grotesque prattling seems to indicate the dislocation of feeling that has begun and is to be continued.

Act ii. sc. 1. Edmund's speech :—

> He replied,
> Thou unpossessing bastard! &c.

Thus the secret poison in Edmund's own heart steals forth; and then observe poor Gloster's—

> Loyal and *natural* boy!

as if praising the crime of Edmund's birth!

Ib. Compare Regan's—

> What, did *my father's* godson seek your life?
> He whom *my father* named?

with the unfeminine violence of her—

> All vengeance comes too short, &c.

and yet no reference to the guilt, but only to the accident, which she uses as an occasion for sneering at her father. Regan is not, in fact, a greater monster than Goneril, but she has the power of casting more venom.

Ib. sc. 2. Cornwall's speech :—

> This is some fellow,
> Who, having been praised for bluntness, doth affect
> A saucy roughness, &c.

In thus placing these profound general truths in the mouths of such men as Cornwall, Edmund, Iago, &c. Shakspeare at once gives them utterance, and yet shows how indefinite their application is.

Ib. sc. 3. Edgar's assumed madness serves the great purpose of taking off part of the shock which would otherwise be caused by the true madness of Lear, and further displays the profound difference between the two. In every attempt at representing madness throughout the whole range of dramatic literature, with the single exception of Lear, it is mere lightheadedness, as especially in Otway. In Edgar's ravings Shakspeare all the while lets you see a fixed purpose, a practical end in view;—in Lear's, there is only the brooding of the one anguish, an eddy without progression.

Ib. sc. 4. Lear's speech:—

> The king would speak with Cornwall; the dear father
> Would with his daughter speak, &c.
> * * * *
> No, but not yet: may be he is not well, &c.

The strong interest now felt by Lear to try to find excuses for his daughter is most pathetic.

Ib. Lear's speech:—

> ——— Beloved Regan,
> Thy sister's naught;—O Regan, she hath tied
> Sharp-tooth'd unkindness, like a vulture, here.
> I can scarce speak to thee;—thou'lt not believe
> Of how deprav'd a quality—O Regan!
> *Reg.* I pray you, Sir, take patience; I have hope,
> You less know how to value her desert,
> Than she to scant her duty.
> *Lear.* Say, how is that?

Nothing is so heart-cutting as a cold unexpected defence or palliation of a cruelty passionately complained of, or so expressive of thorough hard-heartedness. And feel the excessive horror of Regan's 'O, Sir, you are old!'—and then her drawing from that universal object of reverence and indulgence the very reason for her frightful conclusion—

> Say, you have wrong'd her!

All Lear's faults increase our pity for him. We refuse to know them otherwise than as means of his sufferings, and aggravations of his daughter's ingratitude.

Ib. Lear's speech :—

> O, reason not the need: our basest beggars
> Are in the poorest thing superfluous, &c.

Observe that the tranquillity which follows the first stunning of the blow permits Lear to reason.

Act iii. sc. 4. O, what a world's convention of agonies is here! All external nature in a storm, all moral nature convulsed,—the real madness of Lear, the feigned madness of Edgar, the babbling of the Fool, the desperate fidelity of Kent—surely such a scene was never conceived before or since! Take it but as a picture for the eye only, it is more terrific than any which a Michel Angelo, inspired by a Dante, could have conceived, and which none but a Michel Angelo could have executed. Or let it have been uttered to the blind, the howlings of nature would seem converted into the voice of conscious humanity. This scene ends with the first symptoms of positive derangement; and the intervention of the fifth scene is particularly judicious,—the interruption allowing an interval for Lear to appear in full madness in the sixth scene.

Ib. sc. 7. Gloster's blinding :—

What can I say of this scene?—There is my reluctance to think Shakspeare wrong, and yet—

Act iv. sc. 6. Lear's speech :—

> Ha! Goneril!—with a white beard!—They flattered me like a dog; and told me, I had white hairs in my beard, ere the black ones were there. To say *Ay* and *No* to every thing I said!—Ay and No too was no good divinity. When the rain came to wet me once, &c.

The thunder recurs, but still at a greater distance from our feelings.

Ib. sc. 7. Lear's speech :—

> Where have I been? Where am I?—Fair daylight?—
> I am mightily abused.—I should even die with pity
> To see another thus, &c.

How beautifully the affecting return of Lear to reason, and the mild pathos of these speeches prepare the mind for the last sad, yet sweet, consolation of the aged sufferer's death!

HAMLET.

HAMLET was the play, or rather Hamlet himself was the character, in the intuition and exposition of which I first made my turn for philosophical criticism, and especially for insight into the genius of Shakspeare, noticed. This happened first among my acquaintances, as Sir George Beaumont will bear witness; and subsequently, long before Schlegel had delivered at Vienna the lectures on Shakspeare, which he afterwards published, I had given on the same subject eighteen lectures substantially the same, proceeding from the very same point of view, and deducing the same conclusions, so far as I either then agreed, or now agree, with him. I gave these lectures at the Royal Institution, before six or seven hundred auditors of rank and eminence, in the spring of the same year, in which Sir Humphrey Davy, a fellow-lecturer, made his great revolutionary discoveries in chemistry. (*v*) Even in detail the coincidence of Schlegel with my lectures was so extraordinary, that all who at a later period heard the same words, taken by me from my notes of the lectures at the Royal Institution, concluded a borrowing on my part from Schlegel. Mr. Hazlitt, whose hatred of me is in such an inverse ratio to my zealous kindness towards him, as to be defended by his warmest admirer, Charles Lamb—(who, God bless him! besides his characteristic obstinacy of adherence to old friends, as long at least as they are at all down in the world, is linked as by a charm to Hazlitt's conversation),—only as 'frantic;'—Mr. Hazlitt, I say, himself replied to an assertion of my plagiarism from Schlegel in these words;—"That is a lie; for I myself heard the very same character of Hamlet from Coleridge before he went to Germany, and when he had neither read nor could read a page of German!" Now Hazlitt was on a visit to me at my cottage at Nether Stowey, Somerset, in the summer of the year 1798, in the September of which year I first was out of sight of the shores of Great Britain. Recorded by me, S. T. Coleridge, 7th January, 1819.

The seeming inconsistencies in the conduct and character of Hamlet have long exercised the conjectural ingenuity of critics; and, as we are always loth to suppose that the cause of defective apprehension is in ourselves, the mystery has been too commonly explained by the very easy process of setting it down as in fact inexplicable, and by resolving the phenomenon into a misgrowth or *lusus* of the capricious and irregular genius of Shakspeare. The shallow and stupid arrogance of these vulgar and indolent decisions I would fain do my best to expose. I believe the character of Hamlet may be traced to Shakspeare's deep and accurate science in mental philosophy. Indeed, that this character must have some connection with the common fundamental laws of our nature may be assumed from the fact, that Hamlet has been the darling of every country in which the literature of England has been fostered. In order to understand him, it is essential that we should reflect on the constitution of our own minds. Man is distinguished from the brute animals in proportion as thought prevails over sense : but in the healthy processes of the mind, a balance is constantly maintained between the impressions from outward objects and the inward operations of the intellect :—for if there be an overbalance in the contemplative faculty, man thereby becomes the creature of mere meditation, and loses his natural power of action. Now one of Shakspeare's modes of creating characters is, to conceive any one intellectual or moral faculty in morbid excess, and then to place himself, Shakspeare, thus mutilated or diseased, under given circumstances. In Hamlet he seems to have wished to exemplify the moral necessity of a due balance between our attention to the objects of our senses, and our meditation on the workings of our minds,—an *equilibrium* between the real and the imaginary worlds. In Hamlet this balance is disturbed: his thoughts, and the images of his fancy, are far more vivid than his actual perceptions, and his very perceptions, instantly passing through the *medium* of his contemplations, acquire, as they pass, a form and a color not naturally their own. Hence we see a great, an almost enormous, intellectual activity, and a proportionate aversion to real action, consequent upon it, with all its symptoms and accompanying qualities. This character Shakspeare places in circumstances, under which it is obliged to act on the spur of the moment :— Hamlet is brave and careless of death; but he vacillates from sensibility, and procrastinates from thought, and loses the power of action in the energy of resolve. Thus it is that this tragedy presents a direct contrast to that of Macbeth ; the one proceeds with the utmost slowness, the other with a crowded and breathless rapidity. (*w*)

The effect of this overbalance of the imaginative power is beautifully illustrated in the everlasting broodings and superfluous activities of Hamlet's mind, which, unseated from its healthy relation, is constantly occupied with the world within, and abstracted from the world without,—giving substance to shadows, and throwing a mist over all common-place actualities. It is the nature of thought to be indefinite ;—definiteness belongs to external imagery alone. Hence it is that the sense of sublimity arises, not from the sight of an outward object, but from the beholder's reflection upon it ;—not from the sensuous impression, but from the imaginative reflex. Few have seen a celebrated waterfall without feeling something akin to disappointment : it is only subsequently that the image comes back full into the mind, and brings with it a train of grand or beautiful associations. Hamlet feels this ; his senses are in a state of trance, and he looks upon external things as hieroglyphics. His soliloquy—

Oh ! that this too, too solid flesh would melt, &c.

springs from that craving after the indefinite—for that which is not—which most easily besets men of genius ; and the self-delusion common to this temper of mind is finely exemplified in the character which Hamlet gives of himself:—

—It can not be
But I am pigeon-livered, and lack gall
To make oppression bitter.

He mistakes the seeing his chains for the breaking of them, delays action till action is of no use, and dies the victim of mere circumstance and accident. (*x*)

There is a great significancy in the names of Shakspeare's plays. In the Twelfth Night, Midsummer Night's Dream, As You Like It, and Winter's Tale, the total effect is produced by a co-ordination of the characters as in a wreath of flowers. But in Coriolanus, Lear, Romeo and Juliet, Hamlet, Othello, &c., the effect arises from the subordination of all to one, either as the prominent person, or the principal object. Cymbeline is the only exception ; and even that has its advantages in preparing the audience for the chaos of time, place, and costume, by throwing the date back into a fabulous king's reign.

But as of more importance, so more striking, is the judgment displayed by our truly dramatic poet, as well as poet of the drama, in the management of his first scenes. With the single exception of Cymbeline, they either place before us at one glance both the past and the future in some effect, which implies the continuance and full agency of its cause, as in the feuds and party-spirit of the servants of the two houses in the first scene of Romeo and Juliet; or in the degrading passion for shows and public spectacles, and the overwhelming attachment for the newest successful war-chief in the Roman people, already become a populace, contrasted with the jealousy of the nobles in Julius Cæsar;—or they at once commence the action so as to excite a curiosity for the explanation in the following scenes, as in the storm of wind and waves, and the boatswain in the Tempest, instead of anticipating our curiosity, as in most other first scenes, and in too many other first acts;—or they act, by contrast of diction suited to the characters, at once to heighten the effect, and yet to give a naturalness to the language and rhythm of the principal personages, either as that of Prospero and Miranda by the appropriate lowness of the style,—or as in King John, by the equally appropriate stateliness of official harangues or narratives, so that the after blank verse seems to belong to the rank and quality of the speakers, and not to the poet;—or they strike at once the key-note, and give the predominant spirit of the play, as in the Twelfth Night and in Macbeth;—or finally, the first scene comprises all these advantages at once, as in Hamlet.

Compare the easy language of common life, in which this drama commences, with the direful music and wild wayward rhythm and abrupt lyrics of the opening of Macbeth. The tone is quite familiar;—there is no poetic description of night, no elaborate information conveyed by one speaker to another of what both had immediately before their senses—(such as the first distich in Addison's Cato, which is a translation into poetry of 'Past four o'clock and a dark morning!');—and yet nothing bordering on the comic on the one hand, or any striving of the intellect on the other. It is precisely the language of sensation among men who feared no charge of effeminacy for feeling what they had no want of resolution to bear. Yet the armor, the dead silence, the watchfulness that first interrupts it, the welcome relief of the guard, the cold, the broken expressions of compelled attention to bodily feelings still under control—all excellently accord with, and prepare for, the after gradual rise into tragedy;—but, above all, into a tragedy, the interest of which is as eminently *ad et apud intra*, as that of Macbeth is directly *ad extra*.

In all the best attested stories of ghosts and visions, as in that of Brutus, of Archbishop Cranmer, that of Benvenuto Cellini recorded by himself, and the vision of Galileo communicated by him to his favorite pupil Torricelli, the ghost-seers were in a state of cold or chilling damp from without, and of anxiety inwardly. It has been with all of them as with Francisco on his guard,—alone, in the depth and silence of the night;—''twas bitter cold, and they were sick at heart, and *not a mouse stirring*.' The attention to minute sounds,—naturally associated with the recollection of minute objects, and the more familiar and trifling, the more impressive from the unusualness of their producing any impression at all—gives a philosophic pertinency to this last image; but it has likewise its dramatic use and purpose. For its commonness in ordinary conversation tends to produce the sense of reality, and at once hides the poet, and yet approximates the reader or spectator to that state in which the highest poetry will appear, and in its component parts, though not in the whole composition, really is, the language of nature. If I should not speak it, I feel that I should be thinking it;—the voice only is the poet's,—the words are my own. That Shakspeare meant to put an effect in the actor's power in the very first words—"Who's there?"—is evident from the impatience expressed by the startled Francisco in the words that follow—"Nay, answer me: stand and unfold yourself." A brave man is never so peremptory, as when he fears that he is afraid. Observe the gradual transition from the silence and the still recent habit of listening in Francisco's—"I think I hear them"—to the more cheerful call out, which a good actor would observe, in the—"Stand ho! Who is there?" Bernardo's inquiry after Horatio, and the repetition of his name and in his own presence indicate a respect or an eagerness that implies him as one of the persons who are in the foreground; and the skepticism attributed to him,—

> Horatio says, 'tis but our fantasy;
> And will not let belief take hold of him—

prepares us for Hamlet's after-eulogy on him as one whose blood and judgment were happily commingled. The actor should also be careful to distinguish the expectation and gladness of Bernardo's 'Welcome, Horatio!' from the mere courtesy of his 'Welcome, good Marcellus!'

Now observe the admirable indefiniteness of the first opening out of the occasion of all this anxiety. The preparation informative of the audience is just as much as was precisely necessary, and no more;—it begins with the uncertainty appertaining to a question:—

Mar. What! has *this thing* appeared again to-night?—

Even the word 'again' has its *credibilizing* effect. Then Horatio, the representative of the ignorance of the audience, not himself, but by Marcellus to Bernardo, anticipates the common solution—''tis but our fantasy!' upon which Marcellus rises into

This dreaded sight, twice seen of us—

which immediately afterwards becomes 'this apparition,' and that, too, an intelligent spirit, that is, to be spoken to! Then comes the confirmation of Horatio's disbelief;—

Tush! tush! 'twill not appear!—

and the silence, with which the scene opened, is again restored in the shivering feeling of Horatio sitting down, at such a time, and with the two eye-witnesses, to hear a story of a ghost, and that, too, of a ghost which had appeared twice before at the very same hour. In the deep feeling which Bernardo has of the solemn nature of what he is about to relate, he makes an effort to master his own imaginative terrors by an elevation of style,—itself a continuation of the effort,—and by turning off from the apparition, as from something which would force him too deeply into himself, to the outward objects, the realities of nature, which had accompanied it:—

Ber. Last night of all,
When yon same star, that's westward from the pole,
Had made his course to illume that part of heaven
Where now it burns, Marcellus and myself,
The bell then beating one—

This passage seems to contradict the critical law that what is told, makes a faint impression compared with what is beholden; for it does indeed convey to the mind more than the eye can see; whilst the interruption of the narrative at the very moment when we are most intensely listening for the sequel, and have our thoughts diverted from the dreaded sight in expectation of the desired, yet almost dreaded, tale—this gives all the suddenness and surprise of the original appearance ;—

Mar. Peace, break thee off; look, where it comes again !—

Note the judgment displayed in having the two persons present, who, as having seen the Ghost before, are naturally eager in confirming their former opinions,—whilst the skeptic is silent, and after having been twice addressed by his friends, answers with two hasty syllables—'Most like,'—and a confession of horror :—

It harrows me with fear and wonder.

O heaven ! words are wasted on those who feel, and to those who do not feel the exquisite judgment of Shakspeare in this scene, what can be said ?—Hume himself could not but have had faith in this Ghost dramátically, let his anti-ghostism have been as strong as Samson against other ghosts less powerfully raised.

Act i. sc. 1.

Mar. Good now, sit down, and tell me, he that knows
Why this same strict and most observant watch, &c.

How delightfully natural is the transition to the retrospective narrative ! And observe, upon the Ghost's reappearance, how much Horatio's courage is increased by having translated the late individual spectator into general thought and past experience,—and the sympathy of Marcellus and Bernardo with his patriotic surmises in daring to strike at the Ghost ; whilst in a moment, upon its vanishing the former solemn awe-stricken feeling returns upon them :—

We do it wrong, being so majestical,
To offer it the show of violence.—

Ib. Horatio's speech :—

I have heard,
The cock, that is the trumpet to the morn,
Doth with his lofty and shrill sounding throat
Awake the god of day, &c.

No Addison could be more careful to be poetical in diction than Shakspeare in providing the grounds and sources of its propriety. But how to elevate a thing almost mean by its familiarity, young poets may learn in this treatment of the cock-crow.

Ib. Horatio's speech :—

> And, by my advice,
> Let us impart what we have seen to-night
> Unto young Hamlet; for, upon my life,
> The spirit, dumb to us, will speak to him.

Note the unobtrusive and yet fully adequate mode of introducing the main character, 'young Hamlet,' upon whom is transferred all the interest excited for the acts and concerns of the king his father.

Ib. sc. 2. The audience are now relieved by a change of scene to the royal court, in order that Hamlet may not have to take up the leavings of exhaustion. In the king's speech, observe the set and pedantically antithetic form of the sentences when touching that which galled the heels of conscience,—the strain of undignified rhetoric,—and yet in what follows concerning the public weal, a certain appropriate majesty. Indeed was he not a royal brother ?—

Ib. King's speech :—

> And now, Laertes, what's the news with you? &c.

Thus with great art Shakspeare introduces a most important, but still subordinate character first, Laertes, who is yet thus graciously treated in consequence of the assistance given to the election of the late king's brother instead of his son by Polonius..

Ib.

> *Ham.* A little more than kin, and less than kind.
> *King.* How is it that the clouds still hang on you?
> *Ham.* Not so, my lord, I am too much i' the sun.

Hamlet opens his mouth with a playing on words, the complete absence of which throughout characterizes Macbeth. This playing on words may be attributed to many causes or motives, as either to an exuberant activity of mind, as in the higher comedy of Shakspeare generally ;—or to an imitation of it as a mere fashion, as if it were said—' Is not this better than groaning ?' —or to a contemptuous exultation in minds vulgarized and overset by their success, as in the poetic instance of Milton's Devils in the battle ;—or it is the language of resentment, as is familiar to every one who has witnessed the quarrels of the lower orders, where there is invariably a profusion of punning invective, whence, perhaps, nicknames have in a considerable degree sprung up ;—or it is the language of suppressed passion, and especially of a hardly smothered personal dislike. The first and last of these combine in Hamlet's case ; and I have little doubt that Farmer is right in supposing the equivocation carried on in the expression 'too much i' the sun,' or son.

Ib.

Ham. Ay, madam, it is common.

Here observe Hamlet's delicacy to his mother, and how the suppression prepares him for the overflow in the next speech, in which his character is more developed by bringing forward his aversion to externals, and which betrays his habit of brooding over the world within him, coupled with a prodigality of beautiful words, which are the half-embodyings of thought, and are more than thought, and have an outness, a reality *sui generis*, and yet contain their correspondence and shadowy affinity to the images and movements within. Note also Hamlet's silence to the long speech of the king which follows, and his respectful, but general, answer to his mother.

Ib. Hamlet's first soliloquy :—

O, that this too too solid flesh would melt,
Thaw, and resolve itself into a dew ! &c.

This *tædium vitæ* is a common oppression on minds cast in the Hamlet mould, and is caused by disproportionate mental exertion, which necessitates exhaustion of bodily feeling. Where there is a just coincidence of external and internal action, pleasure is always the result ; but where the former is deficient, and the mind's appetency of the ideal is unchecked, realities will seem cold and unmoving. In such cases, passion combines itself with the indefinite alone. In this mood of his mind the relation of the appearance of his father's spirit in arms is made all at once to Hamlet :—it is—Horatio's speech, in particular—a perfect model of the true style of dramatic narrative ;—the purest poetry, and yet in the most natural language, equally remote from the inkhorn and the plough.

Ib. sc. 3. This scene must be regarded as one of Shakspeare's lyric movements in the play, and the skill with which it is interwoven with the dramatic parts is peculiarly an excellence of our poet. You experience the sensation of a pause without the sense of a stop. You will observe in Ophelia's short and general answer to the long speech of Laertes the natural carelessness of innocence, which can not think such a code of cautions and prudences necessary to its own preservation.

Ib. Speech of Polonius:—(in Stockdale's edition.)

> Or (not to crack the wind of the poor phrase)
> Wronging it thus, you'll tender me a fool.

I suspect this 'wronging' is here used much in the same sense as 'wringing' or 'wrenching;' and that the parenthesis should be extended to 'thus.'*

Ib. Speech of Polonius:—

> —— How prodigal the soul
> Lends the tongue vows:—these blazes, daughter, &c.

A spondee has, I doubt not, dropped out of the text. Either insert 'Go to' after 'vows;'—

> Lends the tongue vows: Go to, these blazes, daughter—

or read

> Lends the tongue vows:—These blazes, daughter, mark you—

Shakspeare never introduces a catalectic line without intending an equivalent to the foot omitted in the pauses, or the dwelling emphasis, or the diffused retardation. I do not, however, deny that a good actor might by employing the last-mentioned means, namely, the retardation, or solemn knowing drawl, supply the missing spondee with good effect. But I do not believe that in this or any other of the foregoing speeches of Polonius, Shakspeare meant to bring out the senility or weakness of that personage's mind. In the great ever-recurring dangers and duties of life, where to distinguish the fit objects for the application of the maxims collected by the experience of a long life, requires no fineness of tact, as in the admonitions to his son and daughter, Polonius is uniformly made respectable. But if an actor were

* It is so pointed in the modern editions.—*Ed.*

even capable of catching these shades in the character, the pit and the gallery would be malcontent at their exhibition. It is to Hamlet that Polonius is, and is meant to be, contemptible, because in inwardness and uncontrollable activity of movement, Hamlet's mind is the logical contrary to that of Polonius, and besides, as I have observed before, Hamlet dislikes the man as false to his true allegiance in the matter of the succession to the crown.

Ib. sc. 4. The unimportant conversation with which this scene opens is a proof of Shakspeare's minute knowledge of human nature. It is a well-established fact, that on the brink of any serious enterprise, or event of moment, men almost invariably endeavor to elude the pressure of their own thoughts by turning aside to trivial objects and familiar circumstances: thus this dialogue on the platform begins with remarks on the coldness of the air, and inquiries, obliquely connected, indeed, with the expected hour of the visitation, but thrown out in a seeming vacuity of topics, as to the striking of the clock and so forth. The same desire to escape from the impending thought is carried on in Hamlet's account of, and moralizing on, the Danish custom of wassailing: he runs off from the particular to the universal, and in his repugnance to personal and individual concerns, escapes, as it were, from himself in generalizations, and smothers the impatience and uneasy feelings of the moment in abstract reasoning. Besides this, another purpose is answered;—for by thus entangling the attention of the audience in the nice distinctions and parenthetical sentences of this speech of Hamlet's, Shakspeare takes them completely by surprise on the appearance of the Ghost, which comes upon them in all the suddenness of its visionary character. Indeed, no modern writer would have dared, like Shakspeare, to have preceded this last visitation by two distinct appearances,—or could have contrived that the third should rise upon the former two in impressiveness and solemnity of interest.

But in addition to all the other excellences of Hamlet's speech concerning the wassel-music—so finely revealing the predominant idealism, the ratiocinative meditativeness, of his character—it has the advantage of giving nature and probability to the impassioned continuity of the speech instantly directed to the Ghost. The *momentum* had been given to his mental activity; the full current of the thoughts and words had set in, and the very forgetfulness, in the fervor of his augmentation, of the purpose for which he was there, aided in preventing the appearance from benumbing the mind. Consequently, it acted as a new impulse, —a sudden stroke which increased the velocity of the body already in motion, whilst it altered the direction. The co-presence of Horatio, Marcellus, and Bernardo is most judiciously contrived; for it renders the courage of Hamlet and his impetuous eloquence perfectly intelligible. The knowledge,—the unthought of consciousness,—the sensation,—of human auditors—of flesh and blood sympathists—acts as a support and a stimulation *a tergo*, while the front of the mind, the whole consciousness of the speaker, is filled, yea, absorbed, by the apparition. Add too, that the apparition itself has by its previous appearances been brought nearer to a thing of this world. This accrescence of objectivity in a Ghost that yet retains all its ghostly attributes and fearful subjectivity, is truly wonderful.

Ib. sc. 5. Hamlet's speech:—

> O all you host of heaven! O earth! What else?
> And shall I couple hell?—

I remember nothing equal to this burst unless it be the first speech of Prometheus in the Greek drama, after the exit of Vulcan and the two Afrites. But Shakspeare alone could have produced the vow of Hamlet to make his memory a blank of all maxims and generalized truths, that 'observation had copied there,'—followed immediately by the speaker noting down the generalized fact,

> That one may smile, and smile, and be a villain!

Ib.

> *Mar.* Hillo, ho, ho, my lord!
> *Ham.* Hillo, ho, ho, boy! come bird, come, &c.

This part of the scene after Hamlet's interview with the Ghost has been charged with an improbable eccentricity. But the truth is, that after the mind has been stretched beyond its usual pitch and tone, it must either sink into exhaustion and inanity, or seek relief by change. It is thus well known, that persons conversant in deeds of cruelty contrive to escape from conscience by connecting something of the ludicrous with them, and by inventing grotesque terms and a certain technical phraseology to disguise the horror of their practices. Indeed, paradoxical as it may appear, the terrible by a law of the human mind always touches on the verge of the ludicrous. Both arise from the perception of something out of the common order of things—something, in fact, out of its place; and if from this we can abstract danger, the uncommonness will alone remain, and the sense of the ridiculous be excited. The close alliance of these opposites—they are not contraries—appears from the circumstance, that laughter is equally the expression of extreme anguish and horror as of joy: as there are tears of sorrow and tears of joy, so is there a laugh of terror and a laugh of merriment. These complex causes will naturally have produced in Hamlet the disposition to escape from his own feelings of the overwhelming and supernatural by a wild transition to the ludicrous,—a sort of cunning bravado, bordering on the flights of delirium. For you may, perhaps, observe that Hamlet's wildness is but half false; he plays that subtle trick of pretending to act only when he is very near really being what he acts.

The subterraneous speeches of the Ghost are hardly defensible:—but I would call your attention to the characteristic difference between this Ghost, as a superstition connected with the most mysterious truths of revealed religion,—and Shakspeare's consequent reverence in his treatment of it,—and the foul earthly witcheries and wild language in Macbeth.

Act ii. sc. 1. Polonius and Reynaldo.

In all things dependent on, or rather made up of, fine address, the manner is no more or otherwise rememberable than the light motions, steps, and gestures of youth and health. But this is almost every thing:—no wonder, therefore, if that which can be put down by rule in the memory should appear to us as mere poring, maudlin, cunning,—slyness blinking through the watery eye of superannuation. So in this admirable scene, Polonius, who is throughout the skeleton of his own former skill and statecraft, hunts the trail of policy at a dead scent, supplied by the weak fever-smell in his own nostrils.

Ib. sc. 2. Speech of Polonius:—

> My liege, and madam, to expostulate, &c.

Warburton's note.

Then as to the jingles, and play on words, let us but look into the sermons of Dr. Donne (the wittiest man of that age), and we shall find them full of this vein.

I have, and that most carefully, read Dr. Donne's sermons, and find none of these jingles. The great art of an orator—to make whatever he talks of appear of importance—this, indeed, Donne has effected with consummate skill.

Ib.

Ham. Excellent well;
You are a fishmonger.

That is, you are sent to fish out this secret. This is Hamlet's own meaning.

Ib.

Ham. For if the sun breeds maggots in a dead dog,
Being a god, kissing carrion—

These purposely obscure lines, I rather think, refer to some thought in Hamlet's mind, contrasting the lovely daughter with such a tedious old fool, her father, as he, Hamlet, represents Polonius to himself:—'Why, fool as he is, he is some degrees in rank above a dead dog's carcass; and if the sun, being a god that kisses carrion, can raise life out of a dead dog,—why may not good fortune, that favors fools, have raised a lovely girl out of this dead-alive old fool?' Warburton is often led astray, in his interpretations, by his attention to general positions without the due Shaksperian reference to what is probably passing in the mind of his speaker, characteristic, and expository of his particular character and present mood. The subsequent passage,—

O Jephtha, judge of Israel! what a treasure hadst thou!

is confirmatory of my view of these lines.

Ib.

Ham. You can not, Sir, take from me any thing that I will more willingly part withal; except my life, except my life, except my life.

This repetition strikes me as most admirable.

Ib.

Ham. Then are our beggars, bodies; and our monarchs, and out-stretched heroes, the beggars' shadows.

I do not understand this; and Shakspeare seems to have intended the meaning not to be more than snatched at :—'By my fay, I can not reason !'

Ib.

The rugged Pyrrhus—he whose sable arms, &c.

This admirable substitution of the epic for the dramatic, giving such a reality to the impassioned dramatic diction of Shakspeare's own dialogue, and authorized too, by the actual style of the tragedies before his time (Porrex and Ferrex, Titus Andronicus, &c.), is well worthy of notice. The fancy, that a burlesque was intended, sinks below criticism : the lines, as epic narrative, are superb.

In the thoughts, and even in the separate parts of the diction, this description is highly poetical : in truth, taken by itself, that is its fault that it is too poetical !—the language of lyric vehemence and epic pomp, and not of the drama. But if Shakspeare had made the diction truly dramatic, where would have been the contrast between Hamlet and the play in Hamlet ? (*y*)

Ib.

—— had seen the *mobled* queen, &c.

A mob-cap is still a word in common use for a morning-cap, which conceals the whole head of hair, and passes under the chin. It is nearly the same as the night-cap, that is, it is an imitation of it, so as to answer the purpose ('I am not drest for company'), and yet reconciling it with neatness and perfect purity.

Ib. Hamlet's soliloquy :—

O, what a rogue and peasant slave am I! &c.

This is Shakspeare's own attestation to the truth of the idea of Hamlet which I have before put forth.

Ib.

The spirit that I have seen,
May be a devil : and the devil hath power
To assume a pleasing shape ; yea, and, perhaps
Out of my weakness, and my melancholy,
(As he is very potent with such spirits)
Abuses me to damn me.

See Sir Thomas Brown :—

I believe———that those apparitions and ghosts of departed persons are not the wandering souls of men, but the unquiet walks of devils, prompting and suggesting us unto mischief, blood, and villany, instilling and stealing into our hearts, that the blessed spirits are not at rest in their graves, but wander solicitous of the affairs of the world. *Relig. Med.* pt. i. sec. 37.

Act iii. sc. 1. Hamlet's soliloquy :—

To be, or not to be, that is the question, &c.

This speech is of absolutely universal interest,—and yet to which of all Shakspeare's characters could it have been appropriately given but to Hamlet? For Jaques it would have been too deep, and for Iago too habitual a communion with the heart; which in every man belongs, or ought to belong, to all mankind.

Ib.

That undiscover'd country, from whose bourne
No traveller returns.—

Theobald's note in defence of the supposed contradiction of this in the apparition of the Ghost.

O miserable defender! If it be necessary to remove the apparent contradiction,—if it be not rather a great beauty,—surely it were easy to say, that no traveller returns to this world, as to his home or abiding-place.

Ib.

Ham. Ha, ha! are you honest?
Oph. My lord?
Ham. Are you fair?

Here it is evident that the penetrating Hamlet perceives, from the strange and forced manner of Ophelia, that the sweet girl was not acting a part of her own, but was a decoy; and his after-speeches are not so much directed to her as to the listeners and spies. Such a discovery in a mood so anxious and irritable accounts for a certain harshness in him;—and yet a wild up-working of love, sporting with opposites in a wilful self-tormenting strain of irony, is perceptible throughout. 'I did love you once;'—'I lov'd you not;'—and particularly in his enumeration of the faults of the sex from which Ophelia is so free, that the mere freedom therefrom constitutes her character. Note Shakspeare's charm of composing the female character by the absence of characters, that is, marks and out-jottings.

Ib. Hamlet's speech :—

I say, we will have no more marriages: those that are married already, all but one, shall live: the rest shall keep as they are.

Observe this dallying with the inward purpose, characteristic of one who had not brought his mind to the steady acting point. He would fain sting the uncle's mind ;—but to stab his body !—The soliloquy of Ophelia, which follows, is the perfection of love—so exquisitely unselfish !

Ib. sc. 2. This dialogue of Hamlet with the players is one of the happiest instances of Shakspeare's power of diversifying the scene while he is carrying on the plot.

Ib.

Ham. My lord, you play'd once i' the university, you say ? (*To Polonius.*)

To have kept Hamlet's love for Ophelia before the audience in any direct form, would have made a breach in the unity of the interest ;—but yet to the thoughtful reader it is suggested by his spite to poor Polonius, whom he can not let rest.

Ib. The style of the interlude here is distinguished from the real dialogue by rhyme, as in the first interview with the players by epic verse.

Ib.

Ros. My lord, you once did love me.
Ham. *So* I do still, by these pickers and stealers.

I never heard an actor give this word 'so' its proper emphasis. Shakspeare's meaning is—'lov'd you? Hum!—*so* I do still,' &c. There has been no change in my opinion :—I think as ill of you as I did. Else Hamlet tells an ignoble falsehood, and a useless one, as the last speech to Guildenstern—'Why, look you now,' &c.—proves.

Ib. Hamlet's soliloquy :—

Now could I drink hot blood,
And do such business as the bitter day
Would quake to look on.

The utmost at which Hamlet arrives, is a disposition, a mood, to do something ;—but what to do, is still left undecided, while every word he utters tends to betray his disguise. Yet observe how perfectly equal to any call of the moment is Hamlet, let it only not be for the future.

Ib. sc. 4. Speech of Polonius. Polonius's volunteer obtrusion of himself into this business, while it is appropriate to his character, still itching after former importance, removes all likelihood that Hamlet should suspect his presence, and prevents us from making his death injure Hamlet in our opinion.

Ib. The king's speech :—

> O, my offence is rank, it smells to heaven, &c.

This speech well marks the difference between crime and guilt of habit. The conscience here is still admitted to audience. Nay, even as an audible soliloquy, it is far less improbable than is supposed by such as have watched men only in the beaten road of their feelings. But the final—' all may be well!' is remarkable ;—the degree of merit attributed by the self-flattering soul to its own struggle, though baffled, and to the indefinite half-promise, half-command, to persevere in religious duties. The solution is in the divine *medium* of the Christian doctrine of expiation :—not what you have done, but what you are, must determine.

Ib. Hamlet's speech :—

> Now might I do it, pat, now he is praying:
> And now I'll do it :—And so he goes to heaven :
> And so am I revenged? That would be scann'd, &c.

Dr. Johnson's mistaking of the marks of reluctance and procrastination for impetuous, horror-striking fiendishness !—Of such importance is it to understand the germ of a character. But the interval taken by Hamlet's speech is truly awful ! And then—

> My words fly up, my thoughts remain below:
> Words, without thoughts, never to heaven go,—

O what a lesson concerning the essential difference between wishing and willing, and the folly of all motive-mongering, while the individual self remains !

Ib. sc. 4.

> *Ham.* A bloody deed ;—almost as bad, good mother,
> As kill a king, and marry with his brother.
> *Queen.* As kill a king?

I confess that Shakspeare has left the character of the Queen in an unpleasant perplexity. Was she, or was she not, conscious of the fratricide ?

Act iv. sc. 2.

> *Ros.* Take you me for a sponge, my lord?

Ham. Ay, Sir; that soaks up the King's countenance, his rewards, his authorities, &c.

Hamlet's madness is made to consist in the free utterance of all the thoughts that had passed through his mind before;—in fact, in telling home-truths.

Act iv. sc. 5. Ophelia's singing. O, note the conjunction here of these two thoughts that had never subsisted in disjunction, the love for Hamlet, and her filial love, with the guileless floating on the surface of her pure imagination of the cautions so lately expressed, and the fears not too delicately avowed, by her father and brother, concerning the dangers to which her honor lay exposed. Thought, affliction, passion, murder itself—she turns to favor and prettiness. This play of association is instanced in the close:—

My brother shall know of it, and I thank you for your good counsel.

Ib. Gentleman's speech:—

And as the world were now but to begin
Antiquity forgot, custom not known,
The ratifiers and props of every ward—
They cry, &c.

Fearful and self-suspicious as I always feel, when I seem to see an error of judgment in Shakspeare, yet I can not reconcile the cool, and, as Warburton calls it, 'rational and consequential,' reflection in these lines with the anonymousness, or the alarm, of this Gentleman or Messenger, as he is called in other editions.

Ib. King's speech:—

There's such divinity doth hedge a king,
That treason can but peep to what it would,
Acts little of his will.

Proof, as indeed all else is, that Shakspeare never intended us to see the King with Hamlet's eyes; though, I suspect, the managers have long done so.

Ib. Speech of Laertes:—

To hell, allegiance! vows, to the blackest devil!

Laertes is a *good* character, but, &c. WARBURTON.

Mercy on Warburton's notion of goodness! Please to refer to the seventh scene of this act:—

I will do it;
And for this purpose I'll anoint my sword, &c.

uttered by Laertes after the King's description of Hamlet;—

He being remiss,
Most generous, and free from all contriving,
Will not peruse the foils.

Yet I acknowledge that Shakspeare evidently wishes, as much as possible, to spare the character of Laertes,—to break the extreme turpitude of his consent to become an agent and accomplice of the King's treachery;—and to this end he re-introduces Ophelia at the close of this scene to afford a probable stimulus of passion in her brother.

Ib. sc. 6. Hamlet's capture by the pirates. This is almost the only play of Shakspeare, in which mere accidents, independent of all will, form an essential part of the plot;—but here how judiciously in keeping with the character of the over-meditative Hamlet, ever at last determined by accident or by a fit of passion?

Ib. sc. 7. Note how the King first awakens Laertes's vanity by praising the reporter, and then gratifies it by the report itself and finally points it by—

Sir, this report of his
Did Hamlet so envenom with his envy!—

Ib. King's speech:—

For goodness, growing to a *pleurisy,*
Dies in his own too much.

Theobald's note from Warburton, who conjectures 'plethory.'

I rather think that Shakspeare meant 'pleurisy,' but involved in it the thought of *plethora,* as supposing pleurisy to arise from too much blood; otherwise I can not explain the following line—

And then this *should* is like a spendthrift sigh,
That hurts by easing.

In a stitch in the side every one must have heaved a sigh that 'hurt by easing.'

Since writing the above I feel confirmed that 'pleurisy' is the right word; for I find that in the old medical dictionaries the pleurisy is often called the 'plethory.'

Ib.

> *Queen.* Your sister's drown'd, Laertes.
> *Laer.* Drown'd! O, where?

That Laertes might be excused in some degree for not cooling, the Act concludes with the affecting death of Ophelia,—who in the beginning lay like a little projection of land into a lake or stream, covered with spray-flowers, quietly reflected in the quiet waters, but at length is undermined or loosened, and becomes a fairy isle, and after a brief vagrancy sinks almost without an eddy!

Act v. sc. 1. O, the rich contrast between the Clowns and Hamlet, as two extremes! You see in the former the mockery of logic, and a traditional wit valued, like truth, for its antiquity, and treasured up, like a tune, for use.

Ib. sc. 1 and 2. Shakspeare seems to mean all Hamlet's character to be brought together before his final disappearance from the scene;—his meditative excess in the grave-digging, his yielding to passion with Laertes, his love for Ophelia blazing out, his tendency to generalize on all occasions in the dialogue with Horatio, his fine gentlemanly manners with Osrick, and his and Shakspeare's own fondness for presentiment:

> But thou would'st not think, how ill all's here about my heart: but it is no matter.

NOTES ON MACBETH.

Macbeth stands in contrast throughout with Hamlet; in the manner of opening more especially. In the latter, there is a gradual ascent from the simplest forms of conversation to the language of impassioned intellect,—yet the intellect still remaining the seat of passion: in the former, the invocation is at once made to the imagination and the emotions connected therewith. Hence the movement throughout is the most rapid of all Shakspeare's plays; and hence also, with the exception of the disgusting passage of the Porter (*z*) (Act ii. sc. 3), which I dare pledge myself to demonstrate to be an interpolation of the actors, there is not, to the best of my remembrance, a single pun or play on words in the whole drama. (*aa*) I have previously given an answer to the thousand times repeated charge against Shakspeare upon the subject of his punning, and I here merely mention the fact of the absence of any puns in Macbeth, as justifying a candid doubt at least, whether even in these figures of speech and fanciful modifications of language, Shakspeare may not have followed rules and principles that merit and would stand the test of philosophic examination. And hence, also, there is an entire absence of comedy, nay, even of irony and philosophic contemplation in Macbeth,—the play being wholly and purely tragic. For the same cause, there are no reasonings of equivocal morality, which would have required a more leisurely state and a consequently greater activity of mind;—no sophistry of self-delusion,—except only that previously to the dreadful act, Macbeth mistranslates the recoilings and ominous whispers of conscience into prudential and selfish reasonings, and, after the deed done, the terrors of remorse into fear from external dangers,—like delirious men who run away from the phantoms of their own brains, or, raised by terror to rage, stab the real object that is within their reach:—whilst Lady Macbeth merely endeavors to reconcile his and her own sinkings of heart by anticipations of the worst, and an affected bravado in confronting them. In all the rest, Macbeth's language is the grave utterance of the very heart, conscience-sick, even to the last faintings of moral death. It is the same in all the other characters. The variety arises from rage, caused ever and anon by disruption of anxious thought, and the quick transition of fear into it.

In Hamlet and Macbeth the scene opens with superstition; but in each it is not merely different, but opposite. In the first it is connected with the best and holiest feelings; in the second with the shadowy, turbulent, and unsanctified cravings of the individual will. Nor is the purpose the same; in the one the object is to excite, whilst in the other it is to mark a mind already excited. Superstition, of one sort or another, is natural to victorious generals; the instances are too notorious to need mentioning. There is so much of chance in warfare, and such vast events are connected with the acts of a single individual,—the representative, in truth, of the efforts of myriads, and yet to the public, and, doubtless, to his own feelings, the aggregate of all,—that the proper temperament for generating or receiving superstitious impressions is naturally produced. Hope, the master element of a commanding genius, meeting with an active and combining intellect, and an imagination of just that degree of vividness which disquiets and impels the soul to try to realize its images, greatly increases the creative power of the mind ; and hence the images become a satisfying world of themselves, as is the case in every poet and original philosopher :—but hope fully gratified, and yet the elementary basis of the passion remaining, becomes fear ; and, indeed, the general, who must often feel, even though he may hide it from his own consciousness, how large a share chance had in his successes, may very naturally be irresolute in a new scene, where he knows that all will depend on his own act and election.

The Weird Sisters are as true a creation of Shakspeare's, as his Ariel and Caliban,—fates, furies, and materializing witches being the elements. They are wholly different from any representation of witches in the contemporary writers, and yet presented a sufficient external resemblance to the creatures of vulgar prejudice to act immediately on the audience. Their character consists in the imaginative disconnected from the good ; they are the shadowy obscure and fearfully anomalous of physical nature, the lawless of human nature,—elemental avengers without sex or kin :

> Fair is foul, and foul is fair ;
> Hover thro' the fog and filthy air.

How much it were to be wished in playing Macbeth, that an attempt should be made to introduce the flexile character-mask of the ancient pantomime ;—that Flaxman would contribute his genius to the embodying and making sensuously perceptible that of Shakspeare !

The style and rhythm of the Captain's speeches in the second scene should be illustrated by reference to the interlude in Hamlet, in which the epic is substituted for the tragic, in order to make the latter be felt as the real-life diction. In Macbeth, the poet's object was to raise the mind at once to the high tragic tone, that the audience might be ready for the precipitate consummation of guilt in the early part of the play. The true reason for the first appearance of the Witches is to strike the key-note of the character of the whole drama, as is proved by their re-appearance in the third scene, after such an order of the king's as establishes their supernatural power of information. I say information,—for so it only is as to Glamis and Cawdor ; the 'king hereafter' was still contingent,—still in Macbeth's moral will ; although, if he should yield to the temptation, and thus forfeit his free agency, the link of cause and effect *more physico* would then commence. I need not say, that the general idea is all that can be required from the poet,—not a scholastic logical consistency in all the parts so as to meet metaphysical objectors. But O! how truly Shaksperian is the opening of Macbeth's character given in the *unpossessedness* of Banquo's mind, wholly present to the present object,—an unsullied, unscarified mirror! —And how strictly true to nature it is, that Banquo, and not Macbeth himself, directs our notice to the effect produced on Macbeth's mind, rendered temptable by previous dalliance of the fancy with ambitious thoughts:

> Good Sir, why do you start; and seem to fear
> Things that do sound so fair?

And then, again, still unintroitive, addresses the Witches:—

> I' the name of truth,
> Are ye fantastical, or that indeed
> Which outwardly ye show?

Banquo's questions are those of natural curiosity,—such as a girl would put after hearing a gipsy tell her school-fellow's fortune;—all perfectly general, or rather planless. But Macbeth, lost in thought, raises himself to speech only by the Witches being about to depart:—

> Stay, you imperfect speakers, tell me more:—

and all that follows is reasoning on a problem already discussed in his mind,—on a hope which he welcomes, and the doubts concerning the attainment of which he wishes to have cleared up. Compare his eagerness,—the keen eye with which he has pursued the Witches' evanishing—

> Speak, I charge you!

with the easily satisfied mind of the self-uninterested Banquo —

> The air hath bubbles, as the water has,
> And these are of them:—Whither are they vanish'd?

and then Macbeth's earnest reply,—

> Into the air; and what seem'd corporal, melted
> As breath into the wind.—'*Would they had stay'd!*

Is it too minute to notice the appropriateness of the simile 'as breath,' &c., in a cold climate?

Still again Banquo goes on wondering, like any common spectator:

> Were such things here as we do speak about?

whilst Macbeth persists in recurring to the self-concerning :—

> Your children shall be kings.
> *Ban.* You shall be king.
> *Macb.* And thane of Cawdor too: went it not so?

So surely is the guilt in its germ anterior to the supposed cause, and immediate temptation! Before he can cool, the confirmation of the tempting half of the prophecy arrives and the concatenating tendency of the imagination is fostered by the sudden coincidence :—

> Glamis and thane of Cawdor:
> The greatest is behind.

Oppose this to Banquo's simple surprise :—

> What, can the devil speak true?

Ib. Banquo's speech :—

> That, trusted home,
> Might yet enkindle you unto the crown,
> Besides the thane of Cawdor.

I doubt whether 'enkindle' has not another sense than that of 'stimulating;' I mean of 'kind' and 'kin,' as when rabbits are said to 'kindle.' However, Macbeth no longer hears any thing *ab extra* :—

> Two truths are told,
> As happy prologues to the swelling act
> Of the imperial theme.

Then in the necessity of recollecting himself—

> I thank you, gentlemen.

Then he relapses into himself again, and every word of his soliloquy shows the early birth-date of his guilt. He is all-powerful without strength; he wishes the end, but is irresolute as to the means; conscience distinctly warns him, and he lulls it imperfectly :—

> If chance will have me king, why, chance may crown me
> Without my stir.

Lost in the prospective of his guilt, he turns round alarmed lest others may suspect what is passing in his own mind, and instantly invents the lie of ambition :

> My dull brain was wrought
> With things *forgotten* ;—

And immediately after pours forth the promising courtesies of a usurper in intention :—

> Kind gentlemen, your pains
> Are register'd where every day I turn
> The leaf to read them.

Ib. Macbeth's speech :—

> Present *fears*
> Are less than horrible imaginings.

Warburton's note, and substitution of 'feats' for 'fears.'

Mercy on this most wilful ingenuity of blundering, which, nevertheless, was the very Warburton of Warburton—his inmost being ! 'Fears,' here, are present fear-striking objects, *terribilia adstantia*.

Ib. sc. 4. O ! the affecting beauty of the death of Cawdor, and the presentimental speech of the king :—

> There's no art
> To find the mind's construction in the face:
> He was a gentleman on whom I built
> An absolute trust—

Interrupted by—

> O worthiest cousin !

on the entrance of the deeper traitor for whom Cawdor had made way ! And here in contrast with Duncan's 'plenteous joys,' Macbeth has nothing but the common-places of loyalty, in which he hides himself with 'our duties.' Note the exceeding effort of Macbeth's addresses to the king, his reasoning on his allegiance, and then especially when a new difficulty, the designation of a successor, suggests a new crime. This, however, seems the first distinct notion, as to the plan of realizing his wishes ; and here, therefore, with great propriety, Macbeth's cowardice of his own conscience discloses itself. I always think there is something especially Shaksperian in Duncan's speeches throughout this scene, such pourings forth, such abandonments, compared with the language of vulgar dramatists, whose characters seem to have made their speeches as the actors learn them.

Ib. Duncan's speech :—

> Sons, kinsmen, thanes,
> And you whose places are the nearest, know,
> We will establish our estate upon
> Our eldest Malcolm, whom we name hereafter
> The Prince of Cumberland: which honor must
> Not unaccompanied, invest him only ;
> But signs of nobleness, like stars, shall shine
> On all deservers.

It is a fancy ;—but I can never read this and the following speeches of Macbeth, without involuntarily thinking of the Miltonic Messiah and Satan.

Ib. sc. 5. Macbeth is described by Lady Macbeth so as at the same time to reveal her own character. Could he have every thing he wanted, he would rather have it innocently ;—ignorant, as alas! how many of us are, that he who wishes a temporal end for itself, does in truth will the means ; and hence the danger of indulging fancies. Lady Macbeth, like all in Shakspeare, is a class individualized :—of high rank, left much alone, and feeding herself with day-dreams of ambition, she mistakes the courage of fantasy for the power of bearing the consequences of the realities of guilt. Hers is the mock fortitude of a mind deluded by ambition ; she shames her husband with a superhuman audacity of fancy which she can not support, but sinks in the season of remorse, and dies in suicidal agony. Her speech :—

> Come, all you spirits
> That tend on mortal thoughts, unsex me here, &c.

is that of one who had habitually familiarized her imagination to dreadful conceptions, and was trying to do so still more. Her invocations and requisitions are all the false efforts of a mind accustomed only hitherto to the shadows of the imagination, vivid enough to throw the every-day substances of life into shadow, but never as yet brought into direct contact with their own correspondent realities. She evinces no womanly life, no wifely joy, at the return of her husband, no pleased terror at the thought of his past dangers, whilst Macbeth bursts forth naturally—

My dearest love—

and shrinks from the boldness with which she presents his own thoughts to him. With consummate art she at first uses as incentives the very circumstances, Duncan's coming to their house, &c. which Macbeth's conscience would most probably have adduced to her as motives of abhorrence or repulsion. Yet Macbeth is not prepared :

We will speak further.

Ib. sc. 6. The lyrical movement with which this scene opens, and the free and unengaged mind of Banquo, loving nature, and rewarded in the love itself, form a highly dramatic contrast with the labored rhythm and hypocritical over-much of Lady Macbeth's welcome, in which you can not detect a ray of personal feeling, but all is thrown upon the 'dignities,' the general duty.

Ib. sc. 7. Macbeth's speech :—

We will proceed no further in this business :
He hath honor'd me of late ; and I have bought
Golden opinions from all sorts of people,
Which would be worn now in their newest gloss,
Not cast aside so soon.

Note the inward pangs and warnings of conscience interpreted into prudential reasonings.

Act ii. sc. 1. Banquo's speech :—

A heavy summons lies like lead upon me,
And yet I would not sleep. Merciful powers !
Restrain in me the cursed thoughts, that nature
Gives way to in repose.

The disturbance of an innocent soul by painful suspicions of another's guilty intentions and wishes, and fear of the cursed thoughts of sensual nature.

Ib. sc. 2. Now that the deed is done or doing—now that the first reality commences, Lady Macbeth shrinks. The most simple sound strikes terror, the most natural consequences are horrible, whilst previously every thing, however awful, appeared a mere trifle ; conscience, which before had been hidden to Macbeth in selfish and prudential fears, now rushes in upon him in her own veritable person :

> Methought I heard a voice cry—Sleep no more!
> I could not say Amen,
> When they did say, God bless us!

And see the novelty given to the most familiar images by a new state of feeling.

Ib. sc. 3. This low soliloquy of the Porter and his few speeches afterwards, I believe to have been written for the mob by some other hand, perhaps with Shakspeare's consent ; and that finding it take, he with the remaining ink of a pen otherwise employed, just interpolated the words—

> I'll devil-porter it no further: I had thought to have let in some of all professions, that go the primrose way to th' everlasting bonfire.

Of the rest not one syllable has the ever-present being of Shakspeare.

Act iii. sc. 1. Compare Macbeth's mode of working on the murderers in this place with Schiller's mistaken scene between Butler, Devereux, and Macdonald in Wallenstein (Part ii. act iv. sc. 2). The comic was wholly out of season. Shakspeare never introduces it, but when it may react on the tragedy by harmonious contrast.

Ib. sc. 2. Macbeth's speech :—

> But let the frame of things disjoint, both the worlds suffer,
> Ere we will eat our meal in fear, and sleep
> In the affliction of these terrible dreams
> That shake us nightly.

Ever and ever mistaking the anguish of conscience for fears of selfishness, and thus as a punishment of that selfishness, plunging still deeper in guilt and ruin.

Ib. Macbeth's speech :—

> Be innocent of the knowledge, dearest chuck,
> Till thou applaud the deed.

This is Macbeth's sympathy with his own feelings, and his mistaking his wife's opposite state.

Ib. sc. 4.

> *Macb.* It will have blood, they say; blood will have blood:

Stones have been known to move, and trees to speak;
Augurs and understood relations, have
By maggot-pies, and choughs, and rooks, brought forth
The secret'st man of blood.

The deed is done; but Macbeth receives no comfort, no additional security. He has by guilt torn himself live-asunder from nature, and is, therefore, himself in a preternatural state: no wonder, then, that he is inclined to superstition, and faith in the unknown of signs and tokens, and superhuman agencies.

Act iv. sc. 1.

Len. 'Tis two or three, my lord, that bring you word,
Macduff is fled to England.
Macb. Fled to England?

The acme of the avenging conscience.

Ib. sc. 2. This scene, dreadful as it is, is still a relief, because a variety, because domestic, and therefore soothing, as associated with the only real pleasures of life. The conversation between Lady Macduff and her child heightens the pathos, and is preparatory for the deep tragedy of their assassination. Shakspeare's fondness for children is everywhere shown;—in Prince Arthur, in King John; in the sweet scene in the Winter's Tale between Hermione and her son; nay, even in honest Evans's examination of Mrs. Page's school-boy. To the objection that Shakspeare wounds the moral sense by the unsubdued, undisguised description of the most hateful atrocity—that he tears the feelings without mercy, and even outrages the eye itself with scenes of insupportable horror—I, omitting Titus Andronicus, as not genuine, and excepting the scene of Gloster's blinding in Lear, answer boldly in the name of Shakspeare, not guilty. (*bb*)

Ib. sc. 3. Malcolm's speech:—

Better Macbeth,
Than such a one to reign.

The moral is—the dreadful effects even on the best minds of the soul-sickening sense of insecurity.

Ib. How admirably Macduff's grief is in harmony with the whole play! It rends, not dissolves, the heart. 'The tune of it goes manly.' Thus is Shakspeare always master of himself and of his subject,—a genuine Proteus:—we see all things in him, as images in a calm lake, most distinct, most accurate,—only more splendid, more glorified. This is correctness in the only philosophical sense. But he requires your sympathy and your submission; you must have that recipiency of moral impression without which the purposes and ends of the drama would be frustrated, and the absence of which demonstrates an utter want of all imagination, a deadness to that necessary pleasure of being innocently—shall I say, deluded;—or rather, drawn away from ourselves to the music of noblest thought in harmonious sounds. Happy he, who not only in the public theatre, but in the labors of a profession, and round the light of his own hearth, still carries a heart so pleasure-fraught!

Alas for Macbeth! now all is inward with him; he has no more prudential prospective reasonings. His wife, the only being who could have had any seat in his affections, dies; he puts on despondency, the final heart-armor of the wretched, and would fain think every thing shadowy and unsubstantial, as indeed all things are to those who can not regard them as symbols of goodness:—

> Out, out, brief candle!
> Life's but a walking shadow; a poor player,
> That struts and frets his hour upon the stage,
> And then is heard no more; it is a tale
> Told by an idiot, full of sound and fury,
> Signifying nothing.

NOTES ON THE WINTER'S TALE.

Although, on the whole, this play is exquisitely respondent to its title, and even in the fault I am about to mention, still a winter's tale; yet it seems a mere indolence of the great bard not to have provided in the oracular response (Act ii. sc. 2) some ground for Hermione's seeming death and fifteen years' voluntary concealment. This might have been easily effected by some obscure sentence of the oracle, as for example:—

'Nor shall he ever recover an heir, if he have a wife before that recovery.'

The idea of this delightful drama is a genuine jealousy of disposition, and it should be immediately followed by the perusal of Othello, which is the direct contrast of it in every particular. For jealousy is a vice of the mind, a culpable tendency of the temper, having certain well-known and well-defined effects and concomitants, all of which are visible in Leontes, and, I boldly say, not one of which marks its presence in Othello;—such as, first, an excitability by the most inadequate causes, and an eagerness to snatch at proofs; secondly, a grossness of conception, and a disposition to degrade the object of the passion by sensual fancies and images, thirdly, a sense of shame of his own feelings exhibited in a solitary moodiness of humor, and yet from the violence of the passion forced to utter itself, and therefore catching occasions to ease the mind by ambiguities, equivoques, by talking to those who can not, and who are known not to be able to, understand what is said to them,—in short, by soliloquy in the form of dialogue, and hence a confused, broken, and fragmentary manner; fourthly, a dread of vulgar ridicule, as distinct from a high sense of honor, or a mistaken sense of duty; and lastly, and immediately, consequent on this, a spirit of selfish vindictiveness.

Act i. sc. 1–2.

Observe the easy style of chitchat between Camillo and Archidamus as contrasted with the elevated diction on the introduction of the kings and Hermione in the second scene: and how admirably Polixenes' obstinate refusal to Leontes to stay—

> There is no tongue that moves; none, none i' the world
> So soon as yours, could win me;—

prepares for the effect produced by his afterwards yielding to Hermione;—which is, nevertheless, perfectly natural from mere courtesy of sex, and the exhaustion of the will by former efforts of denial, and well calculated to set in nascent action the jealousy of Leontes. This, when once excited, is unconsciously increased by Hermione:—

> Yet, good deed, Leontes,
> I love thee not a jar o' the clock behind
> What lady she her lord;—

accompanied, as a good actress ought to represent it, by an expression and recoil of apprehension that she had gone too far.

> At my request, he would not:—

The first working of the jealous fit;—

> Too hot, too hot:—

The morbid tendency of Leontes to lay hold of the merest trifles, and his grossness immediately afterwards—

Paddling palms and pinching fingers ;—

followed by his strange loss of self-control in his dialogue with the little boy.

Act iii. sc. 2. Paulina's speech .

That thou betray'dst Polixenes, 'twas nothing;
That did but show thee, of a *fool*, inconstant,
And damnable ingrateful.—

Theobald reads 'soul.'

I think the original word is Shakspeare's. 1. My ear feels it to be Shaksperian; 2. The involved grammar is Shaksperian; —'show thee, being a fool naturally, to have improved thy folly by inconstancy;' 3. The alteration is most flat, and un-Shaksperian. As to the grossness of the abuse—she calls him 'gross and foolish' a few lines below.

Act iv. sc. 2. Speech of Autolycus :—

For the life to come, I sleep out the thought of it.

Fine as this is, and delicately characteristic of one who had lived and been reared in the best society, and had been precipitated from it by dice and drabbing; yet still it strikes against my feelings as a note out of tune, and as not coalescing with that pastoral tint which gives such a charm to this act. It is too Macbeth-like in the 'snapper-up of unconsidered trifles.'

Ib. sc. 3. Perdita's speech :—

From Dis's wagon! daffodils.

An epithet is wanted here, not merely or chiefly for the metre, but for the balance, for the æsthetic logic. Perhaps, 'golden' was the word which would set off the 'violets dim.'

Ib.

Pale primroses
That die unmarried.—

Milton's—

And the rathe primrose that forsaken dies.

Ib. Perdita's speech :—

Even here undone:
I was not much afraid; for once or twice

I was about to speak, and tell him plainly,
The self-same sun, that shines upon his court,
Hides not his visage from our cottage, but
Looks on alike. Wilt please you, Sir, be gone!
(*To Florizel.*)
I told you, what would come of this. Beseech you,
Of your own state take care: this dream of mine,
Being awake, I'll queen it no inch farther,
But milk my ewes, and weep.

O how more than exquisite is this whole speech!—And that profound nature of noble pride and grief venting themselves in a momentary peevishness of resentment toward Florizel:—

——Wilt please you, Sir, be gone!

Ib. Speech of Autolycus:—

Let me have no lying; it becomes none but tradesmen, and they often give us soldiers the lie; but we pay them for it in stamped coin, not stabbing steel;—therefore they do not *give* us the lie.

As we *pay* them, they, therefore, do not *give* it us.

NOTES ON OTHELLO.

Act i. sc. 1.

Admirable is the preparation, so truly and peculiarly Shaksperian, in the introduction of Roderigo, as the dupe on whom Iago shall first exercise his art, and in so doing display his own character. Roderigo, without any fixed principle, but not without the moral notions and sympathies with honor, which his rank and connections had hung upon him, is already well fitted and predisposed for the purpose; for very want of character and strength of passion, like wind loudest in an empty house, constitute his character. The first three lines happily state the nature and foundation of the friendship between him and Iago,—the purse,—as also the contrast of Roderigo's intemperance of mind with Iago's coolness,—the coolness of a preconceiving experimenter. The mere language of protestation—

If ever I did dream of such a matter, abhor me,—

which falling in with the associative link, determines Roderigo's continuation of complaint—

> Thou told'st me, thou didst hold him in thy hate—

elicits at length a true feeling of Iago's mind, the dread of contempt habitual to those, who encourage in themselves, and have their keenest pleasure in, the expression of contempt for others. Observe Iago's high self-opinion, and the moral, that a wicked man will employ real feelings, as well as assume those most alien from his own, as instruments of his purposes :—

> —— And, by the faith of man,
> I know my place, I am worth no worse a place.

I think Tyrwhitt's reading of 'life' for 'wife'—

> A fellow almost damn'd in a fair *wife*—

the true one, as fitting to Iago's contempt for whatever did not display power, and that intellectual power. In what follows, let the reader feel how by and through the glass of two passions, disappointed vanity and envy, the very vices of which he is complaining, are made to act upon him as if they were so many excellences, and the more appropriately, because cunning is always admired and wished for by minds conscious of inward weakness ;—but they act only by half, like music on an inattentive auditor, swelling the thoughts which prevent him from listening to it.

Ib.

> *Rod.* What a full fortune does the *thick-lips* owe,
> If he can carry 't thus.

Roderigo turns off to Othello ; and here comes one, if not the only, seeming justification of our blackamoor or negro Othello. Even if we supposed this an uninterrupted tradition of the theatre, and that Shakspeare himself, from want of scenes, and the experience that nothing could be made too marked for the senses of his audience, had practically sanctioned it,—would this prove aught concerning his own intention as a poet for all ages ? Can we imagine him so utterly ignorant as to make a barbarous negro plead royal birth,—at a time, too, when negroes were not known except as slaves ?—As for Iago's language to Brabantio, it implies merely that Othello was a Moor, that is, black. Though I think the rivalry of Roderigo sufficient to account for his wilful confusion of Moor and Negro,—yet, even if compelled to give this up, I should think it only adapted for the acting of the day, and should complain of an enormity built on a single word, in direct contradiction to Iago's 'Barbary horse.' Besides, if we could in good earnest believe Shakspeare ignorant of the distinction, still why should we adopt one disagreeable possibility instead of a ten times greater and more pleasing probability? It is a common error to mistake the epithets applied by the *dramatis personæ* to each other, as truly descriptive of what the audience ought to see or know. No doubt Desdemona saw Othello's visage in his mind; yet, as we are constituted, and most surely as an English audience was disposed in the beginning of the seventeenth century, it would be something monstrous to conceive this beautiful Venetian girl falling in love with a veritable negro. It would argue a disproportionateness, a want of balance, in Desdemona, which Shakspeare does not appear to have in the least contemplated.

Ib. Brabantio's speech :—

> This accident is not unlike my dream :—

The old careful senator, being caught careless, transfers his caution to his dreaming power at least.

Ib. Iago's speech :—

> —For their souls,
> Another of his fathom they have not,
> To lead their business :—

The forced praise of Othello followed by the bitter hatred of him in this speech! And observe how Brabantio's dream prepares for his recurrence to the notion of philters, and how both prepare for carrying on the plot of the arraignment of Othello on this ground.

Ib. sc. 2.

> *Oth.* 'Tis better as it is.

How well these few words impress at the outset the truth of Othello's own character of himself at the end—'that he was not easily wrought!' His self-government contra-distinguishes him throughout from Leontes.

Ib. Othello's speech :—

> —And my demerits
> May speak, *unbonnetted*—

The argument in Theobald's note, where 'and bonnetted' is

suggested, goes on the assumption that Shakspeare could not use the same word differently in different places ; whereas I should conclude, that as in the passage in Lear the word is employed in its direct meaning, so here it is used metaphorically ; and this is confirmed by what has escaped the editors, that it is not 'I,' but 'my demerits' that may speak unbonnetted,—without the symbol of a petitioning inferior.

Ib. Othello's speech :—

> Please your grace, my ancient;
> A man he is of honesty and trust :
> To his conveyance I assign my wife.

Compare this with the behavior of Leontes to his true friend Camillo.

Ib. sc. 3.

> *Bra.* Look to her, Moor ; have a quick eye to see ;
> She has deceiv'd her father, and may thee.
> *Oth.* My life upon her faith.

In real life, how do we look back to little speeches as presentimental of, or contrasted with, an affecting event ! Even so, Shakspeare, as secure of being read over and over, of becoming a family-friend, provides this passage for his readers, and leaves it to them.

Ib. Iago's speech :—

> Virtue ? a fig ! 'tis in ourselves, that we are thus, or thus, &c.

This speech comprises the passionless character of Iago. It is all will in intellect ; and therefore he is here a bold partisan of a truth, but yet of a truth converted into a falsehood by the absence of all the necessary modifications caused by the frail nature of man. And then comes the last sentiment :—

> Our raging motions, our carnal stings, our unbitted lusts, whereof I take this, that you call—love, to be a sect or scion !

Here is the true Iagoism of, alas ! how many ! Note Iago's pride of mastery in the repetition of 'Go, make money !' to his anticipated dupe, even stronger than his love of lucre : and when Roderigo is completely won—

> I am chang'd. I'll go sell all my land—

when the effect has been fully produced, the repetition of triumph—

> Go to; farewell; put money enough in your purse!

The remainder—Iago's soliloquy—the motive-hunting of a motiveless malignity—how awful it is! Yea, whilst he is still allowed to bear the divine image, it is too fiendish for his own steady view,—for the lonely gaze of a being next to devil, and only not quite devil,—and yet a character which Shakspeare has attempted and executed, without disgust and without scandal!

Dr. Johnson has remarked that little or nothing is wanting to render the Othello a regular tragedy, but to have opened the play with the arrival of Othello in Cyprus, and to have thrown the preceding act into the form of narration. Here, then, is the place to determine, whether such a change would or would not be an improvement;—nay (to throw down the glove with a full challenge), whether the tragedy would or not by such an arrangement become more regular,—that is, more consonant with the rules dictated by universal reason, on the true common-sense of mankind, in its application to the particular case. For in all acts of judgment, it can never be too often recollected, and scarcely too often repeated, that rules are means to ends, and, consequently, that the end must be determined and understood before it can be known what the rules are or ought to be. Now, from a certain species of drama, proposing to itself the accomplishment of certain ends,—these partly arising from the idea of the species itself, but in part, likewise, forced upon the dramatist by accidental circumstances beyond his power to remove or control,—three rules have been abstracted;—in other words, the means most conducive to the attainment of the proposed ends have been generalized, and prescribed under the names of the three unities,—the unity of time, the unity of place, and the unity of action,—which last would, perhaps, have been as appropriately, as well as more intelligibly, entitled the unity of interest. With this last the present question has no immediate concern: in fact, its conjunction with the former two is a mere delusion of words. It is not properly a rule, but in itself the great end not only of the drama, but of the epic poem, the lyric ode, of all poetry, down to the candle-flame cone of an epigram,—nay of poesy in general, as the proper generic term inclusive of all the fine arts as its species. But of the unities of time and place, which alone are entitled to the name of rules, the history of their origin will be their best criterion. You might take the Greek chorus to a place, but you could not bring a place to them without as palpable an equivoque as bringing Birnam wood to Macbeth at Dunsinane. It was the same, though in a less degree, with regard to the unity of time:—the positive fact, not for a moment removed from the senses, the presence, I mean, of the same identical chorus, was a continued measure of time;—and although the imagination may supersede perception, yet it must be granted to be an imperfection—however easily tolerated—to place the two in broad contradiction to each other. In truth, it is a mere accident of terms; for the Trilogy of the Greek theatre was a drama in three acts, and notwithstanding this, what strange contrivances as to place there are in the Aristophanic Frogs. Besides, if the law of mere actual perception is once violated—as it repeatedly is even in the Greek tragedies—why is it more difficult to imagine three hours to be three years than to be a whole day and night?

Act ii. sc. 1.

Observe in how many ways Othello is made, first, our acquaintance, then our friend, then the object of our anxiety, before the deeper interest is to be approached!

Ib.

> *Mont.* But, good lieutenant, is your general wiv'd?
> *Cas.* Most fortunately: he hath achiev'd a maid
> That paragons description, and wild fame;
> One that excels the quirks of blazoning pens,
> And, in the essential vesture of creation,
> Does bear all excellency.

Here is Cassio's warm-hearted, yet perfectly disengaged, praise of Desdemona, and sympathy with the 'most fortunately' wived Othello;—and yet Cassio is an enthusiastic admirer, almost a worshipper, of Desdemona. O, that detestable code that excellence can not be loved in any form that is female, but it must needs be selfish! Observe Othello's 'honest,' and Cassio's 'bold' Iago, and Cassio's full guileless-hearted wishes for the safety and love-raptures of Othello and 'the divine Desdemona.' And also note the exquisite circumstance of Cassio's kissing Iago's wife, as if it ought to be impossible that the dullest auditor should not feel Cassio's religious love of Desdemona's purity. Iago's answers are the sneers which a proud bad intellect feels towards women, and expresses to a wife. Surely it ought to be considered a very exalted compliment to women, that all the sarcasms on them in Shakspeare are put in the mouths of villains.

Ib.

Des. I am not merry; but I do beguile, &c.

The struggle of courtesy in Desdemona to abstract her attention.

Ib.

(*Iago, aside*). He takes her by the palm: Ay, well said, whisper; with as little a web as this, will I ensnare as great a fly as Cassio. Ay, smile upon her, do, &c.

The importance given to trifles, and made fertile by the villany of the observer.

Ib. Iago's dialogue with Roderigo:

This is the rehearsal on the dupe of the traitor's intentions on Othello.

Ib. Iago's soliloquy:—

But partly led to diet my revenge,
For that I do suspect the lusty Moor
Hath leap'd into my seat.

This thought, originally by Iago's own confession a mere suspicion, is now ripening, and gnaws his base nature as his own 'poisonous mineral' is about to gnaw the noble heart of his general.

Ib. sc. 3. Othello's speech:—

I know, Iago,
Thy honesty and love doth mince this matter,
Making it light to Cassio.

Honesty and love! Ay, and who but the reader of the play could think otherwise?

Ib. Iago's soliloquy:—

And what's he then that says—I play the villain?
When this advice is free I give, and honest,
Probable to thinking, and, indeed, the course
To win the Moor again.

He is not, you see, an absolute fiend; or, at least, he wishes to think himself not so.

Act iii. sc. 3.

Des. Before Æmilia here,
I give the warrant of this place.

The over-zeal of innocence in Desdemona.

Ib.

Enter Desdemona and Æmilia.

Oth. If she be false, O, then, heaven mocks itself!
I'll not believe it.

Divine! The effect of innocence and the better genius!

Act v. sc. 3.

Æmil. Why, the wrong is but a wrong i' the world; and having the world for your labor, 'tis a wrong in your own world, and you might quickly make it right.

Warburton's note.

What any other man, who had learning enough, might have quoted as a playful and witty illustration of his remarks against the Calvinistic *thesis*, Warburton gravely attributes to Shakspeare as intentional; and this, too, in the mouth of a lady's woman!

Act v. last scene. Othello's speech :—

——Of one, whose hand,
Like the base *Indian*, threw a pearl away
Richer than all his tribe, &c.

Theobald's note from Warburton.

Thus it is for no-poets to comment on the greatest of poets! To make Othello say that he, who had killed his wife, was like Herod who killed Mariamne!—O, how many beauties, in this one line, were impenetrable to the ever thought-swarming, but idealess, Warburton! Othello wishes to excuse himself on the score of ignorance, and yet not to excuse himself,—to excuse himself by accusing. This struggle of feeling is finely conveyed in the word 'base,' which is applied to the rude Indian, not in his own character, but as the momentary representative of Othello's. 'Indian'—for I retain the old reading—means American, a savage *in genere*.

Finally, let me repeat that Othello does not kill Desdemona in jealousy, but in a conviction forced upon him by the almost superhuman art of Iago, such a conviction as any man would and must have entertained who had believed Iago's honesty as Othello did. We, the audience, know that Iago is a villain from the beginning; but in considering the essence of the Shaksperian Othello, we must perseveringly place ourselves in his situation, and under his circumstances. Then we shall immediately feel the fundamental difference between the solemn agony of the noble Moor, and the wretched fishing jealousies of Leontes, and the morbid suspiciousness of Leonatus, who is, in other respects, a fine character. Othello had no life but in Desdemona:—the belief that she, his angel, had fallen from the heaven of her native innocence, wrought a civil war in his heart. She is his counterpart; and, like him, is almost sanctified in our eyes by her absolute unsuspiciousness, and holy entireness of love. As the curtain drops, which do we pity the most?

Extremum hunc————. There are three powers:—Wit, which discovers partial likeness hidden in general diversity; subtlety, which discovers the diversity concealed in general apparent sameness;—and profundity, which discovers an essential unity under all the semblances of difference.

Give to a subtle man fancy, and he is a wit; to a deep man imagination, and he is a philosopher. Add, again, pleasurable sensibility in the threefold form of sympathy with the interesting in morals, the impressive in form, and the harmonious in sound,—and you have the poet.

But combine all,—wit, subtlety, and fancy, with profundity, imagination, and moral and physical susceptibility of the pleasurable,—and let the object of action be man universal; and we shall have—O, rash prophecy! say, rather, we have—a SHAKSPEARE!

NOTES ON BEN JONSON.

IT would be amusing to collect out of our dramatists from Elizabeth to Charles I. proofs of the manners of the times. One striking symptom of general coarseness of manners, which may co-exist with great refinement of morals, as, alas! *vice versa*, is to be seen in the very frequent allusions to the olfactories with their most disgusting stimulants, and these, too, in the conversation of virtuous ladies. This would not appear so strange to one who had been on terms of familiarity with Sicilian and Italian women of rank: and bad as they may, too many of them, actually be, yet I doubt not that the extreme grossness of their language has impressed many an Englishman of the present era with far darker notions than the same language would have produced in the mind of one of Elizabeth's or James's courtiers. Those who have read Shakspeare only, complain of occasional grossness in his plays; but compare him with his contemporaries, and the inevitable conviction, is that of the exquisite purity of his imagination.

The observation I have prefixed to the Volpone is the key to the faint interest which these noble efforts of intellectual power excite, with the exception of the fragment of the Sad Shepherd; because in that piece only is there any character with whom you can morally sympathize. On the other hand, Measure for Measure is the only play of Shakspeare's in which there are not some one or more characters, generally many, whom you follow with affectionate feeling. For I confess that Isabella, of all Shakspeare's female characters, pleases me the least; and Measure for Measure is, indeed the only one of his genuine works, which is painful to me.

Let me not conclude this remark, however, without a thankful acknowledgment to the *manes* of Ben Jonson, that the more I study his writings, I the more admire them; and the more my study of him resembles that of an ancient classic, in the *minutiæ* of his rhythm, metre, choice of words, forms of connection, and so forth, the more numerous have the points of my admiration become. I may add, too, that both the study and the admiration can not but be disinterested, for to expect therefrom any advantage to the present drama would be ignorance. The latter is utterly heterogeneous from the drama of the Shaksperian age, with a diverse object and contrary principle. The one was to present a model by imitation of real life, taking from real life all that in it which it ought to be, and supplying the rest;—the other is to copy what is, and as it is,—at best a tolerable, but most frequently a blundering, copy. In the former the difference was an essential element; in the latter an involuntary defect. We should think it strange, if a tale in dance were announced, and the actors did not dance at all;—and yet such is modern comedy.

WHALLEY'S PREFACE.

But Johnson was soon sensible, how inconsistent this medley of names and manners was in reason and nature; and with how little propriety it could ever have a place in a legitimate and just picture of real life.

But did Johnson reflect that the very essence of a play, the very language in which it is written, is a fiction to which all the parts must conform? Surely, Greek manners in English should be a still grosser improbability than a Greek name transferred to English manners. Ben's *personæ* are too often not characters, but derangements;—the hopeless patients of a mad-doctor rather,—exhibitions of folly betraying itself in spite of existing reason and prudence. He not poetically, but painfully exaggerates every trait; that is, not by the drollery of the circumstance, but by the excess of the originating feeling.

But to this we might reply, that far from being thought to build his characters upon abstract ideas, he was really accused of representing particular persons then existing; and that even those characters which appear to be the most exaggerated, are said to have had their respective archetypes in nature and life.

This degrades Jonson into a libeller, instead of justifying him as a dramatic poet. *Non quod verum est, sed quod verisimile*, is the dramatist's rule. At all events, the poet who chooses transitory manners, ought to content himself with transitory praise. If his object be reputation, he ought not to expect fame. The utmost he can look forwards to, is to be quoted by, and to enliven the writings of, an antiquarian. Pistol, Nym, and *id genus omne*, do not please us as characters, but are endured as fantastic creations, foils to the native wit of Falstaff.—I say wit emphatically; for this character so often extolled as the masterpiece of humor, neither contains, nor was meant to contain, any humor at all.

WHALLEY'S LIFE OF JONSON.

It is to the honor of Jonson's judgment, that *the greatest poet of our nation* had the same opinion of Donne's genius and wit; and hath preserved part of him from perishing, by putting his thoughts and satire into modern verse.

Videlicet Pope !

He said further to Drummond, Shakspeare wanted art, and sometimes sense ; for in one of his plays he brought in a number of men, saying they had suffered shipwreck in Bohemia, where is no sea near by a hundred miles.

I HAVE often thought Shakspeare justified in this seeming anachronism. In Pagan times a single name of a German kingdom might well be supposed to comprise a hundred miles more than at present. The truth is, these notes of Drummond's are more disgraceful to himself than to Jonson. It would be easy to conjecture how grossly Jonson must have been misunderstood and what he had said in jest, as of Hippocrates, interpreted in earnest. But this is characteristic of a Scotchman ; he has no notion of a jest, unless you tell him—" This is a joke !"—and still less of that finer shade of feeling, the half-and-half, in which Englishmen naturally delight.

EVERY MAN OUT OF HIS HUMOR.

Epilogue.

The throat of war be stopt within her land,
And *turtle-footed* peace dance fairie rings
About her court.

TURTLE-FOOTED is a pretty word, a very pretty word : pray, what does it mean ? Doves, I presume, are not dancers ; and the other sort of turtle, land or sea, green-fat or hawksbill, would, I should suppose, succeed better in slow minuets than in the brisk rondillo. In one sense, to be sure, pigeons and ring-doves could not dance but with *éclat—a claw ?*

POETASTER.

Introduction.

Light ! I salute thee, but with wounded nerves,
Wishing thy golden splendor pitchy darkness.

THERE is no reason to suppose Satan's address to the sun in the Paradise Lost, more than a mere coincidence with these lines ; but were it otherwise, it would be a fine instance, what usurious interest a great genius pays in borrowing. It would not be difficult to give a detailed psychological proof from these constant outbursts of anxious self-assertion, that Jonson was not a genius, a creative power. Subtract that one thing, and you may safely accumulate on his name all other excellences of a capacious, vigorous, agile, and richly-stored intellect.

Act i. sc. 1.

> *Ovid.* While slaves be false, fathers hard, and bawds be whorish—

The roughness noticed by Theobald and Whalley, may be cured by a simple transposition :—

> While fathers hard, slaves false, and bawds be whorish.

Act iv. sc. 3.

> *Crisp.* O—oblatrant—furibund—fatuate—strenuous.
> O—conscious.

It would form an interesting essay, or rather series of essays, in a periodical work, were all the attempts to ridicule new phrases brought together, the proportion observed of words ridiculed which have been adopted, and are now common, such as *strenuous*, *conscious*, &c., and a trial made how far any grounds can be detected, so that one might determine beforehand whether a word was invented under the conditions of assimilability to our language or not. Thus much is certain, that the ridiculers were as often wrong as right ; and Shakspeare himself could not prevent the naturalization of *accommodation*, *remuneration*, &c. ; or Swift the gross abuse even of the word *idea*.

FALL OF SEJANUS.

Act i.

> *Arruntius.* The name Tiberius,
> I hope, will keep, howe'er he hath foregone
> The dignity and power.
> *Silius.* Sure, while he lives.
> *Arr.* And dead, it comes to Drusus. Should he fail,
> To the brave issue of Germanicus ;
> And they are three : too many (ha ?) for him
> To have a plot upon ?
> *Sil.* I do not know

The heart of his designs; but, sure, their face
Looks farther than the present.
  Arr. By the gods,
If I could guess he had but such a thought,
My sword should cleave him down, &c.

The anachronic mixture in this Arruntius of the Roman republican, to whom Tiberius [illegible] [illegible]ared as much a tyrant as Sejanus with his James-and-Charles-the-First zeal for legitimacy of descent in this passage, is amusing. Of our great names Milton was, I think, the first who could properly be called a republican. My recollections of Buchanan's works are too faint to enable me to judge whether the historian is not a fair exception.

Act ii. Speech of Sejanus :—

Adultery! it is the lightest ill
I will commit. A race of wicked acts
Shall flow out of my anger, and o'erspread
The world's wide face, which no posterity
Shall e'er approve, nor yet keep silent, &c.

The more we reflect and examine, examine and reflect, the more astonished shall we be at the immense superiority of Shakspeare over his contemporaries :—and yet what contemporaries! —giant minds indeed! Think of Jonson's erudition, and the force of learned authority in that age; and yet in no genuine part of Shakspeare's works is there to be found such an absurd rant and ventriloquism as this, and too, too many other passages ferruminated by Jonson from Seneca's tragedies and the writings of the later Romans. I call it ventriloquism, because Sejanus is a puppet, out of which the poet makes his own voice appear to come.

Act. v. Scene of the sacrifice to Fortune. This scene is unspeakably irrational. To believe, and yet to scoff at, a present miracle is little less than impossible. Sejanus should have been made to suspect priestcraft and a secret conspiracy against him.

VOLPONE.

This admirable, indeed, but yet more wonderful than admirable play, is from the fertility and vigor of invention, character, language, and sentiment, the strongest proof, how impossible it is to keep up any pleasurable interest in a tale, in which there is no goodness of heart in any of the prominent characters. After the third act, this play becomes not a dead, but a painful, weight on the feelings. Zeluco is an instance of the same truth. Bonario and Celia should have been made in some way or other principals in the plot; which they might have been, and the objects of interest, without having been made characters. In novels, the person, in whose fate you are most interested, is often the least marked character of the whole. If it were possible to lessen the paramountcy of Volpone himself, a most delightful comedy might be produced, by making Celia the ward or niece of Corvino, instead of his wife, and Bonario her lover.

EPICŒNE.

THIS is to my feelings the most entertaining of old Ben's comedies, and, more than any other, would admit of being brought out anew, if under the management of a judicious and stage-understanding play-wright; and an actor, who had studied Morose, might make his fortune.

Act i. sc. 1. Clerimont's speech :—

He would have hanged a pewterer's 'prentice once on a Shrove Tuesday's riot, for being o' that trade, when the rest were *quiet*.

The old copies read *quit*, *i. e.* discharged from working, and gone to divert themselves. Whalley's note.

It should be *quit*, no doubt; but not meaning 'discharged from working,' &c.—but quit, that is, acquitted. The pewterer was at his holiday diversion as well as the other apprentices, and they as forward in the riot as he. But he alone was punished under pretext of the riot, but in fact for his trade.

Act ii. sc. 1.

Morose. Can not I, yet, find out a more compendious method, than by this *trunk*, to save my servants the labor of speech, and mine ears the discord of sounds?

What does 'trunk' mean here and in the 1st scene of the 1st act? Is it a large ear-trumpet?—or rather a tube, such as passes from parlor to kitchen, instead of a bell?

Whalley's note at the end.

Some critics of the last age imagined the character of Morose to be wholly out of nature. But to vindicate our poet, Mr. Dryden tells us from tradition, and we may venture to take his word, that Jonson was really acquainted with a person of this whimsical turn of mind; and as humor is a personal quality, the poet is acquitted from the charge of exhibiting a monster, or an extravagant or unnatural caricature.

If Dryden had not made all additional proof superfluous by his own plays, this very vindication would evince that he had formed a false and vulgar conception of the nature and conditions of the drama and dramatic personation. Ben Jonson would himself have rejected such a plea :—

> For he knew, poet never credit gain'd
> By writing *truths*, but things, like truths, well feign'd.

By 'truths' he means 'facts.' Caricatures are not less so, because they are found existing in real life. Comedy demands characters, and leaves caricatures to farce. The safest and truest defence of old Ben would be to call the Epicæne the best of farces. The defect in Morose, as in other of Jonson's *dramatis personæ*, lies in this :—that the accident is not a prominence growing out of, and nourished by, the character which still circulates in it, but that the character, such as it is, rises out of, or, rather, consists in, the accident. Shakspeare's comic personages have exquisitely characteristic features ; however awry, disproportionate, and laughable they may be, still, like Bardolph's nose, they are features. But Jonson's are, either a man with a huge wen, having a circulation of its own, and which we might conceive amputated, and the patient thereby losing all his character ; or they are mere wens themselves instead of men,—wens personified, or with eyes, nose, and mouth cut out, mandrake fashion.

Nota Bene. All the above, and much more, will have justly been said, if, and whenever, the drama of Jonson is brought into comparisons of rivalry with the Shaksperian. But this should not be. Let its inferiority to the Shaksperian be at once fairly owned,—but at the same time as the inferiority of an altogether different *genus* of the drama. On this ground, old Ben would still maintain his proud height. He, no less than Shakspeare, stands on the summit of his hill, and looks round him like a master,—though his be Lattrig, and Shakspeare's Skiddaw.

THE ALCHEMIST.

Act i. sc. 2. Face's speech :—

> Will take his oath o' the Greek *Xenophon*,
> If need be, in his pocket.

ANOTHER reading is 'Testament.'

Probably, the meaning is—that intending to give false evidence, he carried a Greek Xenophon to pass it off for a Greek Testament, and so avoid perjury—as the Irish do, by contriving to kiss their thumb-nails instead of the book.

Act ii. sc. 2. Mammon's speech :—

> I will have all my beds blown up ; not stuft :
> Down is too hard.

Thus the air-cushions, though perhaps only lately brought into use, were invented in idea in the seventeenth century !

CATILINE'S CONSPIRACY.

A FONDNESS for judging one work by comparison with others, perhaps altogether of a different class, argues a vulgar taste. Yet it is chiefly on this principle that the Catiline has been rated so low. Take it and Sejanus, as compositions of a particular kind, namely, as a mode of relating great historical events in the liveliest and most interesting manner, and I can not help wishing that we had whole volumes of such plays. We might as rationally expect the excitement of the Vicar of Wakefield from Goldsmith's History of England, as that of Lear, Othello, &c. from the Sejanus or Catiline.

Act i. sc. 4.

> *Cat.* Sirrah, what ail you ?
> (*He spies one of his boys not answer.*)
> *Pag.* Nothing.
> *Best.* Somewhat modest.
> *Cat.* Slave, I will strike your soul out with my foot, &c.

This is either an unintelligible, or, in every sense, a most unnatural, passage,—improbable, if not impossible, at the moment of signing and swearing such a conspiracy, to the most libidinous satyr. The very presence of the boys is an outrage to probability. I suspect that these lines down to the words 'throat opens,' should be removed back so as to follow the words 'on this part of the house,' in the speech of Catiline soon after the entry of the conspirators. A total erasure, however, would be the best, or, rather, the only possible, amendment.

Act ii. sc. 2. Sempronia's speech :—

—He is but a new fellow,
An *inmate* here in Rome, as Catiline calls him—

A 'lodger' would have been a happier imitation of the *inquilinus* of Sallust.

Act iv. sc. 6. Speech of Cethegus :—

Can these or such be any aids to us, &c.

What a strange notion Ben must have formed of a determined, remorseless, all-daring fool-hardiness, to have represented it in such a mouthing Tamburlane, and bombastic tongue-bully as this Cethegus of his !

BARTHOLOMEW FAIR.

Induction. Scrivener's speech :—

If there be never a *servant-monster* i' the Fair, who can help it, he says, not a nest of antiques ?

THE best excuse that can be made for Jonson, and in a somewhat less degree for Beaumont and Fletcher, in respect of these base and silly sneers at Shakspeare, is, that his plays were present to men's minds chiefly as acted. They had not a neat edition of them, as we have, so as, by comparing the one with the other, to form a just notion of the mighty mind that produced the whole. At all events, and in every point of view, Jonson stands far higher in a moral light than Beaumont and Fletcher. He was a fair contemporary, and, in his way, and as far as Shakspeare is concerned, an original. But Beaumont and Fletcher were always imitators of, and often borrowers from him, and yet sneer at him with a spite far more malignant than Jonson, who, besides, has made noble compensation by his praises.

Act ii. sc. 3.

Just. I mean a child of the horn-thumb, a babe *of booty,* boy, a cut purse.

Does not this confirm, what the passage itself can not but suggest, the propriety of substituting 'booty' for 'beauty' in Falstaff's speech, Henry IV. pt. i. act i. sc. 2, 'Let not us, &c. ?'

It is not often that old Ben condescends to imitate a modern author; but Master Dan. Knockhum Jordan and his vapors are manifest reflexes of Nym and Pistol.

Ib. sc. 5.

Quarl. She'll make excellent geer for the coachmakers here in Smithfield, to anoint wheels and axletrees with.

Good! but yet it falls short of the speech of a Mr. Johnes, M.P., in the Common Council, on the invasion intended by Bonaparte: 'Houses plundered—then burnt;—sons conscribed—wives and daughters ravished,' &c. &c.—"But as for you, you luxurious Aldermen! with your fat will he grease the wheels of his triumphant chariot!"

Ib. sc. 6.

Cok. Avoid i' your satin doublet, Numps.

This reminds me of Shakspeare's 'Aroint thee, witch!' I find in several books of that age the words *aloigne* and *eloigne*—that is,—'keep your distance!' or 'off with you!' Perhaps 'aroint' was a corruption of 'aloigne' by the vulgar. The common etymology from *ronger* to gnaw seems unsatisfactory.

Act iii. sc. 4.

Quarl. How now, Numps! almost tired i' your protectorship? overparted, overparted?

An odd sort of propheticality in this Numps and old Noll!

Ib. sc. 6. Knockhum's speech:—

He eats with his eyes, as well as his teeth.

A good motto for the Parson in Hogarth's Election Dinner,—who shows how easily he might be reconciled to the Church of Rome, for he worships what he eats.

Act v. sc. 5.

Pup. Di. It is not prophane.
Lan. It is not prophane, he says.

Boy. It is prophane.
Pup. It is not prophane.
Boy. It is prophane.
Pup. It is not prophane.
Lan. Well said, confute him with Not, still.

An imitation of the quarrel between Bacchus and the Frogs in Aristophanes :—

Χορός.
ἀλλὰ μὴν κεκραξόμεσθά γ',
ὁπόσον ἡ φάρυγξ ἂν ἡμῶν
χανδάνῃ, δι' ἡμέρας,
βρεκεκεκὲξ, κοὰξ, κοὰξ.
Διόνυσος.
τούτῳ γὰρ οὐ νικήσετε.
Χορός.
οὐδὲ μὴν ἡμᾶς σὺ πάντως.
Διόνυσος.
οὐδὲ μὴν ὑμεῖς γε δή μ' οὐδέποτε.

THE DEVIL IS AN ASS.

Act i. sc. 1.

Pug. Why any: Fraud,
Or Covetousness, or lady Vanity,
Or old Iniquity, *I'll call him hither.*

The words in italics should probably be given to the master-devil, Satan. Whalley's note.

That is, against all probability, and with a (for Jonson) impossible violation of character. The words plainly belong to Pug, and mark at once his simpleness and his impatience.

Ib. sc. 4. Fitz-dottrel's soliloquy :—

Compare this exquisite piece of sense, satire, and sound philosophy in 1616 with Sir M. Hale's speech from the bench in a trial of a witch many years afterwards.*

Act ii. sc. 1. Meercraft's speech :—

Sir, money's a whore, a bawd, a drudge.—

I doubt not that 'money' was the first word of the line, and has dropped out :—

Money! Sir, money's a, &c.

---

* In 1664, at Bury St. Edmonds on the trial of Rose Cullender and Amy Duny.—*Ed.*

THE STAPLE OF NEWS.

Act iv. sc. 3. Pecunia's speech :—

> No, he would ha' done,
> That lay not in his power: he had the use
> Of your bodies, Band and Wax, and sometimes Statute's.

READ (1815),

> —he had the use of
> Your bodies, &c.

Now, however, I doubt the legitimacy of my transposition of the 'of' from the beginning of this latter line to the end of the one preceding ;—for though it facilitates the metre and reading of the latter line, and is frequent in Massinger, this disjunction of the proposition from its case seems to have been disallowed by Jonson. Perhaps the better reading is—

> O' your bodies, &c.—

the two syllables being slurred into one, or rather snatched, or sucked, up into the emphasized 'your.' In all points of view, therefore, Ben's judgment is just; for in this way, the line can not be read, as metre, without that strong and quick emphasis on 'your' which the sense requires ;—and had not the sense required an emphasis on 'your,' the *tmesis* of the sign of its cases 'of,' 'to,' &c., would destroy almost all boundary between the dramatic verse and prose in comedy :—a lesson not to be rash in conjectural amendments. 1818.

Ib. sc. 4.

> *P. jun.* I love all men of virtue, *frommy* Princess.—

'Frommy,' *fromme*, pious, dutiful, &c.

Act v. sc. 4. Penny-boy sen. and Porter :—

I dare not, will not, think that honest Ben had Lear in his mind in this mock mad scene.

THE NEW INN.

Act i. sc. 1. Host's speech :—

> A heavy purse, and then two turtles, *makes*.—

'Makes,' frequent in old books, and even now used in some counties for mates, or pairs.

Ib. sc. 3. Host's speech :—

> —And for a leap
> O' the vaulting horse, to *play* the vaulting *house*.—

Instead of reading with Whalley 'ply' for 'play,' I would suggest 'horse' for 'house.' The meaning would then be obvious and pertinent. The punlet, or pun-maggot, or pun intentional, 'horse and house,' is below Jonson. The *jeu-de-mots* just below—

> Read a lecture
> Upon *Aqui*nas at St. Thomas à *Water*ings—

had a learned smack in it to season its insipidity.

Ib. sc. 6. Lovel's speech :—

> Then shower'd his bounties on me, like the Hours,
> That open-handed sit upon the clouds,
> And press the liberality of heaven
> Down to the laps of thankful men!

Like many other similar passages in Jonson, this is εἶδος χαλεπὸν ἰδεῖν—a sight which it is difficult to make one's self see,—a picture my fancy can not copy detached from the words.

Act ii. sc. 5. Though it was hard upon old Ben, yet Felton, it must be confessed, was in the right in considering the Fly, Tipto, Bat Burst, &c., of this play mere dotages. Such a scene as this was enough to damn a new play; and Nick Stuff is worse still,—most abominable stuff indeed!

Act iii. sc. 2. Lovel's speech :—

> So knowledge first begets benevolence,
> Benevolence breeds friendship, friendship love.—

Jonson has elsewhere proceeded thus far; but the part most

difficult and delicate, yet, perhaps, not the least capable of being both morally and poetically treated, is the union itself, and what, even in this life, it can be.

NOTES ON BEAUMONT AND FLETCHER.

Seward's Preface. 1750.

The King And No King, too, is extremely spirited in all its characters; Arbaces holds up a mirror to all men of virtuous principles but violent passions. Hence he is, as it were, at once magnanimity and pride, patience and fury, gentleness and rigor, chastity and incest, and is one of the finest mixtures of virtues and vices that any poet has drawn, &c.

These are among the endless instances of the abject state to which psychology had sunk from the reign of Charles I. to the middle of the present reign of George III.; and even now it is but just awaking.

Ib. Seward's comparison of Julia's speech in the Two Gentlemen of Verona, act iv. last scene—

Madam, 'twas Ariadne passioning, &c.

with Aspatia's speech in the Maid's Tragedy—

I stand upon the sea-beach now, &c. Act ii.

and preference of the latter.

It is strange to take an incidental passage of one writer, intended only for a subordinate part, and compare it with the same thought in another writer, who had chosen it for a prominent and principal figure.

Ib. Seward's preference of Alphonso's poisoning in A Wife for a Month, act i. sc. 1, to the passage in King John, act v. sc. 7,—

Poison'd, ill fare! dead, forsook, cast off!

Mr. Seward! Mr. Seward! you may be, and I trust you are, an angel; but you were an ass.

Ib.

Every reader of *taste* will see how superior this is to the quotation from Shakspeare.

Of what taste?

Ib. Seward's classification of the plays:—

Surely Monsieur Thomas, the Chances, Beggar's Bush, and the Pilgrim, should have been placed in the very first class! But the whole attempt ends in a woful failure.

HARRIS'S COMMENDATORY POEM ON FLETCHER.

I'd have a state of wit convok'd, which hath
A *power* to take up on common faith:—

THIS is an instance of that modifying of quantity by emphasis, without which our elder poets can not be scanned. 'Power,' here, instead of being one long syllable—pow'r—must be sounded, not indeed as a spondee, nor yet as a trochee; but as—˘ ᴗ;—the first syllable is 1¼.

We can, indeed, never expect an authentic edition of our elder dramatic poets (for in those times a drama was a poem), until some man undertakes the work, who has studied the philosophy of metre. This has been found the main torch of sound restoration in the Greek dramatists by Bentley, Porson, and their followers;—how much more, then, in writers in our own language! It is true that quantity, an almost iron law with the Greek, is in English rather a subject for a peculiarly fine ear, than any law or even rule; but, then, instead of it, we have, first, accent; secondly, emphasis; and lastly, retardation, and acceleration of the times of syllables according to the meaning of the words, the passion that accompanies them, and even the character of the person that uses them. With due attention to these,—above all, to that, which requires the most attention and the finest taste, the character, Massinger, for example, might be reduced to a rich and yet regular metre. But then the *regulæ* must be first known;—though I will venture to say, that he who does not find a line (not corrupted) of Massinger's flow to the time total of a trimeter catalectic iambic verse, has not read it aright. But by virtue of the last principle—the retardation or acceleration of time—we have the proceleusmatic foot ᴗ ᴗ ᴗ ᴗ, and the *dispondæus*— — — — —, not to mention the *choriambus*, the ionics, pæons, and epitrites. Since Dryden, the metre of our poets leads to the sense: in our elder and more genuine bards, the sense, including the passion, leads to the metre. Read even Donne's satires as he meant them to be read, and as the sense and passion demand, and you will find in the lines a manly harmony.

LIFE OF FLETCHER IN STOCKDALE'S EDITION. 1811.

In general their plots are more regular than Shakspeare's.—

THIS is true, if true at all, only before a court of criticism, which judges one scheme by the laws of another and a diverse one. Shakspeare's plots have their own laws or *regulæ*, and according to these they are regular.

MAID'S TRAGEDY.

Act i. The metrical arrangement is most slovenly throughout.

Strat. As well as masque can be, &c.

and all that follows to 'who is return'd'—is plainly blank verse, and falls easily into it.

Ib. Speech of Melantius :—

These soft and silken wars are not for me :
The music must be shrill, and all confus'd,
That stirs my blood ; and then I dance with arms.

What strange self-trumpeters and tongue-bullies all the brave soldiers of Beaumont and Fletcher are ! Yet I am inclined to think it was the fashion of the age from the Soldier's speech in the Counter Scuffle ; and deeper than the fashion B. and F. did not fathom.

Ib. Speech of Lysippus :—

Yes, but this lady
Walks discontented, with her wat'ry eyes
Bent on the earth, &c.

Opulent as Shakspeare was, and of his opulence prodigal, he yet would not have put this exquisite piece of poetry in the mouth of a no-character, or as addressed to a Melantius. I wish that B. and F. had written poems instead of tragedies.

Ib.

Mel. I might run fiercely, not more hastily,
Upon my foe.

Read

I mīght rŭn *mŏre* fiĕrcelȳ, not more hastily.—

Ib. Speech of Calianax :—

Office! I would I could put it off! I am sure I sweat quite through my office!

The syllable *off* reminds the testy statesman of his robe, and he carries on the image.

Ib. Speech of Melantius :—

—Would that blood,
That sea of blood, that I have lost in fight, &c.

All B. and F.'s generals are pugilists, or cudgel-fighters, that boast of their bottom and of the *claret* they have shed.

Ib. The Masque ;—Cinthia's speech :—

But I will give a greater state and glory,
And raise to time a *noble* memōry
Of what these lovers are.

I suspect that 'nobler,' pronounced as 'nobiler'— ᴗ —, was the poet's word, and that the accent is to be placed on the penultimate of 'memory.' As to the passage—

Yet, while our reign lasts, let us stretch our power, &c.

removed from the text of Cinthia's speech by these foolish editors as unworthy of B. and F.—the first eight lines are not worse, and the last couplet incomparably better, than the stanza retained.

Act ii. Amintor's speech :—

Oh, thou hast nam'd a word, that wipes away
All thoughts revengeful! In that sacred name,
'The king,' there lies a terror.

It is worth noticing that of the three greatest tragedians, Massinger was a democrat, Beaumont and Fletcher the most servile *jure divino* royalists, and Shakspeare a philosopher; if aught personal, an aristocrat.

A KING AND NO KING.

Act iv. Speech of Tigranes :—

> She, that forgat the greatness of her grief
> And miseries, that must follow such mad passions,
> Endless and wild *as* women ! &c.

SEWARD's note and suggestion of 'in.'

It would be amusing to learn from some existing friend of Mr. Seward what he meant, or rather dreamed, in this note. It is certainly a difficult passage, of which there are two solutions ;—one, that the writer was somewhat more injudicious than usual ; —the other, that he was very, very much more profound and Shaksperian than usual. Seward's emendation, at all events, is right and obvious. Were it a passage of Shakspeare, I should not hesitate to interpret it as a characteristic of Tigranes' state of mind, disliking the very virtues, and therefore half-consciously representing them as mere products of the violence of the sex in general in all their whims, and yet forced to admire, and to feel and to express gratitude for, the exertion in his own instance. The inconsistency of the passage would be the consistency of the author. But this is above Beaumont and Fletcher.

THE SCORNFUL LADY.

Act ii. Sir Roger's speech :—

> Did I for this consume my *quarters* in meditations, vows, and woo'd her in heroical epistles ? Did I expound the Owl, and undertake, with labor and expense, the recollection of those thousand pieces, consum'd in cellars and tobacco-shops, of that our honored Englishman, Nic. Broughton ? &c.

STRANGE, that neither Mr. Theobald, nor Mr. Seward, should have seen that this mock heroic speech is in full-mouthed blank verse ! Had they seen this, they would have seen that 'quarters' is a substitution of the players for 'quires' or 'squares' (that is) of paper :—

> Consume my quires in meditations, vows,
> And woo'd her in heroical epistles. *(cc)*

They ought, likewise, to have seen that the abbreviated 'Ni. Br.' of the text was properly 'Mi. Dr.'—and that Michael Drayton, not Nicholas Broughton, is here ridiculed for his poem The Owl and his Heroical Epistles. (*dd*)

Ib. Speech of Younger Loveless:—

> Fill him some wine. Thou dost not see me mov'd, &c.

These Editors ought to have learnt, that scarce an instance occurs in B. and F. of a long speech not in metre. This is plain staring blank verse.

THE CUSTOM OF THE COUNTRY.

I CAN not but think that in a country conquered by a nobler race than the natives, and in which the latter became villains and bondsmen, this custom, *lex merchetæ*, may have been introduced for wise purposes—as of improving the breed, lessening the antipathy of different races, and producing a new bond of relationship between the lord and the tenant, who, as the eldest born, would, at least, have a chance of being, and a probability of being thought, the lord's child. In the West Indies it can not have these effects, because the mulatto is marked by nature different from the father, and because there is no bond, no law, no custom, but of mere debauchery. 1815.

Act i. sc. 1. Rutilio's speech:—

> Yet if you play not fair play, &c.

Evidently to be transposed and read thus:—

> Yet if you play not fair, above board too,
> I'll tell you what—
> I've a foolish engine here:—I say no more—
> But if your Honor's guts are not enchanted—

Licentious as the comic metre of B. and F. is—a far more lawless, and yet far less happy, imitation of the rhythm of animated talk in real life than Massinger's—still it is made worse than it really is by ignorance of the halves, thirds, and two thirds of a line which B. and F. adopted from the Italian and Spanish dramatists. Thus in Rutilio's speech:—

Though I confess
Any man would desire to have her, and by any means, &c.

Correct the whole passage—

Though I confess
Any man would
Desire to have her, and by any means,
At any rate too, yet this common hangman
That hath whipt off a thoūsănd māids' heāds already—
That he should glean the harvest, sticks in my stomach!

In all comic metres the gulping of short syllables, and the abbreviation of syllables ordinarily long by the rapid pronunciation of eagerness and vehemence, are not so much a license, as a law —a faithful copy of nature, and let them be read characteristically, the times will be found nearly equal. Thus the three words marked above make a *choriambus* —⏑ ⏑—, or perhaps a *pæon primus*—⏑ ⏑ ⏑ ; a dactyl, by virtue of comic rapidity, being only equal to an iambus when distinctly pronounced. I have no doubt that all B. and F.'s works might be safely corrected by attention to this rule, and that the editor is entitled to transpositions of all kinds, and to not a few omissions. For the rule of the metre once lost—what was to restrain the actors from interpolation?

THE ELDER BROTHER.

Act i. sc. 2. Charles's speech :—

—For what concerns tillage,
Who better can deliver it than Virgil
In his Georgics? and to cure your herds,
His Bucolics is a master-piece.

FLETCHER was too good a scholar to fall into so gross a blunder, as Messrs. Sympson and Colman suppose. I read the passage thus :—

—For what concerns tillage,
Who better can deliver it than Virgil
In his Gĕōrgĭcs, *or* to cure your herds;
(His Bucolics are a master-piece). But when, &c.

Jealous of Virgil's honor, he is afraid lest, by referring to the

Georgics alone, he might be understood as undervaluing the preceding work. 'Not that I do not admire the Bucolics, too, in their way :—But when, &c.'

Act iii. sc. 3. Charles's speech :—

—She has a face looks like a *story ;*
The *story* of the heavens looks very like her.

Seward reads 'glory ;' and Theobald quotes from Philaster—

That reads the story of a woman's face.—

I can make sense of this passage as little as Mr. Seward ;—the passage from Philaster is nothing to the purpose. Instead of 'a story,' I have sometimes thought of proposing 'Astræa.' (*ee*)

Ib. Angellina's speech :—

—You're old and dim, Sir,
And the shadow of the earth eclips'd your judgment.

Inappropriate to Angellina, but one of the finest lines in our language.

Act iv. sc. 3. Charles's speech :—

And lets the serious part of life run by
As thin neglected sand, whiteness of name.
You must be mine, &c.

Seward's note, and reading—

—Whiteness of name,
You must be mine!

Nonsense! 'Whiteness of name' is in apposition to 'the serious part of life,' and means a deservedly pure reputation. The following line—'You *must* be mine!' means—'Though I do not enjoy you to-day, I shall hereafter, and without reproach.' (*ff*)

THE SPANISH CURATE.

Act iv. sc. 7. Amaranta's speech :—

And still I push'd him on, as he had been *coming.*

PERHAPS the true word is 'conning,' that is, learning, or reading, and therefore inattentive.

WIT WITHOUT MONEY.

Act i. Valentine's speech :—

> One without substance, &c.

THE present text, and that proposed by Seward, are equally vile. I have endeavored to make the lines sense, though the whole is, I suspect, incurable except by bold conjectural reformation. I would read thus :—

> One without substance of herself, that's woman;
> Without the pleasure of her life, that's wanton;
> Tho' she be young, forgetting it; tho' fair,
> Making her glass the eyes of honest men,
> Not her own admiration.

'That's wanton,' or, 'that is to say, wantonness.'

Act ii. Valentine's speech :—

> Of half-a-crown a week for pins and puppets—

As there is a syllable wanting in the measure here. Seward.

A syllable wanting! Had this Seward neither ears nor fingers? The line is a more than usually regular iambic hendecasyllable.

Ib.

> With one man satisfied, with one rein guided;
> With one faith, one content, one bed;
> *Aged*, she makes the wife, preserves the fame and issue;
> A widow is, &c.

Is 'apaid'—contented—too obsolete for B. and F.? If not, we might read it thus :—

> Content with one faith, with one bed apaid,
> She makes the wife, preserves the fame and issue;

Or it may be—

> —with one breed apaid—

that is, satisfied with one set of children, in opposition to—

> A widow is a Christmas-box, &c.

Colman's note on Seward's attempt to put this play into metre.

The editors, and their contemporaries in general, were ignorant of any but the regular iambic verse. A study of the Aristophanic and Plautine metres would have enabled them to reduce B. and F. throughout into metre, except where prose is really intended.

THE HUMOROUS LIEUTENANT.

Act i. sc. 1. Second Ambassador's speech :—

> —When your angers,
> *Like* so many brother billows, rose together,
> And, curling up *your* foaming crests, defied, &c.

THIS worse than superfluous 'like' is very like an interpolation of some matter of fact critic—all *pus, prose atque venenum.* The 'your' in the next line, instead of 'their,' is likewise yours, Mr. Critic !

Act ii. sc. 1. Timon's speech :—

> Another of a new *way* will be look'd at—

We must suspect the poets wrote, 'of a new *day*.' So immediately after,

> —— Time may
> For all his wisdom, yet give us a day.
>
> SEWARD'S NOTE.

For this very reason I more than suspect the contrary.

Ib. sc. 3. Speech of Leucippe :—

> I'll put her into action for a *waistcoat.*

What we call a riding-habit,—some mannish dress.

THE MAD LOVER.

Act iv. Masque of beasts :—

> — This goodly tree,
> An usher that still grew before his lady,
> Wither'd at root: this, for he could not woo,
> A grumbling lawyer: &c.

HERE must have been omitted a line rhyming to 'tree;' and the words of the next line have been transposed :—

— This goodly tree,
Which leafless, and obscur'd with moss you see,
An usher this, that 'fore his lady grew,
Wither'd at root: this, for he could not woo, &c.

THE LOYAL SUBJECT.

It is well worthy of notice, and yet has not been, I believe, noticed hitherto, what a marked difference there exists in the dramatic writers of the Elizabetho-Jacobæan age—(Mercy on me! what a phrase for 'the writers during the reigns of Elizabeth and James I.!')—in respect of their political opinions. Shakspeare, in this as in all other things, himself and alone, gives the permanent politics of human nature, and the only predilection, which appears, shows itself in his contempt of mobs and the populacy. Massinger is a decided Whig;—Beaumont and Fletcher high-flying, passive-obedience Tories. The Spanish dramatists furnished them with this, as with many other ingredients. By-the-by, an accurate and familiar acquaintance with all the productions of the Spanish stage previously to 1620, is an indispensable qualification for an editor of B. and F.;—and with this qualification a most interesting and instructive edition might be given. This edition of Colman's (Stockdale, 1811) is below criticism.

In metre B. and F. are inferior to Shakspeare, on the one hand, as expressing the poetic part of the drama, and to Massinger, on the other, in the art of reconciling metre with the natural rhythm of conversation,—in which, indeed, Massinger is unrivalled. Read him aright, and measure by time, not syllables, and no lines can be more legitimate,—none in which the substitution of equipollent feet, and the modifications by emphasis, are managed with such exquisite judgment. B. and F. are fond of the twelve syllable (not Alexandrine) line, as—

Too many fears 'tis thought too: and to nourish those—

This has, often, a good effect, and is one of the varieties most common in Shakspeare.

RULE A WIFE AND HAVE A WIFE.

Act iii. Old Woman's speech :—

> —I fear he will knock my
> Brains out for lying.

Mr. Seward discards the words 'for lying,' because 'most of the things spoke of Estifania are true, with only a little exaggeration, and because they destroy all appearance of measure.' Colman's Note.

Mr. Seward had his brains out. The humor lies in Estifania's having ordered the Old Woman to tell these tales of her; for though an intriguer, she is not represented as other than chaste; and as to the metre, it is perfectly correct.

Ib.

> *Marg.* As you love me, give way.
> *Leon.* It shall be better, I will give none, madam, &c.

The meaning is: 'It shall be a better way, first;—as it is, I will not give it, or any that you in your present mood would wish.'

THE LAWS OF CANDY.

Act i. Speech of Melitus :—

> Whose insolence and never-yet match'd pride
> Can by no character be well express'd,
> But in her only name, the proud Erota.

Colman's note.

The poet intended no allusion to the word 'Erota' itself; but says that her very name, 'the proud Erota,' became a character and adage; as we say, a quixote or a Brutus: so to say an 'Erota,' expressed female pride and insolence of beauty.

Ib. Speech of Antinous :—

> Of my peculiar honors, not deriv'd
> From *successary*, but purchas'd with my blood.—

The poet doubtless wrote 'successary,' which, though not adopted in our language, would be, on many occasions, as here, a much more significant phrase than ancestry.

THE LITTLE FRENCH LAWYER.

Act i. sc. 1. Dinant's speech :—

> Are you become a patron too? 'Tis a new one,
> No more on't, &c.

Seward reads :—

> Are you become a patron too? *How long*
> *Have you been conning this speech?* 'Tis a new one, &c.

If conjectural emendation, like this, be allowed, we might venture to read —

> Are you become a patron *to a new tune?*

or,

> Are you become a patron? 'Tis a new *tune*.

Ib. (*gg*)

> *Din.* Thou wouldst not willingly
> Live a protested coward, or be call'd one?
> *Cler.* Words are but words.
> *Din.* Nor wouldst thou take a blow?

Seward's note.

O miserable! Dinant sees through Cleremont's gravity, and the actor is to explain it. 'Words are but words,' is the last struggle of affected morality.

VALENTINIAN.

Act i. sc. 3.

It is a real trial of charity to read this scene with tolerable temper towards Fletcher. So very slavish—so reptile—are the feelings and sentiments represented as duties. And yet remember he was a bishop's son, and the duty to God was the supposed basis.

Personals, including body, house, home, and religion;—property, subordination, and inter-community;—these are the fundamentals of society. I mean here, religion negatively taken,—so that the person be not compelled to do or utter, in relation of the soul to God, what would be, in that person, a lie;—such as to force a man to go to church, or to swear that he believes what he does not believe. Religion, positively taken, may be a great and useful privilege, but can not be a right,—were it for this only that it can not be pre-defined. The ground of this distinction between negative and positive religion, as a social right, is plain. No one of my fellow-citizens is encroached on by my not declaring to him what I believe respecting the super-sensual; but should every man be entitled to preach against the preacher, who could hear any preacher? Now it is different in respect of loyalty. There we have positive rights, but not negative rights;—for every pretended negative would be in effect a positive;—as if a soldier had a right to keep to himself, whether he would, or would not, fight. Now, no one of these fundamentals can be rightfully attacked, except when the guardian of it has abused it to subvert one or more of the rest. The reason is, that the guardian, as a fluent, is less than the permanent which he is to guard. He is the temporary and mutable mean, and derives his whole value from the end. In short, as robbery is not high treason, so neither is every unjust act of a king the converse. All must be attacked and endangered. Why? Because the king, as *a.* to A., is a mean to A. or subordination, in a far higher sense than a proprietor, as *b.* to B. is a mean to B. or property.

Act ii. sc. 2. Claudia's speech:—

Chimney-pieces! &c.

The whole of this speech seems corrupt; and if accurately printed,—that is, if the same in all the prior editions, irremediable but by bold conjecture. '*Till* my tackle,' should be, I think, *while*, &c.

Act iii. sc. 1. B. and F. always write as if virtue or goodness were a sort of talisman, or strange something, that might be lost without the least fault on the part of the owner. In short, their chaste ladies value their chastity as a material thing,—not as an act or state of being; and this mere thing being imaginary, no wonder that all their women are represented with the minds of strumpets, except a few irrational humorists, far less capable of exciting our sympathy than a Hindoo, who has had a basin of cow-broth thrown over him;—for this, though a debasing superstition, is still real, and we might pity the poor wretch, though we can not help despising him. But B. and F.'s Lucinas are clumsy fictions. It is too plain that the authors had no one idea of chastity as a virtue, but only such a conception as a blind man might have of the power of seeing, by handling an ox's eye. In The Queen of Corinth, indeed, they talk differently; but it is all talk, and nothing is real in it but the dread of losing a reputation. Hence the frightful contrast between their women (even those who are meant for virtuous) and Shakspeare's. So, for instance, The Maid in the Mill:—a woman must not merely have grown old in brothels, but have chuckled over every abomination committed in them with a rampant sympathy of imagination, to have had her fancy so drunk with the *minutiæ* of lechery as this icy chaste virgin evinces hers to have been.

It would be worth while to note how many of these plays are founded on rapes,—how many on incestuous passions, and how many on mere lunacies. Then their virtuous women are either crazy superstitions of a mere bodily negation of having been acted on, or strumpets in their imaginations and wishes, or, as in this Maid in the Mill, both at the same time. In the men, the love is merely lust in one direction,—exclusive preference of one object. The tyrant's speeches are mostly taken from the mouths of indignant denouncers of the tyrant's character, with the substitution of 'I' for 'he,' and the omission of the prefatory 'he acts as if he thought' so and so. The only feelings they can possibly excite are disgust at the Aeciuses, if regarded as sane loyalists, or compassion, if considered as Bedlamites. So much for their tragedies. But even their comedies are, most of them, disturbed by the fantasticalness, or gross caricature, of the persons or incidents. There are few characters that you can really like,—(even though you should have erased from your mind all the filth which bespatters the most likable of them, as Piniero in The Island Princess for instance)—scarcely one whom you can love. How different this from Shakspeare, who makes one have a sort of sneaking affection even for his Barnardines;—whose very Iagos and Richards are awful, and by the counteracting power of profound intellects, rendered fearful rather than hateful;—and even the exceptions, as Goneril and Regan, are proofs of superlative judgment and the finest moral tact, in being left utter monsters, *nulla virtute redemptæ*, and in being kept out of sight as much as possible,—they being, indeed, only means for the excitement and deepening of noblest emotions towards the Lear, Cordelia, &c. and employed with the severest economy! But even Shakspeare's grossness—that which is really so, independently of the increase in modern times of vicious associations with things indifferent—(for there is a state of manners conceivable so pure, that the language of Hamlet at Ophelia's feet might be a harmless rallying, or playful teasing, of a shame that would exist in Paradise)—at the worst, how diverse in kind is it from Beaumont and Fletcher's! In Shakspeare it is the mere generalities of sex, mere words for the most part, seldom or never distinct images, all head-work, and fancy-drolleries; there is no sensation supposed in the speaker. I need not proceed to contrast this with B. and F.

ROLLO.

THIS is, perhaps, the most energetic of Fletcher's tragedies. He evidently aimed at a new Richard III. in Rollo;—but as in all his other imitations of Shakspeare, he was not philosopher enough to bottom his original. Thus, in Rollo, he has produced a mere personification of outrageous wickedness, with no fundamental characteristic impulses to make either the tyrant's words or actions philosophically intelligible. Hence the most pathetic situations border on the horrible, and what he meant for the terrible, is either hateful, τὸ μισητὸν, or ludicrous. The scene of Baldwin's sentence in the third act is probably the grandest working of passion in all B. and F.'s dramas;—but the very magnificence of filial affection given to Edith, in this noble scene, renders the after-scene—(in imitation of one of the least Shaksperian of all Shakspeare's works, if it be his, the scene between Richard and Lady Anne)—in which Edith is yielding to a few words and tears, not only unnatural, but disgusting. In Shakspeare, Lady Anne is described as a weak, vain, very woman throughout.

Act i. sc. 1.

> *Gis.* He is indeed the perfect character
> Of a good man, and so his actions speak him.

This character of Aubrey, and the whole spirit of this and several other plays of the same authors, are interesting as traits of the morals which it was fashionable to teach in the reigns of James I. and his successor, who died a martyr to them. Stage, pulpit, law, fashion,—all conspired to enslave the realm. Massinger's plays breathe the opposite spirit; Shakspeare's the spirit of wisdom which is for all ages. By-the-by, the Spanish dramatists—Calderon, in particular,—had some influence in this respect, of romantic loyalty to the greatest monsters, as well as in the busy intrigues of B. and F.'s plays.

THE WILDGOOSE CHASE.

Act ii. sc. 1. Belleur's speech :—

> —That wench, methinks,
> If I were but well set on, for she is *a fable*,
> If I were but hounded right, and one to teach me.

Sympson reads 'affable,' which Colman rejects, and says, 'the next line seems to enforce' the reading in the text.

Pity, that the editor did not explain wherein the sense, 'seemingly enforced by the next line,' consists. May the true word be 'a sable,' that is, a black fox, hunted for its precious fur? Or 'at-able,'—as we now say,—'she is come-at-able?'

A WIFE FOR A MONTH.

Act iv. sc. 1. Alphonso's speech :—

> Betwixt the cold bear and the raging lion
> Lies my safe way.

Seward's note and alteration to—

> 'Twixt the cold bears, far from the raging lion—

This Mr. Seward is a blockhead of the provoking species. In his itch for correction, he forgot the words—'lies my safe way!' The Bear is the extreme pole, and thither he would travel over the space contained between it and 'the raging lion.'

THE PILGRIM.

Act iv. sc. 2.

ALINDA's interview with her father is lively, and happily hit off; but this scene with Roderigo is truly excellent. Altogether, indeed, this play holds the first place in B. and F.'s romantic entertainments, *Lustspiele*, which collectively are their happiest performances, and are only inferior to the romance of Shakspeare in the As You Like It, Twelfth Night, &c.

Ib.

> *Alin.* To-day you shall wed Sorrow,
> And Repentance will come to-morrow.

Read 'Penitence,' or else—

> Repentance, she will come to-morrow.

THE QUEEN OF CORINTH.

Act ii. sc. 1.

MERIONE's speech. Had the scene of this tragi-comedy been laid in Hindostan instead of Corinth, and the gods here addressed been the Veeshnoo and Co. of the Indian Pantheon, this rant would not have been much amiss.

In respect of style and versification, this play and the following of Bonduca may be taken as the best, and yet as characteristic, specimens of Beaumont and Fletcher's dramas. I particularly instance the first scene of the Bonduca. Take Shakspeare's Richard II., and having selected some one scene of about the same number of lines, and consisting mostly of long speeches, compare it with the first scene in Bonduca,—not for the idle purpose of finding out which is the better, but in order to see and understand the difference. The latter, that of B. and F., you will find a well-arranged bed of flowers, each having its separate root, and its position determined aforehand by the will of the gardener,—each fresh plant a fresh volition. In the former you see an Indian fig-tree, as described by Milton;—all is growth, evolution, γένεσις;—each line, each word almost, begets the following, and the will of the writer is an interfusion, a continuous agency, and not a series of separate acts. Shakspeare is the height, breadth, and depth of Genius: Beaumont and Fletcher the excellent mechanism, in juxtaposition and succession, of talent.

THE NOBLE GENTLEMAN.

Why have the dramatists of the times of Elizabeth, James I., and the first Charles become almost obsolete, with the exception of Shakspeare? Why do they no longer belong to the English, being once so popular? And why is Shakspeare an exception?—One thing, among fifty, necessary to the full solution is, that they all employed poetry and poetic diction on unpoetic subjects, both characters and situations, especially in their comedy. Now Shakspeare is all, all ideal,—of no time, and therefore for all times. Read, for instance, Marine's panegyric in the first scene of this play:—

> Know
> The eminent court, to them that can be wise,
> And fasten on her blessings, is a sun, &c.

What can be more unnatural and inappropriate—(not only is, but must be felt as such)—than such poetry in the mouth of a silly dupe? In short, the scenes are mock dialogues, in which the poet *solus* plays the ventriloquist, but can not keep down his own way of expressing himself. Heavy complaints have been made respecting the transposing of the old plays by Cibber; but it never occurred to these critics to ask, how it came that no one ever attempted to transpose a comedy of Shakspeare's.

THE CORONATION.

Act i. Speech of Seleucus:—

> Altho' he be my enemy, should any
> Of the gay flies that buzz about the court,
> *Sit* to catch trouts i' the summer, tell me so,
> I durst, &c.

Colman's note.

Pshaw! 'Sit' is either a misprint for 'set,' or the old and still provincial word for 'set,' as the participle passive of 'seat' or 'set.' I have heard an old Somersetshire gardener say:—"Look, Sir! I set these plants here; those yonder I *sit* yesterday."

Act ii. Speech of Arcadius :—

> Nay, some will swear they love their mistress,
> Would hazard lives and fortunes, &c.

Read thus :—

> Nay, some will swear they love their mistress so,
> They would hazard lives and fortunes to preserve
> One of her hairs brighter than Berenice's,
> Or young Apollo's ; and yet, after this, &c.

'Thĕy woŭld hāzard'—furnishes an anapæst for an *iambus.* 'And yet,' which must be read, *a͞nyĕt*, is an instance of the enclitic force in an accented monosyllable. 'Añd yēt,' is a complete *iambus ;* but *anyet* is, like *spirit*, a dibrach ᴗ ᴗ, trocheized, however, by the *arsis* or first accent damping, though not extinguishing, the second.

WIT AT SEVERAL WEAPONS.

Act i. Oldcraft's speech :—

> I'm arm'd at all points, &c.

It would be very easy to restore all this passage to metre, by supplying a sentence of four syllables, which the reasoning almost demands, and by correcting the grammar. Read thus :—

> Arm'd at all points 'gainst treachery, I hold
> My humor firm. If, living, I can see thee
> Thrive by thy wits, I shall have the more courage,
> Dying, to trust thee with my lands. If not,
> The best wit, I can hear of, carries them.
> For since so many in my time and knowledge,
> Rich children of the city, have concluded
> *For lack of wit* in beggary, I'd rather
> Make a wise stranger my executor,
> Than a fool son my heir, and have my lands call'd
> After my wit than name : and that's my nature !

Ib. Oldcraft's speech :—

> To prevent which I have sought out a match for her.

Read

> Which to prevent I've sought a match out for her

Ib. Sir Gregory's speech :—

——Do you think
I'll have any of the wits hang upon me after I am married once?

Read it thus :—

Do you think
That I'll have any of the wits to hang
Upon me after I am married once?

and afterwards—

Is it a fashion in London
To marry a woman, and never to see her?

The superfluous 'to' gives it the Sir Andrew Ague-cheek character.

THE FAIR MAID OF THE INN.

Act ii. Speech of Albertus :—

But, Sir,
By my life, I vow to take assurance from you,
That right hand never more shall strike my son,
* * * * *
Chop his hand off!

In this (as, indeed, in all other respects; but most in this) it is that Shakspeare is so incomparably superior to Fletcher and his friend,—in judgment! What can be conceived more unnatural and motiveless than this brutal resolve? How is it possible to feel the least interest in Albertus afterwards? or in Cesario after his conduct?

THE TWO NOBLE KINSMEN.

On comparing the prison scene of Palamon and Arcite, Act ii. sc. 2, with the dialogue between the same speakers, Act i. sc. 2, I can scarcely retain a doubt as to the first act's having been written by Shakspeare. Assuredly it was not written by B. and F. I hold Jonson more probable than either of these two.

The main presumption, however, for Shakspeare's share in this play rests on a point, to which the sturdy critics of this edition (and indeed all before them) were blind,—that is, the construction of the blank verse, which proves beyond all doubt an intentional imitation, if not the proper hand, of Shakspeare. Now, whatever improbability there is in the former (which supposes Fletcher conscious of the inferiority, the too poematic *minus*-dramatic nature, of his versification, and of which there is neither proof, nor likelihood), adds so much to the probability of the latter. On the other hand, the harshness of many of these very passages, a harshness unrelieved by any lyrical inter-breathings, and still more the want of profundity in the thoughts, keep me from an absolute decision.

Act i. sc. 3. Emilia's speech :—

> —— Since his depart, his *sports*,
> Tho' craving seriousness and skill, &c.

I conjecture 'imports,' that is, duties or offices of importance. The flow of the versification in this speech seems to demand the trochaic ending — ∪ ; while the text blends jingle and *hisses* to the annoyance of less sensitive ears than Fletcher's—not to say, Shakspeare's.

THE WOMAN HATER.

Act i. sc. 2.

This scene from the beginning is prose printed as blank verse, down to the line—

> E'en all the valiant stomachs in the court—

where the verse recommences. This transition from the prose to the verse enhances, and indeed forms, the comic effect. (*hh*) Lazarillo concludes his soliloquy with a hymn to the goddess of plenty.

EXTRACTS OF TWO LETTERS

OF MR. H. C. ROBINSON, GIVING SOME ACCOUNT OF TWO LECTURES OF MR. COLERIDGE, DELIVERED IN MAY, 1808. (*ii*)

May 7th, 1808.

My dear Friend,

On receiving your threatening letter I inclosed it in a note to Coleridge, and on calling upon him before the lecture, found a letter for me, &c. He has offered to give me admission constantly ; I shall accept his offer whenever I can, and give you a weekly letter on the subject. I shall not pretend to tell you *what* he says, but mention the topics he runs over. Every thing he observes on morals will be as familiar to you as all he says on criticism is to me ; for he has adopted in all respects the German doctrines : and it is a useful lesson to me how those doctrines are to be clothed with original illustrations, and adapted to an English audience.

The extraordinary lecture on Education was most excellent, delivered with great animation, and *extorting* praise from those, whose prejudices he was mercilessly attacking : he kept his audience on the rack of pleasure and offence two whole hours and ten minutes ; and few went away during the lecture. He began by establishing a common-place distinction neatly between the *objects* and the *means* of education, which he observed to be " perhaps almost the only safe way of being useful." Omitting a tirade, which you can well supply, on the object of Education, I come to the means of forming the character, the cardinal rules of early education. These are, First, to work by love and so generate love : Secondly, to habituate the mind to intellectual accuracy or truth : Thirdly, to excite power. 1. He enforced a great truth strikingly. " My experience tells me, that little is taught or communicated by contest or dispute, but every thing by sympathy and love." " Collision elicits truth only from the hardest head." " I hold motives to be of little influence compared with feelings." He apologized for early prejudices with a self-correction—" and yet what nobler judgment is there than that a child should listen with faith, the principle of all good things, to his father or preceptor." Digressing on Rousseau he told an anecdote pleasantly : *se non è vero è ben trovato.* A friend had defended the negative education of Rousseau. Coleridge led him into his miserably neglected garden, choked with weeds. " What is this ?" said he. " Only a garden," C. replied, " educated according to Rousseau's principles !"

On punishment he pleaded the cause of humanity eloquently. He noticed the good arising from the corporal inflictions of our great schools, in the Spartan fortitude it excited ; in the generous sympathy and friendship it awakened ; and in the point of honor it enforced. Yet, on the other hand, he showed this very reference to honor to be a great evil as a substitute for virtue and principle. School-boys, he observed, lived in civil war with their masters. They are disgraced by a lie told to their fellows ; it is an honor to impose on the common enemy : thus the mind is prepared for every falsehood and injustice, when the interest of the party, when honor requires it. On disgraceful punishments, such as fools-caps, &c. he spoke with great indignation, and declared that even now his life is embittered by the recollection of ignominious punishment he suffered when a child ; it comes to him in disease, and when his mind is dejected. This part was delivered with fervor. Could all the pedagogues of the United Kingdom have been before him ! 2. On Truth too he was very judicious : he advised beginning with the enforcement of great accuracy of assertion in young children. The parent, he observed, who should hear his child call a round leaf long, would do well to fetch one instantly. Thus tutored to render words conformable with ideas, the child would have the *habit* of truth before he had any *notion* or *thought* of *moral* truth. "We should not early begin with impressing ideas of virtue, goodness, &c. which the child could not comprehend." Then he digressed *à l'Allemagne* on the distinction between obscure ideas and clear notions.* Our notions resemble the index and hand of the dial ; our feelings are the hidden springs which impel the machine ; with this difference that notions and feelings react on each other reciprocally. The veneration for the Supreme Being, sense of mysterious existence, was not to be profaned by the intrusion of clear notions. Here he was applauded by those who do not pretend to understand religion, while the Socinians of course felt profound contempt for the lecturer. I find from my notes, that C. was not very methodical : you will therefore excuse my not being more so

1. 2. "Stimulate the heart to love and the mind to be early accurate, and all other virtues will rise of their own accord, and all vices will be thrown out." When treating of punishments, he dared to represent the text, "He that spareth the rod spoileth the child," as a source of much evil. He feelingly urged the repugnance of infancy to quiet and gloom, and the duty of attending to such indications, observing that the severe notions entertained of Religion were more pernicious than all that had been written by Voltaire and such "paltry scribblers." Considering this phrase as the gilding of the pill I let it pass. Coleridge is right in the main, but Voltaire is no paltry scribbler. *Apropos*, I was every twenty minutes provoked with the lecturer for little

* Conceptions ?—S. C.

unworthy compliances—for occasional conformity. But *n'importe.* He says such a number of things, both good and useful at the same time, that I can tolerate these drawbacks or rather makeweights. 3. In speaking of education as a mean of strengthening the character, he opposed our system of "cramming" children, and especially satirized the moral rules for juvenile readers lately introduced. "I infinitely prefer The Seven Champions of Christendom, Jack the Giant-killer, and such like : for at least they make the child forget himself: but when in your good-child stories, a little boy comes in and says, 'Mamma, I met a poor beggar-man and gave him the sixpence you gave me yesterday. Did I do right?' 'O yes, my dear, to be sure you did :'—This is not virtue but vanity :—Such lessons do not teach goodness, but, if I might hazard such a word, *goodiness.*" What Goody he referred to, I know not, for he praised Mrs. Trimmer afterwards. He added, "The lesson to be inculcated should be, let the child be good and know it not." "Instructors should be careful not to let the intellect die of plethora."

The latter part of the lecture was taken up with a defence of education for the Poor, &c. &c. He lugged in most unnecessarily an attack upon Malthus, and was as unfair in his representation as Hazlitt in his answer. He also noticed Cobbett, &c. In the end he eulogized Dr. Bell's plan of education, and concluded by a severe attack upon Lancaster for having stolen from Dr. Bell all that is good in his plans :—expatiated with warmth on the barbarous, ignominious punishments introduced by Lancaster, &c. &c. He concluded by gratulating himself on living in this age. "For I have seen what infinite good *one* man can do by persevering in his efforts to resist evil and spread good over human life : and if I were called upon to say, which two men in my own time, had been most extensively useful, and who had done most for humanity, I should say Mr. Clarkson and Dr. Bell. (*kk*) I can not answer for the terms of this sentence : the surprise I felt at the sudden introduction of the name of Clarkson perhaps made me lose the immediately preceding words.

May 15th, 1808.

MY DEAR FRIEND,

Be assured you have imposed upon me no burthensome task. To write to you is as much a relief from my ordinary employment as it would be for a man to write with his right hand who should have been condemned as a penance to write with his left. Yet what we might do against our will, becomes our will at last, and perhaps I feel some awkwardness when I leave the dry, uninteresting and mechanical works of the office to discourse with you on Coleridge's lectures ; I find I am a bad reporter, and that I have not the art of condensing the spirit of an hour's declamation into a page of post paper. However, you will kindly accept all I can give you.

I have only two lectures to speak about, and shall not pretend to speak of them in the order in which Coleridge spoke, since there was no order in his speaking. I came in late one day and found him in the midst of a deduction of the origin of the fine arts from the necessities of our being, which a friend who accompanied me could make neither head nor tail of, because he had not studied German metaphysics.

The first "free art" of man (Architecture) arose from the impulse to make his habitation beautiful. The second arose from the instinct to provide himself food. The third was the love of dress. Here C. atoned for his metaphysics by his gallantry ; he declared that the passion for dress in females has been the great cause of the civilization of mankind. "When I behold the ornaments which adorn a beautiful woman, I see the mirror of that instinct which leads man not to be content with what is necessary or useful, but impels him to the beautiful." 4. From the necessity of self-defence springs the military art, and this has produced the keenest sense of honor, the finest sensibility, the character of a gentleman. 5. The ornaments of speech are eloquence and poetry. Here C. distinguished these arts by the characteristic, that poetry is a general impulse :—he might have said, it gives the character of what is universal to what still remains particular. Eloquence impels to particular acts. "Let us rise against Philip," said the Athenians when Demosthenes sat down, for Demosthenes had been eloquent. Apropos, Kant observes that the oration treats an affair of business, as if it were a thing of imagination, while the poet handles a work of fancy, as if it were a matter of business. Kant speaks (and Schiller expatiates on this) of the method of the two artists. C. refers to the principle of the arts, but both assertions amount to the same thing. In this same lecture Coleridge contrived to work into his speech

Kant's admirably profound definition of the *naïf*, that it is *nature putting art to shame;* and he also digressed into a vehement but well-merited declamation against those *soi-disant* philosophers, who deny the nobler powers of man, his idealizing poetic faculty, and degrade him to the beast: and declared he could not think of Buffon without horror;—an assertion with which I sympathize, and which is far less exceptionable than his abuse of Voltaire.

Here are metaphysics enough for the present. Now for a critical remark or two.—Of Shakspeare C. observed, that he alone preserved the individuality of his characters without losing his own. High moral feeling is to be deduced from, though it is not in, Shakspeare, for the sentiment of his age was less pure than that of the preceding. Not a *vicious* passage in all Shakspeare, though there are many which are gross (for grossness depends on the age). Shakspeare surpasses all poets, 1st, in the purity of his female characters. (N.B. He declared his conviction that no part of Richard III. except the character of Richard, was written by Shakspeare, doubtless with a silent reference to the disgusting character of Lady Anne.) They have no Platonic refinement, but are perfect wives, mothers, &c. Secondly, he is admirable for the close union of morality and passion. Shakspeare conceived that these should never be separated; in this differing from the Greek who reserved the chorus for the morality. The truth he teaches he told in character and with passion. They are the "sparks from heated iron." They have all a higher worth than their insulated sententious import bespeaks. A third characteristic is this, that Shakspeare's observation was preceded by contemplation. "He first conceived what the forms of things must be, and then went humbly to the oracle of nature to ask whether he was right. He inquired of her as a sovereign: he did not gossip with her. Shakspeare describes feelings which no observation could teach. Shakspeare made himself all characters—he left out parts of himself and supplied what might have been in himself—nothing was given him but the canvass. ("This fact does honor to human nature, for it shows that the seeds of all that is noble and good are in man: they require only to be developed.") This canvass which Shakspeare used, formed his stories. The absurdity of his tales has often been a reproach to Shakspeare from those who did not comprehend him, as Johnson, Pope, &c. But Shakspeare had nothing to do with the probability of the histories. It was enough for him that they had found their way among the people. Every body admitted them to be true, though childish in the extreme. There was once upon a time a king who had three daughters, and he said to them, "tell me how you love me, and I will give my kingdom to her that loves me best." And so one daughter said, &c. &c. From such stuff as this Shakspeare has produced the most *wonderful* work of human genius, as in Othello he produced the most *perfect* work. "In the three first acts he carried human feelings to the utmost height, therefore in the two following they seem to sink and become feeble: as, after the bursting of the storm, we behold the scattered clouds dispersed over the heavens."

Coleridge's digressions are not the worst parts of his lectures, or rather, he is always digressing. He quoted Mrs. Barbauld under the appellation of "an amiable lady," who had asked how Richardson was inferior to Shakspeare? Richardson, he allowed, evinces an exquisite perception of minute feeling, but there is a want of harmony, a vulgarity in his sentiment; he is *only* interesting. Shakspeare on the contrary elevates and instructs. Instead of referring to our ordinary situations and common feelings he emancipates us from them, and when most remote from ordinary life is most interesting. I should observe, this depreciation of the interesting in poetry is one of the most characteristic features of the new German criticism. It is always opposed by Schiller to the beautiful, and is considered as a very subordinate merit indeed. Hence the severity of the attacks on Kotzebue, who certainly is more interesting to nineteen out of twenty than Shakspeare. C. took occasion, on mentioning Richardson to express his opinions of the immorality of his novels. The lower passions of our nature are kept through seven or eight volumes, in a hot-bed of interest. Fielding's is far less pernicious; "for the gusts of laughter drive away sensuality."

P.S. Coleridge called Voltaire "a petty scribbler." I oppose to this common-place, in which aversion is compounded with contempt, Goethe's profound and cutting remark: "It has been found that certain monarchs unite all the talents and powers of their race. It was thus with Louis XIV.: and it is so with authors. In this sense it may be said that Voltaire is the greatest of all conceivable Frenchmen." I abhor Bonaparte as the gates of hell, yet I smile at the drivellers who cry out *c'est un bon caporal*. Damn 'em both if you will, but don't despise them.

PROSPECTUS OF LECTURES IN 1811.

LONDON PHILOSOPHICAL SOCIETY, SCOTS CORPORATION HALL, CRANE COURT, FLEET STREET.

MR. COLERIDGE will commence on Monday, Nov. 18th, a Course of Lectures on Shakspeare and Milton, in Illustration of the principles of Poetry, and their Application as grounds of criticism to the most popular works of later English Poets, those of the Living included.

After an introductory Lecture on false criticism (especially in Poetry), and on its causes : two thirds of the remaining course will be assigned, 1st, to a philosophical analysis and explanation of all the principal *characters* of our great Dramatist, as Othello, Falstaff, Richard III., Iago, Hamlet, &c. : and 2d, to a critical *comparison* of Shakspeare, in respect of Diction, Imagery, Management of the Passions, Judgment in the construction of his Dramas, in short of all that belongs to him as a Poet, and as a dramatic Poet, with his contemporaries, or immediate successors, Jonson, Beaumont and Fletcher, Ford, Massinger, &c., in the endeavor to determine what of Shakspeare's merits and defects are common to him with other writers of the same age, and what remain peculiar to his own Genius.

The course will extend to fifteen Lectures, which will be given on Monday and Thursday evenings successively. The Lectures to commence at half-past seven o'clock.

A COURSE OF LECTURES.

PROSPECTUS.

THERE are few families, at present, in the higher and middle-classes of English society, in which literary topics and the productions of the Fine Arts, in some one or other of their various forms, do not occasionally take their turn in contributing to the entertainment of the social board, and the amusement of the circle at the fire-side. The acquisitions and attainments of the intellect ought, indeed, to hold a very inferior rank in our estimation, opposed to moral worth, or even to professional and specific skill, prudence, and industry. But why should they be opposed, when they may be made subservient merely by being subordinated? It can rarely happen, that a man of social disposition, altogether a stranger to subjects of taste (almost the only ones on which persons of both sexes can converse with a common interest), should pass through the world without at times feeling dissatisfied with himself. The best proof of this is to be found in the marked anxiety which men, who have succeeded in life without the aid of these accomplishments, show in securing them to their children. A young man of ingenuous mind will not wilfully deprive himself of any species of respect. He will wish to feel himself on a level with the average of the society in which he lives, though he may be ambitious of distinguishing himself only in his own immediate pursuit or occupation.

Under this conviction, the following Course of Lectures was planned. The several titles will best explain the particular subjects and purposes of each: but the main objects proposed, as the result of all, are the two following:

1. To convey, in a form best fitted to render them impressive at the time, and remembered afterwards, rules and principles of sound judgment, with a kind and degree of connected information, such as the hearers can not generally be supposed likely to form, collect, and arrange for themselves by their own unassisted studies. It might be presumption to say, that any important part of these Lectures could not be derived from books ; but none, I trust, in supposing, that the same information could not be so surely or conveniently acquired from such books as are of commonest occurrence, or with that quantity of time and attention which can be reasonably expected, or even wisely desired, of men engaged in business and the active duties of the world.

2. Under a strong persuasion that little of real value is derived by persons in general from a wide and various reading ; but still more deeply convinced as to the actual mischief of unconnected and promiscuous reading, and that it is sure, in a greater or less degree, to enervate even where it does not likewise inflate ; I hope to satisfy many an ingenuous mind, seriously interested in its own development and cultivation, how moderate a number of volumes, if only they be judiciously chosen, will suffice for the attainment of every wise and desirable purpose ; that is, in addition to those which he studies for specific and professional purposes. It is saying less than the truth to affirm, that an excellent book (and the remark holds almost equally good of a Raphael as of a Milton) is like a well-chosen and well-tended fruit-tree. Its fruits are not of one season only. With the due and natural intervals, we may recur to it year after year, and it will supply the same nourishment and the same gratification, if only we ourselves return to it with the same healthful appetite.

The subjects of the Lectures are indeed very different; but not (in the strict sense of the term) diverse ; they are various, rather than miscellaneous. There is this bond of connection common to them all,—that the mental pleasure which they are calculated to excite, is not dependent on accidents of fashion, place, or age, or the events or the customs of the day ; but commensurate with the good sense, taste, and feeling, to the cultivation of which they themselves so largely contribute, as being all in kind, though not all in the same degree, productions of genius.

What it would be arrogant to promise, I may yet be permitted to hope,—that the execution will prove correspondent and adequate to the plan. Assuredly, my best efforts have not been wanting so to select and prepare the materials, that, at the conclusion of the Lectures, an attentive auditor, who should consent to aid his future recollection by a few notes taken either during each Lecture, or soon after, would rarely feel himself, for the time to come, excluded from taking an intelligent interest in any general conversation likely to occur in mixed society.

SYLLABUS OF THE COURSE.

I. January 27, 1818.—On the manners, morals, literature, philosophy, religion, and the state of society in general, in European Christendom, from the eighth to the fifteenth century (that is, from A.D. 700, to A.D. 1400), more particularly in reference to England, France, Italy, and Germany; in other words, a portrait of the so-called dark ages of Europe.

II. January 30.—On the tales and metrical romances common, for the most part, to England, Germany, and the north of France, and on the English songs and ballads, continued to the reign of Charles I. A few selections will be made from the Swedish, Danish, and German languages, translated for the purpose by the Lecturer.

III. February 3.—Chaucer and Spenser; of Petrarch; of Ariosto, Pulei, and Boiardo.

IV. V. VI. February 6, 10, 13.—On the dramatic works of Shakspeare. In these Lectures will be comprised the substance of Mr. Coleridge's former courses on the same subject, enlarged and varied by subsequent study and reflection.

VII. February 17.—On Ben Jonson, Beaumont and Fletcher, and Massinger; with the probable causes of the cessation of dramatic poetry in England with Shirley and Otway, soon after the restoration of Charles II.

VIII. February 20.—Of the life and all the works of Cervantes, but chiefly of his Don Quixote. The ridicule of knight errantry shown to have been but a secondary object in the mind of the author, and not the principal cause of the delight which the work continues to give to all nations, and under all the revolutions of manners and opinions.

IX. February 24.—On Rabelais, Swift, and Sterne: on the

nature and constituents of genuine Humor, and on the distinctions of the Humorous from the Witty, the Fanciful, the Droll, and the Old.

X. February 27.—Of Donne, Dante, and Milton.

XI. March 3.—On the Arabian Nights' Entertainments, and on the romantic use of the supernatural in poetry, and in works of fiction not poetical. On the conditions and regulations under which such books may be employed advantageously in the earlier periods of education.

XII. March 6.—On tales of witches, apparitions, &c. as distinguished from the magic and magicians of Asiatic origin. The probable sources of the former, and of the belief in them in certain ages and classes of men. Criteria by which mistaken and exaggerated facts may be distinguished from absolute falsehood and imposture. Lastly, the causes of the terror and interest which stories of ghosts and witches inspire, in early life at least, whether believed or not.

XIII. March 10.—On color, sound, and form, in Nature, as connected with poesy: the word "Poesy" used as the generic or class term, including poetry, music, painting, statuary, and ideal architecture, as its species. The reciprocal relations of poetry and philosophy to each other; and of both to religion, and the moral sense.

XIV. March 13.—On the corruptions of the English language since the reign of Queen Anne in our style of writing prose. A few easy rules for the attainment of a manly, unaffected, and pure language, in our genuine mother tongue, whether for the purpose of writing, oratory, or conversation.

LECTURE I.*

GENERAL CHARACTER OF THE GOTHIC MIND IN THE MIDDLE AGES.

Mr. Coleridge began by treating of the races of mankind as descended from Shem, Ham, and Japhet, and therein of the early condition of man in his antique form. He then dwelt on the

* From Mr. Green's note taken at the delivery.—*Ed.*

pre-eminence of the Greeks in Art and Philosophy, and noticed the suitableness of polytheism to small, insulated states, in which patriotism acted as a substitute for religion, in destroying or suspending self. Afterwards, in consequence of the extension of the Roman empire, some universal or common spirit became necessary for the conservation of the vast body, and this common spirit was, in fact, produced in Christianity. The causes of the decline of the Roman empire were in operation long before the time of the actual overthrow; that overthrow had been foreseen by many eminent Romans, especially by Seneca. In fact, there was under the empire an Italian and a German party in Rome, and in the end the latter prevailed.

He then proceeded to describe the generic character of the Northern nations, and defined it as an independence of the whole in the freedom of the individual, noticing their respect for women, and their consequent chivalrous spirit in war; and how evidently the participation in the general council laid the foundation of the representative form of government, the only rational mode of preserving individual liberty in opposition to the licentious democracy of the ancient republics.

He called our attention to the peculiarity of their art, and showed how it entirely depended on a symbolical expression of the infinite,—which is not vastness, nor immensity, nor perfection, but whatever can not be circumscribed within the limits of actual, sensuous being. In the ancient art, on the contrary, every thing was finite and material. Accordingly, sculpture was not attempted by the Gothic races till the ancient specimens were discovered, whilst painting and architecture were of native growth amongst them. In the earliest specimens of the paintings of modern ages, as in those of Giotto and his associates in the cemetery at Pisa, this complexity, variety, and symbolical character are evident, and are more fully developed in the mightier works of Michel Angelo and Raffael. The contemplation of the works of antique art excites a feeling of elevated beauty, and exalted notions of the human self; but the Gothic architecture impresses the beholder with a sense of self-annihilation; he becomes, as it were, a part of the work contemplated. An endless complexity and variety are united into one whole, the plan of which is not distinct from the execution. A Gothic cathedral is the petrifaction of our religion. The only work of truly modern sculpture is the Moses of Michael Angelo.

The Northern nations were prepared by their own previous religion for Christianity ; they, for the most part, received it gladly, and it took root as in a native soil. The deference to woman, characteristic of the Gothic races, combined itself with devotion in the idea of the Virgin Mother, and gave rise to many beautiful associations.*

Mr. C. remarked how Gothic an instrument in origin and character the organ was.

He also enlarged on the influence of female character on our education, the first impressions of our childhood being derived from women. Amongst oriental nations, he said, the only distinction was between lord and slave. With the antique Greeks, the will of every one conflicting with the will of all, produced licentiousness; with the modern descendants from the northern stocks, both these extremes were shut out, to reappear mixed and condensed into this principle or temper ;—submission, but with free choice, illustrated in chivalrous devotion to women as such, in attachment to the sovereign, &c.

LECTURE II.†

GENERAL CHARACTER OF THE GOTHIC LITERATURE AND ART.

In my last lecture I stated that the descendants of Japhet and Shem peopled Europe and Asia, fulfilling in their distribution the prophecies of Scripture, while the descendants of Ham passed into Africa, there also actually verifying the interdiction pronounced against them. The Keltic and Teutonic nations occupied that part of Europe, which is now France, Britain, Germany, Sweden, Denmark, &c. They were in general a hardy race,

* The reader may compare the last two paragraphs with the first of Schlegel's Prelections on Dramatic Art and Literature—Vol. i. pp. 10–16. 2d. edit.—and with Schelling *Ueber das Verhältniss der bildenden Künste*, p. 377 ; though the resemblance in thought is but general.

† From Mr. William Hammond's note taken at the delivery.—*Ed.*

possessing great fortitude, and capable of great endurance. The Romans slowly conquered the more southerly portion of their tribes, and succeeded only by their superior arts, their policy, and better discipline. After a time, when the Goths,—to use the name of the noblest and most historical of the Teutonic tribes,—had acquired some knowledge of these arts from mixing with their conquerors, they invaded the Roman territories. The hardy habits, the steady perseverance, the better faith of the enduring Goth rendered him too formidable an enemy for the corrupt Roman, who was more inclined to purchase the subjection of his enemy, than to go through the suffering necessary to secure it. The conquest of the Romans gave to the Goths the Christian religion as it was then existing in Italy; and the light and graceful building of Grecian, or Roman-Greek order, became singularly combined with the massy architecture of the Goths, as wild and varied as the forest vegetation which it resembled. The Greek art is beautiful. When I enter a Greek Church, my eye is charmed, and my mind elated; I feel exalted, and proud that I am a man. But the Gothic art is sublime. On entering a cathedral, I am filled with devotion and with awe; I am lost to the actualities that surround me, and my whole being expands into the infinite; earth and air, nature and art, all swell up into eternity, and the only sensible impression left, is 'that I am nothing!' This religion, while it tended to soften the manners of the Northern tribes, was at the same time highly congenial to their nature. The Goths are free from the stain of hero-worship. Gazing on their rugged mountains, surrounded by impassable forests, accustomed to gloomy seasons, they lived in the bosom of nature, and worshipped an invisible and unknown deity. Firm in his faith, domestic in his habits, the life of the Goth was simple and dignified, yet tender and affectionate.

The Greeks were remarkable for complacency and completion; they delighted in whatever pleased the eye; to them it was not enough to have merely the idea of a divinity, they must have it placed before them, shaped in the most perfect symmetry, and presented with the nicest judgment: and if we look upon any Greek production of art, the beauty of its parts, and the harmony of their union, the complete and complacent effect of the whole, are the striking characteristics. It is the same in their poetry. In Homer you have a poem perfect in its form, whether originally so, or from the labor of after-critics, I know not; his descriptions are pictures brought vividly before you, and as far as the eye and understanding are concerned, I am indeed gratified. But if I wish my feelings to be affected, if I wish my heart to be touched, if I wish to melt into sentiment and tenderness, I must turn to the heroic songs of the Goths, to the poetry of the middle ages. The worship of statues in Greece had, in a civil sense, its advantage, and disadvantage; advantage, in promoting statuary and the arts; disadvantage, in bringing their gods too much on a level with human beings, and thence depriving them of their dignity, and gradually giving rise to skepticism and ridicule. But no statue, no artificial emblem, could satisfy the Northman's mind; the dark, wild imagery of nature which surrounded him, and the freedom of his life, gave his mind a tendency to the infinite, so that he found rest in that which presented no end, and derived satisfaction from that which was indistinct.

We have few and uncertain vestiges of Gothic literature till the time of Theodoric, who encouraged his subjects to write, and who made a collection of their poems. These consisted chiefly of heroic songs, sung at the Court; for at that time this was the custom. Charlemagne, in the beginning of the ninth century, greatly encouraged letters, and made a further collection of the poems of his time, among which were several epic poems of great merit; or rather in strictness there was a vast cycle of heroic poems, or minstrelsies, from and out of which separate poems were composed. The form of poetry was, however, for the most part, the metrical romance and heroic tale. Charlemagne's army, or a large division of it, was utterly destroyed in the Pyrenees, when returning from a successful attack on the Arabs of Navarre and Arragon; yet the name of Roncesvalles became famous in the songs of the Gothic poets. The Greeks and Romans would not have done this; they would not have recorded in heroic verse the death and defeat of their fellow-countrymen. But the Goths, firm in their faith, with a constancy not to be shaken, celebrated those brave men who died for their religion and their country! What, though they had been defeated, they died without fear, as they had lived without reproach; they left no stain on their names, for they fell fighting for their God, their liberty, and their rights; and the song that sang that day's reverse animated them to future victory and certain vengeance.

I must now turn to our great monarch, Alfred, one of the most august characters that any age has ever produced; and when I picture him after the toils of government and the dangers of battle, seated by a solitary lamp, translating the holy scriptures into the Saxon tongue,—when I reflect on his moderation in success, on his fortitude and perseverance in difficulty and defeat, and on the wisdom and extensive nature of his legislation, I am really at a loss which part of this great man's character most to admire. Yet above all, I see the grandeur, the freedom, the mildness, the domestic unity, the universal character of the middle ages condensed into Alfred's glorious institution of the trial by jury. I gaze upon it as the immortal symbol of that age;—an age called indeed dark; but how could that age be considered dark, which solved the difficult problem of universal liberty, freed man from the shackles of tyranny, and subjected his actions to the decision of twelve of his fellow-countrymen? The liberty of the Greeks was a phenomenon, a meteor, which blazed for a short time, and then sank into eternal darkness. It was a combination of most opposite materials, slavery and liberty. Such can neither be happy nor lasting. The Goths on the other hand said, You shall be our Emperor; but we must be Princes on our own estates, and over them you shall have no power! The Vassals said to their Prince, We will serve you in your wars, and defend your castle; but we must have liberty in our own circle, our cottage, our cattle, our proportion of land. The Cities said, We acknowledge you for our Emperor; but we must have our walls and our strongholds, and be governed by our own laws. Thus all combined, yet all were separate; all served, yet all were free. Such a government could not exist in a dark age. Our ancestors may not indeed have been deep in the metaphysics of the schools; they may not have shone in the fine arts; but much knowledge of human nature, much practical wisdom must have existed amongst them, when this admirable constitution was formed; and I believe it is a decided truth, though certainly an awful lesson, that nations are not the most happy at the time when literature and the arts flourish the most among them.

The translations I had promised in my syllabus I shall defer to the end of the course, when I shall give a single lecture of recitations illustrative of the different ages of poetry. There is one Northern tale I will relate, as it is one from which Shakspeare derived that strongly marked and extraordinary scene between Richard III. and the Lady Anne. It may not be equal to that in strength and genius, but it is, undoubtedly, superior in decorum and delicacy.

A Knight had slain a Prince, the lord of a strong castle, in combat. He afterwards contrived to get into the castle, where he obtained an interview with the Princess's attendant, whose life he had saved in some encounter; he told her of his love for her mistress, and won her to his interest. She then slowly and gradually worked on her mistress's mind, spoke of the beauty of his person, the fire of his eyes, the sweetness of his voice, his valor in the field, his gentleness in the court; in short, by watching her opportunities, she at last filled the Princess's soul with this one image; she became restless; sleep forsook her; her curiosity to see this Knight became strong; but her maid still deferred the interview, till at length she confessed she was in love with him;—the Knight is then introduced, and the nuptials are quickly celebrated.

In this age there was a tendency in writers to the droll and the grotesque, and in the little dramas which at that time existed, there were singular instances of these. It was the disease of the age. It is a remarkable fact that Luther and Melancthon, the great religious reformers of that day, should have strongly recommended, for the education of children, dramas, which at present would be considered highly indecorous, if not bordering on a deeper sin. From one which they particularly recommended, I will give a few extracts; more I should not think it right to do. The play opens with Adam and Eve washing and dressing their children to appear before the Lord, who is coming from heaven to hear them repeat the Lord's Prayer, Belief, &c. In the next scene the Lord appears seated like a schoolmaster, with the children standing round, when Cain, who is behind hand, and a sad pickle, comes running in with a bloody nose and his hat on. Adam says, "What, with your hat on!" Cain then goes up to shake hands with the Almighty, when Adam says (giving him a cuff), "Ah, would you give your left hand to the Lord?" At length Cain takes his place in the class, and it becomes his turn to say the Lord's Prayer. At this time the Devil (a constant attendant at that time) makes his appearance, and getting behind Cain, whispers in his ear; instead of the Lord's Prayer, Cain gives it so changed by the transposition of the words, that the meaning is reversed; yet this is so artfully done by the author, that it is exactly as an obstinate child would answer, who knows his lesson, yet does not choose to say it. In the last scene, horses in rich trappings and carriages covered with gold are introduced, and the good children are to ride in them and be Lord Mayors, Lords, &c.; Cain and the bad ones are to be made cobblers and tinkers, and only to associate with such.

This, with numberless others, was written by Hans Sachs. Our simple ancestors, firm in their faith, and pure in their morals, were only amused by these pleasantries, as they seemed to them, and neither they nor the reformers feared their having any influence hostile to religion. When I was many years back in the north of Germany, there were several innocent superstitions in practice. Among others, at Christmas presents used to be given to the children by the parents, and they were delivered on Christmas-day by a person who personated, and was supposed by the children to be, Christ: early on Christmas morning he called, knocking loudly at the door, and (having received his instructions) left presents for the good and a rod for the bad. Those who have since been in Germany have found this custom relinquished; it was considered profane and irrational. Yet they have not found the children better, nor the mothers more careful of their offspring; they have not found their devotion more fervent, their faith more strong, nor their morality more pure.*

LECTURE III.

THE TROUBADOURS—BOCCACCIO—PETRARCH—PULCI—CHAUCER—SPENSER.

The last Lecture was allotted to an investigation into the origin and character of a species of poetry, the least influenced of any by the literature of Greece and Rome,—that in which

* See this custom of Knecht Rupert more minutely described in Mr. Coleridge's own letter from Germany, published in The Friend, II. p. 335. *Ed.*

the portion contributed by the Gothic conquerors, the predilections and general tone or habit of thought and feeling, brought by our remote ancestors with them from the forests of Germany, or the deep dells and rocky mountains of Norway, are the most prominent. In the present Lecture I must introduce you to a species of poetry, which had its birth-place near the centre of Roman glory, and in which, as might be anticipated, the influences of the Greek and Roman muse are far more conspicuous, —as great, indeed, as the efforts of intentional imitation on the part of the poets themselves could render them. But happily for us and for their own fame, the intention of the writers as men is often at complete variance with the genius of the same men as poets. To the force of their intention we owe their mythological ornaments, and the greater definiteness of their imagery; and their passion for the beautiful, the voluptuous, and the artificial, we must in part attribute to the same intention, but in part likewise to their natural dispositions and tastes. For the same climate and many of the same circumstances were acting on them, which had acted on the great classics, whom they were endeavoring to imitate. But the love of the marvellous, the deeper sensibility, the higher reverence for womanhood, the characteristic spirit of sentiment and courtesy,—these were the heirlooms of nature, which still regained the ascendant, whenever the use of the living mother-language enabled the inspired poet to appear instead of the toilsome scholar.

From this same union, in which the soul (if I may dare so express myself) was Gothic, while the outward forms and a majority of the words themselves, were the reliques of the Roman, arose the Romance, or romantic language, in which the Troubadours or Love-singers of Provence sang and wrote, and the different dialects of which have been modified into the modern Italian, Spanish, and Portuguese; while the language of the Trouveurs, Trouveres, or Norman-French poets, forms the intermediate link between the Romance or modified Roman, and the Teutonic, including the Dutch, Danish, Swedish, and the upper and lower German, as being the modified Gothic. And as the northernmost extreme of the Norman-French, or that part of the link in which it formed on the Teutonic, we must take the Norman-English minstrels and metrical romances, from the greater predominance of the Anglo-Saxon Gothic in the derivation of the words. I mean, that the language of the English metrical romance is less romanized, and has fewer words, not originally of a northern origin, than the same romances in the Norman-French; which is the more striking, because the former were for the most part translated from the latter; the authors of which seem to have eminently merited their name of Trouveres, or inventors. Thus then we have a chain with two rings or staples: —at the southern end there is the Roman, or Latin; at the northern end the Keltic, Teutonic, or Gothic; and the links beginning with the southern end, are the Romance, including the Provençal, the Italian, Spanish, and Portuguese, with their different dialects, then the Norman-French, and lastly the English.

My object in adverting to the Italian poets, is not so much for their own sakes, in which point of view Dante and Ariosto alone would have required separate Lectures, but for the elucidation of the merits of our countrymen, as to what extent we must consider them as fortunate imitators of their Italian predecessors, and in what points they have the higher claims of original genius. Of Dante, I am to speak elsewhere. Of Boccaccio, who has little interest as a metrical poet in any respect, and none for my present purpose, except, perhaps, as the reputed inventor or introducer of the octave stanza in his Teseide, it will be sufficient to say, that we owe to him the subjects of numerous poems taken from his famous tales, the happy art of narration, and the still greater merit of a depth and fineness in the workings of the passions, in which last excellence, as likewise in the wild and imaginative character of the situations, his almost neglected romances appear to me greatly to excel his far-famed Decameron. To him, too, we owe the more doubtful merit of having introduced into the Italian prose, and by the authority of his name and the influence of his example, more or less throughout Europe, the long interwoven periods, and architectural structure which arose from the very nature of their language in the Greek writers, but which already in the Latin orators and historians, had betrayed a species of effort, a foreign something, which had been superinduced on the language, instead of growing out of it; and which was far too alien from that individualizing and confederating, yet not blending, character of the North, to become permanent, although its magnificence and stateliness were objects of admiration and occasional imitation. This style diminished the control of the writer over the inner feelings of men, and created too great a chasm between the body and the life; and hence especially it was abandoned by Luther.

But lastly, to Boccaccio's sanction we must trace a large portion of the mythological pedantry and incongruous paganisms, which for so long a period deformed the poetry, even of the truest poets. To such an extravagance did Boccaccio himself carry this folly, that in a romance of chivalry he has uniformly styled God the Father Jupiter, our Saviour Apollo, and the Evil Being Pluto. But for this there might be some excuse pleaded. I dare make none for the gross and disgusting licentiousness, the daring profaneness, which rendered the Decameron of Boccaccio the parent of a hundred worse children, fit to be classed among the enemies of the human race; which poisons Ariosto—(for that I may not speak oftener than necessary of so odious a subject, I mention it here once for all)—which interposes a painful mixture in the humor of Chaucer, and which has once or twice seduced even our pure-minded Spenser into a grossness, as heterogeneous from the spirit of his great poem, as it was alien to the delicacy of his morals.

PETRARCH.

Born at Arezzo, 1304.—Died 1374.

Petrarch was the final blossom and perfection of the Troubadours.

NOTES ON PETRARCH'S* SONNETS, CANZONES, &c.

VOL. I.

GOOD.

Sonnet. 1. Voi, ch' ascoltate, &c.
7. La gola, e 'l sonno, &c.
11. Se la mia vita, &c.
12. Quando fra l'altre, &c.

* These notes, by Mr. C., are written in a Petrarch in my possession, and are of some date before 1812. It is hoped that they will not seem ill placed here.—*Ed.*

18. Vergognando talor, &c.
25. Quanto più m' avvicino, &c.
28. Solo e pensoso, &c.
29. S' io credessi, &c.
CANZ. 14. Sì è debile il filo, &c.

PLEASING.

BALL. 1. Lassare il velo, &c.
CANZ. 1. Nel dolce tempo, &c.

This poem was imitated by our old Herbert;* it is ridiculous in the thoughts, but simple and sweet in diction.

DIGNIFIED.

CANZ. 2. O aspettata in ciel, &c.
9. Gentil mia Donna, &c.

The first half of this ninth canzone is exquisite; and in canzone 8, the nine lines beginning

O poggi, O valli, &c.

to *cura*, are expressed with vigor and chastity.

CANZ. 9. Daquel dì innanzi a me medesmo piacqui
Empiendo d'un pensier' alto, e soave
Quel core, *ond' hanno i begli occhi la chiave.*

Note.—O that the Pope would take these eternal keys, which so forever turn the bolts on the finest passages of true passion!

VOL. II.

CANZ. 1. Che debb' io far? &c.

Very good; but not equal, I think, to Canzone 2,

Amor, se vuoi ch' i' torni, &c.

though less faulty. With the omission of half-a-dozen conceits and Petrarchisms of *hooks*, *baits*, *flames*, and *torches*, this second canzone is a bold and impassioned lyric, and leaves no doubt in my mind of Petrarch's having possessed a true poetic genius. *Utinam deleri possint sequentia:*—

* If George Herbert is meant, I can find nothing like an imitation of this canzone in his poems.—*Ed.*

L. 17—19. ——— e la soave fiamma
Ch' ancor, lasso! m' infiamma
Essendo spenta, or che fea dunque ardendo?

L. 54—56. ——— ov' erano a tutt' ore
Disposti gli ami ov' io fui preso, e l'esca
Ch' i' bramo sempre.

L. 76—79. ——— onde l' accese
Saette uscivan d' invisibil foco,
E ragion temean poco;
Chè contra 'l ciel non val difesa umana.

And the lines 86, 87.
Poser' in dubbio, a cui
Devesse il pregio di più laude darsi—

are rather flatly worded.

LUIGI PULCI.

Born at Florence, 1431.—Died about 1487.

Pulci was of one of the noblest families in Florence, reported to be one of the Frankish stocks which remained in that city after the departure of Charlemagne:—

Pulcia Gallorum soboles descendit in urbem,
Clara quidem bello, sacris nec inhospita Musis.
Verino de illustrat. Cort. Flor. ii. v. 118.

Members of this family were five times elected to the Priorate, one of the highest honors of the republic. Pulci had two brothers, and one of their wives, Antonia, who were all poets:—

Carminibus patriis notissima Pulcia proles;
Quis non hanc urbem Musarum dicat amicam,
Si tres producat fratres domus una poetas?
Ib. ii. v. 241.

Luigi married Lucrezia di Uberto, of the Albizzi family, and was intimate with the great men of his time, but more especially with Angelo Politian, and Lorenzo the Magnificent. His Morgante has been attributed, in part at least,* to the assistance of Marsilius Ficinus, and by others the whole has been attributed to Politian. The first conjecture is utterly improbable; the last

* Meaning the 25th canto.—*Ed.*

is possible, indeed, on account of the licentiousness of the poem; but there are no direct grounds for believing it. The Morgante Maggiore is the first proper romance; although, perhaps, Pulci had the Teseide before him. The story is taken from the fabulous history of Turpin; and if the author had any distinct object, it seems to have been that of making himself merry with the absurdities of the old romancers. The Morgante sometimes makes you think of Rabelais. It contains the most remarkable guess or allusion upon the subject of America that can be found in any book published before the discovery.* The well-known passage in the tragic Seneca is not to be compared with it. The *copia verborum* of the mother Florentine tongue, and the easiness

* The reference is, of course, to the following stanzas:—

Disse Astarotte: un error lungo e fioco
Per molti secol non ben conosciuto,
Fa che si dice d' Ercol le colonne,
E che più là molti periti sonne.
Sappi che questa opinione è vana;
Perchè più oltre navicar si puote,
Però che l' acqua in ogni parte è piana,
Benchè la terra abbi forma di ruote:
Era più grossa allor la gente humana;
Talche potrebbe arrosirne le gote
Ercule ancor d' aver posti que' segni,
Perchè più oltre passeranno i legni.
E puossi andar giù ne l' altro emisperio,
Però che al centro ogni cosa reprime;
Sì che la terra per divin misterio
Sospesa sta fra le stelle sublime,
E là giù son città, castella, e imperio;
Ma nol cognobbon quelle genti prime:
Vedi che il sol di camminar s' affretta,
Dove io ti dico che là giù s' aspetta.
E come un segno surge in Oriente,
Un altro cade con mirabil arte,
Come si vede qua ne l' Occidente,
Però che il ciel giustamente comparte;
Antipodi appellata è quella gente;
Adora il sole e Jupiterre e Marte,
E piante e animal come voi hanno,
E spesso insieme gran battaglie fanno.

C. xxv. st. 228, &c.

The Morgante was printed in 1488.—*Ed.* Another very curious antici-

of his style, afterwards brought to perfection by Berni, are the chief merits of Pulci; his chief demerit is his heartless spirit of jest and buffoonery, by which sovereigns and their courtiers were flattered by the degradation of nature, and the *impossibilification* of a pretended virtue.

CHAUCER.

Born in London, 1328.—Died 1400.*

CHAUCER must be read with an eye to the Norman-French Trouveres, of whom he is the best representative in English. He had great powers of invention. As in Shakspeare, his characters represent classes, but in a different manner; Shakspeare's characters are the representatives of the interior nature of humanity, in which some element has become so predominant as to destroy the health of the mind; whereas Chaucer's are rather representatives of classes of manners. He is therefore more led to individualize in a mere personal sense. Observe Chaucer's love of nature; and how happily the subject of his main work is chosen. When you reflect that the company in the Decameron have retired to a place of safety, from the raging of a pestilence, their mirth provokes a sense of their unfeelingness; whereas in Chaucer nothing of this sort occurs, and the scheme of a party on a pilgrimage, with different ends and occupations, aptly allows of the greatest variety of expression in the tales.

SPENSER.

Born in London, 1553.—Died 1599.

THERE is this difference, among many others, betwen Shakspeare and Spenser:—Shakspeare is never colored by the customs of his age; what appears of contemporary character in him

pation, said to have been first noticed by Amerigo Vespucci, occurs in Dante's *Purgatorio:*

I mi volsi a man destra e posi mente
All 'altro polo: e vidi quattro stelle
Non viste mai, fuor ch' alla prima gente.
C. l. l. 22–4.

* From Mr. Green's note.—*Ed.*

is merely negative; it is just not something else. He has none of the fictitious realities of the classics, none of the grotesquenesses of chivalry, none of the allegory of the middle ages; there is no sectarianism either of politics or religion, no miser, no witch,—no common witch,—no astrology—nothing impermanent of however long duration; but he stands like the yew-tree in Lorton vale, which has known so many ages that it belongs to none in particular; a living image of endless self-reproduction, like the immortal tree of Malabar. In Spenser the spirit of chivalry is entirely predominant, although with a much greater infusion of the poet's own individual self into it than is found in any other writer. He has the wit of the southern with the deeper inwardness of the northern genius.

No one can appreciate Spenser without some reflection on the nature of allegorical writing. The mere etymological meaning of the word, allegory,—to talk of one thing and thereby convey another,—is too wide. The true sense is this,—the employment of one set of agents and images to convey in disguise a moral meaning, with a likeness to the imagination, but with a difference to the understanding,—those agents and images being so combined as to form a homogeneous whole. This distinguishes it from metaphor, which is part of an allegory. But allegory is not properly distinguishable from fable, otherwise than as the first includes the second, as a genus its species; for in a fable there must be nothing but what is universally known and acknowledged, but in an allegory there may be that which is new and not previously admitted. The pictures of the great masters, especially of the Italian schools, are genuine allegories. Amongst the classics, the multitude of their gods either precluded allegory altogether, or else made every thing allegory, as in the Hesiodic Theogonia; for you can scarcely distinguish between power and the personification of power. The Cupid and Psyche of, or found in, Apuleius, is a phænomenon. It is the Platonic mode of accounting for the fall of man. The Battle of the Soul* by Prudentius is an early instance of Christian allegory.

Narrative allegory is distinguished from mythology as reality from symbôl; it is, in short, the proper intermedium between person and personification. Where it is too strongly individualized, it ceases to be allegory; this is often felt in the Pilgrim's

* Psychomachia.—*Ed.*

Progress, where the characters are real persons with nick-names. Perhaps one of the most curious warnings against another attempt at narrative allegory on a great scale, may be found in Tasso's account of what he himself intended in and by his Jerusalem Delivered.

As characteristic of Spenser, I would call your particular attention in the first place to the indescribable sweetness and fluent projection of his verse, very clearly distinguishable from the deeper and more interwoven harmonies of Shakspeare and Milton. This stanza is a good instance of what I mean :—

Yet she, most faithfull ladie, all this while
Forsaken, wofull, solitarie mayd,
Far from all peoples preace, as in exile,
In wildernesse and wastfull deserts strayd
To seeke her knight; who, subtily betrayd
Through that late vision which th' enchaunter wrought,
Had her abandond; she, of nought affrayd,
Through woods and wastnes wide him daily sought,
Yet wished tydinges none of him unto her brought.

F. Qu. B. i. c. 3, st. 3.

2. Combined with this sweetness and fluency, the scientific construction of the metre of the Faery Queene is very noticeable. One of Spenser's arts is that of alliteration, and he uses it with great effect in doubling the impression of an image :—

In *w*ildernesse and *w*astful deserts—
Through *w*oods and *w*astnes *w*ilde,—
They passe the bitter waves of Acheron,
Where many soules sit *w*ailing *w*oefully,
And come to *f*iery *f*lood of *Ph*legeton,
Whereas the damned ghosts in torments fry,
And with *s*harp *s*hrilling *s*hrieks doth bootlesse cry,—&c.

He is particularly given to an alternate alliteration, which is, perhaps, when well used, a great secret in melody :—

A *r*amping lyon *r*ushed suddenly,—
And *s*ad to *s*ee her *s*orrowful constraint,—
And on the grasse her *d*aintie *l*imbes *d*id *l*ay,—&c.

You can not read a page of the Faery Queene, if you read for that purpose, without perceiving the intentional alliterativeness of the words ; and yet so skilfully is this managed, that it never strikes any unwarned ear as artificial, or other than the result of the necessary movement of the verse.

3. Spenser displays great skill in harmonizing his descriptions of external nature and actual incidents with the allegorical character and epic activity of the poem. Take these two beautiful passages as illustrations of what I mean :—

By this the northerne wagoner had set
His sevenfol teme behind the stedfast starre
That was in ocean waves yet never wet,
But firme is fixt, and sendeth light from farre
To all that in the wide deepe wandring arre ;
And chearefull chaunticlere with his note shrill
Had warned once, that Phœbus' fiery carre
In hast was climbing up the easterne hill,
Full envious that Night so long his roome did fill;

When those accursed messengers of hell,
That feigning dreame, and that faire-forged spright
Came, &c. B. i. c. 2, st. 1.

* * *

At last, the golden orientall gate
Of greatest Heaven gan to open fayre ;
And Phœbus, fresh as brydegrome to his mate,
Came dauncing forth, shaking his deawie hayre ;
And hurld his glistring beams through gloomy ayre.
Which when the wakeful Elfe perceiv'd, streightway
He started up, and did him selfe prepayre
In sunbright armes and battailons array ;
For with that Pagan proud he combat will that day.

Ib. c. 5, st. 2.

Observe also the exceeding vividness of Spenser's descriptions. They are not, in the true sense of the word, picturesque ; but are composed of a wondrous series of images, as in our dreams. Compare the following passage with any thing you may remember *in pari materia* in Milton or Shakspeare :—

His haughtie helmet, horrid all with gold,
Both glorious brightnesse and great terrour bredd;
For all the crest a dragon did enfold
With greedie pawes, and over all did spredd
His golden winges; his dreadfull hideous hedd,
Close couched on the bever, seemd to throw
From flaming mouth bright sparkles fiery redd,
That suddeine horrour to faint hartes did show;
And scaly tayle was stretcht adowne his back full low.

Upon the top of all his loftie crest
A bounch of haires discolourd diversly,
With sprinkled pearle and gold full richly drest,
Did shake, and seemd to daunce for jollitie;
Like to an almond tree ymounted hye
On top of greene Selinis all alone,
With blossoms brave bedecked daintily,
Whose tender locks do tremble every one
At everie little breath that under heaven is blowne.

Ib. c. 7, st. 31–2.

4. You will take especial note of the marvellous independence and true imaginative absence of all particular space or time in the Faery Queene. It is in the domains neither of history or geography; it is ignorant of all artificial boundary, all material obstacles; it is truly in land of Faery, that is, of mental space. The poet has placed you in a dream, a charmed sleep, and you neither wish, nor have the power, to inquire where you are, or how you got there. It reminds me of some lines of my own:—

Oh! would to Alla!
The raven or the sea-mew were appointed
To bring me food!—or rather that my soul
Might draw in life from the universal air!
It were a lot divine in some small skiff
Along some ocean's boundless solitude
To float forever with a careless course
And think myself the only being alive!

Remorse, Act iv. sc. 3.

Indeed Spenser himself, in the conduct of his great poem, may be represented under the same image, his symbolizing purpose being his mariner's compass:—

As pilot well expert in perilous wave,
That to a stedfast starre his course hath bent,
When foggy mistes or cloudy tempests have
The faithfull light of that faire lampe yblent,
And coverd Heaven with hideous dreriment;
Upon his card and compas firmes his eye,
The maysters of his long experiment,
And to them does the steddy helme apply,
Bidding his winged vessell fairely forward fly.

B. ii. c. 7, st. 1.

So the poet through the realms of allegory.

5. You should note the quintessential character of Christian

chivalry in all his characters, but more especially in his women. The Greeks, except, perhaps, in Homer, seem to have had no way of making their women interesting, but by unsexing them, as in the instances of the tragic Medea, Electra, &c. Contrast such characters with Spenser's Una, who exhibits no prominent feature, has no particularization, but produces the same feeling that a statue does, when contemplated at a distance :—

From her fayre head her fillet she undight,
And layd her stole aside : her angels face,
As the great eye of Heaven, shyned bright,
And made a sunshine in the shady place ;
Did never mortal eye behold such heavenly grace.
B. i. c. 3, st. 4.

6. In Spenser we see the brightest and purest form of that nationality which was so common a characteristic of our elder poets. There is nothing unamiable, nothing contemptuous of others, in it. To glorify their country—to elevate England into a queen, an empress of the heart—this was their passion and object ; and how dear and important an object it was or may be, let Spain, in the recollection of her Cid, declare ! There is a great magic in national names. What a damper to all interest is a list of native East Indian merchants ! Unknown names are non-conductors ; they stop all sympathy. No one of our poets has touched this string more exquisitely than Spenser ; especially in his chronicle of the British Kings (B. ii. c. 10), and the marriage of the Thames with the Medway (B. iv. c. 11), in both which passages the mere names constitute half the pleasure we receive. To the same feeling we must in particular attribute Spenser's sweet reference to Ireland :—

Ne thence the Irishe rivers absent were ;
Sith no lesse famous than the rest they be, &c. Ib.
*   *   *   *   *   *   *   *
And Mulla mine, whose waves I whilom taught to weep.
Ib.

And there is a beautiful passage of the same sort in the Colin Clout's Come Home Again :—

" One day," quoth he, " I sat, as was my trade,
Under the foot of Mole," &c.

Lastly, the great and prevailing character of Spenser's mind is fancy under the conditions of imagination, as an ever-present but not always active power. He has an imaginative fancy, but he has not imagination, in kind or degree, as Shakspeare and Milton have ; the boldest effort of his powers in this way is the character of Talus.* Add to this a feminine tenderness and almost maidenly purity of feeling, and above all, a deep moral earnestness which produces a believing sympathy and acquiescence in the reader, and you have a tolerably adequate view of Spenser's intellectual being.

LECTURE VII.

BEN JONSON, BEAUMONT AND FLETCHER, AND MASSINGER

A CONTEMPORARY is rather an ambiguous term, when applied to authors. It may simply mean that one man lived and wrote while another was yet alive, however deeply the former may have been indebted to the latter as his model. There have been instances in the literary world that might remind a botanist of a singular sort of parasite plant, which rises above ground, independent and unsupported, an apparent original; but trace its roots, and you will find the fibres all terminating in the root of another plant at an unsuspected distance, which, perhaps, from want of sun and genial soil, and the loss of sap, has scarcely been able to peep above the ground.—Or the word may mean those whose compositions were contemporaneous in such a sense as to preclude all likelihood of the one having borrowed from the other. In the latter sense, I should call Ben Jonson a contemporary of Shakspeare, though he long survived him ; while I should prefer the phrase of immediate successors for Beaumont and Fletcher, and Massinger, though they too were Shakspeare's contemporaries in the former sense.

* B. 5. Legend of Artegall.—*Ed.*

BEN JONSON.*

Born, 1574.—Died, 1637.

BEN JONSON is original; he is, indeed, the only one of the great dramatists of that day who was not either directly produced, or very greatly modified, by Shakspeare. In truth, he differs from our great master in every thing—in form and in substance—and betrays no tokens of his proximity. He is not original in the same way as Shakspeare is original; but after a fashion of his own, Ben Jonson is most truly original.

The characters in his plays are, in the strictest sense of the term, abstractions. Some very prominent feature is taken from the whole man, and that single feature or humor is made the basis upon which the entire character is built up. Ben Jonson's *dramatis personæ* are almost as fixed as the masks of the ancient actors; you know from the first scene—sometimes from the list of names—exactly what every one of them is to be. He was a very accurately observing man; but he cared only to observe what was external or open to, and likely to impress, the senses. He individualizes, not so much, if at all, by the exhibition of moral or intellectual differences, as by the varieties and contrasts of manners, modes of speech and tricks of temper; as in such characters as Puntarvolo, Bobadill, &c.

I believe there is not one whim or affectation in common life noted in any memoir of that age which may not be found drawn and framed in some corner or other of Ben Jonson's dramas; and they have this merit, in common with Hogarth's prints, that not a single circumstance is introduced in them which does not play upon, and help to bring out, the dominant humor or humors of the piece. Indeed I ought very particularly to call your attention to the extraordinary skill shown by Ben Jonson in contriving situations for the display of his characters.† In fact, his care and anxiety in this matter led him to do what scarcely any of the dramatists of that age did—that is, invent his plots. It is not a first perusal that suffices for the full perception of the elaborate artifice of the plots of the Alchemist and the Silent Woman;—

* From Mr. Green's note.—*Ed.*

† "In Jonson's comic inventions," says Schlegel, "a spirit of observation is manifested more than fancy."—Vol. iv. p. 93.

that of the former is absolute perfection for a necessary entanglement, and an unexpected, yet natural, evolution

Ben Jonson exhibits a sterling English diction, and he has with great skill contrived varieties of construction; but his style is rarely sweet or harmonious, in consequence of his labor at point and strength being so evident. In all his works, in verse or prose, there is an extraordinary opulence of thought; but it is the produce of an amassing power in the author, and not of a growth from within. Indeed a large proportion of Ben Jonson's thoughts may be traced to classic or obscure modern writers, by those who are learned and curious enough to follow the steps of this robust, surly, and observing dramatist.

BEAUMONT. Born, 1586.*—Died, 1615–16.
FLETCHER. Born, 1579.—Died, 1625.

Mr. Weber, to whose taste, industry, and appropriate erudition, we owe, I will not say the best (for that would be saying little), but a good, edition of Beaumont and Fletcher, has complimented the Philaster, which he himself describes as inferior to the Maid's Tragedy by the same writers, as but little below the noblest of Shakspeare's plays, Lear, Macbeth, Othello, &c., and consequently implying the equality, at least, of the Maid's Tragedy;—and an eminent living critic,—who in the manly wit, strong sterling sense, and robust style of his original works, had presented the best possible credentials of office, as *chargé d'affaires* of literature in general,—and who by his edition of Massinger—a work in which there was more for an editor to do, and in which more was actually well done, than in any similar work within my knowledge—has proved an especial right of authority in the appreciation of dramatic poetry, and hath potentially a double voice with the public in his own right and in that of the critical synod, where, as *princeps senatus*, he possesses it by his prerogative,—has affirmed that Shakspeare's superiority to his contemporaries

* Mr. Dyce thinks that "Beaumont's birth ought to be fixed at a somewhat earlier date," because, in the Funeral Certificate on the decease of his father, dated 22d April, 1598, he is said to be *of the age of thirteen years or more;* and because "at the age of twelve, 4th February, 1596–7," according to Wood's Ath. Oxon, "he was admitted a gentleman-commoner of Broadgates Hall."

rests on his superior wit alone, while in all the other, and, as I should deem, higher excellencies of the drama, character, pathos, depth of thought, &c. he is equalled by Beaumont and Fletcher, Ben Jonson, and Massinger !*

Of wit I am engaged to treat in another Lecture. It is a genus of many species ; and at present I shall only say, that the species which is predominant in Shakspeare, is so completely Shaksperian, and in its essence so interwoven with all his other characteristic excellencies, that I am equally incapable of comprehending, both how it can be detached from his other powers, and how, being disparate in kind from the wit of contemporary dramatists, it can be compared with theirs in degree. And again —the detachment and the practicability of the comparison being granted—I should, I confess, be rather inclined to concede the contrary ;—and in the most common species of wit, and in the ordinary application of the term, to yield this particular palm to Beaumont and Fletcher, whom here and hereafter I take as one poet with two names—leaving undivided what a rare love and still rarer congeniality have united. At least, I have never been able to distinguish the presence of Fletcher during the life of Beaumont, nor the absence of Beaumont during the survival of Fletcher.

But waiving, or rather deferring this question, I protest against the remainder of the position *in toto*. And indeed, whilst I can never, I trust, show myself blind to the various merits of Jonson, Beaumont and Fletcher, and Massinger, or insensible to the greatness of the merits which they possess in common, or to the specific excellencies which give to each of the three a worth of his own—I confess, that one main object of this Lecture was to prove that Shakspeare's eminence is his own, and not that of his age ;—even as the pine-apple, the melon, and the gourd may grow on the same bed ;—yea, the same circumstances of warmth and soil may be necessary to their full development, yet do not account for the golden hue, the ambrosial flavor, the perfect shape of the pine-apple, or the tufted crown on its head. Would that those, who seek to twist it off, could but promise us in this instance to make it the germ of an equal successor !

What had a grammatical and logical consistency for the ear—what could be put together and represented to the eye—these

* See Mr. Gifford's introduction to his edition of Massinger.—*Ed.*

poets took from the ear and eye, unchecked by any intuition of an inward impossibility;—just as a man might put together a quarter of an orange, a quarter of an apple, and the like of a lemon and a pomegranate, and make it look like one round diverse-colored fruit. But nature, which works from within by evolution and assimilation according to a law, can not do so, nor could Shakspeare; for he too worked in the spirit of nature, by evolving the germ from within by the imaginative power according to an idea. For as the power of seeing is to light, so is an idea in mind to a law in nature. They are correlatives, which suppose each other.

The plays of Beaumont and Fletcher are mere aggregations without unity; in the Shaksperian drama there is a vitality which grows and evolves itself from within—a key-note which guides and controls the harmonies throughout. What is Lear?—It is storm and tempest—the thunder at first grumbling in the far horizon, then gathering around us, and at length bursting in fury over our heads—succeeded by a breaking of the clouds for a while, a last flash of lightning, the closing in of night, and the single hope of darkness! And Romeo and Juliet?—It is a spring day, gusty and beautiful in the morn, and closing like an April evening with the song of the nightingale;*—whilst Macbeth is deep and earthy—composed to the subterranean music of a troubled conscience, which converts every thing into the wild and fearful!

Doubtless from mere observation, or from the occasional similarity of the writer's own character, more or less in Beaumont and Fletcher, and other such writers will happen to be in correspondence with nature, and still more in apparent compatibility with it. But yet the false source is always discoverable, first by the gross contradictions to nature in so many other parts, and secondly, by the want of the impression which Shakspeare makes, that the thing said not only might have been said, but that nothing else could be substituted, so as to excite the same sense of its exquisite propriety. I have always thought the conduct and expressions of Othello and Iago in the last scene, when Iago is

* Was der Duft eines südlichen Frühlings berauschendes, der Gesang der Nachtigall sehnsüchtiges, das erste Aufblühung der Rose wollüstiges hat, das athmet aus diesem Gedicht.—Schlegel's *Dram. Vorlesungen.* Vol. iii. p. 107.

brought in prisoner, a wonderful instance of Shakspeare's consummate judgment :—

> *Oth.* I look down towards his feet ;—but that's a fable.
> If that thou be'st a devil, I can not kill thee.
> *Iago.* I bleed, Sir ; but not kill'd.
> *Oth.* I am not sorry neither.

Think what a volley of execrations and defiances Beaumont and Fletcher would have poured forth here !

Indeed Massinger and Ben Jonson are both more perfect in their kind than Beaumont and Fletcher ; the former in the story and affecting incidents ; the latter in the exhibition of manners and peculiarities, whims in language, and vanities of appearance.

There is, however, a diversity of the most dangerous kind here. Shakspeare shaped his characters out of the nature within ; but we can not so safely say, out of his own nature as an individual person. No ! this latter is itself but a *natura naturata*—an effect, a product, not a power. It was Shakspeare's prerogative to have the universal, which is potentially in each particular, opened out to him, the *homo generalis*, not as an abstraction from observation of a variety of men, but as the substance capable of endless modifications, of which his own personal existence was but one, and to use this one as the eye that beheld the other, and as the tongue that could convey the discovery. There is no greater or more common vice in dramatic writers than to draw out of themselves. How I—alone and in the self-sufficiency of my study, as all men are apt to be proud in their dreams—should like to be talking *king !* Shakspeare, in composing, had no *I*, but the *I* representative. In Beaumont and Fletcher you have descriptions of characters by the poet rather than the characters themselves : we are told, and impressively told, of their being ; but we rarely or never feel that they actually are.

Beaumont and Fletcher are the most lyrical of our dramatists. I think their comedies the best part of their works, although there are scenes of very deep tragic interest in some of their plays. I particularly recommend Monsieur Thomas for good pure comic humor.

There is, occasionally, considerable license in their dramas ; and this opens a subject much needing vindication and sound exposition, but which is beset with such difficulties for a Lecturer, that I must pass it by. Only as far as Shakspeare is concerned, I own, I can with less pain admit a fault in him than beg an excuse for it. I will not, therefore, attempt to palliate the grossness that actually exists in his plays by the customs of his age, or by the far greater coarseness of all his contemporaries, excepting Spenser, who is himself not wholly blameless, though nearly so;—for I place Shakspeare's merit on being of no age. But I would clear away what is, in my judgment, not his, as that scene of the Porter* in Macbeth, and many other such passages, and abstract what is coarse in manners only, and all that which from the frequency of our own vices, we associate with his words. If this were truly done, little that could be justly reprehensible would remain. Compare the vile comments, offensive and defensive, on Pope's

Lust thro' some gentle strainers, &c.

with the worst thing in Shakspeare, or even in Beaumont and Fletcher; and then consider how unfair the attack is on our old dramatists; especially because it is an attack that can not be properly answered in that presence in which an answer would be most desirable, from the painful nature of one part of the position; but this very pain is almost a demonstration of its falsehood!

MASSINGER.

Born at Salisbury, 1584.—Died, 1640.

With regard to Massinger, observe,

1. The vein of satire on the times; but this is not as in Shakspeare, where the natures evolve themselves according to their incidental disproportions, from excess, deficiency, or mislocation, of one or more of the component elements; but is merely satire on what is attributed to them by others.

2. His excellent metre—a better model for dramatists in general to imitate than Shakspeare's,—even if a dramatic taste existed in the frequenters of the stage, and could be gratified in the present size and management, or rather mismanagement, of the two patent theatres. I do not mean that Massinger's verse is superior to Shakspeare's or equal to it. Far from it; but it is

* Act ii. sc. 3.

much more easily constructed, and may be more successfully adopted by writers in the present day. It is the nearest approach to the language of real life at all compatible with a fixed metre. In Massinger, as all our poets before Dryden, in order to make harmonious verse in the reading, it is absolutely necessary that the meaning should be understood;—when the meaning is once seen, then the harmony is perfect. Whereas in Pope and in most of the writers who followed in his school, it is the mechanical metre which determines the sense.

3. The impropriety, and indecorum of demeanor in his favorite characters, as in Bertoldo in the Maid of Honor, who is a swaggerer, talking to his sovereign what no sovereign could endure, and to gentlemen what no gentlemen would answer without pulling his nose.

4. Shakspeare's Ague-cheek, Osric, &c., are displayed through others, in the course of social intercourse, by the mode of their performing some office in which they are employed; but Massinger's *Sylli* come forward to declare themselves fools *ab arbitrium auctoris*, and so the diction always needs the *subintelligitur* ('the man looks as if he thought so and so,') expressed in the language of the satirist, and not in that of the man himself:—

> *Sylli.* You may, madam,
> Perhaps, believe that I in this use art
> To make you dote upon me, by exposing
> My more than most rare features to your view;
> But I, as I have ever done, deal simply,
> A mark of sweet simplicity, ever noted
> In the family of the Syllis. Therefore, lady,
> Look not with too much contemplation on me;
> If you do, you are in the suds.
>
> Maid of Honor, Act i. sc. 2.

The author mixes his own feelings and judgments concerning the presumed fool; but the man himself, till mad, fights up against them, and betrays, by his attempts to modify them, that he is no fool at all, but one gifted with activity and copiousness of thought, image and expression, which belong not to a fool, but to a man of wit making himself merry with his own character.

5. There is an utter want of preparation in the decisive acts of Massinger's characters, as in Camiola and Aurelia in the Maid of Honor. Why? Because the *dramatis personæ* were all

planned each by itself. Whereas in Shakspeare, the play is *syngenesia;* each character has, indeed, a life of its own, and is an *individuum* of itself, but yet an organ of the whole, as the heart in the human body. Shakspeare was a great comparative anatomist.

Hence Massinger and all, indeed, but Shakspeare, take a dislike to their own characters, and spite themselves upon them by making them talk like fools or monsters; as Fulgentio in his visit to Camiola (Act ii. sc. 2). Hence too, in Massinger, the continued flings at kings, courtiers, and all the favorites of fortune, like one who had enough of intellect to see injustice in his own inferiority in the share of the good things of life, but not genius enough to rise above it, and forget himself. Beaumont and Fletcher have the same vice in the opposite pole, a servility of sentiment and a spirit of partisanship with the monarchical faction.

6. From the want of a guiding point in Massinger's characters, you never know what they are about. In fact they have no character.

7. Note the faultiness of his soliloquies, with connectives and arrangements that have no other motive but the fear lest the audience should not understand him.

8. A play of Massinger's produces no one single effect, whether arising from the spirit of the whole, as in the As You Like It; or from any one indisputably prominent character, as Hamlet. It is just "which you like best, gentlemen!"

9. The unnaturally irrational passions and strange whims of feeling which Massinger delights to draw, deprive the reader of all sound interest in the characters;—as in Mathias in the Picture, and in other instances.

10. The comic scenes in Massinger not only do not harmonize with the tragic, not only interrupt the feeling, but degrade the characters that are to form any part in the action of the piece, so as to render them unfit for any tragic interest. At least, they do not concern, or act upon, or modify, the principal characters. As when a gentleman is insulted by a mere blackguard,—it is the same as if any other accident of nature had occurred, a pig run under his legs, or his horse thrown him. There is no dramatic interest in it.

I like Massinger's comedies better than his tragedies, although where the situation requires it, he often rises into the truly tragic and pathetic. He excels in narration, and for the most part displays his mere story with skill. But he is not a poet of high imagination; he is like a Flemish painter, in whose delineations objects appear as they do in nature, have the same force and truth, and produce the same effect upon the spectator. But Shakspeare is beyond this; he always by metaphors and figures involves in the thing considered a universe of past and possible experiences; he mingles earth, sea and air, gives a soul to every thing, and at the same time that he inspires human feelings, adds a dignity in his images to human nature itself:—

Full many a glorious morning have I seen
Flatter the mountain tops with sovereign eye;
Kissing with golden face the meadows green,
Gilding pale streams with heavenly alchymy, &c.

33d Sonnet.

NOTES ON MASSINGER.

Have I not overrated Gifford's edition of Massinger?—Not,—if I have, as but just is, main reference to the restitution of the text; but yes, perhaps, if I were talking of the notes. These are more often wrong than right. In the Maid of Honor, act i. sc. 5, Astutio describes Fulgentio as "A gentleman, yet no lord." Gifford supposes a transposition of the press for "No gentleman, yet a lord." But this would have no connection with what follows; and we have only to recollect that "lord" means a lord of lands, to see that the after-lines are explanatory. He is a man of high birth, but no landed property;—as to the former, he is a distant branch of the blood royal;—as to the latter, his whole rent lies in a narrow compass, the king's ear! In the same scene the text stands:

Bert. No! they are useful
For your *imitation;*—I remember you, &c.;—

and Gifford condemns Mason's conjecture of 'initiation' as void of meaning and harmony. Now my ear deceives me if 'initiation' be not the right word. In fact, 'imitation' is utterly impertinent to all that follows. Bertoldo tells Antonio that he had been initiated in the manners suited to the court by two or three sacred beauties, and that as similar experience would be equally useful for his initiation into the camp. Not a word of his imitation. Besides, I say the rhythm requires 'initiation,' and is lame as the verse now stands.

* Two or three tales, each in itself independent of the others, and united only by making the persons that are the agents in the story the *relations* of those in the other, as when a bind-weed or thread is twined round a bunch of flowers, each having its own root—and this novel narrative in *dialogue*—such is the *character* of Massinger's plays.—That the juxtaposition and the tying together by a common thread, which goes round this and round that, and then round them all, twine and intertwine, are contrived ingeniously—that the component tales are well chosen, and the whole well and conspicuously told; so as to excite and sustain the mind by kindling and keeping alive the curiosity of the reader—that the language is most pure, equally free from bookishness and from vulgarism, from the peculiarities of the School, and the transiencies of fashion, whether fine or coarse; that the rhythm and metre are incomparably good, and form the very model of dramatic versification, flexible and seeming to rise out of the passions, so that whenever a line sounds immetrical, the speaker may be certain he has recited it amiss, either that he has misplaced or misproportioned the emphasis, or neglected the acceleration or retardation of the voice in the pauses (all which the mood or passion would have produced in the real Agent, and therefore demand from the Actor or {translator / emulator}) and that read aright the blank verse is not less smooth than varied, a rich harmony, puzzling the fingers, but satisfying the ear—these are Massinger's characteristic merits.

Among the varieties of blank verse Massinger is fond of the anapæst in the first and third foot, as:

" Tŏ yoŭr mōre | thăn m̄as | cŭlinĕ reā | sŏn
thāt | cŏmmānds 'ĕm|| —"†
The Guardian, Act i. sc. 2.

* The notes on Massinger which follow were transcribed from a copy of that dramatist's works, belonging to Mr. Gillman. I do not know whence the first was taken by the original editor.

† Gifford divides the lines in question thus:

"Command my sensual appetites.
Calip. As vassals to
Your more than masculine reason, that commands them."

But it is obviously better to make the first line end with "vassals," so as to

Likewise of the second Pæon (◡ – ◡◡) in the first foot followed by four trochees (– ◡) as :

"Sŏ greēdĭlȳ | lōng fŏr, | knōw thĕir |
tĭtĭll | ātiŏns." Ib. ib.

The emphasis too has a decided influence on the metre, and, contrary to the metres of the Greek and Roman classics, at least to all their more common sorts of verse, as the hexameter and hex and pentameter, Alchaic, Sapphic, &c. has an essential agency on the character of the feet and power of the verse. One instance only of this I recollect in Theocritus :

τα μη̄ κᾰλᾰ κᾰλᾰ πεφᾰνται,

unless Homer's Ἄρες, Ἄρες, may (as I believe) be deemed another—For I can not bring my ear to believe that Homer would have perpetrated such a cacophony as Ὤρες, Ἄρες.

"In feār | my chaasteetee | may be | suspected." | Ib. ib.

In short, musical notes are required to explain Massinger—metres in addition to prosody. When a speech is interrupted, or one of the characters speaks aside, the last syllable of the former speech and first of the succeeding Massinger counts but for one, because both are supposed to be spoken at the same moment.

"And felt the sweetness *of't.*"
"*How* her mouth runs over."
Ib. ib.

Emphasis itself is twofold, the *rap* and the *drawl*, or the emphasis by quality of sound, and that by quantity—the hammer, and the spatula—the latter over 2, 3, 4 syllables or even a whole line. It is in this that the actors and speakers are generally speaking defective, they can not equilibrate an emphasis, or spread it over a number of syllables, all emphasized, sometimes equally, sometimes unequally.

give it only the one over-running syllable, which is so common in the last foot.

LECTURE VIII.

DON QUIXOTE.

CERVANTES.

Born at Madrid, 1547 ;—Shakspeare, 1564 ; both put off mortality on the same day, the 23d of April, 1616,—the one in the sixty-ninth, the other in the fifty-second, year of his life. The resemblance in their physiognomies is striking, but with a predominance of acuteness in Cervantes, and of reflection in Shakspeare, which is the specific difference between the Spanish and English characters of mind.

I. The nature and eminence of Symbolical writing ;—

II. Madness, and its different sorts (considered without pretension to medical science) ;—

To each of these, or at least to my own notions respecting them, I must devote a few words of explanation, in order to render the after-critique on Don Quixote, the master-work of Cervantes' and his country's genius, easily and throughout intelligible. This is not the least valuable, though it may most often be felt by us both as the heaviest and least entertaining portion of these critical disquisitions : for without it, I must have foregone one at least of the two appropriate objects of a Lecture, that of interesting you during its delivery, and of leaving behind in your minds the germs of after-thought, and the materials for future enjoyment. To have been assured by several of my intelligent auditors that they have reperused Hamlet or Othello with increased satisfaction in consequence of the new points of view in which I had placed those characters—is the highest compliment I could receive or desire ; and should the address of this evening open out a new source of pleasure, or enlarge the former in your perusal of Don Quixote, it will compensate for the failure of any personal or temporary object.

I. The Symbolical can not, perhaps, be better defined in distinction from the Allegorical, than that it is always itself a part of that, of the whole of which it is the representative.—"Here comes a sail"—(that is, a ship) is a symbolical expression. "Behold our lion!" when we speak of some gallant soldier, is allegorical. Of most importance to our present subject is this point, that the latter (the allegory) can not be other than spoken consciously;—whereas in the former (the symbol) it is very possible that the general truth represented may be working unconsciously in the writer's mind during the construction of the symbol;—and it proves itself by being produced out of his own mind,—as the Don Quixote out of the perfectly sane mind of Cervantes; and not by outward observation, or historically. The advantage of symbolical writing over allegory is, that it presumes no disjunction of faculties, but simple predominance.

II. Madness may be divided as—

1. hypochondriasis; or, the man is out of his senses.
2. derangement of the understanding; or, the man is out of his wits.
3. loss of reason.
4. frenzy, or derangement of the sensations.

Cervantes's own preface to Don Quixote is a perfect model of the gentle, everywhere intelligible, irony in the best essays of the Tatler and the Spectator. Equally natural and easy, Cervantes is more spirited than Addison; whilst he blends with the terseness of Swift, an exquisite flow and music of style, and above all, contrasts with the latter by the sweet temper of a superior mind, which saw the follies of mankind, and was even at the moment suffering severely under hard mistreatment;* and yet seems everywhere to have but one thought as the undersong—"Brethren! with all your faults I love you still!"—or as a mother that chides the child she loves, with one hand holds up the rod, and with the other wipes off each tear as it drops!

Don Quixote was neither fettered to the earth by want, nor holden in its embraces by wealth;—of which, with the temperance natural to his country, as a Spaniard, he had both far too little, and somewhat too much, to be under any necessity of think-

* *Bien como quien se engendrò en una carcel, donde toda incomodidad tiene su assiento, y todo triste ruido hace su habitacion.* Like one you may suppose born in a prison, where every inconvenience keeps its residence, and every dismal sound its habitation. Pref. Jarvis's Tr.—*Ed.*

ing about it. His age too, fifty, may be well supposed to prevent his mind from being tempted out of itself by any of the lower passions;—while his habits, as a very early riser and a keen sportsman, were such as kept his spare body in serviceable subjection to his will, and yet by the play of hope that accompanies pursuit, not only permitted, but assisted, his fancy in shaping what it would. Nor must we omit his meagreness and entire featureliness, face and frame, which Cervantes gives us at once: "It is said that his surname was *Quixada* or *Quesada*," &c.—even in this trifle showing an exquisite judgment;—just once insinuating the association of *lantern-jaws* into the reader's mind, yet not retaining it obtrusively like the names in old farces and in the Pilgrim's Progress,—but taking for the regular appellative one which had the no meaning of a proper name in real life, and which yet was capable of recalling a number of very different, but all pertinent, recollections, as old armor, the precious metals hidden in the ore, &c. Don Quixote's leanness and featureliness are happy exponents of the excess of the formative or imaginative in him, contrasted with Sancho's plump rotundity, and recipiency of external impression.

He has no knowledge of the sciences or scientific arts which give to the meanest portions of matter an intellectual interest, and which enable the mind to decipher in the world of the senses the invisible agency—that alone, of which the world's phenomena are the effects and manifestations,—and thus, as in a mirror, to contemplate its own reflex, its life in the powers, its imagination in the symbolic forms, its moral instincts in the final causes, and its reason in the laws of material nature: but—estranged from all the motives to observation from self-interest—the persons that surround him too few and too familiar to enter into any connection with his thoughts, or to require any adaptation of his conduct to their particular characters or relations to himself—his judgment lies fallow, with nothing to excite, nothing to employ it. Yet,—and here is the point, where genius even of the most perfect kind, allotted but to few in the course of many ages, does not preclude the necessity in part, and in part counterbalance the craving by sanity of judgment, without which genius either can not be, or can not at least manifest itself,—the dependency of our nature asks for some confirmation from without, though it be only from the shadows of other men's fictions.

Too uninformed, and with too narrow a sphere of power and opportunity to rise into the scientific artist, or to be himself a patron of art, and with too deep a principle, and too much innocence to become a mere projector, Don Quixote has recourse to romances :—

His curiosity and extravagant fondness herein arrived at that pitch, that he sold many acres of arable land to purchase books of knight-errantry, and carried home all he could lay hands on of that kind !—C. 1.

The more remote these romances were from the language of common life, the more akin on that very account were they to the shapeless dreams and strivings of his own mind ;—a mind, which possessed not the highest order of genius which lives in an atmosphere of power over mankind, but that minor kind which, in its restlessness, seeks for a vivid representative of its own wishes, and substitutes the movements of that objective puppet for an exercise of actual power in and by itself. The more wild and improbable these romances were, the more were they akin to his will, which had been in the habit of acting as an unlimited monarch over the creations of his fancy ! Hence observe how the startling of the remaining common sense, like a glimmering before its death, in the notice of the impossible-improbable of Don Belianis, is dismissed by Don Quixote as impertinent—

*He had some doubt** as to the dreadful wounds which Don Belianis gave and received : for he imagined, that notwithstanding the most expert surgeons had cured him, his face and whole body must still be full of seams and scars. *Nevertheless*† he commended in his author the concluding his book with a promise of that unfinishable adventure !—C. 1.

Hence also his first intention to turn author ; but who, with such a restless struggle within him, would content himself with writing in a remote village among apathists and ignorants ? During his colloquies with the village-priest and the barber-surgeon, in which the fervor of critical controversy feeds the passion and gives reality to its object—what more natural than that the mental striving should become an eddy ?—madness may perhaps be defined as the circling in a stream which should be progressive and adaptive ; Don Quixote grows at length to be a man out of his wits ; his understanding is deranged ; and hence without the least deviation from the truth of nature, without losing

* *No estaba muy bien con.—Ed.* † *Pero con todo.—Ed.*

the least trait of personal individuality, he becomes a substantial living allegory, or personification of the reason and the moral sense, divested of the judgment and the understanding. Sancho is the converse. He is the common sense without reason or imagination; and Cervantes not only shows the excellence and power of reason in Don Quixote, but in both him and Sancho the mischiefs resulting from a severance of the two main constituents of sound intellectual and moral action. Put him and his master together, and they form a perfect intellect; but they are separated and without cement; and hence each having a need of the other for its own completeness, each has at times a mastery over the other. For the common sense, although it may see the practical inapplicability of the dictates of the imagination or abstract reason, yet can not help submitting to them. These two characters possess the world, alternately and interchangeably the cheater and the cheated. To impersonate them, and to combine the permanent with the individual, is one of the highest creations of genius, and has been achieved by Cervantes and Shakspeare, almost alone.

Observations on particular passages,— .

B. i. c. 1. But not altogether approving of his having broken it to pieces with so much ease, to secure himself from the like danger for the future, he made it over again, fencing it with small bars of iron within, in such a manner, *that he rested satisfied of its strength; and without caring to make a fresh experiment on it, he approved and looked upon it as a most excellent helmet.*

His not trying his improved skull-cap is an exquisite trait of human character, founded on the oppugnancy of the soul in such a state to any disturbance by doubt of its own broodings. Even the long deliberation about his horse's name is full of meaning; —for in these day-dreams the greater part of the history passes and is carried on in words, which look forward to other words as what will be said of them.

Ib. Near the place where he lived, there dwelt a very comely country lass, with whom he had formerly been in love; though, as it is supposed, she never knew it, nor troubled herself about it.

The nascent love for the country lass, but without any attempt at utterance, or an opportunity of knowing her except as the hint—the ὅτι ἔστι—of the inward imagination, is happily conceived in both parts;—first, as confirmative of the shrinking back of the mind on itself, and its dread of having a cherished image destroyed by its own judgment; and secondly, as showing how necessarily love is the passion of novels. Novels are to love as fairy tales to dreams. I never knew but two men of taste and feeling who could not understand why I was delighted with the Arabian Nights' Tales, and they were likewise the only persons in my knowledge who scarcely remembered having ever dreamed. Magic and war—itself a magic—are the day-dreams of childhood; love is the day-dream of youth, and early manhood.

C. 2. "Scarcely had ruddy Phœbus spread the golden tresses of his beauteous hair over the face of the wide and spacious earth; and scarcely had the little painted birds, with the sweet and mellifluous harmony of their forked tongues, saluted the approach of rosy Aurora, who, quitting the soft couch of her jealous husband, disclosed herself to mortals through the gates of the Mauchegan horizon; when the renowned Don Quixote," &c.

How happily already is the abstraction from the senses, from observation, and the consequent confusion of the judgment, marked in this description! The knight is describing objects immediate to his senses and sensations without borrowing a single trait from either. Would it be difficult to find parallel descriptions in Dryden's plays and in those of his successors?

C. 3. The host is here happily conceived as one who, from his past life as a sharper, was capable of entering into and humoring the knight, and so perfectly in character, that he precludes a considerable source of improbability in the future narrative, by enforcing upon Don Quixote the necessity of taking money with him.

C. 3. "Ho, there, whoever thou art, rash knight, that approachest to touch the arms of the most valorous adventurer that ever girded sword," &c.

Don Quixote's high eulogiums upon himself—"the most valorous adventurer!"—but it is not himself that he has before him, but the idol of his imagination, the imaginary being whom he is acting. And this, that it is entirely a third person, excuses his heart from the otherwise inevitable charge of selfish vanity; and so by madness itself he preserves our esteem, and renders those actions natural by which he, the first person, deserves it.

C. 4. Andres and his master.

The manner in which Don Quixote redressed this wrong, is a picture of the true revolutionary passion in its first honest state, while it is yet only a bewilderment of the understanding. You have a benevolence limitless in its prayers, which are in fact aspirations towards omnipotence; but between it and beneficence, the bridge of judgment—that is, of measurement of personal power—intervenes, and must be passed. Otherwise you will be bruised by the leap into the chasm, or be drowned in the revolutionary river, and drag others with you to the same fate.

C. 4. Merchants of Toledo.

When they were come so near as to be seen and heard, Don Quixote raised his voice, and with arrogant air cried out: "Let the whole world stand; if the whole world does not confess that there is not in the whole world a damsel more beautiful than," &c.

Now mark the presumption which follows the self-complacency of the last act! That was an honest attempt to redress a real wrong; this is an arbitrary determination to enforce a Brissotine or Rousseau's ideal on all his fellow-creatures.

Let the whole world stand!

'If there had been any experience in proof of the excellence of our code, where would be our superiority in this enlightened age?'

"No? the business is that without seeing her, you believe, confess, affirm, swear, and maintain it; *and if not, I challenge you all to battle.*"*

Next see the persecution and fury excited by opposition however moderate! The only words listened to are those, that, without their context and their conditionals, and transformed into positive assertions, might give some shadow of excuse for the violence shown! This rich story ends, to the compassion of the men in their senses, in a sound rib-roasting of the idealist by the muleteer, the mob. And happy for thee, poor knight! that the mob were against thee! For had they been with thee, by the change of the moon and of them, thy head would have been off.

C. 5. first part—The idealist recollects the causes that had been necessary to the reverse, and attempts to remove them—too late. He is beaten and disgraced.

* *Donde no, conmigo sois en battalla, gente descomunal!—Ed.*

C. 6. This chapter on Don Quixote's library proves that the author did not wish to destroy the romances, but to cause them to be read as romances—that is, for their merits as poetry.

C. 7. Among other things, Don Quixote told him, he should dispose himself to go with him willingly;—for some time or other such an adventure might present, that an island might be won, in the turn of a hand, and he be left governor thereof.

At length the promises of the imaginative reason begin to act on the plump, sensual, honest, common-sense accomplice,—but unhappily not in the same person, and without the *copula* of the judgment,—in hopes of the substantial good things, of which the former contemplated only the glory and the colors.

C. 7. Sancho Panza went riding upon his ass, like any patriarch, with his wallet and leathern bottle, and with a vehement desire to find himself governor of the island which his master had promised him.

The first relief from regular labor is so pleasant to poor Sancho!

C. 8. "I no gentleman! I swear by the great God, thou liest, as I am a Christian. Biscainer by land, gentleman by sea, gentleman for the devil, and thou liest: look then if thou hast any thing else to say."

This Biscainer is an excellent image of the prejudices and bigotry provoked by the idealism of a speculator. This story happily detects the trick which our imagination plays in the description of single combats: only change the preconception of the magnificence of the combatants, and all is gone.

B. ii. c. 2. "Be pleased, my lord Don Quixote, to bestow upon me the government of that island," &c.

Sancho's eagerness for his government, the nascent lust of actual democracy, or isocracy!

C. 2. "But tell me, on your life, have you ever seen a more valorous knight than I, upon the whole face of the known earth? Have you read in story of any other, who has, or ever had, more bravery in assailing, more breath in holding out, more dexterity in wounding, or more address in giving a fall?"—"The truth is," answered Sancho, "that I never read any history at all; for I can neither read nor write; but what I dare affirm is, that I never served a bolder master," &c.

This appeal to Sancho, and Sancho's answer, are exquisitely

humorous. It is impossible not to think of the French bulletins and proclamations. Remark the necessity under which we are of being sympathized with, fly as high into abstraction as we may, and how constantly the imagination is recalled to the ground of our common humanity! And note a little further on, the knight's easy vaunting of his balsam, and his quietly deferring the making and application of it.

C. 3. The speech before the goatherds:

> "Happy times and happy ages," &c.*

Note the rhythm of this, and the admirable beauty and wisdom of the thoughts in themselves, but the total want of judgment in Don Quixote's addressing them to such an audience.

B. iii. c. 3. Don Quixote's balsam, and the vomiting and consequent relief; an excellent hit at *panacea nostrums*, which cure the patient by his being himself cured of the medicine by revolting nature.

> C. 4. "Peace! and have patience, the day will come," &c.

The perpetual promises of the imagination!

> Ib. "Your Worship," said Sancho, "would make a bettér preacher than knight errant!"

Exactly so. This is the true moral.

C. 6. The uncommon beauty of the description in the commencement of this chapter. In truth, the whole of it seems to put all nature in its heights and its humiliations before us.

Ib. Sancho's story of the goats:

> "Make account, he carried them all over," said Don Quixote, "and do not be going and coming in this manner; for at this rate, you will not have done carrying them over in a twelvemonth." "How many are passed already?" said Sancho, &c.

Observe the happy contrast between the all-generalizing mind of the mad knight, and Sancho's all-particularizing memory. How admirable a symbol of the dependence of all *copula* on the higher powers of the mind, with the single exception of the succession in time and the accidental relations of space. Men of mere common sense have no theory or means of making one fact

* *Dichosa edad y siglos dichosos aquellos, &c.—Ed.*

more important or prominent than the rest; if they lose one link, all is lost. Compare Mrs. Quickly and the Tapster.* And note also Sancho's good heart, when his master is about to leave him. Don Quixote's conduct upon discovering the fulling-hammers, proves he was meant to be in his senses. Nothing can be better conceived than his fit of passion at Sancho's laughing, and his sophism of self-justification by the courage he had shown.

Sancho is by this time cured, through experience, as far as his own errors are concerned; yet still is he lured on by the unconquerable awe of his master's superiority, even when he is cheating him.

C. 8. The adventure of the Galley-slaves. I think this is the only passage of moment in which Cervantes slips the mask of his hero, and speaks for himself.

C. 9. Don Quixote desired to have it, and bade him take the money, and keep it for himself. Sancho kissed his hands for the favor, &c.

Observe Sancho's eagerness to avail himself of the permission of his master, who, in the war sports of knight-errantry, had, without any selfish dishonesty, overlooked the *meum* and *tuum*. Sancho's selfishness is modified by his involuntary goodness of heart, and Don Quixote's flighty goodness is debased by the involuntary or unconscious selfishness of his vanity and self-applause.

C. 10. Cardenio is the madman of passion, who meets and easily overthrows for the moment the madman of imagination. And note the contagion of madness of any kind, upon Don Quixote's interruption of Cardenio's story.

C. 11. Perhaps the best specimen of Sancho's proverbializing is this:—

"And I (Don Q.) say again, they lie, and will lie two hundred times more, all who say, or think her so." "I neither say, nor think so," answered Sancho; "let those who say it, eat the lie, and swallow it with their bread: whether they were guilty or no, they have given an account to God before now: I come from my vineyard, I know nothing; I am no friend to inquiring into other men's lives; *for* he that buys and lies shall find the lie left in his purse behind; *besides*, naked was I born, and naked I remain; I neither win nor lose; if they were guilty, what is that to me? Many think to find bacon, where there is not so much as a pin to hang it on: *but* who can hedge in the cuckoo? *Especially*, do they spare God himself?"

* See The Friend, II. p. 416.—*Ed.*

Ib. "And it is no great matter, if it be in another hand; for by what I remember, Dulcinea can neither write nor read," &c.

The wonderful twilight of the mind! and mark Cervantes's courage in daring to present it, and trust to a distant posterity for an appreciation of its truth to nature.

P. ii. b. iii. c. 9. Sancho's account of what he had seen on Clavileno is a counterpart in his style to Don Quixote's adventures in the cave of Montesinos. This last is the only impeachment of the knight's moral character; Cervantes just gives one instance of the veracity failing before the strong cravings of the imagination for something real and external; the picture would not have been complete without this; and yet it is so well managed, that the reader has no unpleasant sense of Don Quixote having told a lie. It is evident that he hardly knows whether it was a dream or not; and goes to the enchanter to inquire the real nature of the adventure.

SUMMARY OF CERVANTES.

A Castilian of refined manners; a gentleman, true to religion, and true to honor.

A scholar and a soldier, and fought under the banners of Don John of Austria, at Lepanto, lost his arm and was captured.

Endured slavery not only with fortitude, but with mirth; and by the superiority of nature, mastered and overawed his barbarian owner.

Finally ransomed, he resumed his native destiny, the awful task of achieving fame; and for that reason died poor and a prisoner, while nobles and kings over their goblets of gold gave relish to their pleasures by the charms of his divine genius. He was the inventor of novels for the Spaniards, and in his Persilis and Sigismunda, the English may find the germ of their Robinson Crusoe.

The world was a drama to him. His own thoughts, in spite of poverty and sickness, perpetuated for him the feelings of youth. He painted only what he knew and had looked into, but he knew and had looked into much indeed; and his imagination was ever at hand to adapt and modify the world of his experience. Of delicious love he fabled, yet with stainless virtue.

LECTURE IX.

ON THE DISTINCTIONS OF THE WITTY, THE DROLL, THE ODD, AND THE HUMOROUS; THE NATURE AND CONSTITUENTS OF HUMOR;—RABELAIS—SWIFT—STERNE.

I.

PERHAPS the most important of our intellectual operations are those of detecting the difference in similar, and the identity in dissimilar, things. Out of the latter operation it is that wit arises; and it, generically regarded, consists in presenting thoughts or images in an unusual connection with each other, for the purpose of exciting pleasure by the surprise. This connection may be real; and there is in fact a scientific wit; though where the object, consciously entertained, is truth, and not amusement, we commonly give it some higher name. But in wit popularly understood, the connection may be, and for the most part is, apparent only, and transitory; and this connection may be by thoughts, or by words, or by images. The first is our Butler's especial eminence; the second, Voltaire's; the third, which we oftener call fancy, constitutes the larger and more peculiar part of the wit of Shakspeare. You can scarcely turn to a single speech of Falstaff's without finding instances of it. Nor does wit always cease to deserve the name by being transient, or incapable of analysis. I may add that the wit of thoughts belongs eminently to the Italians, that of words to the French, and that of images to the English.

II. Where the laughable is its own end, and neither inference, nor moral is intended, or where at least the writer would wish it so to appear, there arises what we call drollery. The pure, unmixed, ludicrous, or laughable belongs exclusively to the understanding, and must be presented under the form of the senses; it lies within the spheres of the eye and the ear, and hence is allied to the fancy. It does not appertain to the reason or the moral sense, and accordingly is alien to the imagination. I think Aristotle has already excellently defined* the laughable, τὸ γελοῖον, as consisting of, or depending on, what is out of its proper time and place, yet without danger or pain. Here the *impropriety*—τὸ ἄτοπον—is the positive qualification; the *dangerlessness*—τὸ ἀκίνδυνον—the negative. Neither the understanding without an object of the senses, as for example, a mere notional error, or idiocy;—nor any external object, unless attributed to the understanding, can produce the poetically laughable. Nay, even in ridiculous positions of the body laughed at by the vulgar, there is a subtle personification always going on, which acts on the, perhaps, unconscious mind of the spectator as a symbol of intellectual character. And hence arises the imperfect and awkward effect of comic stories of animals; because although the understanding is satisfied in them, the senses are not. Hence too, it is, that the true ludicrous is its own end. When serious satire commences, or satire that is felt as serious, however comically drest, free and genuine laughter ceases; it becomes sardonic. This you experience in reading Young, and also not unfrequently in Butler. The true comic is the blossom of the nettle.

III. When words or images are placed in unusual juxtaposition rather than connection, and are so placed merely because the juxtaposition is unusual—we have the odd or the grotesque; the occasional use of which in the minor ornaments of architecture, is an interesting problem for a student in the psychology of the Fine Arts.

IV. In the simply laughable there is a mere disproportion between a definite act and a definite purpose or end, or a disproportion of the end itself to the rank or circumstances of the definite person; but humor is of more difficult description. I must try to define it in the first place by its points of diversity from the

* He elsewhere commends this Def: "To resolve laughter into an expression of contempt is contrary to fact, and laughable enough. Laughter is a convulsion of the nerves, and it seems as if nature cut short the rapid thrill of pleasure on the nerves by a sudden convulsion of them to prevent the sensation becoming painful—*Aristotle's Def*, is *as good as can be.* Surprise at perceiving any thing out of its usual place when the unusualness is not accompanied by a sense of serious danger. *Such* surprise is always pleasurable, and it is observable that surprise accompanied with circumstances of danger becomes Tragic. Hence *Farce* may often *border* on *Tragedy;* indeed *Farce* is *nearer Tragedy* in *its Essence* than *Comedy is.*"

Table Talk.

former species. Humor does not, like the different kinds of wit, which is impersonal, consist wholly in the understanding and the senses. No combination of thoughts, words, or images will of itself constitute humor, unless some peculiarity of individual temperament and character be indicated thereby, as the cause of the same. Compare the Comedies of Congreve with the Falstaff in Henry IV. or with Sterne's Corporal Trim, Uncle Toby, and Mr. Shandy, or with some of Steele's charming papers in the Tatler, and you will feel the difference better than I can express it. Thus again (to take an instance from the different works of the same writer), in Smollett's Strap, his Lieutenant Bowling, his Morgan the honest Welshman, and his Matthew Bramble, we have exquisite humor,—while in his Peregrine Pickle we find an abundance of drollery, which too often degenerates into mere oddity ; in short, we find that a number of things are put together to counterfeit humor, but that there is no growth from within. And this indeed is the origin of the word, derived from the humoral pathology, and excellently described by Ben Jonson :

So in every human body,
The choler, melancholy, phlegm, and blood,
By reason that they flow continually
In some one part, and are not continent,
Receive the name of humors. Now thus far
It may, by metaphor, apply itself
Unto the general disposition :
As when some one peculiar quality
Doth so possess a man, that it doth draw
All his effects, his spirits, and his powers,
In their confluctions, all to run one way,
This may be truly said to be a humor.*

Hence we may explain the congeniality of humor with pathos, so exquisite in Sterne and Smollett, and hence also the tender feeling which we always have for, and associate with, the humors or hobby-horses of a man. First, we respect a humorist, because absence of interested motives is the groundwork of the character, although the imagination of an interest may exist in the individual himself, as if a remarkably simple-hearted man should pride himself on his knowledge of the world, and how well he can manage it :—and secondly, there always is in a genuine humor

* Every Man Out Of His Humor. Prologue.

an acknowledgment of the hollowness and farce of the world, and its disproportion to the godlike within us. And it follows immediately from this, that whenever particular acts have reference to particular selfish motives, the humorous bursts into the indignant and abhorring ; whilst all follies not selfish are pardoned or palliated. The danger of this habit, in respect of pure morality, is strongly exemplified in Sterne.

This would be enough, and indeed less than this has passed, for a sufficient account of humor, if we did not recollect that not every predominance of character, even where not precluded by the moral sense, as in criminal dispositions, constitutes what we mean by a humorist, or the presentation of its produce, humor. What then is it ? Is it manifold ? Or is there some one humorific point common to all that can be called humorous ?—I am not prepared to answer this fully, even if my time permitted : but I think there is ;—and that it consists in a certain reference to the general and the universal, by which the finite great is brought into identity with the little, or the little with the finite great, so as to make both nothing in comparison with the infinite. The little is made great, and the great little in order to destroy both ; because all is equal in contrast with the infinite. "It is not without reason, brother Toby, that learned men write dialogues on long noses."* I would suggest, therefore, that whenever a finite is contemplated in reference to the infinite, whether consciously or unconsciously, humor essentially arises. In the highest humor, at least, there is always a reference to, and a connection with, some general power not finite, in the form of some finite ridiculously disproportionate in our feelings to that of which it is, nevertheless, the representative, or by which it is to be displayed. Humorous writers, therefore, as Sterne in particular, delight, after much preparation, to end in nothing, or in a direct contradiction.

That there is some truth in this definition, or origination of humor, is evident ; for you can not conceive a humorous man who does not give some disproportionate generality, or even a universality to his hobby-horse, as is the case with Mr. Shandy ; or at least there is an absence of any interest but what arises from the humor itself, as in my Uncle Toby, and it is the idea of the soul, of its undefined capacity and dignity, that gives the sting to any absorption of it by any one pursuit, and this not in respect of the

* Trist. Sh. vol. iii. c. 37.

humorist as a mere member of society for a particular, however mistaken, interest, but as a man.

The English humor is the most thoughtful, the Spanish the most ethereal—the most ideal—of modern literature. Amongst the classic ancients there was little or no humor in the foregoing sense of the term. Socrates, or Plato under his name, gives some notion of humor in the Banquet, when he argues that tragedy and comedy rest upon the same ground. But humor properly took its rise in the middle ages; and the Devil, the Vice of the mysteries, incorporates the modern humor in its elements. It is a spirit measured by disproportionate finites. The Devil is not, indeed, perfectly humorous; but that is only because he is the extreme of all humor.

RABELAIS.*

Born at Chinon, 1483–4.—Died, 1553.

One can not help regretting that no friend of Rabelais (and surely friends he must have had) has left an authentic account of him. His buffoonery was not merely Brutus' rough stick, which contained a rod of gold; it was necessary as an amulet against the monks and bigots. Beyond a doubt, he was among the deepest as well as boldest thinkers of his age. Never was a more plausible, and seldom, I am persuaded, a less appropriate line than the thousand times quoted,

> Rabelais laughing in his easy chair—

of Mr. Pope. The caricature of his filth and zanyism proves how fully he both knew and felt the danger in which he stood. I could write a treatise in proof and praise of the morality and moral elevation of Rabelais' work which would make the church stare, and the conventicle groan, and yet should be the truth, and nothing but the truth. I class Rabelais with the creative minds of the world, Shakspeare, Dante, Cervantes, &c.

All Rabelais' personages are phantasmagoric allegories, but Panurge above all. He is throughout the πανουϱγία,—the wis-

* No note remains of that part of this Lecture which treated of Rabelais. This seems, therefore, a convenient place for the reception of some remarks written by Mr. C. in Mr. Gillman's copy of Rabelais, about the year 1825. See Table Talk, VI. p. 333.—*Ed.*

dom, that is, the cunning of the human animal,—the understanding, as the faculty of means to purposes without ultimate ends, in the most comprehensive sense, and including art, sensuous fancy, and all the passions of the understanding. It is impossible to read Rabelais without an admiration mixed with wonder at the depth and extent of his learning, his multifarious knowledge, and original observation beyond what books could in that age have supplied him with.

B. iii. c. 9. How Panurge asketh counsel of Pantagruel, whether he should marry, yea or no.

Note this incomparable chapter. Pantagruel stands for the reason as contra-distinguished from the understanding and choice, that is, from Panurge; and the humor consists in the latter asking advice of the former on a subject in which the reason can only give the inevitable conclusion, the syllogistic *ergo*, from the premisses provided by the understanding itself, which puts each case so as of necessity to predetermine the verdict thereon. This chapter, independently of the allegory, is an exquisite satire on the spirit in which people commonly ask advice.

SWIFT.*

Born in Dublin, 1667.—Died, 1745.

In Swift's writings there is a false misanthropy grounded upon an exclusive contemplation of the vices and follies of mankind, and this misanthropic tone is also disfigured or brutalized by his obtrusion of physical dirt and coarseness. I think Gulliver's Travels the great work of Swift. In the voyages to Lilliput and Brobdingnag he displays the littleness and moral contemptibility of human nature; in that to the Houyhnhnms he represents the disgusting spectacle of man with the understanding only, without the reason or the moral feeling, and in his horse he gives the misanthropic ideal of man—that is, a being virtuous from rule and duty, but untouched by the principle of love.

* From Mr. Green's note.—*Ed.*

STERNE.

Born at Clonmel, 1713.—Died, 1768.

WITH regard to Sterne, and the charge of licentiousness which presses so seriously upon his character as a writer, I would remark that there is a sort of knowingness, the wit of which depends—1st, on the modesty it gives pain to; or, 2dly, on the innocence and innocent ignorance over which it triumphs; or, 3dly, on a certain oscillation in the individual's own mind between the remaining good and the encroaching evil of his nature—a sort of dallying with the devil—a fluxionary act of combining courage and cowardice, as when a man snuffs a candle with his fingers for the first time, or better still, perhaps, like that trembling daring with which a child touches a hot tea urn, because it has been forbidden; so that the mind has in its own white and black angel the same or similar amusement, as may be supposed to take place between an old debauchee and a prude,—she feeling resentment, on the one hand, from a prudential anxiety to preserve appearances and have a character, and, on the other, an inward sympathy with the enemy. We have only to suppose society innocent, and then nine tenths of this sort of wit would be like a stone that falls in snow, making no sound because exciting no resistance; the remainder rests on its being an offence against the good manners of human nature itself.

This source, unworthy as it is, may doubtless be combined with wit, drollery, fancy, and even humor, and we have only to regret the misalliance; but that the latter are quite distinct from the former, may be made evident by abstracting in our imagination the morality of the characters of Mr. Shandy, my Uncle Toby, and Trim, which are all antagonists to this spurious sort of wit, from the rest of Tristram Shandy. And by supposing, instead of them, the presence of two or three callous debauchees. The result will be pure disgust. Sterne can not be too severely censured for thus using the best dispositions of our nature as the panders and condiments for the basest.

The excellencies of Sterne consist—

1. In bringing forward into distinct consciousness those minutiæ of thought and feeling which appear trifles, yet have an importance for the moment, and which almost every man feels in one

way or other. Thus is produced the novelty of an individual peculiarity, together with the interest of a something that belongs to our common nature. In short, Sterne seizes happily on those points, in which every man is more or less a humorist. And, indeed, to be a little more subtle, the propensity to notice these things does itself constitute the humorist, and the superadded power of so presenting them to men in general gives us the man of humor. Hence the difference of the man of humor, the effect of whose portraits does not depend on the felt presence of himself, as a humorist, as in the instances of Cervantes and Shakspeare—nay, of Rabelais too; and of the humorist, the effect of whose works does very much depend on the sense of his own oddity, as in Sterne's case, and perhaps Swift's; though Swift again would require a separate classification.

2. In the traits of human nature, which so easily assume a particular cast and color from individual character. Hence this excellence and the pathos connected with it quickly pass into humor, and form the ground of it. See particularly the beautiful passage, so well known, of Uncle Toby's catching and liberating the fly:

> "Go,"—says he, one day at dinner, to an overgrown one which had buzzed about his nose, and tormented him cruelly all dinner-time, and which, after infinite attempts, he had caught at last, as it flew by him;—"I'll not hurt thee," says my Uncle Toby, rising from his chair, and going across the room, with the fly in his hand,—"I'll not hurt a hair of thy head:—Go," says he, lifting up the sash, and opening his hand as he spoke, to let it escape;—"go, poor devil, get thee gone, why should I hurt thee? This world is surely wide enough to hold both thee and me." Vol. ii. ch. 12.

Observe in this incident how individual character may be given by the mere delicacy of presentation and elevation in degree of a common good quality, humanity, which in itself would not be characteristic at all.

3. In Mr. Shandy's character,—the essence of which is a craving for sympathy in exact proportion to the oddity and unsympathizability of what he proposes;—this coupled with an instinctive desire to be at least disputed with, or rather both in one, to dispute and yet to agree—and holding as worst of all—to acquiesce without either resistance or sympathy. This is charmingly, indeed, profoundly conceived, and is psychologically and ethically true of all Mr. Shandies. Note, too, how the contrasts of charac-

ter, which are always either balanced or remedied, increase the love between the brothers.

4. No writer is so happy as Sterne in the unexaggerated and truly natural representation of that species of slander, which consists in gossiping about our neighbors, as whetstones of our moral discrimination ; as if they were conscience-blocks which we used in our apprenticeship, in order not to waste such precious materials as our own consciences in the trimming and shaping of ourselves by self-examination :—

> Alas o'day !—had Mrs. Shandy (poor gentlewoman !) had but her wish in going up to town just to lie in and come down again ; which, they say, she begged and prayed for upon her bare knees, and which, in my opinion, considering the fortune which Mr. Shandy got with her, was no such mighty natter to have complied with, the lady and her babe might both of them aave been alive at this hour. Vol. i. c. 18.

5. When you have secured a man's likings and prejudices in your favor, you may then safely appeal to his impartial judgment. In the following passage not only is acute sense shrouded in wit, out a life and a character are added which exalt the whole into the dramatic :—

> "I see plainly, Sir, by your looks" (or as the case happened) my father vould say—"that you do not heartily subscribe to this opinion—which, to hose," he would add, "who have not carefully sifted it to the bottom,—I own has an air more of fancy than of solid reasoning in it ; and yet, my dear Sir, if I may presume to know your character, I am morally assured I hould hazard little in stating a case to you, not as a party in the dispute, out as a judge, and trusting my appeal upon it to your good sense and candid disquisition in this matter ; you are a person free from as many narrow prejudices of education as most men ; and, if I may presume to penetrate arther into you, of a liberality of genius above bearing down an opinion, nerely because it wants friends. Your son,—your dear son,—from whose weet and open temper you have so much to expect,—your Billy, Sir !—vould you, for the world, have called him JUDAS ? Would you, my dear Sir," he would say, laying his hand upon your breast, with the genteelest ddress,—and in that soft and irresistible *piano* of voice, which the nature f the *argumentum ad hominem* absolutely requires,—"Would you, Sir, if *Jew* of a godfather had proposed the name for your child, and offered you is purse along with it, would you have consented to such a desecration of im ? O my God !" he would say, looking up, "if I know your temper ightly, Sir, you are incapable of it ;—you would have trampled upon the ffer ;—you would have thrown the temptation at the tempter's head with bhorrence. Your greatness of mind in this action, which I admire, with

that generous contempt of money, which you show me in the whole transaction, is really noble ;—and what renders it more so, is the principle of it ;—the workings of a parent's love upon the truth and conviction of this very hypothesis, namely, that were your son called Judas,—the sordid and treacherous idea, so inseparable from the name, would have accompanied him through life like his shadow, and in the end made a miser and a rascal of him, in spite, Sir, of your example." Vol. i. c. 19.

6. There is great physiognomic tact in Sterne. See it particularly displayed in his description of Dr. Slop, accompanied with all that happiest use of drapery and attitude, which at once give reality by individualizing and vividness by unusual, yet probable, combinations :—

Imagine to yourself a little squat uncourtly figure of a Doctor Slop, of about four feet and a half perpendicular height, with a breadth of back, and a sesquipedality of belly, which might have done honor to a sergeant in the horseguards.

* * * * * * * *

Imagine such a one ;—for such, I say, were the outlines of Doctor Slop's figure, coming slowly along, foot by foot, waddling through the dirt upon the *vertebræ* of a little diminutive pony, of a pretty color—but of strength—alack! scarce able to have made an amble of it, under such a fardel, had the roads been in an ambling condition :—they were not. Imagine to yourself Obadiah mounted upon a strong monster of a coach-horse, pricked into a full gallop, and making all practicable speed the adverse way. Vol. ii c. 9.

7. I think there is more humor in the single remark, which I have quoted before—"Learned men, brother Toby, don't write dialogues upon long noses for nothing!"—than in the whole Slawkenburghian tale that follows, which is mere oddity interspersed with drollery.

8. Note Sterne's assertion of, and faith in a moral good in the characters of Trim, Toby, &c. as contrasted with the cold skepticism of motives which is the stamp of the Jacobin spirit. Vol v. c. 9.

9. You must bear in mind, in order to do justice to Rabelais and Sterne, that by right of humoristic universality each part is essentially a whole in itself. Hence the digressive spirit is no mere wantonness, but in fact the very form and vehicle of their genius. The connection, such as was needed, is given by the continuity of the characters.

Instances of different forms of wit, taken largely:

1. "Why are you reading romances at your age?"—"Why, I used to be fond of history, but I have given it up—it was so grossly improbable."

2. "Pray, sir, do it!—although you have promised me."

3. The Spartan mother's—

"Return with, or on, thy shield."

"My sword is too short!"—"Take a step forwarder."

4. The Gasconade:—

"I believe you, Sir! but you will excuse my repeating it on account of my provincial accent."

5. Pasquil on Pope Urban, who had employed a committee to rip up the old errors of his predecessors.

Some one placed a pair of spurs on the heels of the statue of St. Peter, and a label from the opposite statue of St. Paul, on the same bridge:—

St. Paul. "Whither then are you bound?"

St. Peter. "I apprehend danger here;—they'll soon call me in question for denying my Master."

St. Paul. "Nay, then, I had better be off too; for they'll question me for having persecuted the Christians, before my conversion."

6. Speaking of the small German potentates, I dictated the phrase—*officious for equivalents.* This my amanuensis wrote—*fishing for elephants;*—which, as I observed at the time, was a sort of Noah's angling, that could hardly have occurred, except at the commencement of the Deluge.

LECTURE X.

DONNE—DANTE—MILTON—PARADISE LOST.

DONNE.*

Born in London, 1573.—Died, 1631.

I.

With Donne, whose muse on dromedary trots,
Wreathe iron pokers into true-love knots;
Rhyme's sturdy cripple, fancy's maze and clue,
Wit's forge and fire-blast, meaning's press and screw.

II.

See lewdness and theology combin'd,—
A cynic and a sycophantic mind;
A fancy shar'd party per pale between
Death's heads and skeletons, and Aretine!—
Not his peculiar defect or crime,
But the true current mintage of the time.
Such were the establish'd signs and tokens given
To mark a loyal churchman, sound and even,
Free from papistic and fanatic leaven.

The wit of Donne, the wit of Butler, the wit of Pope, the wit of Congreve, the wit of Sheridan—how many disparate things are here expressed by one and the same word, Wit!—Wonder-exciting vigor, intenseness and peculiarity of thought, using at will the almost boundless stores of a capacious memory, and exercised on subjects, where we have no right to expect it—this is

* Nothing remains of what was said on Donne in this Lecture. Here, therefore, as in previous like instances, the gap is filled up with some notes written by Mr. Coleridge in a volume of Chalmer's Poets, belonging to Mr. Gillman. The verses were added in pencil to the collection of commendatory lines; No. I. is Mr. C.'s; the publication of No. II. I trust the all-accomplished author will, under the circumstances, pardon. Numerous and elaborate notes by Mr. Coleridge on Donne's Sermons are in existence, and will be published hereafter.—*Ed.*

the wit of Donne! The four others I am just in the mood to describe and inter-distinguish;—what a pity that the marginal space will not let me!

> My face in thine eye, thine in mine appears,
> And true plain hearts do in the faces rest;
> Where can we find two fitter hemispheres
> Without sharp north, without declining west?
>
> Good-Morrow, v. 15, &c.

The sense is:—Our mutual loves may in many respects be fitly compared to corresponding hemispheres; but as no simile squares (*nihile simile est idem*), so here the simile fails, for there is nothing in our loves that corresponds to the cold north, or the declining west, which in two hemispheres must necessarily be supposed. But an ellipse of such length will scarcely rescue the line from the charge of nonsense or a bull. *January*, 1829.

Woman's constancy.

A misnomer. The title ought to be—

Mutual Inconstancy.

> Whether both th' Indias of spice and *mine*, &c.
>
> Sun Rising, v. 17.

> And see at night thy western land of *mine*, &c.
>
> Progress of the Soul, 1 Song, 2 st.

This use of the word *mine* specifically for mines of gold, silver, or precious stones, is, I believe, peculiar to Donne.

DANTE.

Born at Florence, 1265.—Died, 1321.

As I remarked in a former Lecture on a different subject (for subjects the most diverse in literature have still their tangents), the Gothic character, and its good and evil fruits, appeared less in Italy than in any other part of European Christendom. There was accordingly much less romance, as that word is commonly understood; or, perhaps, more truly stated, there was romance instead of chivalry. In Italy, an earlier imitation of, and a more evident and intentional blending with, the Latin literature took place than elsewhere. The operation of the feudal system, too, was incalculably weaker, of that singular chain of independent interdependents, the principle of which was a confederacy for the preservation of individual, consistently with general, freedom. In short, Italy, in the time of Dante, was an after-birth of eldest Greece, a renewal or a reflex of the old Italy under its kings and first Roman consuls, a net-work of free little republics, with the same domestic feuds, civil wars, and party spirit—the same vices and virtues produced on a similarly narrow theatre—the existing state of things being, as in all small democracies, under the working and direction of certain individuals, to whose will even the laws were swayed;—whilst at the same time the singular spectacle was exhibited amidst all this confusion of the flourishing of commerce, and the protection and encouragement of letters and arts. Never was the commercial spirit so well reconciled to the nobler principles of social polity as in Florence. It tended there to union and permanence and elevation—not as the overbalance of it in England is now doing, to dislocation, change and moral degradation. The intensest patriotism reigned in these communities, but confined and attached exclusively to the small locality of the patriot's birth and residence; whereas in the true Gothic feudalism, country was nothing but the preservation of personal independence. But then, on the other hand, as a counterbalance to these disuniting elements, there was in Dante's Italy, as in Greece, a much greater uniformity of religion common to all than amongst the northern nations.

Upon these hints the history of the republican æras of ancient Greece and modern Italy ought to be written. There are three kinds or stages of historic narrative;—1. that of the annalist or chronicler, who deals merely in facts and events arranged in order of time, having no principle of selection, no plan of arrangement, and whose work properly constitutes a supplement to the poetical writings of romance or heroic legends:—2. that of the writer who takes his stand on some moral point, and selects a series of events for the express purpose of illustrating it, and in whose hands the narrative of the selected events is modified by the principle of selection;—as Thucydides, whose object was to describe the evils of democratic and aristocratic partisanships;—or Polybius, whose design was to show the social benefits resulting from the triumph and grandeur of Rome, in public institutions and military discipline ;—or Tacitus, whose secret aim was to exhibit the pressure and corruptions of despotism; in all which writers and others like them, the ground-object of the historian colors with artificial lights the facts which he relates :—3. and which in idea is the grandest—the most truly founded in philosophy—there is the Herodotean history, which is not composed with reference to any particular causes, but attempts to describe human nature itself on a great scale as a portion of the drama of providence, the free will of man resisting the destiny of events—for the individuals often succeeding against it, but for the race always yielding to it, and in the resistance itself invariably affording means towards the completion of the ultimate result. Mitford's history is a good and useful work; but in his zeal against democratic government, Mitford forgot, or never saw, that ancient Greece was not, nor ought ever to be considered, a permanent thing, but that it existed, in the disposition of providence, as a proclaimer of ideal truths, and that everlasting proclamation being made, that its functions were naturally at an end.

However, in the height of such a state of society in Italy, Dante was born and flourished; and was himself eminently a picture of the age in which he lived. But of more importance even than this, to a right understanding of Dante, is the consideration that the scholastic philosophy was then at its acme even in itself; but more especially in Italy, where it never prevailed so exclusively as northward of the Alps. It is impossible to understand the genius of Dante, and difficult to understand his poem, without some knowledge of the characters, studies, and writings of the schoolmen of the twelfth, thirteenth, and fourteenth centuries. For Dante was the living link between religion and philosophy; he philosophized the religion and Christianized the philosophy of Italy; and, in this poetic union of religion and philosophy, he became the ground of transition into the mixed Platonism and Aristotelianism of the Schools, under which, by numerous minute articles of faith and ceremony, Christianity became a craft of hair-splitting, and was ultimately degraded into a complete *fetisch* worship, divorced from philosophy, and made up of a faith without thought, and a credulity directed by passion. Afterwards, indeed, philosophy revived under condition of defending this very superstition; and, in so doing, it necessarily led the way to its subversion, and that in exact proportion to the influence of the philosophic schools. Hence it did its work most completely in Germany, then in England, next in France, then in Spain, least of all in Italy. We must, therefore, take the poetry of Dante as Christianized, but without the further Gothic accession of proper chivalry. It was at a somewhat later period, that the importations from the East, through the Venetian commerce and the crusading armaments, exercised a peculiarly strong influence on Italy.

In studying Dante, therefore, we must consider carefully the differences produced, first, by allegory being substituted for polytheism; and secondly and mainly, by the opposition of Christianity to the spirit of pagan Greece, which receiving the very names of its gods from Egypt, soon deprived them of all that was universal. The Greeks changed the ideas into finites, and these finites into *anthropomorphi*, or forms of men. Hence their religion, their poetry, nay, their very pictures, became statuesque. With them the form was the end. The reverse of this was the natural effect of Christianity; in which finites, even the human form, must, in order to satisfy the mind, be brought into connection with, and be in fact symbolical of, the infinite; and must be considered in some enduring, however shadowy and indistinct, point of view, as the vehicle or representative of moral truth.

Hence resulted two great effects; a combination of poetry with doctrine, and, by turning the mind inward on its own essence instead of letting it act only on its outward circumstances and communities, a combination of poetry with sentiment. And it is this inwardness or subjectivity, which principally and most fundamentally distinguishes all the classic from all the modern poetry. Compare the passage in the Iliad (Z′. vi. 119–236) in which Diomed and Glaucus change arms,—

> Χεῖράς τ' ἀλλήγων λαβέτην καὶ πιστώσαντο—
> They took each other by the hand, and pledged friendship—

with the scene in Ariosto (Orlando Furioso, c. i. st. 20–22), where Rinaldo and Ferrauto fight and afterwards make it up:—

> Al Pagan la proposta non dispiacque:
> Così fu differita la tenzone;
> E tal tregua tra lor subito nacque,
> Sì l' odio e l' ira va in oblivione,

Che 'l Pagano al partir dalle fresche acque
Non lasciò a piede il buon figliuol d' Amone;
Con preghi invita, e al fin lo toglie in groppa,
E per l' orme d' Angelica galoppa.

Here Homer would have left it. But the Christian poet has his own feelings to express, and goes on:—

Oh gran bontà de' cavalieri antiqui!
Eran rivali, eran di fè diversi,
E si sentian degli aspri colpi iniqui
Per tutta la persona anco dolersi;
E pur per selve oscure e calli obbliqui
Insieme van senza sospetto aversi!

And here you will observe, that the reaction of Ariosto's own feelings on the image or act is more fore-grounded (to use a painter's phrase) than the image or act itself.

The two different modes in which the imagination is acted on by the ancient and modern poetry, may be illustrated by the parallel effects caused by the contemplation of the Greek or Roman-Greek architecture, compared with the Gothic. In the Pantheon, the whole is perceived in a perceived harmony with the parts which compose it; and generally you will remember that where the parts preserve any distinct individuality, there simple beauty, or beauty simply, arises; but where the parts melt undistinguished into the whole, there majestic beauty, or majesty, is the result. In York Minster, the parts, the grotesques, are in themselves very sharply distinct and separate, and this distinction and separation of the parts is counterbalanced only by the multitude and variety of those parts, by which the attention is bewildered;—whilst the whole, or that there is a whole produced, is altogether a feeling in which the several thousand distinct impressions lose themselves as in a universal solvent. Hence in a Gothic cathedral, as in a prospect from a mountain's top, there is indeed a unity, an awful oneness;—but it is, because all distinction evades the eye. And just such is the distinction between the Antigone of Sophocles and the Hamlet of Shakspeare.*

The Divina Commedia is a system of moral, political, and theological truths, with arbitrary personal exemplifications, which are not, in my opinion, allegorical. I do not even feel convinced

* See Lect. i. p. 234, and note: and compare with Schelling's *Dram. Vorlesung.* Lect. i. vol. i. p. 10.

that the punishments in the Inferno are strictly allegorical. I rather take them to have been in Dante's mind *quasi*-allegorical, or conceived in analogy to pure allegory.

I have said, that a combination of poetry with doctrines, is one of the characteristics of the Christian muse ; but I think Dante has not succeeded in effecting this combination nearly so well as Milton.

This comparative failure of Dante, as also some other peculiarities of his mind, *in malam partem*, must be immediately attributed to the state of North Italy in his time, which is vividly represented in Dante's life ; a state of intense democratical partisanship, in which an exaggerated importance was attached to individuals, and which whilst it afforded a vast field for the intellect, opened also a boundless arena for the passions, and in which envy, jealousy, hatred, and other malignant feelings, could and did assume the form of patriotism, even to the individual's own conscience.

All this common, and, as it were, natural partisanship, was aggravated and colored by the Guelf and Ghibelline factions ; and, in part explanation of Dante's adherence to the latter, you must particularly remark, that the Pope had recently territorialized his authority to a great extent, and that this increase of territorial power in the church, was by no means the same beneficial movement for the citizens of free republics, as the parallel advance in other countries was for those who groaned as vassals under the oppression of the circumjacent baronial castles.*

By way of preparation to a satisfactory perusal of the Divina Commedia, I will now proceed to state what I consider to be Dante's chief excellences as a poet. And I begin with

I. Style—the vividness, logical connection, strength and energy of which can not be surpassed. In this I think Dante superior to Milton ; and his style is accordingly more imitable than Milton's, and does to this day exercise a greater influence on the literature of his country. You can not read Dante without feeling a gush of manliness of thought within you. Dante was very sensible of his own excellence in this particular, and speaks of poets as guardians of the vast armory of language, which is the intermediate something between matter and spirit :—

* Mr. Coleridge here notes : "I will, if I can, here make an historical movement, and pay a proper compliment to Mr. Hallam."—*Ed.*

Or se' tu quel Virgilio, e quella fonte,
Che spande di parlar sì largo fiume?
Risposi lui con vergognosa fronte.
O degli altri poeti onore e lume,
Vagliami 'l lungo studio e 'l grande amore,
Che m' han fatto cercar lo tuo volume.
Tu se' lo mio maestro, e 'l mio autore:
Tu se' solo colui, da cu' io tolsi
Lo bello stile, che m' ha fatto onore.
Inf. c. 1, v. 79.

"And art thou then that Virgil, that well-spring,
From which such copious floods of eloquence
Have issued?" I, with front abash'd, replied:
"Glory and light of all the tuneful train!
May it avail me, that I long with zeal
Have sought thy volume, and with love immense
Have conn'd it o'er. My master, thou, and guide!
Thou he from whom I have alone deriv'd
That style, which for its beauty into fame
Exalts me." CARY

Indeed there was a passion and a miracle of words in the twelfth and thirteenth centuries, after the long slumber of language in barbarism, which gave an almost romantic character, a virtuous quality and power, to what was read in a book, independently of the thoughts or images contained in it. This feeling is very often perceptible in Dante.

II. The Images in Dante are not only taken from obvious nature, and are all intelligible to all, but are ever conjoined with the universal feeling received from nature, and therefore affect the general feelings of all men. And in this respect, Dante's excellence is very great, and may be contrasted with the idiosyncrasies of some meritorious modern poets, who attempt an eruditeness, the result of particular feelings. Consider the simplicity, I may say plainness, of the following simile, and how differently we should in all probability deal with it at the present day:—

Quale i fioretti dal notturno gelo
Chinati e chiusi, poi che 'l sol gl' imbianca,
Si drizzan tutti aperti in loro stelo,—
Fal mi fec' io di mia virtute stanca:
Inf. c. 2, v. 127.

As florets, by the frosty air of night
Bent down and clos'd, when day has blanch'd their leaves,

Rise all unfolded on their spiry stems,—
So was my fainting vigor new restor'd.
CARY.*

III. Consider the wonderful profoundness of the whole third canto of the Inferno; and especially of the inscription over Hell-gate:—

Per me si va, &c.—

which can only be explained by a meditation on the true nature of religion; that is,—reason *plus* the understanding. I say profoundness rather than sublimity; for Dante does not so much elevate your thoughts as send them down deeper. In this canto all the images are distinct, and even vividly distinct; but there is a total impression of infinity; the wholeness is not in vision or conception, but in an inner feeling of totality, and absolute being.

IV. In picturesqueness, Dante is beyond all other poets, modern, or ancient, and more in the stern style of Pindar, than of any other. Michel Angelo is said to have made a design for every page of the Divina Commedia. As super-excellent in this respect, I would note the conclusion of the third canto of the Inferno:—

Ed ecco verso noi venir per nave
Un vecchio bianco per antico pelo
Gridando: guai a voi anime prave: &c.
Ver. 82, &c.
* * * * * *
And lo! toward us in a bark
Comes on an old man, hoary white with eld,
Crying, "Woe to you, wicked spirits!"
* * * * * *
CARY.

Caron dimonio con occhi di bragia
Loro accennando, tutte le raccoglie:
Batte col remo qualunque s' adagia.
Come d' autunno si levan le foglie
L' una appresso dell' altra, infin che 'l ramo
Rende alla terra tutte le sue spoglie;
Similemente il mal seme d' Adamo,
Gittansi di quel lito ad una ad una
Per cenni, com' augel per suo richiamo.
Ver. 100, &c.

---

* Mr. Coleridge here notes: "Here to speak of Mr. Cary's translation."—*Ed.*

———Charon, demoniac form,
With eyes of burning coal, collects them all,
Beck'ning, and each that lingers, with his oar
Strikes. As fall off the light autumnal leaves,
One still another following, till the bough
Strews all its honors on the earth beneath;—
E'en in like manner Adam's evil brood
Cast themselves one by one down from the shore
Each at a beck, as falcon at his call. CARY.

And this passage, which I think admirably picturesque:—

Ma poco valse, che l' ale al sospetto
Non potero avanzar: quegli andò sotto,
E quei drizzò, volando, suso il petto:
Non altrimenti l' anitra di botto,
Quando 'l falcon s' appressa, giù s' attuffa,
Ed ei ritorna su crucciato e rotto.
Irato Calcabrina della buffa,
Volando dietro gli tenne, invaghito,
Che quei campasse, per aver la zuffa:
E come 'l barattier fu disparito,
Così volse gli artigli al suo compagno,
E fu con lui sovra 'l fosso ghermito.
Ma l' altro fu bene sparvier grifagno
Ad artigliar ben lui, e amedue
Cadder nel mezzo del bollente stagno.
Lo caldo sghermidor subito fue:
Ma però di levarsi era niente,
Sì aveano inviscate l' ale sue.
Infer. c. xxii. ver. 127, &c.

But little it avail'd: terror outstripp'd
His following flight: the other plung'd beneath,
And he with upward pinion rais'd his breast:
E'en thus the water-fowl, when she perceives
The falcon near, dives instant down, while he
Enrag'd and spent retires. That mockery
In Calcabrina fury stirr'd, who flew
After him, with desire of strife inflam'd;
And, for the barterer had 'scap'd, so turn'd
His talons on his comrade. O'er the dyke
In grapple close they join'd; but th' other prov'd
A goshawk, able to rend well his foe;
And in the boiling lake both fell. The heat
Was umpire soon between them, but in vain
To lift themselves they strove, so fast were glued
Their pennons. CARY.

V. Very closely connected with this picturesqueness, is the topographic reality of Dante's journey through Hell. You should note and dwell on this as one of his great charms, and which gives a striking peculiarity to his poetic power. He thus takes the thousand delusive forms of a nature worse than chaos, having no reality but from the passions which they excite, and compels them into the service of the permanent. Observe the exceeding truth of these lines:—

Noi ricidemmo 'l cerchio all' altra riva,
Sovr' una fonte che bolle, e riversa,
Per un fossato che da lei diriva.
L' acqua era buja molto più che persa:
E noi in compagnia dell' onde bige
Entrammo giù per una via diversa.
Una palude fa, ch' ha nome Stige,
Questo tristo ruscel, quando è disceso
Al piè delle maligne piagge grige.
Ed io che di mirar mi stava inteso,—
Vidi genti fangose in quel pantano
Ignude tutte, e con sembiante offeso.
Questi si percotean non pur con mano,
Ma con la testa, e col petto, e co' piedi,
Troncandosi co' denti a brano a brano.
* * * * *
Così girammo della lorda pozza
Grand' arco tra la ripa secca e 'l mezzo,
Con gli occhi volti a chi del fango ingozza:
Venimmo appiè d' una torre al dassezzo.
C. vii. ver. 100 and 127.

——We the circle cross'd
To the next steep, arriving at a well,
That boiling pours itself down to a foss
Sluic'd from its source. Far murkier was the wave
Than sablest grain: and we in company
Of th' inky waters, journeying by their side,
Enter'd, though by a different track, beneath.
Into a lake, the Stygian nam'd, expands
The dismal stream, when it hath reach'd the foot
Of the gray wither'd cliffs. Intent I stood
To gaze, and in the marsh sunk, descried
A miry tribe, all naked, and with looks
Betok'ning rage. They with their hands alone
Struck not, but with the head, the breast, the feet,
Cutting each other piecemeal with their fangs.
* * * * * * *

——————Our route
Thus compass'd, we a segment widely stretch'd
Between the dry embankment and the cove
Of the loath'd pool, turning meanwhile our eyes
Downward on those who gulp'd its muddy lees;
Nor stopp'd, till to a tower's low base we came.
CARY.

VI. For Dante's power,—his absolute mastery over, although rare exhibition of, the pathetic, I can do no more than refer to the passages on Francesca di Rimini (Infer. C. v. ver. 73 to the end), and on Ugolino (Infer. C. xxxiii. ver. 1 to 75). They are so well known, and rightly so admired, that it would be pedantry to analyze their composition; but you will note that the first is the pathos of passion, the second that of affection; and yet even in the first, you seem to perceive that the lovers have sacrificed their passion to the cherishing of a deep and rememberable impression.

VII. As to going into the endless subtle beauties of Dante, that is impossible; but I can not help citing the first triplet of the twenty-ninth canto of the Inferno:—

La molta gente e le diverse piaghe
Avean le luci mie sì inebriate,
Che dello stare a piangere eran vaghe.

So were mine eyes inebriate with the view
Of the vast multitude, whom various wounds
Disfigur'd, that they long'd to stay and weep.
CARY.

Nor have I now room for any specific comparison of Dante with Milton. But if I had, I would institute it upon the ground of the last canto of the Inferno from the 1st to the 69th line, and from the 106th to the end. And in this comparison I should notice Dante's occasional fault of becoming grotesque from being too graphic without imagination; as in his Lucifer compared with Milton's Satan. Indeed he is sometimes horrible rather than terrible,—falling into the μισητὸν instead of the δεινὸν of Longinus;* in other words, many of his images excite bodily disgust, and not moral fear. But here, as in other cases, you may perceive that the faults of great authors are generally excellencies carried to an excess.

* De Subl. l. ix.

MILTON.

Born in London, 1608.—Died, 1674.

If we divide the period from the accession of Elizabeth to the Protectorate of Cromwell into two unequal portions, the first ending with the death of James I., the other comprehending the reign of Charles and the brief glories of the Republic, we are forcibly struck with a difference in the character of the illustrious actors, by whom each period is rendered severally memorable. Or rather, the difference in the characters of the great men in each period, leads us to make this division. Eminent as the intellectual powers were that were displayed in both; yet in the number of great men, in the various sorts of excellence, and not merely in the variety but almost diversity of talents united in the same individual, the age of Charles falls short of its predecessor; and the stars of the Parliament, keen as their radiance was, in fulness and richness of lustre, yield to the constellation at the court of Elizabeth;—which can only be paralleled by Greece in her brightest moment, when the titles of the poet, the philosopher, the historian, the statesman, and the general not seldom formed a garland round the same head, as in the instances of our Sidneys and Raleighs. But then, on the other hand, there was a vehemence of will, an enthusiasm of principle, a depth and an earnestness of spirit, which the charms of individual fame and personal aggrandizement could not pacify,—an aspiration after reality, permanence, and general good,—in short, a moral grandeur in the latter period, with which the low intrigues, Machiavellic maxims, and selfish and servile ambition of the former, stand in painful contrast.

The causes of this it belongs not to the present occasion to detail at length; but a mere allusion to the quick succession of revolutions in religion, breeding a political indifference in the mass of men to religion itself, the enormous increase of the royal power in consequence of the humiliation of the nobility and the clergy—the transference of the papal authority to the crown,—the unfixed state of Elizabeth's own opinions, whose inclinations were as popish as her interests were protestant—the controversial extravagance and practical imbecility of her successor—will help to explain the former period; and the persecutions that had given a life-and-soul-interest to the disputes so imprudently fostered by James,—the ardor of a conscious increase of power in the commons, and the greater austerity of manners and maxims, the natural product and most formidable weapon of religious disputation, not merely in conjunction, but in closest combination, with newly-awakened political and republican zeal, these perhaps account for the character of the latter æra.

In the close of the former period, and during the bloom of the latter, the poet Milton was educated and formed ; and he survived the latter, and all the fond hopes and aspirations which had been its life ; and so in evil days, standing as the representative of the combined excellence of both periods, he produced the Paradise Lost as by an after-throe of nature. "There are some persons" (observes a divine, a contemporary of Milton's), "of whom the grace of God takes early hold, and the good spirit inhabiting them, carries them on in an even constancy through innocence into virtue, their Christianity bearing equal date with their manhood, and reason and religion, like warp and woof, running together, make up one web of a wise and exemplary life. This (he adds) is a most happy case, wherever it happens ; for, besides that there is no sweeter or more lovely thing on earth than the early buds of piety, which drew from our Saviour signal affection to the beloved disciple, it is better to have no wound than to experience the most sovereign balsam, which, if it work a cure, yet usually leaves a scar behind." Although it was and is my intention to defer the consideration of Milton's own character to the conclusion of this Lecture, yet I could not prevail on myself to approach the Paradise Lost without impressing on your minds the conditions under which such a work was in fact producible at all, the original genius having been assumed as the immediate agent and efficient cause ; and these conditions I find in the character of the times and in his own character. The age in which the foundations of his mind were laid, was congenial to it as one golden æra of profound erudition and individual genius ;—that in which the superstructure was carried up, was no less favorable to it by a sternness of discipline and a show of self-control, highly flattering to the imaginative dignity of an heir of fame, and which won Milton over from the dear-loved delights of academic groves and cathedral aisles to the anti-prelatic party. It acted on him too, no doubt, and modified his studies by a characteristic controversial spirit (his presentation of God is tinted with it)—a spirit not less busy indeed in political than in theological and ecclesiastical dispute, but carrying on the former almost always, more or less, in the guise of the latter. And so far as Pope's censure* of our poet—that he makes God the Father a school divine—is just, we must attribute it to the character of his age, from which the men of genius, who escaped, escaped by a worse disease, the licentious indifference of a Frenchified court.

Such was the *nidus* or soil which constituted, in the strict sense of the word, the circumstances of Milton's mind. In his mind itself there were purity and piety absolute; an imagination to which neither the past nor the present were interesting, except as far as they called forth and enlivened the great ideal, in which and for which he lived; a keen love of truth, which, after many weary pursuits, found a harbor in the sublime listening to the still voice in his own spirit, and as keen a love of his country, which, after a disappointment still more depressive, expanded and soared into a love of man as a probationer of immortality. These were, these alone could be, the conditions under which such a work as the Paradise Lost could be conceived and accomplished. By a life-long study Milton had known—

What was of use to know,
What best to say could say, to do had done.
His actions to his words agreed, his words
To his large heart gave utterance due, his heart
Contain'd of good, wise, fair, the perfect shape;

And he left the imperishable total, as a bequest to the ages coming, in the PARADISE LOST.†

Difficult as I shall find it to turn over these leaves without catching some passage, which would tempt me to stop, I propose to consider, 1st, the general plan and arrangement of the work; 2dly, the subject with its difficulties and advantages;—3dly, the poet's object, the spirit in the letter, the ἐνθύμιον ἐν μύθῳ, the true

* Table Talk, VI. p. 490.

† Here Mr. C. notes: "Not perhaps here, but towards, or as, the conclusion, to chastise the fashionable notion that poetry is a relaxation or amusement, one of the superfluous toys and luxuries of the intellect! To contrast the permanence of poems with the transiency and fleeting moral effects of empires, and what are called, great events."—*Ed.*

school-divinity; and lastly, the characteristic excellencies of the poem, in what they consist, and by what means they were produced.

1. As to the plan and ordonnance of the Poem.

Compare it with the Iliad, many of the books of which might change places without any injury to the thread of the story. Indeed, I doubt the original existence of the Iliad as one poem; it seems more probable that it was put together about the time of the Pisistratidæ. The Iliad—and, more or less, all epic poems, the subjects of which are taken from history—have no rounded conclusion; they remain, after all, but single chapters from the volume of history, although they are ornamental chapters. Consider the exquisite simplicity of the Paradise Lost. It and it alone really possesses a beginning, a middle, and an end; it has the totality of the poem as distinguished from the *ab ovo* birth and parentage, or straight line, of history.

2. As to the subject.

In Homer, the supposed importance of the subject, as the first effort of confederated Greece, is an after-thought of the critics; and the interest, such as it is, derived from the events themselves, as distinguished from the manner of representing them, is very languid to all but Greeks. It is a Greek poem. The superiority of the Paradise Lost is obvious in this respect, that the interest transcends the limits of a nation. But we do not generally dwell on this excellence of the Paradise Lost, because it seems attributable to Christianity itself;—yet in fact the interest is wider than Christendom, and comprehends the Jewish and Mohammedan worlds;—nay, still further, inasmuch as it represents the origin of evil, and the combat of evil and good, it contains matter of deep interest to all mankind, as forming the basis of all religion, and the true occasion of all philosophy whatsoever.

The Fall of man is the subject; Satan is the cause; man's blissful state the immediate object of his enmity and attack; man is warned by an angel who gives him an account of all that was requisite to be known, to make the warning at once intelligible and awful, then the temptation ensues, and the Fall; then the immediate sensible consequence; then the consolation, wherein an angel presents a vision of the history of man with the ultimate triumph of the Redeemer. Nothing is touched in this vision but what is of general interest in religion; any thing else would have been improper.

The inferiority of Klopstock's Messiah is inexpressible. I admit the prerogative of poetic feeling, and poetic faith; but I can not suspend the judgment even for a moment. A poem may in one sense be a dream, but it must be a waking dream. In Milton you have a religious faith combined with the moral nature; it is an efflux; you go along with it. In Klopstock there is a wilfulness; he makes things so and so. The feigned speeches and events in the Messiah shock us like falsehoods; but nothing of that sort is felt in the Paradise Lost, in which no particulars, at least very few indeed, are touched which can come into collision or juxtaposition with recorded matter.

But notwithstanding the advantages in Milton's subject, there were concomitant insuperable difficulties, and Milton has exhibited marvellous skill in keeping most of them out of sight. High poetry is the translation of reality into the ideal under the predicament of succession of time only. The poet is an historian, upon condition of moral power being the only force in the universe. The very grandeur of his subject ministered a difficulty to Milton. The statement of a being of high intellect, warring against the supreme Being, seems to contradict the idea of a supreme Being. Milton precludes our feeling this, as much as possible, by keeping the peculiar attributes of divinity less in sight, making them to a certain extent allegorical only. Again poetry implies the language of excitement; yet how to reconcile such language with God! Hence Milton confines the poetic passion in God's speeches to the language of Scripture; and once only allows the *passio vera*, or *quasi humana* to appear, in the passage, where the Father contemplates his own likeness in the Son before the battle:—

> Go then, thou Mightiest, in thy Father's might,
> Ascend my chariot, guide the rapid wheels
> That shake Heaven's basis, bring forth all my war,
> My bow and thunder; my almighty arms
> Gird on, and sword upon thy puissant thigh;
> Pursue these sons of darkness, drive them out
> From all Heaven's bounds into the utter deep:
> There let them learn, as likes them, to despise
> God and Messiah his anointed king.

B. vi. v. 710.

3. As to Milton's object:

It was to justify the ways of God to man! The controversial spirit observable in many parts of the poem, especially in God's speeches, is immediately attributable to the great controversy of that age, the origination of evil. The Arminians considered it a mere calamity. The Calvinists took away all human will. Milton asserted the will, but declared for the enslavement of the will out of an act of the will itself. There are three powers in us, which distinguish us from the beasts that perish:—1, reason; 2, the power of viewing universal truth; and 3, the power of contracting universal truth into particulars. Religion is the will in the reason, and love in the will.

The character of Satan is pride and sensual indulgence, finding in self the sole motive of action. It is the character so often seen *in little* on the political stage. It exhibits all the restlessness, temerity, and cunning which have marked the mighty hunters of mankind from Nimrod to Napoleon. The common fascination of men is, that these great men, as they are called, must act from some great motive. Milton has carefully marked in his Satan the intense selfishness, the alcohol of egotism, which would rather reign in hell than serve in heaven. To place this lust of self in opposition to denial of self or duty, and to show what exertions it would make, and what pains endure to accomplish its end, is Milton's particular object in the character of Satan. But around this character he has thrown a singularity of daring, a grandeur of sufferance, and a ruined splendor, which constitute the very height of poetic sublimity.

Lastly, as to the execution:—

The language and versification of the Paradise Lost are peculiar in being so much more necessarily correspondent to each than those in any other poem or poet. The connection of the sentences and the position of the words are exquisitely artificial; but the position is rather according to the logic of passion or universal logic, than to the logic of grammar. Milton attempted to make the English language obey the logic of passion, as perfectly as the Greek and Latin. Hence the occasional harshness in the construction.

Sublimity is the pre-eminent characteristic of the Paradise Lost. It is not an arithmetical sublime like Klopstock's, whose rule always is to treat what we might think large as contemptibly small.

Klopstock mistakes bigness for greatness. There is a greatness arising from images of effort and daring, and also from those of moral endurance; in Milton both are united. The fallen angels are human passions, invested with a dramatic reality.

The apostrophe to light at the commencement of the third book is particularly beautiful as an intermediate link between Hell and Heaven; and observe, how the second and third book support the subjective character of the poem. In all modern poetry in Christendom there is an under consciousness of a sinful nature, a fleeting away of external things, the mind or subject greater than the object, the reflective character predominant. In the Paradise Lost the sublimest parts are the revelations of Milton's own mind, producing itself and evolving its own greatness; and this is so truly so, that when that which is merely entertaining for its objective beauty is introduced, it at first seems a discord.

In the description of Paradise itself, you have Milton's sunny side as a man; here his descriptive powers are exercised to the utmost, and he draws deep upon his Italian resources. In the description of Eve, and throughout this part of the poem, the poet is predominant over the theologian. Dress is the symbol of the Fall, but the mark of intellect; and the metaphysics of dress are, the hiding what is not symbolic and displaying by discrimination what is. The love of Adam and Eve in Paradise is of the highest merit—not phantomatic, and yet removed from every thing degrading. It is the sentiment of one rational being towards another made tender by a specific difference in that which is essentially the same in both; it is a union of opposites, a giving and receiving mutually of the permanent in either, a completion of each in the other.

Milton is not a picturesque, but a musical, poet; although he has this merit, that the object chosen by him for any particular foreground always remains prominent to the end, enriched, but not encumbered, by the opulence of descriptive details furnished by an exhaustless imagination. I wish the Paradise Lost were more carefully read and studied than I can see any ground for believing it is, especially those parts which, from the habit of always looking for a story in poetry, are scarcely read at all,—as for example, Adam's vision of future events in the 11th and 12th books. No one can rise from the perusal of this immortal poem without a deep sense of the grandeur and the purity of Milton's soul, or without feeling how susceptible of domestic enjoyments he really was, notwithstanding the discomforts which actually resulted from an apparently unhappy choice in marriage. He was, as every truly great poet has ever been, a good man; but finding it impossible to realize his own aspirations, either in religion or politics, or society, he gave up his heart to the living spirit and light within him, and avenged himself on the world by enriching it with this record of his own transcendent ideal.

NOTES ON MILTON. 1807.*

(Hayley quotes the following passage:—)

"Time serves not now, and, perhaps, I might seem too profuse to give any certain account of what the mind at home, in the spacious circuit of her musing, hath liberty to propose to herself, though of highest hope and hardest attempting; whether that epic form, whereof the two poems of Homer, and those other two of Virgil and Tasso, are a diffuse, and *the book of Job a brief, model.*"—P. 69.

THESE latter words deserve particular notice. I do not doubt that Milton intended his Paradise Lost as an epic of the first class, and that the poetic dialogue of the Book of Job was his model for the general scheme of his Paradise Regained. Readers would not be disappointed in this latter poem, if they proceeded to a perusal of it with a proper preconception of the kind of interest intended to be excited in that admirable work. In its kind, it is the most perfect poem extant, though its kind may be inferior in interest—being in its essence didactic—to that other sort, in which instruction is conveyed more effectively, because less directly, in connection with stronger and more pleasurable emotions, and thereby in a closer affinity with action. But might we not as rationally object to an accomplished woman's conversing, however agreeably, because it has happened that we have received a keener pleasure from her singing to the harp? *Si genus sit probo et sapienti viro haud indignum, et si poema sit in suo genere perfectum, satis est. Quod si hoc auctor idem altioribus*

* These notes were written by Mr. Coleridge in a copy of Hayley's Life of Milton (4to. 1796), belonging to Mr. Poole. By him they were communicated, and this seems the fittest place for their publication.—*Ed.*

numeris et carmini diviniori ipsum per se divinum superaddiderit, mehercule satis est, et plusquam satis. I can not, however, but wish that the answer of Jesus to Satan in the 4th book, (v. 285)—

> Think not but that I know these things; or think
> I know them not, not therefore am I short
> Of knowing what I ought, &c.

had breathed the spirit of Hayley's noble quotation rather than the narrow bigotry of Gregory the Great. The passage is, indeed, excellent, and is partially true; but partial truth is the worst mode of conveying falsehood.

Hayley, p. 75. "The sincerest friends of Milton may here agree with Johnson, who speaks of *his controversial merriment as disgusting.*"

The man who reads a work meant for immediate effect on one age with the notions and feelings of another, may be a refined gentleman, but must be a sorry critic. He who possesses imagination enough to live with his forefathers, and, leaving comparative reflection for an after-moment, to give himself up during the first perusal to the feelings of a contemporary, if not a partisan, will, I dare aver, rarely find any part of Milton's prose works disgusting.

(Hayley, p. 104. Hayley is speaking of the passage in Milton's Answer to Icon Basilice, in which he accuses Charles of taking his Prayer in captivity from Pamela's prayer in the 3d book of Sidney's Arcadia. The passage begins,—

"But this king, not content with that which, although in a thing holy, is no holy theft, to attribute to his own making other men's whole prayers," &c. Symmons' ed., 1806, p. 407.)

Assuredly, I regret that Milton should have written this passage; and yet the adoption of a prayer from a romance on such an occasion does not evince a delicate or deeply sincere mind. We are the creatures of association. There are some excellent moral and even serious lines in Hudibras; but what if a clergyman should adorn his sermon with a quotation from that poem! Would the abstract propriety of the verses leave him "honorably acquitted?" The Christian baptism of a line in Virgil is so far from being a parallel, that it is ridiculously inappropriate,—an absurdity as glaring as that of the bigoted Puritans, who objected to some of the noblest and most scriptural prayers ever dictated by wisdom and piety, simply because the Roman Catholics had used them.

Hayley, p. 107. "The ambition of Milton," &c.

I do not approve the so frequent use of this word relatively to Milton. Indeed the fondness for ingrafting a good sense on the word "ambition," is not a Christian impulse in general.

Hayley, p. 110. "Milton himself seems to have thought it allowable in literary contention to vilify, &c. the character of an opponent; but surely this doctrine is unworthy," &c.

If ever it were allowable, in this case it was especially so. But these general observations, without meditation on the particular times and the genius of the times, are most often as unjust as they are always superficial.

(Hayley, p. 133. Hayley is speaking of Milton's panegyric on Cromwell's government:—)

Besides, however Milton might and did regret the immediate necessity, yet what alternative was there? Was it not better that Cromwell should usurp power, to protect religious freedom at least, than that the Presbyterians should usurp it to introduce a religious persecution,—extending the notion of spiritual concerns so far as to leave no freedom even to a man's bedchamber?

(Hayley, p. 250. Hayley's conjectures on the origin of the Paradise Lost:—)

If Milton borrowed a hint from any writer, it was more probably from Strada's Prolusions, in which the Fall of the Angels is pointed out as the noblest subject for a Christian poet.* The more dissimilar the detailed images are, the more likely it is that a great genius should catch the general idea.

* The reference seems generally to be to the 5th Prolusion of the 1st Book. *Hic arcus hac tela, quibus olim in magno illo Superum tumultu princeps armorum Michael confixit auctorem proditionis; hic fulmina humanæ mentis terror.* * * * * *In nubibus armatas bello legiones instruam, atque inde pro re nata auxiliares ad terram copias evocabo.* * * * * * *Hic mihi Cœlites, quos esse ferunt elementorum tutelares, prima illa corpora miscebunt.—Sec. 4.—Ed.*

(Hayl. p. 294. Extracts from the Adamo of Andreini :

“ Lucifero. Che dal mio centro oscuro
Mi chiama a rimirar cotanta luce ?

Who from my dark abyss
Calls me to gaze on this *excess of light ?*”

The words in italics are an unfair translation. They may suggest that Milton really had read and did imitate this drama. The original is, ‘ in so great light.’ Indeed the whole version is affectedly and inaccurately Miltonic.

Ib. v. 11. Che di fango opre festi—
Forming thy works of *dust* (no, dirt)—

Ib. v. 17. Tessa pur stella a stella,
V’ aggiunga e luna, e sole.—

Let him unite above
Star upon star, moon, sun.

Let him weave star to star,
Then join both moon and sun !

Ib. v. 21. Ch ’al fin con biasmo e scorno
Vana l’opra sarà, vano il sudore !

Since in the end division
Shall prove his works and all his efforts vain.

Since finally with censure and disdain
Vain shall the work be, and his toil be vain !

1796.*

The reader of Milton must be always on his duty: he is surrounded with sense ; it rises in every line ; every word is to the purpose. There are no lazy intervals ; all has been considered, and demands and merits observation. If this be called obscurity, let it be remembered that it is such an obscurity as is a compliment to the reader ; not that vicious obscurity, which proceeds from a muddled head.

* From a common-place book of Mr. C.’s, communicated by Mr. J. M. Gutch.—*Ed.*

LECTURE XI.*

ASIATIC AND GREEK MYTHOLOGIES—ROBINSON CRUSOE—USE OF WORKS OF IMAGINATION IN EDUCATION.

A CONFOUNDING of God with Nature, and an incapacity of finding unity in the manifold and infinity in the individual,—these are the origin of polytheism. The most perfect instance of this kind of theism is that of early Greece ; other nations seem to have either transcended, or come short of, the old Hellenic standard,—a mythology in itself fundamentally allegorical, and typical of the powers and functions of nature, but subsequently mixed up with a deification of great men and hero-worship,—so that finally the original idea became inextricably combined with the form and attributes of some legendary individual. In Asia, probably from the greater unity of the government and the still surviving influence of patriarchal tradition, the idea of the unity of God, in a distorted reflection of the Mosaic scheme, was much more generally preserved ; and accordingly all other super or ultra-human beings could only be represented as ministers of, or rebels against, his will. The Asiatic genii and fairies are, therefore, always endowed with moral qualities, and distinguishable as malignant or benevolent to man. It is this uniform attribution of fixed moral qualities to the supernatural agents of eastern mythology that particularly separates them from the divinities of old Greece.

Yet it is not altogether improbable that in the Samothracian or Cabeiric mysteries the link between the Asiatic and Greek popular schemes of mythology lay concealed. Of these mysteries there are conflicting accounts, and, perhaps, there were variations of doctrine in the lapse of ages and intercourse with other systems. But, upon a review of all that is left to us on this subject

* Partly from Mr. Green's note.—*Ed.*

Compare with the doctrine of this lecture, Schelling's *Ueber die Gottheiten von Samothrace*, and Creutzer's criticism of it, together with his own account of the eldest religion of Greece : *Symbolik, Sechstes Capitel.* Werke, 2 Th. 53, 302–377.—*Am. Ed.*

in the writings of the ancients, we may, I think, make out thus much of an interesting fact,—that *Cabiri*, impliedly at least, meant *socii*, *complices*, having a hypostatic or fundamental union with, or relation to, each other; that these mysterious divinities were, ultimately at least, divided into a higher and lower triad; that the lower triad, *primi quia infimi*, consisted of the old Titanic deities or powers of nature, under the obscure names of *Axieros*, *Axiokersos* and *Axiokersa*, representing symbolically different modifications of animal desire or material action, such as hunger, thirst, and fire, without consciousness; that the higher triad, *ultimi quia superiores*, consisted of Jupiter (Pallas, or Apollo, or Bacchus, or Mercury, mystically called *Cadmilos*) and Venus, representing, as before, the νοῦς or reason, the λόγος or word or communicative power, and the ἔρως or love; that the *Cadmilos* or Mercury, they manifested, communicated, or sent, appeared not only in his proper person as second of the higher triad, but also as a mediator between the higher and lower triad, and so there were seven divinities; and, indeed, according to some authorities, it might seem that the *Cadmilos* acted once as a mediator of the higher, and once of the lower, triad, and that so there were eight Cabeiric divinities. The lower or Titanic powers being subdued, chaos ceased, and creation began in the reign of the divinities of mind and love; but the chaotic gods still existed in the abyss, and the notion of evoking them was the origin, the idea, of the Greek necromancy.

These mysteries, like all the others, were certainly in connection with either the Phœnician or Egyptian systems, perhaps with both. Hence the old Cabeiric powers were soon made to answer the corresponding popular divinities; and the lower triad was called by the uninitiated, Ceres, Vulcan, or Pluto, and Proserpine, and the *Cadmilos* became Mercury. It is not without ground that I direct your attention, under these circumstances to the probable derivation of some portion of this most remarkable system from patriarchal tradition, and to the connection of the Cabeiri with the Kabbala.

The Samothracian mysteries continued in celebrity till some time after the commencement of the Christian era.* But they

* In the reign of Tiberius, A.D. 18, Germanicus attempted to visit Samothrace;—*illum in regressu sacra Samothracum visere nitentem obvii aquilones depulere.* Tacit. Ann. ii. c. 54.—*Ed.*

gradually sank with the rest of the ancient system of mythology, to which, in fact, they did not properly belong. The peculiar doctrines, however, were preserved in the memories of the initiated, and handed down by individuals. No doubt they were propagated in Europe, and it is not improbable that Paracelsus received many of his opinions from such persons, and I think a connection may be traced between him and Jacob Behmen.

The Asiatic supernatural beings are all produced by imagining an excessive magnitude, or an excessive smallness combined with great power; and the broken associations, which must have given rise to such conceptions, are the sources of the interest which they inspire, as exhibiting, through the working of the imagination, the idea of power in the will. This is delightfully exemplified in the Arabian Nights' Entertainments, and indeed, more or less, in other works of the same kind. In all these there is the same activity of mind as in dreaming, that is—an exertion of the fancy in the combination and recombination of familiar objects so as to produce novel and wonderful imagery. To this must be added that these tales cause no deep feeling of a moral kind—whether of religion or love; but an impulse of motion is communicated to the mind without excitement, and this is the reason of their being so generally read and admired.

I think it not unlikely that the Milesian Tales contained the germs of many of those now in the Arabian Nights; indeed it is scarcely possible to doubt that the Greek Empire must have left deep impression on the Persian intellect. So also many of the Roman Catholic legends are taken from Apuleius. In that exquisite story of Cupid and Psyche, the allegory is of no injury to the dramatic vividness of the tale. It is evidently a philosophic attempt to parry Christianity with a *quasi*-Platonic account of the fall and redemption of the soul.

The charm of De Foe's works, especially of Robinson Crusoe, is founded on the same principle. It always interests, never agitates. Crusoe himself is merely a representative of humanity in general; neither his intellectual or his moral qualities set him above the middle degree of mankind; his only prominent characteristic is the spirit of enterprise and wandering, which is, nevertheless, a very common disposition. You will observe that all that is wonderful in this tale is the result of external circumstances—of things which fortune brings to Crusoe's hand.

NOTES ON ROBINSON CRUSOE.*

Vol. i. p. 17. But my ill fate pushed me on now with an obstinacy that nothing could resist; and though I had several times loud calls from my reason, and my more composed judgment to go home, yet I had no power to do it. I know not what to call this, nor will I urge that it is a secret over-ruling decree that hurries us on to be the instruments of our own destruction, even though it be before us, and that we rush upon it with our eyes open.

THE wise only possess ideas; the greater part of mankind are possessed by them. Robinson Crusoe was not conscious of the master-impulse, even because it was his master, and had taken, as he says, full possession of him. When once the mind, in despite of the remonstrating conscience, has abandoned its free power to a haunting impulse or idea, then whatever tends to give depth and vividness to this idea or indefinite imagination, increases its despotism, and in the same proportion renders the reason and free will ineffectual. Now, fearful calamities, sufferings, horrors, and hair-breadth escapes will have this effect, far more than even sensual pleasure and prosperous incidents. Hence the evil consequences of sin in such cases, instead of retracting or deterring the sinner, goad him on to his destruction. This is the moral of Shakspeare's Macbeth, and the true solution of this paragraph,—not any overruling decree of divine wrath, but the tyranny of the sinner's own evil imagination, which he has voluntarily chosen as his master.

Compare the contemptuous Swift with the contemned De Foe, and how superior will the latter be found! But by what test?—Even by this; that the writer who makes me sympathize with his presentations with the whole of my being, is more estimable than he who calls forth, and appeals but to, a part of my being—my sense of the ludicrous, for instance. De Foe's excellence it is, to make me forget my specific class, character, and circumstances, and to raise me while I read him, into the universal man.

P. 80. I smiled to myself at the sight of this money: "O drug!" said I

* These notes were written by Mr. C. in Mr. Gillman's copy of Robinson Crusoe, in the summer of 1830. The references in the text are to Major's edition, 1831.—*Ed.*

aloud, &c. *However, upon second thoughts, I took it away;* and wrapping all this in a piece of canvass, &c.

Worthy of Shakspeare !—and yet the simple semicolon after it, the instant passing on without the least pause of reflex consciousness, is more exquisite and masterlike than the touch itself. A meaner writer, a Marmontel, would have put an (!) after '*away*,' and have commenced a fresh paragraph. 30th July, 1830.

P. 111. And I must confess, my religious thankfulness to God's providence began to abate too, upon the discovering that all this was nothing but what was common; though I ought to have been as thankful for so strange and unforeseen a providence, as if it had been miraculous.

To make men feel the truth of this is one characteristic object of the miracles worked by Moses;—in them the providence is miraculous, the miracles providential.

P. 126. The growing up of the corn, as is hinted in my Journal, had, at first, some little influence upon me, and began to affect me with seriousness, as long as I thought it had something miraculous in it, &c.

By far the ablest vindication of miracles which I have met with. It is indeed the true ground, the proper purpose and intention of a miracle.

P. 141. To think that this was all my own, that I was king and lord of all this country indefeasibly, &c.

By the by, what is the law of England respecting this? Suppose I had discovered, or been wrecked on an uninhabited island, would it be mine or the king's?

P. 223. I considered—that as I could not foresee what the ends of divine wisdom might be in all this, so I was not to dispute his sovereignty, who, as I was his creature, had an undoubted right, by creation, to govern and dispose of me absolutely as he thought fit, &c.

I could never understand this reasoning, grounded on a complete misapprehension of St. Paul's image of the potter, Rom. ix., or rather I do fully understand the absurdity of it. The susceptibility of pain and pleasure, of good and evil, constitutes a right in every creature endowed therewith in relation to every rational and moral being,—*à fortiori*, therefore, to the Supreme Reason, to the absolutely good Being. Remember Davenant's verses :—

Doth it our reason's mutinies appease
To say, the potter may his own clay mould
To every use, or in what shape he please,
At first not counsell'd, nor at last controll'd?

Power's hand can neither easy be, nor strict
To lifeless clay, which ease nor torment knows,
And where it can not favor or afflict,
It neither justice or injustice shows.

But souls have life, and life eternal too:
Therefore if doom'd before they can offend,
It seems to show what heavenly power can do,
But does not in that deed that power commend.

Death of Astragon, st. 88, &c.

P. 232–3. And this I must observe with grief too, that the discomposure of my mind had too great impressions also upon the religious parts of my thoughts,—praying to God being properly an act of the mind, not of the body.

As justly conceived as it is beautifully expressed. And a mighty motive for habitual prayer; for this can not but greatly facilitate the performance of rational prayer even in moments of urgent distress.

P. 244. That this would justify the conduct of the Spaniards in all their barbarities practised in America.

De Foe was a true philanthropist, who had risen above the antipathies of nationality; but he was evidently partial to the Spanish character, which, however, it is not, I fear, possible to acquit of cruelty. Witness the Netherlands, the Inquisition, the late Guerilla warfare, &c.

P. 249. That I shall not discuss, and perhaps can not account for; but certainly they are a proof of the converse of spirits, &c.

This reminds me of a conversation I once overheard. "How a statement so injurious to Mr. A. and so contrary to the truth, should have been made to you by Mr. B. I do not pretend to account for;—only I know of my own knowledge that B. is an inveterate liar, and has long borne malice against Mr. A.; and I can prove that he has repeatedly declared that in some way or other he would do Mr. A. a mischief."

P. 254. The place I was in was a most delightful cavity or grotto of its kind, as could be expected, though perfectly dark; the floor was dry and level, and had a sort of small loose gravel on it, &c.

How accurate an observer of nature De Foe was! The reader will at once recognize Professor Buckland's caves and the diluvial gravel.

P. 308. I entered into a long discourse with him about the devil, the original of him, his rebellion against God, his enmity to man, the reason of it, his setting himself up in the dark parts of the world to be worshipped instead of God, &c.

I presume that Milton's Paradise Lost must have been bound up with one of Crusoe's Bibles; otherwise I should be puzzled to know where he found all this history of the Old Gentleman. Not a word of it in the Bible itself, I am quite sure. But to be serious. De Foe did not reflect that all these difficulties are attached to a mere fiction, or, at the best, an allegory, supported by a few popular phrases and figures of speech used incidentally or dramatically by the Evangelists,—and that the existence of a personal, intelligent, evil being, the counterpart and antagonist of God, is in direct contradiction to the most express declarations of Holy Writ. "*Shall there be evil in a city, and the Lord hath not done it?*" Amos iii. 6. "*I make peace and create evil.*" Isa. xlv. 7. This is the deep mystery of the abyss of God.

Vol. ii. p. 3. I have often heard persons of good judgment say, * * * that there is no such thing as a spirit appearing, a ghost walking, and the like, &c.

I can not conceive a better definition of Body than "spirit appearing," or of a flesh-and-blood man than a rational spirit apparent. But a spirit *per se* appearing, is tantamount to a spirit appearing without its appearances. And as for ghosts, it is enough for a man of common sense to observe, that a ghost and a shadow are concluded in the same definition, that is, visibility without tangibility.

P. 9. She was, in a few words, the stay of all my affairs, the centre of all my enterprises, &c.

The stay of his affairs, the centre of his interests, the regulator of his schemes and movements, whom it soothed his pride to submit to, and in complying with whose wishes the conscious sensation of his acting will increased the impulse, while it disguised the coercion, of duty!—the clinging dependent, yet the strong supporter—the comforter, the comfort, and the soul's living home! This is De Foe's comprehensive character of the wife, as she should be; and, to the honor of womanhood be it spoken, there are few neighborhoods in which one name at least might not be found for the portrait.

The exquisite paragraphs in this and the next page, in addition to others scattered, though with a sparing hand, through his novels, afford sufficient proof that De Foe was a first-rate master of periodic style; but with sound judgment, and the fine tact of genius, he has avoided it as adverse to, nay, incompatible with, the every-day matter-of-fact realness, which form the charm and the character of all his romances. The Robinson Crusoe is like the vision of a happy night-mair, such as a denizen of Elysium might be supposed to have from a little excess in his nectar and ambrosia supper. Our imagination is kept in full play, excited to the highest; yet all the while we are touching, or touched by, common flesh and blood.

P. 67. The ungrateful creatures began to be as insolent and troublesome as before, &c.

How should it be otherwise? They were idle; and when we will not sow corn, the devil will be sure to sow weeds, nightshade, henbane, and devil's bit.

P. 82. That hardened villain was so far from denying it, that he said it was true, and ——— him they would do it still before they had done with them.

Observe when a man has once abandoned himself to wickedness, he can not stop, and does not join the devils till he has become a devil himself. Rebelling against his conscience he becomes the slave of his own furious will.

One excellence of De Foe, amongst many, is his sacrifice of lesser interest to the greater because more universal. Had he (as without any improbability he might have done) given his Robinson Crusoe any of the turn for natural history, which forms so striking and delightful a feature in the equally uneducated Dampier;—had he made him find out qualities and uses in the before (to him) unknown plants of the island, discover, for instance a substitute for hops, or describe birds, &c.—many delightful pages and incidents might have enriched the book ;—but then Crusoe would have ceased to be the universal representative, the person for whom every reader could substitute himself. But now nothing is done, thought, suffered, or desired, but what every man can imagine himself doing, thinking, feeling, or wishing for. Even so very easy a problem as that of finding a substitute for ink, is with exquisite judgment made to baffle Crusoe's inventive faculties. And in what he does, he arrives at no excellence ; he does not make basket-work like Will Atkins ; the carpentering, tailoring, pottery, &c., are all just what will answer his purposes, and those are confined to needs that all men have, and comforts that all men desire. Crusoe rises only to the point to which all men may be made to feel that they might, and that they ought to, rise in religion—to resignation, dependence on, and thankful acknowledgment of, the divine mercy and goodness.

In the education of children, love is first to be instilled, and out of love obedience is to be educed. Then impulse and power should be given to the intellect, and the ends of a moral being be exhibited. For this object thus much is effected by works of imagination ;—that they carry the mind out of self, and show the possible of the good and the great in the human character. The height, whatever it may be, of the imaginative standard will do no harm; we are commanded to imitate one who is inimitable. We should address ourselves to those faculties in a child's mind, which are first awakened by nature, and consequently first admit of cultivation, that is to say, the memory and the imagination.* The comparing power, the judgment, is not at that age active, and ought not to be forcibly excited, as is too frequently and mistakenly done in the modern systems of education, which can only lead to selfish views, debtor and creditor principles of virtue, and an inflated sense of merit. In the imagination of man exist the

* He (Sir W. Scott) "detested and despised the whole generation of modern children's books in which the attempt is made to convey accurate notions of scientific minutiæ, delighting cordially on the other hand in those of the preceding age, which addressing themselves chiefly to the *imagination* obtain *through it*, as he believed, the best chance of stirring our graver faculties also."—*Life of Scott.*

seeds of all moral and scientific improvement; chemistry was first alchemy, and out of astrology sprang astronomy. In the childhood of those sciences the imagination opened a way, and furnished materials, on which the ratiocinative powers in a maturer state operated with success. The imagination is the distinguishing characteristic of man as a progressive being; and I repeat that it ought to be carefully guided and strengthened as the indispensable means and instrument of continued amelioration and refinement. Men of genius and goodness are generally restless in their minds in the present, and this, because they are by a law of their nature unremittingly regarding themselves in the future, and contemplating the possible of moral and intellectual advance towards perfection. Thus we live by hope and faith; thus we are for the most part able to realize what we will, and thus we accomplish the end of our being. The contemplation of futurity inspires humility of soul in our judgment of the present.

I think the memory of children can not, in reason, be too much stored with the objects and facts of natural history. God opens the images of nature, like the leaves of a book, before the eyes of his creature, Man—and teaches him all that is grand and beautiful in the foaming cataract, the glassy lake, and the floating mist.

The common modern novel, in which there is no imagination, but a miserable struggle to excite and gratify mere curiosity, ought, in my judgment, to be wholly forbidden to children. Novel-reading of this sort is especially injurious to the growth of the imagination, the judgment, and the morals, especially to the latter, because it excites mere feelings without at the same time ministering an impulse to action. Women are good novelists, but indifferent poets; and this because they rarely or never thoroughly distinguish between fact and fiction. In the jumble of the two lies the secret of the modern novel, which is the *medium aliquid* between them, having just so much of fiction as to obscure the fact, and so much of fact as to render the fiction insipid. The perusal of a fashionable lady's novel, is to me very much like looking at the scenery and decorations of a theatre by broad daylight. The source of the common fondness for novels of this sort rests in that dislike of vacancy, and that love of sloth, which are inherent in the human mind; they afford excitement without producing reaction. By reaction I mean an activity of the intellectual faculties, which shows itself in consequent reasoning and observation, and originates action and conduct according to a principle. Thus, the act of thinking presents two sides for contemplation—that of external causality, in which the train of thought may be considered as the result of outward impressions, of accidental combinations, of fancy, or the associations of the memory—and on the other hand, that of internal causality, or of the energy of the will on the mind itself. Thought, therefore, might thus be regarded as passive or active; and the same faculties may in a popular sense be expressed as perception or observation, fancy or imagination, memory or recollection.

LECTURE XII.

DREAMS—APPARITIONS—ALCHEMISTS—PERSONALITY OF THE EVIL BEING—BODILY IDENTITY.

It is a general, but, as it appears to me, a mistaken opinion, that in our ordinary dreams we judge the objects to be real. I say our ordinary dreams;—because as to the night-mair the opinion is to a considerable extent just. But the night-mair is not a mere dream, but takes place when the waking state of the brain is recommencing, and most often during a rapid alternation, a twinkling, as it were, of sleeping and waking;—while either from pressure on, or from some derangement in, the stomach or other digestive organs acting on the external skin (which is still in sympathy with the stomach and bowels), and benumbing it, the sensations sent up to the brain by double touch (that is, when my own hand touches my side or breast), are so faint as to be merely equivalent to the sensation given by single touch, as when another person's hand touches me. The mind, therefore, which at all times, with and without our distinct consciousness, seeks for, and assumes, some outward cause for every impression from without, and which in sleep, by aid of the imaginative faculty, converts its judgment respecting the cause into a personal image as being the cause—the mind, I say, in this case, deceived by past experience, attributes the painful sensation received to a corresponding agent—an assassin, for instance, stabbing at the side, or a goblin sitting on the breast. Add too that the impressions of the bed, curtains, room, &c., received by the eyes in the half-moments of their opening, blend with, and give vividness and appropriate distance to, the dream image which returns when they close again; and thus we unite the actual perceptions, or their immediate reliques, with the phantoms of the inward sense; and in this manner so confound the half-waking, half-sleeping, reasoning power, that we actually do pass a positive judgment on the reality of what we see and hear, though often accompanied by doubt and self-questioning, which, as I have myself experienced, will at all times become strong enough, even before we awake, to convince us that it is what it is—namely, the night-mair.

In ordinary dreams we do not judge the objects to be real;—we simply do not determine that they are unreal. The sensations which they seem to produce, are in truth the causes and occasions of the images; of which there are two obvious proofs: first, that in dreams the strangest and most sudden metamorphoses do not create any sensation of surprise: and the second, that as to the most dreadful images, which during the dream were accompanied with agonies of terror, we merely awake, or turn round on the other side, and off fly both image and agony, which would be impossible if the sensations were produced by the images. This has always appeared to me an absolute demonstration of the true nature of ghosts and apparitions—such I mean of the tribe as were not pure inventions. Fifty years ago (and to this day in the ruder parts of Great Britain and Ireland, in almost every kitchen and in too many parlors it is nearly the same) you might meet persons who would assure you in the most solemn manner, so that you could not doubt their veracity at least, that they had seen an apparition of such and such a person,—in many cases, that the apparition had spoken to them; and they would describe themselves as having been in an agony of terror. They would tell you the story in perfect health. Now take the other class of facts, in which real ghosts have appeared;—I mean, where figures have been dressed up for the purpose of passing for apparitions:—in every instance I have known or heard of (and I have collected very many) the consequence has been either sudden death, or fits, or idiocy, or mania, or a brain fever. Whence comes the difference? evidently from this,—that in the one case the whole of the nervous system has been by slight internal causes gradually and all together brought into a certain state, the sensation of which is extravagantly exaggerated during sleep, and of which the images are the mere effects and exponents, as the motions of the weather-cock are of the wind;—while in the other case, the image rushing through the senses upon a nervous system, wholly unprepared, actually causes the sensation, which is sometimes powerful enough to produce a total check, and almost always a lesion or inflammation. Who has not witnessed the difference in shock when we have leaped down half-a-dozen steps intentionally, and that of having missed a single stair. How comparatively severe the latter is! The fact really is, as to apparitions, that the terror produces the image instead of the contrary; for *in omnem actum perceptionis influit imaginatio*, as says Wolfe.

O, strange is the self-power of the imagination—when painful sensations have made it their interpreter, or returning gladsomeness or convalescence has made its chilled and evanished figures and landscape bud, blossom, and live in scarlet, green, and snowy white (like the fire-screen inscribed with the nitrate and muriate of cobalt)—strange is the power to represent the events and circumstances, even to the anguish or the triumph of the *quasi*-credent soul, while the necessary conditions, the only possible causes of such contingencies, are known to be in fact quite hopeless;—yea, when the pure mind would recoil from the eve-lengthened shadow of an approaching hope, as from a crime:—and yet the effect shall have place, and substance, and living energy, and, on a blue islet of ether, in a whole sky of blackest cloudage, shine like a firstling of creation!

To return, however, to apparitions, and by way of an amusing illustration of the nature and value of even contemporary testimony upon such subjects, I will present you with a passage, literally translated by my friend, Mr. Southey, from the well-known work of Bernal Dias, one of the companions of Cortez, in the conquest of Mexico:

Here it is that Gomara says, that Francisco de Morla rode forward on a dappled gray horse, before Cortes and the cavalry came up, and that the apostle St. Iago, or St. Peter, was there. I must say that all our works and victories are by the hand of our Lord Jesus Christ, and that in this battle there were for each of us so many Indians, that they could have covered us with handfuls of earth, if it had not been that the great mercy of God helped us in every thing. And it may be that he of whom Gomara speaks, was the glorious Santiago or San Pedro, and I, as a sinner, was not worthy to see him; but he whom I saw there and knew, was Francisco de Morla on a chestnut horse, who came up with Cortes. And it seems to me that now while I am writing this, the whole war is represented before these sinful eyes, just in the manner as we then went through it. And though I, as an unworthy sinner, might not deserve to see either of these glorious apostles, there were in our company above four hundred soldiers and Cortes, and many other knights; and it would have been talked of and testified, and they would have made a church when they peopled the town, which would have been called Santiago de la Vittoria, or San Pedro de la Vittoria, as it is now called, Santa Maria de la Vittoria. And if it was, as Gomara says, bad Christians must we have been when our Lord God sent us his holy apostles, not to acknowledge his great mercy, and venerate his church daily. And would to God, it had been, as the Chronicler says!—but till I read his Chronicle, I never heard such a thing from any of the conquerors who were there.

Now, what if the odd accident of such a man as Bernal Dias' writing a history had not taken place! Gomara's account, the account of a contemporary, which yet must have been read by scores who were present, would have remained uncontradicted. I remember the story of a man, whom the devil met and talked with, but left at a particular lane;—the man followed him with his eyes, and when the devil got to the turning or bend of the lane, he vanished! The devil was upon this occasion drest in a blue coat, plush waistcoat, leather breeches and boots, and talked and looked just like a common man, except as to a particular lock of hair which he had. "And how do you know then that it was the devil?" "How do I know," replied the fellow,—"why, if it had not been the devil, being drest as he was, and looking as he did, why should I have been sore stricken with fright when I first saw him? and why should I be in such a tremble all the while he talked? And, moreover, he had a particular sort of a kind of a look, and when I groaned and said, upon every question he asked me, Lord have mercy upon me! or, Christ have mercy upon me! it was plain enough that he did not like it, and so he left me!"—The man was quite sober when he related this story; but as it happened to him on his return from market, it is probable that he was then muddled. As for myself, I was actually seen in Newgate in the winter of 1798;—the person who saw me there, said he asked my name of Mr. A. B. a known acquaintance of mine, who told him that it was young Coleridge, who had married the eldest Miss ——. "Will you go to Newgate, Sir?" said my friend; "for I assure you that Mr. C. is now in Germany." "Very willingly," replied the other, and away they went to Newgate, and sent for A. B. "Coleridge," cried he, "in Newgate! God forbid!" I said, "young Col—— who married the eldest Miss ——." The names were something similar. And yet this person had himself really seen me at one of my lectures.

I remember, upon the occasion of my inhaling the nitrous oxide at the Royal Institution, about five minutes afterwards, a gentleman came from the other side of the theatre and said to me,—"Was it not ravishingly delightful, Sir?"—"It was highly pleasurable, no doubt."—"Was it not very like sweet music?"—"I can not say I perceived any analogy to it."—"Did you not say it was very like Mrs. Billington singing by your ear?"—"No, Sir, I said that while I was breathing the gas, there was a singing in my ears."

To return, however, to dreams, I not only believe, for the reasons given, but have more than once actually experienced that the most fearful forms, when produced simply by association, instead of causing fear, operate no other effect than the same would do if they had passed through my mind as thoughts, while I was composing a faery tale; the whole depending on the wise and gracious law in our nature, that the actual bodily sensations, called forth according to the law of association by thoughts and images of the mind, never greatly transcend the limits of pleasurable feeling in a tolerably healthy frame, unless when an act of the judgment supervenes and interprets them as purporting instant danger to ourselves.

* There have been very strange and incredible stories told of and by the alchemists. Perhaps in some of them there may have been a specific form of mania, originating in the constant intension of the mind on an imaginary end, associated with an immense variety of means, all of them substances not familiar to men in general, and in forms strange and unlike to those of ordinary nature. Sometimes, it seems as if the alchemists wrote like

* From Mr. Green's note.

the Pythagoreans on music, imagining a metaphysical and inaudible music as the basis of the audible. It is clear that by sulphur they meant the solar rays or light, and by mercury the principle of ponderability, so that their theory was the same with that of the Heraclitic physics, or the modern German *Naturphilosophie*, which deduces all things from light and gravitation, each being bipolar; gravitation = north and south, or attraction and repulsion; light = east and west, or contraction and dilation; and gold being the tetrad, or interpenetration of both, as water was the dyad of light, and iron the dyad of gravitation.

It is, probably, unjust to accuse the alchemists generally of dabbling with attempts at magic in the common sense of the term. The supposed exercise of magical power always involved some moral guilt, directly or indirectly, as in stealing a piece of meat to lay on warts, touching humors with the hand of an executed person, &c. Rites of this sort and other practices of sorcery have always been regarded with trembling abhorrence by all nations, even the most ignorant, as by the Africans, the Hudson's Bay people, and others. The alchemists were, no doubt, often considered as dealers in art magic, and many of them were not unwilling that such a belief should be prevalent; and the more earnest among them evidently looked at their association of substances, fumigations, and other chemical operations as merely ceremonial, and seem, therefore, to have had a deeper meaning, that of evoking a latent power. It would be profitable to make a collection of all the cases of cures by magical charms and incantations; much useful information might, probably, be derived from it; for it is to be observed that such rites are the form in which medical knowledge would be preserved amongst a barbarous and ignorant people.

NOTE.* June, 1827.

The apocryphal book of Tobit consists of a very simple, but beautiful and interesting, family-memoir, into which some later Jewish poet or fabulist of Alexandria wove the ridiculous and frigid machinery, borrowed from the popular superstitions of the Greeks (though, probably, of Egyptian origin), and accommodated, clumsily enough, to the purer monotheism of the Mosaic law.

* Written in a copy of Mr. Hillhouse's Hadad.—*Ed.*

The Rape of the Lock is another instance of a simple tale thus enlarged at a later period, though in this case by the same author, and with a very different result. Now unless Mr. Hillhouse is Romanist enough to receive this nursery-tale garnish of a domestic incident as grave history and holy writ (for which, even from learned Roman Catholics, he would gain more credit as a very obedient child of the Church than as a biblical critic), he will find it no easy matter to support this assertion of his by the passages of Scripture here referred to, consistently with any sane interpretation of their import and purpose.

I. The Fallen Spirits.

This is the mythological form, or, if you will, the symbolical representation, of a profound idea necessary as the *præ-suppositum* of the Christian scheme, or a postulate of reason, indispensable, if we would render the existence of a world of finites compatible with the assumption of a super-mundane God, not one with the world. In short, this idea is the condition under which alone the reason of man can retain the doctrine of an infinite and absolute Being, and yet keep clear of pantheism as exhibited by Benedict Spinosa.

II. The Egyptian Magicians.

This whole narrative is probably a relic of the old diplomatic *lingua-arcana*, or state-symbolique—in which the prediction of events is expressed as the immediate causing of them. Thus the prophet is said to destroy the city, the destruction of which he predicts. The word which our version renders by "*enchantments*" signifies "flames or burnings," by which it is probable that the Egyptians were able to deceive the spectators, and substitute serpents for staves. See Parkhurst *in voce*.

And with regard to the possessions in the Gospels, bear in mind first of all, that spirits are not necessarily souls or *I's* (*ichheiten* or *self-consciousnesses*), and that the most ludicrous absurdities would follow from taking them as such in the Gospel instances; and secondly, that the Evangelist, who has recorded the most of these incidents, himself speaks of one of these possessed persons as a lunatic:—(*σεληνιάζεται—ἐξῆλθεν ἀπ' αὐτοῦ τὸ δαιμόνιον*. Matt. xvii. 15, 18) while St. John names them not at all, but seems to include them under the description of diseased or deranged persons. That madness may result from spiritual causes, and not only or principally from physical ailments, may readily be admitted. Is not our will itself a spiritual power? Is it not the spirit of the man? The mind of a rational and responsible being (that is, of a free-agent) is a spirit, though it does not follow that all spirits are minds. Who shall dare determine what spiritual influences may not arise out of the collective evil wills of wicked men? Even the bestial life, sinless in animals and their nature, may when awakened in the man, and by his own act admitted into his will, become a spiritual influence. He receives a nature into his will, which by this very act becomes a corrupt will; and *vice versa*, this will becomes his nature, and thus a corrupt nature. This may be conceded; and this is all that the recorded words of our Saviour absolutely require in order to receive an appropriate sense; but this is altogether different from making spirits to be devils, and devils self-conscious individuals.

NOTES.* March, 1824.

A Christian's conflicts and conquests, p. 459. By the devil we are to understand that apostate spirit which fell from God, and is always designing to hale down others from God also. The Old Dragon (mentioned in the Revelation) with his tail drew down the third part of the stars of heaven, and cast them to the earth.

How much is it to be regretted, that so enlightened and able a divine as Smith, had not philosophically and scripturally enucleated this so difficult, yet important question,—respecting the personal existence of the evil principle; that is, whether as τὸ θεῖον of paganism is ὁ θεὸς in Christianity, so the τὸ πονηρὸν is to be ὁ πονηρὸς,—and whether this is an express doctrine of Christ, and not merely a Jewish dogma left undisturbed to fade away under the increasing light of the Gospel, instead of assuming the former, and confirming the position by a verse from a poetic tissue of visual symbols,—a verse alien from the subject, and by which the Apocalypt enigmatized the Neronian persecutions and the apostasy through fear occasioned by it in a large number of converts.

Ib. p. 463. When we say, the devil is continually busy with us, I mean not only some apostate spirit as one particular being, but that spirit of

---

* Written in a copy of "Select Discourses by John Smith, of Queen's College, Cambridge, 1660," and communicated by the Rev. Edward Coleridge.—*Ed.*

apostasy which is lodged in all men's natures; and this may seem particularly to be aimed at in this place, if we observe the context:—as the scripture speaks of Christ not only as a particular person, but as a divine principle in holy souls.

Indeed the devil is not only the name of one particular thing, but a nature.

May I not venture to suspect that this was Smith's own belief and judgment? and that his conversion of the Satan, that is, *circuitor*, or minister of police (what our Sterne calls the accusing angel) in the prologue to Job into the devil was a mere condescension to the prevailing prejudice? Here, however, he speaks like himself, and like a true religious philosopher, who felt that the personality of evil spirits is a trifling question, compared with the personality of the evil principle. This is indeed most momentous.

Note on a Passage in the Life of Henry Earl of Morland. 20th June, 1827.

The defect of this and all similar theories that I am acquainted with, or rather, let me say, the desideratum, is the neglect of a previous definition of the term "body." What do you mean by it? The immediate grounds of a man's size, visibility, tangibility, &c.?—But these are in a continual flux even as a column of smoke. The material particles of carbon, nitrogen, oxygen, hydrogen, lime, phosphorus, sulphur, soda, iron, that constitute the ponderable organism in May, 1827, at the moment of Pollio's death in his 70th year, have no better claim to be called his "body" than the numerical particles of the same names that constituted the ponderable mass in May, 1787, in Pollio's prime of manhood in his 30th year;—the latter no less than the former go into the grave, that is, suffer dissolution, the one in a series, the other simultaneously. The result to the particles is precisely the same in both, and of both therefore we must say with holy Paul—"*Thou fool! that which thou sowest, thou sowest not that body that shall be,*" &c. Neither this nor that is the body that abideth. Abideth, I say; for that which riseth again must have remained, though perhaps in an inert state.—It is not dead, but sleepeth;—that is, it is not dissolved any more than the exterior or phenomenal organism appears to us dissolved when it lieth in apparent inactivity during our sleep.

Sound reasoning this, to the best of my judgment, as far as it goes But how are we to explain the reaction of this fluxional body on the animal? In each moment the particles by the informing force of the living principle constitute an organ not only of motion and sense, but of consciousness. The organ plays on the organist. How is this conceivable? The solution requires a depth, stillness, and subtlety of spirit not only for its discovery, but even for the understanding of it when discovered, and in the most appropriate words enunciated. I can merely give a hint. The particles themselves must have an interior and gravitate being, and the multeity must be a removable or at least suspensible accident.

LECTURE XIII.*

ON POESY OR ART. (*ll*)

MAN communicates by articulation of sounds, and paramountly by the memory in the ear; nature, by the impression of bounds and surfaces on the eye, and through the eye it gives significance and appropriation, and thus the conditions of memory, or the capability of being remembered, to sounds, smells, &c. Now Art, used collectively for painting, sculpture, architecture, and music, is the mediatress between, and reconciler of, nature and man. (*mm*) It is, therefore, the power of humanizing nature, of infusing the thoughts and passions of man into every thing which is the object of his contemplation; color, form, motion, and sound are the elements which it combines, and it stamps them into unity in the mould of a moral idea.

The primary art is writing;—primary, if we regard the purposes abstracted from the different modes of realizing it, those steps of progression of which the instances are still visible in the lower degrees of civilization. First, there is mere gesticulation; then rosaries or *wampun;* then picture-language; then hiero-

* For the Notes to this Lecture, containing references to Schelling's oration on the Forming or Imaging Arts, with extracts from the same, see the end of the volume.

glyphics, and finally alphabetic letters. These all consist of a translation of man into nature, of a substitution of the visible for the audible.

The so-called music of savage tribes as little deserves the name of art for the understanding as the ear warrants it for music. Its lowest state is a mere expression of passion by sounds which the passion itself necessitates;—the highest amounts to no more than a voluntary reproduction of these sounds in the absence of the occasioning causes, so as to give the pleasure of contrast,—for example, by the various outcries of battle in the song of security and triumph. Poetry also is purely human; for all its materials are from the mind, and all its products are for the mind. But it is the apotheosis of the former state, in which by excitement of the associative power passion itself imitates order, and the order resulting produces a pleasurable passion, and thus it elevates the mind by making its feelings the object of its reflection. So likewise, whilst it recalls the sights and sounds that had accompanied the occasions of the original passions, poetry impregnates them with an interest not their own by means of the passions, and yet tempers the passion by the calming power which all distinct images exert on the human soul. In this way poetry is the preparation for art, inasmuch as it avails itself of the forms of nature to recall, to express, and to modify the thoughts and feelings of the mind. Still, however, poetry can only act through the intervention of articulate speech, which is so peculiarly human, that in all languages it constitutes the ordinary phrase by which man and nature are contra-distinguished. It is the original force of the word 'brute;' and even 'mute' and 'dumb' do not convey the absence of sound, but the absence of articulated sounds.

As soon as the human mind is intelligibly addressed by an outward image exclusively of articulate speech, so soon does art commence. But please to observe that I have laid particular stress on the words 'human mind,' meaning to exclude thereby all results common to man and all other sentient creatures, and consequently confining myself to the effect produced by the congruity of the animal impression with the reflective powers of the mind; so that not the thing presented, but that which is represented by the thing shall be the source of the pleasure. In this sense nature itself is to a religious observer the art of God; and for the same cause art itself might be defined as of a middle quality between a thought and a thing, or, as I said before, the union and reconciliation of that which is nature with that which is exclusively human. It is the figured language of thought, and is distinguished from nature by the unity of all the parts in one thought or idea. Hence nature itself would give us the impression of a work of art if we could see the thought which is present at once in the whole and in every part; and a work of art will be just in proportion as it adequately conveys the thought, and rich in proportion to the variety of parts which it holds in unity.

If, therefore, the term 'mute' be taken as opposed not to sound but to articulate speech, the old definition of painting will in fact be the true and best definition of the Fine Arts in general, that is, *muta poesis*, mute poesy, and so of course poesy. (*nn*) And, as all languages perfect themselves by a gradual process of desynonymizing words originally equivalent, I have cherished the wish to use the word 'poesy' as the generic or common term, and to distinguish that species of poetry which is not *muta poesis* by its usual name 'poetry;' while of all the other species which collectively form the Fine Arts, there would remain this as the common definition,—that they all, like poetry, are to express intellectual purposes, thoughts, conceptions, and sentiments which have their origin in the human mind, not, however, as poetry does, by means of articulate speech, but as nature or the divine art does, by form, color, magnitude, proportion, or by sound, that is, silently or musically. (*oo*)

Well! it may be said—but who has ever thought otherwise! We all know that art is the imitatress of nature. And, doubtless, the truths which I hope to convey, would be barren truisms, if all men meant the same by the words 'imitate' and 'nature.' (*pp*) But it would be flattering mankind at large, to presume that such is the fact. First, to imitate. The impression on the wax is not an imitation, but a copy, of the seal; the seal itself is an imitation. But, further, in order to form a philosophic conception, we must seek for the kind, as the heat in ice, invisible light, &c., whilst, for practical purposes, we must have reference to the degree. It is sufficient that philosophically we understand that in all imitation two elements must co-exist, and not only co-exist, but must be perceived as co-existing. These two constituent elements are likeness and unlikeness, or sameness and difference, and in all genuine creations of art there must be a union of these disparates. The artist may take his point of view where he pleases, provided that the desired effect be perceptibly produced,—that there be likeness in the difference, difference in the likeness, and a reconcilement of both in one. If there be likeness to nature without any check of difference, the result is disgusting, and the more complete the delusion, the more loathsome the effect. (*qq*) Why are such simulations of nature, as wax-work figures of men and women, so disagreeable? Because, not finding the motion and the life which we expected, we are shocked as by a falsehood, every circumstance of detail, which before induced us to be interested, making the distance from truth more palpable. You set out with a supposed reality, and are disappointed and disgusted with the deception; whilst, in respect to a work of genuine imitation, you begin with an acknowledged total difference, and then every touch of nature gives you the pleasure of an approximation to truth. The fundamental principle of all this is undoubtedly the horror of falsehood and the love of truth inherent in the human breast. The Greek tragic dance rested on these principles, and I can deeply sympathize in imagination with the Greeks in this favorite part of their theatrical exhibitions, when I call to mind the pleasure I felt in beholding the combat of the Horatii and Curiatii most exquisitely danced in Italy to the music of Cimarosa.

Secondly, as to nature. We must imitate nature! yes, but what in nature,—all and every thing? No, the beautiful in nature. (*rr*) And what then is the beautiful? What is beauty? It is, in the abstract, the unity of the manifold, the coalescence of the diverse; in the concrete, it is the union of the shapely (*formosum*) with the vital. In the dead organic it depends on regularity of form, the first and lowest species of which is the triangle with all its modifications, as in crystals, architecture, &c.; in the living organic it is not mere regularity of form, which would produce a sense of formality; neither is it subservient to any thing beside itself. (ss) It may be present in a disagreeable object, in which the proportion of the parts constitutes a whole; it does not arise from association, as the agreeable does, but sometimes lies in the rupture of association; it is not different to different individuals and nations, as has been said, nor is it connected with the ideas of the good, or the fit, or the useful. The sense of beauty is intuitive, and beauty itself is all that inspires pleasure without, and aloof from, and even contrarily to, interest.

If the artist copies the mere nature, the *natura naturata*, what idle rivalry! If he proceeds only from a given form, which is supposed to answer to the notion of beauty, what an emptiness, what an unreality there always is in his productions, as in Cipriani's pictures! Believe me, you must master the essence, the *natura naturans*, which presupposes a bond between nature in the higher sense and the soul of man. (*tt*)

The wisdom in nature is distinguished from that in man, by the co-instantaneity of the plan and the execution; the thought and the product are one, or are given at once; but there is no reflex act, and hence there is no moral responsibility. In man there is reflexion, freedom, and choice; he is, therefore, the head of the visible creation. (*uu*) In the objects of nature are presented, as in a mirror, all the possible elements, steps, and processes of intellect antecedent to consciousness, and therefore to the full development of the intelligential act; and man's mind is the very focus of all the rays of intellect which are scattered throughout the images of nature. Now so to place these images, totalized, and fitted to the limits of the human mind, as to elicit from, and to superinduce upon, the forms themselves the moral reflections to which they approximate, to make the external internal, the internal external, to make nature thought, and thought nature,—this is the mystery of genius in the Fine Arts. Dare I add that the genius must act on the feeling, that body is but a striving to become mind, that it is mind in its essence! (*vv*)

In every work of art there is a reconcilement of the external with the internal; the conscious is so impressed on the unconscious as to appear in it; as compare mere letters inscribed on a tomb with figures themselves constituting the tomb. He who combines the two is the man of genius; and for that reason he must partake of both. Hence there is in genius itself an unconscious activity; nay, that is the genius in the man of genius. (*ww*) And this is the true exposition of the rule that the artist must first eloign himself from nature in order to return to her with full effect. Why this? Because if he were to begin by mere painful copying, he would produce masks only, not forms breathing life. He must out of his own mind create forms according to the severe laws of the intellect, in order to generate in himself that co-ordination of freedom and law, that involution of obedience in the prescript, and of the prescript in the impulse to obey, which assimilates him to nature, and enables him to understand her. He merely absents himself for a season from her, that his own spirit, which has the same ground with nature, may learn her unspoken language in its main radicals, before he approaches to her endless compositions of them. (*xx*) Yes, not to acquire cold notions—lifeless technical rules—but living and life-producing ideas, which shall contain their own evidence, the certainty that they are essentially one with the germinal causes in nature—his consciousness being the focus and mirror of both,—for this does the artist for a time abandon the external real in order to return to it with a complete sympathy with its internal and actual. For of all we see, hear, feel and touch the substance is and must be in ourselves; and therefore there is no alternative in reason between the dreary (and thank heaven! almost impossible) belief that every thing around us is but a phantom, or that the life which is in us is in them likewise;* and that to know is to resemble, when we speak of objects out of ourselves, even as within ourselves to learn is, according to Plato, only to recollect;—the only effective answer to which, that I have been fortunate enough to meet with, is that which Pope has consecrated for future use in the line—

And coxcombs vanquish Berkeley with a grin!

The artist must imitate that which is within the thing, that which is active through form and figure, and discourses to us by symbols the *Natur-geist*, or spirit of nature, as we unconsciously imitate those whom we love; for so only can he hope to produce any work truly natural in the object and truly human in the effect. (*yy*) The idea which puts the form together can not itself be the form. It is above form, and is its essence, the universal in the individual, or the individuality itself,—the glance and the exponent of the indwelling power. (*zz*)

Each thing that lives has its moment of self-exposition, and so has each period of each thing, if we remove the disturbing forces

* See the *Biographia Literaria* of Mr. Coleridge, chap. xii. p. 322, and Schelling's *Transcendental Idealism*.

of accident. To do this is the business of ideal art, whether in images of childhood, youth, or age, in man or in woman. (*aaa*) Hence a good portrait is the abstract of the personal; it is not the likeness for actual comparison, but for recollection. This explains why the likeness of a very good portrait is not always recognized; because some persons never abstract, and amongst these are especially to be numbered the near relations and friends of the subject, in consequence of the constant pressure and check exercised on their minds by the actual presence of the original. And each thing that only appears to live has also its possible position of relation to life, as nature herself testifies, who, where she can not be, prophesies her being in the crystallized metal, or the inhaling plant.

The charm, the indispensable requisite, of sculpture is unity of effect. But painting rests in a material remoter from nature, and its compass is therefore greater. (*bbb*) Light and shade give external, as well as internal, being even with all its accidents, whilst sculpture is confined to the latter. And here I may observe that the subjects chosen for works of art, whether in sculpture or painting, should be such as really are capable of being expressed and conveyed within the limits of those arts. Moreover they ought to be such as will affect the spectator by their truth, their beauty, or their sublimity, and therefore they may be addressed to the judgment, the senses, or the reason. The peculiarity of the impression which they may make, may be derived either from color and form, or from proportion and fitness, or from the excitement of the moral feelings; or all these may be combined. Such works as do combine these sources of effect must have the preference in dignity.

Imitation of the antique may be too exclusive, and may produce an injurious effect on modern sculpture;—1st, generally, because such an imitation can not fail to have a tendency to keep the attention fixed on externals rather than on the thought within;—2dly, because, accordingly, it leads the artist to rest satisfied with that which is always imperfect, namely, bodily form, and circumscribes his views of mental expression to the ideas of power and grandeur only;—3dly, because it induces an effort to combine together two incongruous things, that is to say, modern feelings in antique forms;—4thly, because it speaks in a language, as it were, learned and dead, the tones of which, being unfamiliar, leave the common spectator cold and unimpressed; (*ccc*)—and lastly, because it necessarily causes a neglect of thoughts, emotions and images of profounder interest and more exalted dignity, as motherly, sisterly, and brotherly love, piety, devotion, the divine become human,—the Virgin, the Apostle, the Christ. The artist's principle in the statue of a great man should be the illustration of departed merit; and I can not but think that a skilful adoption of modern habiliments would, in many instances, give a variety and force of effect which a bigoted adherence to Greek or Roman costume precludes. It is, I believe, from artists finding Greek models unfit for several important modern purposes, that we see so many allegorical figures on monuments and elsewhere. Painting was, as it were, a new art, and being unshackled by old models it chose its own subjects, and took an eagle's flight. And a new field seems opened for modern sculpture in the symbolical expression of the ends of life, as in Guy's monument, Chantrey's children in Worcester Cathedral, &c.

Architecture exhibits the greatest extent of the difference from nature which may exist in works of art. It involves all the powers of design, and is sculpture and painting inclusively. It shows the greatness of man, and should at the same time teach him humility.

Music is the most entirely human of the fine arts, and has the fewest *analoga* in nature. Its first delightfulness is simple accordance with the ear; but it is an associated thing, and recalls the deep emotions of the past with an intellectual sense of proportion. Every human feeling is greater and larger than the exciting cause,—a proof, I think, that man is designed for a higher state of existence; and this is deeply implied in music, in which there is always something more and beyond the immediate expression.

With regard to works in all the branches of the fine arts, I may remark that the pleasure arising from novelty must of course be allowed its due place and weight. This pleasure consists in the identity of two opposite elements, that is to say—sameness and variety. If in the midst of the variety there be not some fixed object for the attention, the unceasing succession of the variety will prevent the mind from observing the difference of the individual objects; and the only thing remaining will be the succession, which will then produce precisely the same effect as sameness. This we experience when we let the trees or hedges pass before the fixed eye during a rapid movement in a carriage, or on the other hand, when we suffer a file of soldiers or ranks of men in procession to go on before us without resting the eye on any one in particular. In order to derive pleasure from the occupation of the mind, the principle of unity must always be present, so that in the midst of the multeity the centripetal force be never suspended, nor the sense be fatigued by the predominance of the centrifugal force. This unity in multeity I have elsewhere stated as the principle of beauty. It is equally the source of pleasure in variety, and in fact a higher term including both. What is the seclusive or distinguishing term between them

Remember that there is a difference between form as proceeding, and shape as superinduced ;—the latteris either the death or the imprisonment of the thing ;—the former is its self-witnessing and self-effected sphere of agency. (*ddd*) Art would or should be the abridgment of nature. Now the fulness of nature is without character, as water is purest when without taste, smell, or color ; (*eee*) but this is the highest, the apex only,—it is not the whole. The object of art is to give the whole *ad hominem ;* hence each step of nature hath its ideal, and hence the possibility of a climax up to the perfect form of a harmonized chaos.

To the idea of life victory or strife is necessary ; as virtue consists not simply in the absence of vices, but in the overcoming of them. So it is in beauty. The sight of what is subordinated and conquered heightens the strength and the pleasure ; and this should be exhibited by the artist either inclusively in his figure, or else out of it and beside it to act by way of supplement and contrast. And with a view to this, remark the seeming identity of body and mind in infants, and thence the loveliness of the former ; the commencing separation in boyhood, and the struggle of equilibrium in youth : thence onward the body is first simply indifferent ; then demanding the translucency of the mind not to be worse than indifferent ; and finally all that presents the body as body becoming almost of an excremental nature.

LECTURE XIV.

ON STYLE.

I HAVE, I believe, formerly observed with regard to the character of the governments of the East, that their tendency was despotic, that is, towards unity; whilst that of the Greek governments, on the other hand, leaned to the manifold and the popular, the unity in them being purely ideal, namely of all as an identification of the whole. In the northern or Gothic nations the aim and purpose of the government were the preservation of the rights and interests of the individual in conjunction with those of the whole. The individual interest was sacred. In the character and tendency of the Greek and Gothic languages there is precisely the same relative difference. In Greek the sentences are long, and the structure architectural, so that each part or clause is insignificant when compared with the whole. The result is every thing, the steps and processes nothing. But in the Gothic and, generally, in what we call the modern, languages, the structure is short, simple, and complete in each part, and the connection of the parts with the sum total of the discourse is maintained by the sequency of the logic, or the community of feelings excited between the writer and his readers. As an instance equally delightful and complete, of what may be called the Gothic structure as contra-distinguished from that of the Greeks, let me cite a part of our famous Chaucer's character of a parish priest as he should be. Can it ever be quoted too often?

A good man thér was of religiöun
That was a pouré Parsone of a toun,
But riche he was of holy thought and werk,
He was alsó a lerned man, a clerk,
That Cristés gospel trewély wolde preche;
His párishens[1] devoutly wolde he teche;

[1] Parishioners.

Benigne he was, and wonder[1] diligent,
And in adversite ful patient,
And swiche[2] he was ypreved[3] often sithes[4];
Ful loth were him to cursen for his tithes,
But rather wolde he yeven[5] out of doute
Unto his pouré párishens aboute
Of hís offríng, and eke of his substánce;
He coude in litel thing have suffisance:
Wide was his parish, and houses fer asonder,
But he ne[6] left nought for no rain ne[7] thonder,
In sikenesse and in mischief to visíte
The ferrest[8] in his parish moche and lite[9]
Upon his fete, and in his hand a staf:
This noble ensample to his shepe he yaf,[10]
That first he wrought, and afterward he taught,
Out of the gospel he the wordês caught,
And this figúre he added yet thereto,
That if gold rusté, what should iren do.
He setté not his benefice to hire,
And lette[11] his shepe accombred[12] in the mire,
And ran untó Londón untó Seint Poules,
To seken him a chantérie for soules,
Or with a brotherhede to be withold,
But dwelt at home, and kepté wel his fold,
So that the wolf ne made it not miscarie:
He was a shepherd and no mercenarie;
And though he holy were and vertuous,
He was to sinful men not dispitous,[13]
Ne of his speché dangerous ne digne,[14]
But in his teching discrete and benigne,
To drawen folk to heven with fairénesse,
By good ensample was his besinesse;
But it were any persone obstinat,
What so he were of high or low estat,
Him wolde he snibben[15] sharply for the nones:
A better preest I trowe that no wher non is;
He waited after no pompe ne reverence,
He maked him no spiced conscience,
But Cristés love and his apostles' twelve
He taught, but first he folwed it himselve.*

Such change as really took place in the style of our litera-

[1] Wondrous. [2] Such. [3] Proved. [4] Times.
[5] Give or have given. [6] Not. [7] Nor. [8] Farthest.
[9] Great and small. [10] Gave. [11] Left. [12] Encumbered.
[13] Despiteous. [14] Proud. [15] Reprove.

* Prologue to Canterbury Tales.

ture after Chaucer's time is with difficulty perceptible, on account of the dearth of writers, during the civil wars of the fifteenth century. But the transition was not very great; and accordingly we find in Latimer and our other venerable authors about the time of Edward VI. as in Luther, the general characteristics of the earliest manner;—that is, every part popular, and the discourse addressed to all degrees of intellect;—the sentences short, the tone vehement, and the connection of the whole produced by honesty and singleness of purpose, intensity of passion, and pervading importance of the subject.

Another and a very different species of style is that which was derived from, and founded on, the admiration and cultivation of the classical writers, and which was more exclusively addressed to the learned class in society. I have previously mentioned Boccaccio as the original Italian introducer of this manner, and the great models of it in English are Hooker, Bacon, Milton, and Taylor, although it may be traced in many other authors of that age. In all these the language is dignified but plain, genuine English, although elevated and brightened by superiority of intellect in the writer. Individual words themselves are always used by them in their precise meaning, without either affectation or slipslop. The letters and state papers of Sir Francis Walsingham are remarkable for excellence in style of this description. In Jeremy Taylor the sentences are often extremely long, and yet are generally so perspicuous in consequence of their logical structure, that they require no perusal to be understood; and it is for the most part the same in Milton and Hooker.

Take the following sentence as a specimen of the sort of style to which I have been alluding:—

> Concerning Faith, the principal object whereof is that eternal verity which hath discovered the treasures of hidden wisdom in Christ; concerning Hope, the highest object whereof is that everlasting goodness which in Christ doth quicken the dead; concerning Charity, the final object whereof is that incomprehensible beauty which shineth in the countenance of Christ, the Son of the living God: concerning these virtues, the first of which beginning here with a weak apprehension of things not seen, endeth with the intuitive vision of God in the world to come; the second beginning here with a trembling expectation of things far removed, and as yet but only heard of, endeth with real and actual fruition of that which no tongue can express; the third beginning here with a weak inclination of heart towards

him unto whom we are not able to approach, endeth with endless union, the mystery whereof is higher than the reach of the thoughts of men; concerning that Faith, Hope, and Charity, without which there can be no salvation, was there ever any mention made saving only in that Law which God himself hath from Heaven revealed? There is not in the world a syllable muttered with certain truth concerning any of these three, more than hath been supernaturally received from the mouth of the eternal God.

Eccles. Pol. i. s. 11.

The unity in these writers is produced by the unity of the subject, and the perpetual growth and evolution of the thoughts, one generating, and explaining, and justifying, the place of another, not, as it is in Seneca, where the thoughts, striking as they are, are merely strung together like beads, without any causation or progression. The words are selected because they are the most appropriate, regard being had to the dignity of the total impression, and no merely big phrases are used where plain ones would have sufficed, even in the most learned of their works.

There is some truth in a remark, which I believe was made by Sir Joshua Reynolds, that the greatest man is he who forms the taste of a nation, and that the next greatest is he who corrupts it. The true classical style of Hooker and his fellows was easily open to corruption; and Sir Thomas Brown it was, who, though a writer of great genius, first effectually injured the literary taste of the nation by his introduction of learned words, merely because they were learned. It would be difficult to describe Brown adequately; exuberant in conception and conceit, dignified, hyperlatinistic, a quiet and sublime enthusiast; yet a fantast, a humorist, a brain with a twist; egotistic like Montaigne, yet with a feeling heart and an active curiosity, which, however, too often degenerates into a hunting after oddities. In his *Hydriotaphia*, and, indeed, almost all his works, the entireness of his mental action is very observable; he metamorphoses every thing, be it what it may, into the subject under consideration. But Sir Thomas Brown with all his faults had a genuine idiom; and it is the existence of an individual idiom in each, that makes the principal writers before the Restoration the great patterns or integers of English style. In them the precise intended meaning of a word can never be mistaken; whereas in the latter writers, as especially in Pope, the use of words is for the most part purely arbitrary, so that the context will rarely show the true specific sense, but only that something of the sort is designed. A perusal of the authorities cited by Johnson in his dictionary under any leading word, will give you a lively sense of this declension in etymological truth of expression in the writers after the Restoration, or perhaps, strictly, after the middle of the reign of Charles II.

The general characteristic of the style of our literature down to the period which I have just mentioned, was gravity, and in Milton and some other writers of his day there are perceptible traces of the sternness of republicanism. Soon after the Restoration a material change took place, and the cause of royalism was graced, sometimes disgraced, by every shade of lightness of manner. A free and easy style was considered as a test of loyalty, or at all events, as a badge of the cavalier party; you may detect it occasionally even in Barrow, who is, however, in general remarkable for dignity and logical sequency of expression; but in L'Estrange, Collyer, and the writers of that class, this easy manner was carried out to the utmost extreme of slang and ribaldry. Yet still the works, even of these last authors, have considerable merit in one point of view; their language is level to the understandings of all men; it is an actual transcript of the colloquialism of the day, and is accordingly full of life and reality. Roger North's life of his brother, the Lord Keeper, is the most valuable specimen of this class of our literature; it is delightful, and much beyond any other of the writings of his contemporaries.

From the common opinion that the English style attained its greatest perfection in and about Queen Anne's reign I altogether dissent; not only because it is in one species alone in which it can be pretended that the writers of that age excelled their predecessors; but also because the specimens themselves are not equal, upon sound principles of judgment, to much that had been produced before. The classical structure of Hooker—the impetuous, thought-agglomerating flood of Taylor—to these there is no pretence of a parallel; and for mere ease and grace, is Cowley inferior to Addison, being as he is so much more thoughtful and full of fancy? Cowley, with the omission of a quaintness here and there, is probably the best model of style for modern imitation in general. Taylor's periods have been frequently attempted by his admirers; you may, perhaps, just catch the turn of a simile or single image, but to write in the real manner of Jeremy Taylor would require as mighty a mind as his. Many parts of Algernon Sidney's treatises afford excellent exemplars of a good modern practical style; and Dryden in his prose works is a still better model, if you add a stricter and purer grammar. It is, indeed, worthy of remark that all our great poets have been good prose writers, as Chaucer, Spenser, Milton; and this probably arose from their just sense of metre. For a true poet will never confound verse and prose; whereas it is almost characteristic of indifferent prose writers that they should be constantly slipping into scraps of metre. Swift's style is, in its line, perfect; the manner is a complete expression of the matter, the terms appropriate, and the artifice concealed. It is simplicity in the true sense of the word.

After the Revolution, the spirit of the nation became much more commercial than it had been before; a learned body, or clerisy, as such, gradually disappeared, and literature in general began to be addressed to the common miscellaneous public. That public had become accustomed to, and required, a strong stimulus; and to meet the requisitions of the public taste, a style was produced which by combining triteness of thought with singularity and excess of manner of expression, was calculated at once to soothe ignorance and to flatter vanity. The thought was carefully kept down to the immediate apprehension of the commonest understanding, and the dress was as anxiously arranged for the purpose of making the thought appear something very profound. The essence of this style consisted in a mock antithesis, that is, an opposition of mere sounds, in a rage for personification, the abstract made animate, far-fetched metaphors, strange phrases, metrical scraps, in every thing, in short, but genuine prose. Style is, of course, nothing else but the art of conveying the meaning appropriately and with perspicuity, whatever that meaning may be, and one criterion of style is that it shall not be translatable without injury to the meaning. Johnson's style has pleased many from the very fault of being perpetually translatable; he creates an impression of cleverness by never saying any thing in a common way. The best specimen of this manner is in Junius, because his antithesis is less merely verbal than Johnson's. Gibbon's manner is the worst of all; it has every fault of which this peculiar style is capable. Tacitus is an example of it in Latin; in coming from Cicero you feel the *falsetto* imme-diately.

In order to form a good style, the primary rule and condition is, not to attempt to express ourselves in language before we thoroughly know our own meaning:—when a man perfectly understands himself, appropriate diction will generally be at his command either in writing or speaking. In such cases the thoughts and the words are associated. In the next place preciseness in the use of terms is required, and the test is whether you can translate the phrase adequately into simpler terms, regard being had to the feeling of the whole passage. Try this upon Shakspeare, or Milton, and see if you can substitute other simpler words in any given passage without a violation of the meaning or tone. The source of bad writing is the desire to be something more than a man of sense,—the straining to be thought a genius; and it is just the same in speech-making. If men would only say what they have to say in plain terms, how much more eloquent they would be! Another rule is to avoid converting mere abstractions into persons. I believe you will very rarely find in any great writer before the Revolution the possessive case of an inanimate noun used in prose instead of the dependent case, as 'the watch's hand,' for 'the hand of the watch.' The possessive or Saxon genitive was confined to persons, or at least to animated subjects. And I can not conclude this Lecture without insisting on the importance of accuracy of style as being near akin to veracity and truthful habits of mind; he who thinks loosely will write loosely, and, perhaps, there is some moral inconvenience in the common forms of our grammars which give our children so many obscure terms for material distinctions. Let me also exhort you to careful examination of what you read, if it be worth any perusal at all; such an examination will be a safeguard from fanaticism, the universal origin of which is in the contemplation of phenomena without investigation into their causes.

ON THE PROMETHEUS OF ÆSCHYLUS.

An Essay, preparatory to a series of disquisitions respecting the Egyptian, in connection with the sacerdotal, theology, and in contrast with the mysteries of ancient Greece. Read at the Royal Society of Literature. May 18, 1825.

THE French *savans* who went to Egypt in the train of Bonaparte, Denon, Fourrier, and Dupuis (it has been asserted), triumphantly vindicated the chronology of Herodotus, on the authority of documents that can not lie;—namely, the inscriptions and sculptures on those enormous masses of architecture, that might seem to have been built in the wish of rivalling the mountains, and at some unknown future to answer the same purpose, that is, to stand the gigantic tombstones of an elder world. It is decided, say the critics, whose words I have before cited, that the present division of the zodiac had been already arranged by the Egyptians fifteen thousand years before the Christian era, and according to an inscription 'which can not lie,' the temple of Esne is of eight thousand years' standing.

Now, in the first place, among a people who had placed their national pride in their antiquity, I do not see the impossibility of an inscription lying; and, secondly, as little can I see the improbability of a modern interpreter misunderstanding it; and lastly, the incredibility of a French infidel's partaking of both defects, is still less evident to my understanding. The inscriptions may be, and in some instances, very probably are, of later date than the temples themselves,—the offspring of vanity or priestly rivalry, or of certain astrological theories; or the temples themselves may have been built in the place of former and ruder structures, of an earlier and ruder period, and not impossibly under a different scheme of hieroglyphic or significant characters; and these may have been intentionally, or ignorantly, miscopied or mistranslated.

But more than all the preceding,—I can not but persuade myself, that for a man of sound judgment and enlightened common sense—a man with whom the demonstrable laws of the human mind, and the rules generalized from the great mass of facts respecting human nature, weigh more than any two or three detached documents or narrations, of whatever authority the narrator may be, and however difficult it may be to bring positive proofs against the antiquity of the documents—I can not but persuade myself, I say, that for such a man, the relation preserved in the first book of the Pentateuch,—and which, in perfect accordance with all analogous experience, with all the facts of history, and all that the principles of political economy would lead us to anticipate, conveys to us the rapid progress in civilization and splendor from Abraham and Abimelech to Joseph and Pharaoh,—will be worth a whole library of such inferences.

I am aware that it is almost universal to speak of the gross idolatry of Egypt; nay, that arguments have been grounded on this assumption in proof of the divine origin of the Mosaic monotheism. But first, if by this we are to understand that the great doctrine of the one Supreme Being was first revealed to the Hebrew legislator, his own inspired writings supply abundant and direct confutation of the position. Of certain astrological superstitions,—of certain talismans connected with star-magic,—plates and images constructed in supposed harmony with the movements and influences of celestial bodies,—there doubtless exist hints, if not direct proofs, both in the Mosaic writings, and those next to these in antiquity. But of plain idolatry in Egypt, or the existence of a polytheistic religion, represented by various idols, each signifying a several deity, I can find no decisive proof in the Pentateuch; and when I collate these with the books of the prophets, and the other inspired writings subsequent to the Mosaic, I can not but regard the absence of any such proof in the latter, compared with the numerous and powerful assertions, or evident implications, of Egyptian idolatry in the former, both as an argument of incomparatively greater value in support of the age and authenticity of the Pentateuch; and as a strong presumption in favor of the hypothesis on which I shall in part ground the theory which will pervade this series of disquisitions;—namely, that the sacerdotal religion of Egypt had, during the interval from Abimelech to Moses, degenerated from the patriarchal monotheism into a pantheism, cosmotheism, or worship of the world as God.

The reason or pretext, assigned by the Hebrew legislator to Pharaoh for leading his countrymen into the wilderness to join with their brethren, the tribes who still sojourned in the nomadic state, namely, that their sacrifices would be an abomination to the Egyptians, may be urged as inconsistent with, nay, as confuting this hypothesis. But to this I reply, first, that the worship of the ox and cow was not, in and of itself, and necessarily, a contravention of the first commandment, though a very gross breach of the second;—for it is most certain that the ten tribes worshipped the Jehovah, the God of Abraham, Isaac, and Jacob, under the same or similar symbols:—secondly that the cow, or Isis, and the Io of the Greeks, truly represented, in the first instance, the earth or productive nature, and afterwards the mundane religion grounded on the worship of nature, or the τὸ πᾶν, as God. In after-times, the ox or bull was added, representing the sun, or generative force of nature, according to the habit of male and female deities, which spread almost over the whole world,—the positive and negative forces in the science of superstition;—for the pantheism of the sage necessarily engenders polytheism as the popular creed. But lastly, a very sufficient reason may, I think, be assigned for the choice of the ox or cow, as representing the very life of nature, by the first legislators of Egypt, and for the similar sacred character in the Brachmanic tribes of Hindostan. The progress from savagery to civilization is evidently first from the hunting to the pastoral state, a process which even now is going on, within our own times, among the South American Indians in the vast tracts between Buenos Ayres and the Andes: but the second and the most important step, is from the pastoral, or wandering, to the agricultural, or fixed, state. Now, if even for men born and reared under European civilization, the charms of a wandering life have been found so great a temptation, that few who have taken to it have been induced to return (see the confession in the preamble to the statute respecting the gipsies);* —how much greater must have been the danger of relapse in the first formation of fixed states with a condensed population? And what stronger prevention could the ingenuity of the priestly kings—(for the priestly is ever the first form of government)—devise, than to have made the ox or cow the representatives of the divine principle in the world, and, as such, an object of adoration, the wilful destruction of which was sacrilege?—For this

* The Act meant is probably the 5 Eliz. c. 20, enforcing the two previous Acts of Henry VIII. and Philip and Mary, and reciting that natural born Englishmen had 'become of the fellowship of the said vagabonds, by transforming or disguising themselves in their apparel,' &c.—*Ed.*

rendered a return to the pastoral state impossible ; in which the flesh of these animals and the milk formed almost the exclusive food of mankind ; while, in the meantime, by once compelling and habituating men to the use of a vegetable diet, it enforced the laborious cultivation of the soil, and both produced and permitted a vast and condensed population. In the process and continued subdivisions of polytheism, this great sacred Word,—for so the consecrated animals were called, ἱεροὶ λόγοι,—became multiplied, till almost every power and supposed attribute of nature had its symbol in some consecrated animal from the beetle to the hawk. Wherever the powers of nature had found a cycle for themselves, in which the powers still produced the same phenomenon during a given period, whether in the motions of the heavenly orbs, or in the smallest living organic body, there the Egyptian sages predicated life and mind. Time, cyclical time, was their abstraction of the deity, and their holidays were their gods.

The diversity between theism and pantheism may be most simply and generally expressed in the following *formula*, in which the material universe is expressed by W, and the deity by G.

$$W - G = 0;$$

or the World without God is an impossible conception. This position is common to theist and pantheist. But the pantheist adds the converse—

$$G - W = 0;$$

for which the theist substitutes—

$$G - W = G;$$

or that—

$\overline{G = G}$, anterior and irrelative to the existence of the world, is equal to $G + W$.*

Before the mountains were, Thou art.—I am not about to lead the society beyond the bounds of my subject into divinity or theology in the professional sense. But without a precise definition of pantheism, without a clear insight into the essential dis-

* Mr. Coleridge was in the constant habit of expressing himself on paper by the algebraic symbols. They have an uncouth look in the text of an ordinary essay, and I have sometimes ventured to render them by the equivalent words. But most of the readers of these volumes will know that — means *less by*, or, *without ;* + *more by*, or, *in addition to ;* = *equal to*, or, *the same as.—Ed.*

tinction between it and the theism of the Scriptures, it appears to me impossible to understand either the import or the history of the polytheism of the great historical nations. I beg leave, therefore, to repeat, and to carry on my former position, that the religion of Egypt, at the time of the Exodus of the Hebrews, was a pantheism, on the point of passing into that polytheism, of which it afterwards afforded a specimen, gross and distasteful even to polytheists themselves of other nations.

The objects which, on my appointment as Royal Associate of the Royal Society of Literature, I proposed to myself were, 1st. The elucidation of the purpose of the Greek drama, and the relations in which it stood to the mysteries on the one hand, and to the state or sacerdotal religion on the other :—2d. The connection of the Greek tragic poets with philosophy as the peculiar offspring of Greek genius :—3d. The connection of the Homeric and cyclical poets with the popular religion of the Greeks: and, lastly from all these,—namely, the mysteries, the sacerdotal religion, their philosophy before and after Socrates, the stage, the Homeric poetry and the legendary belief of the people, and from the sources and productive causes in the derivation and confluence of the tribes that finally shaped themselves into a nation of Greeks—to give a juster and more distinct view of this singular people, and of the place which they occupied in the history of the world, and the great scheme of divine providence, than I have hitherto seen,—or rather let me say, than it appears to me possible to give by any other process.

The present Essay, however, I devote to the purpose of removing, or at least invalidating, one objection that I may reasonably anticipate, and which may be conveyed in the following question :—What proof have you of the fact of any connection between the Greek drama, and either the mysteries, or the philosophy, of Greece ? What proof that it was the office of the tragic poet, under a disguise of the sacerdotal religion, mixed with the legendary or popular belief, to reveal as much of the mysteries interpreted by philosophy, as would counteract the demoralizing effects of the state religion, without compromising the tranquillity of the state itself, or weakening that paramount reverence, without which a republic (such I mean, as the republics of ancient Greece were) could not exist ?

I know no better way in which I can reply to this objection, than by giving, as my proof and instance, the Prometheus of Æschylus, accompanied with an exposition of what I believe to be the intention of the poet, and the mythic import of the work; of which it may be truly said, that it is more properly tragedy itself in the plenitude of the idea, than a particular tragic poem; and as a preface to this exposition, and for the twin purpose of rendering it intelligible, and of explaining its connection with the whole scheme of my Essays, I entreat permission to insert a quotation from a work of my own, which has indeed been in print for many years, but which few of my auditors will probably have heard of, and still fewer, if any, have read.

"As the representative of the youth and approaching manhood of the human intellect we have ancient Greece, from Orpheus, Linus, Musæus, and the other mythological bards, or, perhaps, the brotherhoods impersonated under those names, to the time when the republics lost their independence, and their learned men sank into copyists of, and commentators on, the works of their forefathers. That we include these as educated under a distinct providential, though not miraculous, dispensation, will surprise no one, who reflects, that in whatever has a permanent operation on the destinies and intellectual condition of mankind at large,—that in all which has been manifestly employed as a co-agent in the mightiest revolution of the moral world, the propagation of the Gospel, and in the intellectual progress of mankind in the restoration of philosophy, science, and the ingenuous arts—it were irreligion not to acknowledge the hand of divine providence. The periods, too, join on to each other. The earliest Greeks took up the religious and lyrical poetry of the Hebrews; and the schools of the prophets were, however partially and imperfectly, represented by the mysteries derived through the corrupt channel of the Phœnicians! With these secret schools of physiological theology, the mythical poets were doubtless in connection, and it was these schools which prevented polytheism from producing all its natural barbarizing effects. The mysteries and the mythical hymns and pæans shaped themselves gradually into epic poetry and history on the one hand, and into the ethical tragedy and philosophy on the other. Under their protection, and that of a youthful liberty, secretly controlled by a species of internal theocracy, the sciences, and the sterner kinds of the fine arts, that is, architecture and statuary, grew up together, followed, indeed, by painting, but a statuesque, and austerely idealized, painting, which did not degenerate into mere copies of the sense, till the process for which Greece existed had been completed."*

The Greeks alone brought forth philosophy in the proper and contra-distinguishable sense of the term, which we may compare to the coronation medal with its symbolic characters, as contrasted with the coins, issued under the same sovereign, current in the market. In the primary sense, philosophy had for its aim and proper subject the τὰ περὶ ἀρχῶν, *de originibus rerum*, as far as man proposes to discover the same in and by the pure reason alone. This, I say, was the offspring of Greece, and elsewhere adopted only. The pre-disposition appears in their earliest poetry.

The first object (or subject-matter) of Greek philosophizing was in some measure philosophy itself;—not, indeed, as a product, but as the producing power—the productivity. Great minds turned inward on the fact of the diversity between man and beast; a superiority of kind in addition to that of degree; the latter, that is, the difference in degree comprehending the more enlarged sphere and the multifold application of faculties common to man and brute animals;—even this being in great measure a transfusion from the former, namely, from the superiority in kind;—for only by its co-existence with reason, free will, self-consciousness, the contra-distinguishing attributes of man, does the instinctive intelligence manifested in the ant, the dog, the elephant, &c. become human understanding. It is a truth with which Heraclitus, the senior, but yet contemporary, of Æschylus, appears, from the few genuine fragments of his writings that are yet extant, to have been deeply impressed,—that the mere understanding in man, considered as the power of adapting means to immediate purposes, differs, indeed, from the intelligence displayed by other animals, and not in degree only; but yet does not differ by any excellence which it derives from itself, or by any inherent diversity, but solely in consequence of a combination with far higher powers of a diverse kind in one and the same subject.

Long before the entire separation of metaphysics from poetry, that is, while yet poesy, in all its several species of verse, music, statuary, &c. continued mythic;—while yet poetry remained the union of the sensuous and the philosophic mind;—the efficient

* The Friend, Essay ix. II. p. 442.

presence of the latter in the *synthesis* of the two, had manifested itself in the sublime *mythus* περὶ γενέσεως τοῦ νοῦ ἐν ἀνθρωποῖς, concerning the *genesis*, or birth of the νους or reason in man. This the most venerable, and perhaps the most ancient, of Grecian *mythi*, is a philosopheme, the very same in subject-matter with the earliest records of the Hebrews, but most characteristically different in tone and conception;—for the patriarchal religion, as the antithesis of pantheism, was necessarily personal; and the doctrines of a faith, the first ground of which, and the primary enunciation, is the eternal I AM, must be in part historic, and must assume the historic form. Hence the Hebrew record is a narrative, and the first instance of the fact is given as the origin of the fact.

That a profound truth—a truth that is, indeed, the grand and indispensable condition of all moral responsibility—is involved in this characteristic of the sacred narrative, I am not alone persuaded, but distinctly aware. This, however, does not preclude us from seeing, nay, as an additional mark of the wisdom that inspired the sacred historian, it rather supplies a motive to us, impels and authorizes us, to see, in the form of the vehicle of the truth, an accommodation to the then childhood of the human race. Under this impression we may, I trust, safely consider the narration,—introduced, as it is here introduced, for the purpose of explaining a mere work of the unaided mind of man by comparison,—as an ἔπος ἱερογλυφικὸν,—and as such (apparently, I mean, not actually) a *synthesis* of poesy and philosophy, characteristic of the childhood of nations.

In the Greek we see already the dawn of approaching manhood. The substance, the stuff, is philosophy; the form only is poetry. The Prometheus is a *philosophema* ταυτηγορικὸν,—the tree of knowledge of good and evil,—an allegory, a προπαίδευμα, though the noblest and the most pregnant of its kind.

The generation of the νοῦς, or pure reason in man. 1. It was superadded or infused, *a supra* to mark that it was no mere evolution of the animal basis;—that it could not have grown out of the other faculties of man, his life, sense, understanding, as the flower grows out of the stem, having pre-existed potentially in the seed: 2. The νοῦς, or fire, was 'stolen,'—to mark its *hetero*— or rather its *allo*-geneity, that is, its diversity, its difference in kind, from the faculties which are common to man with the nobler animals : 3. And stolen from Heaven,'—to mark its superiority in kind, as well as its essential diversity : 4. And it was a 'spark,'—to mark that it is not subject to any modifying reaction from that on which it immediately acts ; that it suffers no change, and receives no accession, from the inferior, but multiplies itself by conversion, without being alloyed by, or amalgamated with, that which it potentiates, ennobles, and transmutes : 5. And lastly (in order to imply the homogeneity of the donor and of the gift), it was stolen by a 'god,' and a god of the race before the dynasty of Jove,—Jove the binder of reluctant powers, the coercer and entrancer of free spirits under the fetters of shape, and mass, and passive mobility ; but likewise by a god of the same race and essence with Jove, and linked of yore in closest and friendliest intimacy with him. This, to mark the pre-existence, in order of thought, of the *nous*, as spiritual, both to the objects of sense, and to their products, formed as it were, by the precipitation, or, if I may dare adopt the bold language of Leibnitz, by a coagulation of spirit.* In other words this derivation of the spark from above, and from a god anterior to the Jovial dynasty—(that is, to the submersion of spirits in material forms),—was intended to mark the transcendency of the *nous*, the contra-distinctive faculty of man, as timeless, ἄχρονόν τι, and, in this negative sense, eternal. It signified, I say, its superiority to, and its diversity from, all things that subsist in space and time, nay, even those which, though spaceless, yet partake of time, namely, souls or understandings. For the soul, or understanding, if it be defined physiologically as the principle of sensibility, irritability, and growth, together with the functions of the organs, which are at once the representations and the instruments of these, must be considered *in genere*, though not in degree or dignity, common to man and the inferior animals. It was the spirit, the *nous*, which man alone possessed. And I must be permitted to suggest that this notion deserves some respect, were it only that it can show a semblance, at least, of sanction from a far higher authority.

* Schelling ascribes this expression, which I have not been able to find in the words of Leibnitz, to Hemsterhuis : "When Leibnitz," says he, "calls matter the sleep-state of the Monads, or when Hemsterhuis calls it *curdled spirit,—den geronnenen Geist.*—In fact, matter is no other than spirit contemplated in the equilibrium of its activities."—*Transl. Transsc. Ideal.* p. 190.—S. C.

The Greeks agreed with the cosmogonies of the East in deriving all sensible forms from the indistinguishable. The latter we find designated as the τὸ ἄμορφον, the ὕδωρ προκοσμικὸν, the χάος, as the essentially unintelligible, yet necessarily presumed, basis or sub-position of all positions. That it is, scientifically considered, an indispensable idea for the human mind, just as the mathematical point, &c. for the geometrician ;—of this the various systems of our geologists and cosmogonists, from Burnet to La Place, afford strong presumption. As an idea, it must be interpreted as a striving of the mind to distinguish being from existence—or potential being, the ground of being containing the possibility of existence, from being actualized. In the language of the mysteries, it was the *esurience*, the πόθος or *desideratum*, the unfuelled fire, the Ceres, the ever-seeking maternal goddess, the origin and interpretation of whose name is found in the Hebrew root signifying hunger, and thence capacity. It was, in short, an effort to represent the universal ground of all differences distinct or opposite, but in relation to which all *antithesis* as well as all *antitheta*, existed only potentially. This was the container and withholder (such is the primitive sense of the Hebrew word rendered darkness (Gen. i, 2)) out of which light, that is, the *lux lucifica*, as distinguished from *lumen seu lux phænomenalis* was produced ;—say, rather, that which, producing itself into light as the one pole or antagonist power, remained in the other pole as darkness, that is, gravity, or the principle of mass, or wholeness without distinction of parts.

And here the peculiar, the philosophic, genius of Greece began its fœtal throb. Here it individualized itself in contradistinction from the Hebrew archæology, on the one side, and from the Phœnician, on the other. The Phœnician confounded the indistinguishable with the absolute, the *Alpha* and *Omega*, the ineffable *causa sui*. It confounded, I say, the multeity below intellect, that is, unintelligible from defect of the subject, with the absolute identity above all intellect, that is, transcending comprehension by the plenitude of its excellence. With the Phœnician sages the cosmogony was their theogony and *vice versa*. Hence, too, flowed their theurgic rites, their magic, their worship (*cultus et apotheosis*) of the plastic forces, chemical and vital, and these, or their notions respecting these, formed the hidden meaning, the soul, as it were, of which the popular and civil worship was the body with its drapery.

The Hebrew wisdom imperatively asserts an unbeginning creative One, who neither became the world; nor is the world eternally; nor made the world out of himself by emanation, or evolution;—but who willed it, and it was! *Τὰ ἄθεα ἐγένετο, καὶ ἐγένετο χάος*,—and this chaos, the eternal will, by the spirit and the word, or express *fiat*—again acting as the impregnant, distinctive, and ordonnant power—enabled to become a world—*κοσμεῖσθαι*. So must it be when a religion, that shall preclude superstition on the one hand, and brute indifference on the other, is to be true for the meditative sage, yet intelligible, or at least apprehensible, for all but the fools in heart.

The Greek philosopheme, preserved for us in the Æschylean Prometheus, stands midway betwixt both, yet is distinct in kind from either. With the Hebrew or purer Semitic, it assumes an X Y Z—(I take these letters in their algebraic application)—an indeterminate *Elohim*, antecedent to the matter of the world, *ὕλη ἄκοσμος*—no less than to the *ὕλη κεκοσμημένη*. In this point, likewise, the Greek accorded with the Semitic, and differed from the Phœnician—that it held the antecedent X Y Z to be supersensuous and divine. But on the other hand, it coincides with the Phœnician in considering this antecedent ground of corporeal matter—*τῶν σωμάτων καὶ τοῦ σωματικοῦ*,—not so properly the cause of the latter, as the occasion and the still continuing substance. *Materia substat adhuc.* The corporeal was supposed co-essential with the antecedent of its corporeity. Matter, as distinguished from body, was a *non ens*, a simple apparition, *id quod mere videtur;* but to body the elder physico-theology of the Greeks allowed a participation in entity. It was *spiritus ipse, oppressus, dormiens, et diversis modis somnians.* In short, body was the productive power suspended, and as it were, quenched in the product. This may be rendered plainer by reflecting, that, in the pure Semitic scheme there are four terms introduced in the solution of the problem, 1. the beginning, self-sufficing, and immutable Creator; 2. the antecedent night as the identity, or including germ, of the light and darkness, that is, gravity; 3. the chaos; and 4. the material world resulting from the powers communicated by the divine *fiat*. In the Phœnician scheme there are in fact but two—a self-organizing chaos, and the omniform nature as the result. In the Greek scheme we have three terms, 1. the *hyle* ὕλη, which holds the place of the chaos, or the waters, in the true system ; 2. τὰ σώματα, answering to the Mosaic heaven and earth ; and 3. the Saturnian χρόνοι ὑπερχρόνιοι,—which answer to the antecedent darkness of the Mosaic scheme, but to which the elder physico-theologists attributed a self-polarizing power—a *natura gemina quæ fit et facit, agit et patitur.* In other words, the *Elohim* of the Greeks were still but a *natura deorum,* τὸ θεῖον, in which a vague plurality adhered ; or if any unity was imagined, it was not personal—not a unity of excellence, but simply an expression of the negative—that which was to pass, but which had not yet passed, into distinct form.

All this will seem strange and obscure at first reading—perhaps fantastic. But it will only seem so. Dry and prolix, indeed, it is to me in the writing, full as much as it can be to others in the attempt to understand it. But I know that, once mastered, the idea will be the key to the whole cypher of the Æschylean mythology. The sum stated in the terms of philosophic logic is this: First, what Moses appropriated to the chaos itself: what Moses made passive and a *materia subjecta et lucis et tenebrarum,* the containing προθέμενον of the *thesis* and *antithesis ;*—this the Greek placed anterior to the chaos ;—the chaos itself being the struggle between the *hyperchronia,* the ἰδέαι πρόνομοι, as the unevolved, unproduced, *prothesis,* of which ἰδέα καὶ νόμος—(idea and law)—are the *thesis* and *antithesis.* (I use the word 'produced' in the mathematical sense, as a point elongating itself to a bipolar line.) Secondly, what Moses establishes, not merely as a transcendant *Monas,* but as an individual Ἑνὰς likewise ;—this the Greek took as a harmony, θεοὶ ἀθάνατοι, τὸ θεῖον, as distinguished from ὁ θεὸς—or, to adopt the more expressive language of the Pythagoreans and cabalists *numen numerantis;* and these are to be contemplated as the identity.

Now according to the Greek philosopheme or *mythus,* in these, or in this identity, there arose a war, schism, or division, that is, a polarization into *thesis* and *antithesis.* In consequence of this schism in the τὸ θεῖον, the *thesis* becomes *nomos,* or law, and the *antithesis* becomes *idea,* but so that the *nomos* is *nomos,* because, and only because, the *idea* is *idea :* the *nomos* is not idea, only because the idea has not become *nomos.* And this *not* must be heedfully borne in mind through the whole interpretation of this most profound and pregnant philosopheme. The *nomos* is essentially idea, but essentially it is idea *substans*, that is, *id quod stat subtus*, understanding *sensu generalissimo*. The *idea*, which now is no longer idea, has substantiated itself, become real as opposed to idea, and is henceforward, therefore, *substans in substantiato*. The first product of its energy is the thing itself: *ipsa se posuit et jam facta est ens positum*. Still, however, its productive energy is not exhausted in this product, but overflows, or is effluent, as the specific forces, properties, faculties, of the product. It re-appears, in short, in the body, as the function of the body. As a sufficient illustration, though it can not be offered as a perfect instance, take the following.

'In the world we see everywhere evidences of a unity, which the component parts are so far from explaining, that they necessarily presuppose it as the cause and condition of their existing as those parts, or even of their existing at all. This antecedent unity, or cause and principle of each union, it has, since the time of Bacon and Kepler, been customary to call a law. This crocus, for instance, or any flower the reader may have in sight or choose to bring before his fancy;—that the root, stem, leaves, petals, &c. cohere as one plant, is owing to an antecedent power or principle in the seed, which existed before a single particle of the matters that constitute the size and visibility of the crocus had been attracted from the surrounding soil, air, and moisture. Shall we turn to the seed? Here too the same necessity meets us, an antecedent unity (I speak not of the parent plant, but of an agency antecedent in order of operance, yet remaining present as the conservative and reproductive power), must here too be supposed. Analyze the seed with the finest tools, and let the solar microscope come in aid of your senses—what do you find? means and instruments, a wondrous fairy-tale of nature, magazines of food, stores of various sorts, pipes, spiracles, defences—a house of many chambers, and the owner and inhabitant invisible.* Now, compare a plant thus contemplated with an animal. In the former, the productive energy exhausts itself, and as it were, sleeps in the product or *organismus*—in its root, stem, foliage, blossoms, seed. Its balsams, gums, resins, *aromata*, and all other bases of its sensible qualities, are, it is well known,

* Aids to Reflection. Moral and Religious Aphorisms. Aphorism VI. —*Ed.*

mere excretions from the vegetable, eliminated, as lifeless, from the actual plant. The qualities are not its properties, but the properties, or far rather, the dispersion and volatilization of these extruded and rejected bases. But in the animal it is otherwise. Here the antecedent unity—the productive and self-realizing idea—strives, with partial success, to re-emancipate itself from its product, and seeks once again to become *idea :* vainly indeed: for in order to this, it must be retrogressive, and it hath subjected itself to the fates, the evolvers of the endless thread—to the stern necessity of progression. *Idea* itself it can not become, but it may in long and graduated process, become an image, an ANALOGON, an anti-type of IDEA. And this εἴδωλον may approximate to a perfect likeness. *Quod est simile nequit esse idem.* Thus, in the lower animals, we see this process of emancipation commence with the intermediate link, or that which forms the transition from properties to faculties, namely, with sensation. Then the faculties of sense, locomotion, construction, as, for instance, webs, hives, nests, &c. Then the functions; as of instinct, memory, fancy, instinctive intelligence, or understanding, as it exists in the most intelligent animals. Thus the idea (henceforward no more idea, but irrecoverable by its own fatal act) commences the process of its own transmutation, as *substans in substantiato*, as the *enteleche*, or the *vis formatrix*, and it finishes the process as *substans e substantiato*, that is, as the understanding.

If, for the purpose of elucidating this process, I might be allowed to imitate the symbolic language of the algebraists, and thus to regard the successive steps of the process as so many powers and dignities of the *nomos* or law, the scheme would be represented thus :—

$$\text{Nomos}^1 = \text{Product} : N^2 = \text{Property} : N^3 = \text{Faculty} :$$
$$N^4 = \text{Function} : N^5 = \text{Understanding} ;\text{—}$$

which is, indeed, in one sense, itself a *nomos*, inasmuch as it is the index of the *nomos*, as well as its highest function ; but, like the hand of a watch, it is likewise a *nomizomenon*. It is a verb, but still a verb passive.

On the other hand, idea is so far co-essential with *nomos*, that by its co-existence—(not confluence)—with the *nomos* ἐν νομιζομένοις (with the *organismus* and its faculties and functions in the man), it becomes itself a *nomos*. But, observe, a *nomos autonomos*, or containing its law in itself likewise;—even as the *nomos* produces for its highest product the understanding, so the idea, in its opposition and, of course, its correspondence to the *nomos*, begets in itself an *analogon* to product; and this is self-consciousness. But as the product can never become idea, so neither can the idea (if it is to remain idea) become or generate a distinct product. This *analogon* of product is to be itself; but were it indeed and substantially a product, it would cease to be self. It would be an object for a subject, not (as it is and must be) an object that is its own subject, and *vice versa;* a conception which, if the uncombining and infusile genius of our language allowed it, might be expressed by the term subject-object. Now, idea, taken in indissoluble connection with this *analogon* of product is mind, that which knows itself, and the existence of which may be inferred, but can not appear or become a *phenomenon*.

By the benignity of Providence, the truths of most importance in themselves, and which it most concerns us to know, are familiar to us, even from childhood. Well for us if we do not abuse this privilege, and mistake the familiarity of words which convey these truths, for a clear understanding of the truths themselves! If the preceding disquisition, with all its subtlety and all its obscurity, should answer no other purpose, it will still have been neither purposeless, nor devoid of utility, should it only lead us to sympathize with the strivings of the human intellect, awakened to the infinite importance of the inward oracle *γνῶθι σεαυτόν*—and almost instinctively shaping its course of search in conformity with the Platonic intimation—*ψυχῆς φύσιν ἀξίως λόγου κατανοῆσαι οἴει δυνατὸν εἶναι, ἄνευ τῆς τοῦ ὅλου φύσεως*; but be this as it may, the groundwork of the Æschylean *mythus* is laid in the definition of idea and law, as correlatives that mutually interpret each the other;—an idea, with the adequate power of realizing itself being a law, and a law considered abstractedly from, or in the absence of, the power of manifesting itself in its appropriate product being an idea. Whether this be true philosophy, is not the question. The school of Aristotle would, of course, deny, the Platonic affirm it; for in this consists the difference of the two schools. Both acknowledge ideas as distinct from the mere generalizations from objects of sense: both would define an idea as an *ens rationale*, to which there can be no adequate correspondent in sensible experience. But, according to Aristotle, ideas are regulative only, and exist only as functions of the mind :—according to Plato, they are constitutive likewise, and one in essence with the power and life of nature ;—ἐν λόγῳ ζωὴ ἦν, καὶ ἡ ζωὴ ἦν τὸ φῶς τῶν ἀνθρώπων. And this I assert was the philosophy of the mythic poets, who, like Æschylus, adapted the secret doctrines of the mysteries as the (not always safely disguised) antidote to the debasing influences of the religion of the state.

But to return and conclude this preliminary explanation. We have only to substitute the term will, and the term constitutive power, for *nomos* or law, and the process is the same. Permit me to represent the identity or *prothesis* by the letter Z and the *thesis* and *antithesis* by X and Y respectively. Then I say X by not being Y, but in consequence of being the correlative opposite of Y, is will ; and Y, by not being X, but the correlative and opposite of X, is nature, *natura naturans*, νόμος φυσικός. Hence we may see the necessity of contemplating the idea now as identical with the reason, and now as one with the will, and now as both in one, in which last case I shall, for convenience' sake, employ the term *Nous*, the rational will, the practical reason.

We are now out of the holy jungle of transcendental metaphysics ; if indeed, the reader's patience shall have had strength and persistency enough to allow me to exclaim—

Ivimus ambo
Per densas umbras : at tenet umbra Deum.

Not that I regard the foregoing as articles of faith, or as all true ; —I have implied the contrary by contrasting it with, at least, by showing its disparateness from, the Mosaic, which, *bona fide*, I do regard as the truth. But I believe there is much, and profound, truth in it, *supra captum* ψιλοσόφων, *qui non agnoscunt divinum, ideoque nec naturam, nisi nomine, agnoscunt ; sed res cunctas ex sensuali corporeo cogitant, quibus hac ex causa interiora clausa manent, et simul cum illis exteriora quæ proxima interioribus sunt !* And with no less confidence do I believe that the positions above given, true or false, are contained in the Promethean *mythus*.

In this *mythus*, Jove is the impersonated representation or symbol of the *nomos*—*Jupiter est quodcunque vides.* He is the *mens agitans molem*, but at the same time, the *molem corpoream ponens et constituens*. And so far the Greek philosopheme does not differ essentially from the cosmotheism, or identification of God with the universe, in which consisted the first apostasy of mankind after the flood, when they combined to raise a temple to the heavens, and which is still the favored religion of the Chinese. Prometheus, in like manner, is the impersonated representative of Idea, or of the same power as Jove, but contemplated as independent and not immersed in the product,—as law *minus* the productive energy. As such it is next to be seen what the several significances of each must or may be according to the philosophic conception ; and of which significances, therefore, should we find in the philosopheme a correspondent to each, we shall be entitled to assert that such are the meanings of the fable. And first of Jove :—

Jove represents 1. *Nomos* generally, as opposed to Idea or *Nous:* 2. *Nomos archinomos*, now as the father, now as the sovereign, and now as the includer and representative of the *νόμοι οὐράνιοι κοσμικοί*, or *dii majores*, who had joined or come over to Jove in the first schism : 3. *Nomos* *δαμνητής*—the subjugator of the spirits, of the *ἰδέαι πρόνομοι*, who, thus subjugated, became *νόμοι ὑπονόμιοι ὑποσπόνδοι*, *Titanes pacati, dii minores*, that is, the elements considered as powers reduced to obedience under yet higher powers than themselves : 4. *Nomos* *πολιτικός*, law in the Pauline sense, *νόμος ἀλλοτριόνομος* in antithesis to *νόμος αὐτόνομος*.

COROLLARY.

It is in this sense that Jove's jealous, ever-quarrelsome spouse represents the political sacerdotal *cultus*, the church, in short, of republican paganism ;—a church by law established for the mere purposes of the particular state, unennobled by the consciousness of instrumentality to higher purposes ;—at once unenlightened and unchecked by revelation. Most gratefully ought we to acknowledge that since the completion of our constitution in 1688, we may, with unflattering truth, elucidate the spirit and character of such a church by the contrast of the institution, to which England owes the larger portion of its superiority in that, in which alone superiority is an unmixed blessing,—the diffused cultivation of its inhabitants. But previously to this period, I shall offend no enlightened man if I say without distinction of parties—*intra muros peccatur et extra*;—that the history of Christendom presents us with too many illustrations of this Junonian jealousy, this factious harassing of the sovereign power as soon as the latter betrayed any symptoms of a disposition to its true policy, namely, to privilege and perpetuate that which is best,—to tolerate the tolerable,—and to restrain none but those who would restrain all, and subjugate even the state itself. But while truth extorts this confession, it, at the same time, requires that it should be accompanied by an avowal of the fact, that the spirit is a relic of Paganism; and with a bitter smile would an Æschylus or a Plato in the shades, listen to a Gibbon or a Hume vaunting the mild and tolerant spirit of the state religions of ancient Greece or Rome. Here we have the sense of Jove's intrigues with Europa, Io, &c., whom the god, in his own nature a general lover, had successively taken under his protection. And here, too, see the full appropriateness of this part of the *mythus*, in which symbol fades away into allegory, but yet in reference to the working cause, as grounded in humanity, and always existing either actually or potentially, and thus never ceases wholly to be a symbol or tautegory.

Prometheus represents, 1. *sensu generali*, Idea πρόνομος, and in this sense he is a θεὸς ὁμόφυλος, a fellow-tribesman both of the *dii majores*, with Jove at their head, and of the Titans or *dii pacati*: 2. He represents Idea φιλόνομος, νομοδείκτης; and in this sense the former friend and counsellor of Jove or *Nous uranius*: 3. Λόγος φιλάνθρωπος, the divine humanity, the humane God, who retained unseen, kept back, or (in the *catachresis* characteristic of the Phœnicio-Grecian mythology) stole, a portion or *ignicula* from the living spirit of law, which remained with the celestial gods unexpended ἐν τῷ νομίζεσθαι. He gave that which, according to the whole analogy of things, should have existed as pure divinity, the sole property and birth-right of the *Dii Joviales*, the *Uranions*, or was conceded to inferior beings as a *substans in substantiato*. This spark divine Prometheus gave to an elect, a favored animal, not as a *substans* or understanding, commensurate with, and confined by, the constitution and conditions of this particular organism, but as *aliquid superstans, liberum, non subactum, invictum, impacatum*, μὴ νομιζόμενον. This gift, by which we are to understand reason theoretical and practical, was therefore a *νόμος αὐτόνομος*—unapproachable and unmodifiable by the animal basis—that is, by the pre-existing *substans* with its products, the animal *organismus* with its faculties and functions; but yet endowed with the power of potentiating, ennobling, and prescribing to, the substance; and hence, therefore, a *νόμος νομοπειθής*, *lex legisuada:* 4. By a transition, ordinary even in allegory, and appropriate to mythic symbol, but especially significant in the present case—the transition, I mean, from the giver to the gift—the giver, in very truth, being the gift, 'whence the soul receives reason; and reason is her being,' says our Milton. Reason is from God, and God is reason, *mens ipsissima.*

5. Prometheus represents, *Nous ἐν ἀνθρώπῳ—νοῦς ἀγωνιστής.* Thus contemplated, the *Nous* is of necessity, powerless; for all power, that is, productivity, or productive energy, is in Law, that is, *νόμος ἀλλοτριόνομος*:* still, however, the Idea in the Law, the *numerus numerans* become *νόμος*, is the principle of the Law; and if with Law dwells power, so with the knowledge or the Idea *scientialis* of the Law, dwells prophecy and foresight. A perfect astronomical time-piece in relation to the motions of the heavenly bodies, or the magnet in the mariner's compass in relation to the magnetism of the earth, is a sufficient illustration.

6. Both *νόμος* and Idea (or *Nous*) are the *verbum;* but, as in the former, it is *verbum fiat* 'the Word of the Lord,'—in the latter it must be the *verbum fiet* or, 'the Word of the Lord in the mouth of the prophet.' *Pari argumento*, as the knowledge is therefore not power, the power is not knowledge. The *νόμος*, the *Ζεὺς παντοκράτωρ*, seeks to learn, and, as it were, to wrest the secret, the hateful secret, of his own fate, namely, the transitoriness adherent to all antithesis; for the identity or the absolute is alone eternal. This secret Jove would extort from the *Nous*, or Prometheus, which is the sixth representment of Prometheus.

7. Introduce but the least of real as opposed to *ideal*, the least speck of positive existence, even though it were but the mote in a sunbeam, into the sciential *contemplamen* or theorem, and it ceases to be science. *Ratio desinit esse pura ratio et fit discursus, stat subter et fit ὑποθετικὸν:—non superstat.* The *Nous* is bound to a rock, the immovable firmness of which is indisso-

* I scarcely need say, that I use the word *ἀλλοτριόνομος* as a participle active, as exercising law on another, not as receiving law from another, though the latter is the classical force (I suppose) of the word.

lubly connected with its barrenness, its non-productivity. Were it productive it would be *Nomos;* but it is *Nous*, because it is not *Nomos*.

8. Solitary ἀβάτῳ ἐν ἐρημίᾳ. Now I say that the *Nous*, notwithstanding its diversity from the *Nomizomeni*, is yet, relatively to their supposed original essence, πᾶσι τοῖς νομιζομένοις ταυτογενής, of the same race or *radix:* though in another sense, namely, in relation to the πᾶν θεῖον—the pantheistic *Elohim*, it is conceived anterior to the schism, and to the conquest and enthronization of Jove who succeeded. Hence the Prometheus of the great tragedian is θεὸς συγγενής. The kindred deities come to him, some to soothe, to condole; others to give weak, yet friendly, counsels of submission; others to tempt, or insult. The most prominent of the latter, and the most odious to the imprisoned and insulated *Nous*, is Hermes, the impersonation of interest with the entrancing and serpentine *Caduceus*, and, as interest or motives intervening between the reason and its immediate self-determinations, with the antipathies to the νόμος αὐτονόμος. The Hermes impersonates the eloquence of cupidity, the cajolement of power regnant; and in a larger sense, custom, the irrational in language, ῥήματα τὰ ῥητόρικα, the fluent, from ῥέω—the rhetorical in opposition to λόγοι, τὰ νοητά. But, primarily, the Hermes is the symbol of interest. He is the messenger, the inter-nuncio, in the low but expressive phrase, the go-between, to beguile or insult. And for the other visitors of Prometheus, the elementary powers, or spirits of the elements, *Titanes pacati*, θεοὶ ὑπονόμιοι, vassal potentates, and their solicitations, the noblest interpretation will be given, if I repeat the lines of our great contemporary poet:—

> Earth fills her lap with pleasures of her own:
> Yearnings she hath in her own natural kind,
> And e'en with something of a mother's mind,
> And no unworthy aim,
> The homely nurse doth all she can
> To make her foster-child, her inmate, Man
> Forget the glories he hath known
> And that imperial palace whence he came:—
>
> WORDSWORTH.

which exquisite language is prefigured in coarser clay, indeed, and with a less lofty spirit, but yet excellently in their kind, and even more fortunately for the illustration and ornament of the present commentary, in the fifth, sixth, and seventh stanzas of Dr. Henry More's poem on the Pre-existence of the Soul :—

Thus groping after our own centre's near
And proper substance, we grew dark, contract,
Swallow'd up of earthly life! Ne what we were
Of old, thro' ignorance can we detect.
Like noble babe, by fate or friends' neglect
Left to the care of sorry salvage wight,
Grown up to manly years can not conject
His own true parentage, nor read aright
What father him begot, what womb him brought to light.

So we, as stranger infants elsewhere born,
Can not divine from what spring we did flow ;
Ne dare these base alliances to scorn,
Nor lift ourselves a whit from hence below ;
Ne strive our parentage again to know,
Ne dream we once of any other stock,
Since foster'd upon Rhea's* knees we grow,
In Satyrs' arms with many a mow and mock
Oft danced ; and hairy Pan our cradle oft hath rock'd!

But Pan nor Rhea be our parentage!
We been the offspring of the all-seeing Nous, &c.

To express the supersensual character of the reason, its abstraction from sensation, we find the Prometheus *ἀτερπῆ*,—while in the yearnings accompanied with the remorse incident to, and only possible in consequence of the Nous being, the rational, self-conscious, and therefore responsible will, he is *γυπὶ διακναιόμενος*.

If to these contemplations we add the control and despotism exercised on the free reason by Jupiter in his symbolical character, as *νόμος πολιτικὸς* ;—by custom (Hermes) ; by necessity, *βία καὶ κρατὸς* ;—by the mechanic arts and powers, *συγγενεῖς τῷ Νοῷ* though they are, and which are symbolized in Hephaistos,—we shall see at once the propriety of the title, Prometheus, *δεσμώτης*.

9. Nature, or *Zeus* as the *νόμος ἐν νομιζομένοις*, knows herself only, can only come to a knowledge of herself, in man! And

* Rhea (from *ῥέω*, *fluo*), that is, the earth as the transitory, the ever-flowing nature, the flux and sum of *phenomena*, or objects of the outward sense, in contra-distinction from the earth as Vesta, as the firmamental law that sustains and disposes the apparent world! The Satyrs represent the sports and appetences of the sensuous nature (*φρόνημα σαρκὸς*)—Pan, or the total life of the earth, the presence of all in each, the universal *organismus* of bodies and bodily energy.

even in man, only as man is supernatural, above nature, noetic. But this knowledge man refuses to communicate: that is, the human understanding alone is at once self-conscious and conscious of nature. And this high prerogative it owes exclusively to its being an assessor of the reason. Yet even the human understanding in its height of place seeks vainly to appropriate the ideas of the pure reason, which it can only represent by *idola*. Here, then, the *Nous* stands as Prometheus, ἀντίπαλος, *renuens* —in hostile opposition to Jupiter *Inquisitor*.

10. Yet, finally, against the obstacles and even under the fostering influences of the *Nomos*, τοῦ νομίμου, a son of Jove himself, but a descendant from Io, the mundane religion, as contradistinguished from the sacerdotal *cultus*, or religion of the state, an Alcides *Liberator* will arise, and the *Nous* or divine principle in man, will be Prometheus ἐλευθερώμενος.

Did my limits or time permit me to trace the persecutions, wanderings, and migrations of the Io, the mundane religion, through the whole map marked out by the tragic poet, the coincidences would bring the truth, the unarbitrariness, of the preceding exposition as near to demonstration as can rationally be required on a question of history, that must, for the greater part, be answered by combination of scattered facts. But this part of my subject, together with a particular exemplification of the light which my theory throws both on the sense and the beauty of numerous passages of this stupendous poem, I must reserve for a future communication.

NOTES.*

v. 15. φάραγγι:—'in a coomb, or combe.'

v. 17.

ἐξωριάζειν γὰρ πατρὸς λόγους βαρύ.

εὐωριάζειν, as the editor confesses, is a word introduced into the text against the authority of all editions and manuscripts. I should prefer ἐξωριάζειν, notwithstanding its being a ἅπαξ λεγόμενον. The εὐ—seems to my tact too free and easy a word;— and yet our 'to trifle with' appears the exact meaning.

* Written in Bp. Blomfield's edition, and communicated by Mr. Cary.— *Ed.*

SUMMARY OF AN ESSAY

ON THE FUNDAMENTAL POSITION OF THE MYSTERIES IN RELATION TO GREEK TRAGEDY.

THE Position, to the establishment of which Mr. Coleridge regards his essay as the Prolegomena, is : that the Greek Tragedy stood in the same relation to the Mysteries, as the Epic Song, and the Fine Arts to the Temple Worship, or the Religion of the State ; that the proper function of the Tragic Poet was under the disguise of popular superstitions, and using the popular Mythology as his stuff and drapery to communicate so much and no more of the doctrines preserved in the Mysteries as should counteract the demoralizing influence of the state religion, without disturbing the public tranquillity, or weakening the reverence for the laws, or bringing into contempt the ancestral and local usages and traditions on which the patriotism of the citizens mainly rested, or that nationality in its intensest form which was little less than essential in the constitution of a Greek republic. To establish this position it was necessary to explain the nature of these secret doctrines, or at least the fundamental principles of the faith and philosophy of Elensis and Samothrace. The Samothracian Mysteries Mr. Coleridge supposes to have been of Phœnician origin, and both these and the Elensinian to have retained the religious belief of the more ancient inhabitants of the Peloponnesus, prior to their union with the Hellenes and the Egyptian colonies : that it comprised sundry relics and fragments of the Patriarchal Faith, the traditions historical and prophetic of the Noetic Family, though corrupted and depraved by their combinations with the system of Pantheism, or the Worship of the Universe as God (*Jupiter est quodcunque vides*), which Mr. Coleridge contends to have been the first great Apostasy of the Ancient World. But a religion founded on Pantheism, is of necessity a religion founded on philosophy, *i. e.* an attempt to determine the origin of nature by the unaided strength of the human intellect, however unsound and false that philosophy may have been. And of this the sacred books of the Indian Priests afford at once proof and instance. Again : the earlier the date of any philosophic scheme, the more *subjective* will it be found—in other words the earliest reasoners sought in their own minds the form, measure, and substance of all other power. Abstracting from whatever was individual and accidental, from whatever distinguished one human mind from another, they fixed their attention exclusively on the characters which belong to all rational beings, and which therefore they contemplated as mind itself, mind in its essence. And however averse a scholar of the present day may be to these first fruits of speculative thought, as metaphysics, a knowledge of their contents and distinctive tenets is indispensable as history. At all events without this knowledge he will in vain attempt to understand the spirit and genius of the arts, institutions, and governing minds of ancient Greece. The difficulty of comprehending any scheme of opinion is proportionate to its greater or lesser unlikeness to the principles and modes of reasoning in which our own minds have been formed. Where the difference is so great as almost to amount to contrariety, no clearness in the exhibition of the scheme will remove the sense, or rather, perhaps, the *sensation*, of strangeness from the hearer's mind. Even beyond its utmost demerits it will appear obscure, unreal, visionary. This difficulty the author anticipates as an obstacle to the ready comprehension of the first principles of the eldest philosophy, and the esoteric doctrines of the Mysteries ; but to the necessity of overcoming this the only obstacle, the thoughtful inquirer must resign himself, as the condition under which alone he may expect to solve a series of problems the most interesting of all that the records of ancient history propose or suggest.

The fundamental position of the Mysteries, Mr. Coleridge contends, consists in affirming that the productive powers or laws of nature are essentially the same with the active powers of the mind—in other words, that mind, or Nous, under which term they combine the universal attributes of reason and will, is a principle of forms and patterns, endued with a tendency to manifest itself as such; and that this mind or eternal essence exists in two modes of being. Namely, either the form and the productive power, which gives it outward and phænomenal reality, are united in equal and adequate proportions, in which case it is what the eldest philosophers, and the moderns in imitation of them, call a *law* of nature ; or the *form* remaining the same, but with the productive power in unequal or inadequate proportions, whether the diminution be effected by the mind's own act or original determination not to put forth this inherent power, or whether the power have been repressed, and as it were driven inward by the violence of a superior force from without,—and in this case it was called by the most Ancient School "Intelligible Number," by a later School "Idea," or *Mind*—κατ' ἐξοχην. To this position a second was added, namely, that the form could not put forth its productive or self-realizing power without ceasing at the same moment to exist *for* itself,—*i. e.* to exist, and know itself as existing. The formative power was as it were alienated from itself and absorbed in the product. It existed as an instinctive, essentially intelligential, but not self-knowing, power. It was law, Jupiter, or (when contemplated plurally) the Dii Majores. On the other hand, to possess its own being consciously, the form must remain single and only inwardly productive. To exist *for* itself, it must continue to exist *by* itself. It must be an *idea;* but an idea in the primary sense of the term, the sense attached to it by the oldest Italian School and by Plato,—not as a synonyme of, but in contra-distinction from, image, conception or notion: as a true entity of all entities the most actual, of all essences the most essential.

Now on this Antithesis of idea and law, that is of mind as an unproductive but self-knowing power, and of mind as a productive but unconscious power, the whole religion of pantheism as disclosed in the Mysteries turns, as on its axis, bi-polar.

FRAGMENT OF AN ESSAY ON TASTE. 1810.

The same arguments that decide the question, whether taste has any fixed principles, may probably lead to a determination of what those principles are. First, then, what is taste in its metaphorical sense, or, which will be the easiest mode of arriving at the same solution, what is there in the primary sense of the word, which may give to its metaphorical meaning an import different from that of sight or hearing, on the one hand, and of touch or smell on the other? And this question seems the more natural, because in correct language we confine beauty, the main subject of taste, to objects of sight and combinations of sounds, and never, except sportively or by abuse of words, speak of a beautiful flavor, or a beautiful scent.

Now the analysis of our senses in the commonest books of anthropology has drawn our attention to the distinction between the perfectly organic, and the mixed senses;—the first presenting objects, as distinct from the perception;—the last as blending the perception with the sense of the object. Our eyes and ears—(I am not now considering what is or is not the case really, but only that of which we are regularly conscious as appearances), our eyes most often appear to us perfect organs of the sentient principle, and wholly in action, and our hearing so much more so than the three other senses, and in all the ordinary exertions of that sense, perhaps, equally so with the sight, that all languages place them in one class, and express their different modifications by nearly the same metaphors. The three remaining senses appear in part passive, and combine with the perception of the outward object a distinct sense of our own life. Taste, therefore, as opposed to vision and sound, will teach us to expect in its metaphorical use a certain reference of any given object to our own being, and not merely a distinct notion of the object in itself, or in its independent properties. From the sense of touch, on the other hand, it is distinguishable by adding to this reference to our vital being some degree of enjoyment, or the contrary,—some perceptible impulse from pleasure or pain to complacency or dislike. The sense of smell, indeed, might perhaps have furnished a metaphor of the same import with that of taste; but the latter was naturally chosen by the majority of civilized nations on account of the greater frequency, importance, and dignity of its employment or exertion in human nature.

By taste, therefore, as applied to the fine arts, we must be supposed to mean an intellectual perception of any object blended with a distinct reference to our own sensibility of pain or pleasure, or, *vice versa*, a sense of enjoyment or dislike co-instantaneously combined with, and appearing to proceed from, some intellectual perception of the object;—intellectual perception, I say; for otherwise it would be a definition of taste in its primary rather than in its metaphorical sense. Briefly, taste is a metaphor taken from one of our mixed senses, and applied to objects of the more purely organic senses, and of our moral sense, when we would imply the co-existence of immediate personal dislike or complacency. In this definition of taste, therefore, is involved the definition of fine arts, namely, as being such the chief and discriminative purpose of which it is to gratify the taste,—that is, not merely to connect, but to combine and unite, a sense of immediate pleasure in ourselves, with the perception of external arrangement.

The great question, therefore, whether taste in any one of the fine arts has any fixed principle or ideal, will find its solution in the ascertainment of two facts:—first, whether in every determination of the taste concerning any work of the fine arts, the individual does not, with or even against the approbation of his general judgment, involuntarily claim that all other minds ought to think and feel the same; whether the common expressions, 'I dare say I may be wrong, but that is my particular taste;'—are uttered as an offering of courtesy, as a sacrifice to the undoubted fact of our individual fallibility, or are spoken with perfect sincerity, not only of the reason but of the whole feeling, with the same entireness of mind and heart, with which we concede a right to every person to differ from another in his preference of bodily tastes and flavors. If we should find ourselves compelled to deny this, and to admit that, notwithstanding the consciousness of our liability to error, and in spite of all those many individual experiences which may have strengthened the consciousness, each man does at the moment so far legislate for all men, as to believe of necessity that he is either right or wrong, and that if it be right for him, it is universally right,—we must then proceed to ascertain:—secondly, whether the source of these phenomena is at all to be found in those parts of our nature, in which each intellect is representative of all,—and whether wholly, or partially. No person of common reflection demands even in feeling, that what tastes pleasant to him ought to produce the same effect on all living beings; but every man does and must expect and demand the universal acquiescence of all intelligent beings in every conviction of his understanding.

* * * * * * *

FRAGMENT OF AN ESSAY ON BEAUTY. 1818.

THE only necessary, but this the absolutely necessary, prerequisite to a full insight into the grounds of the beauty in the objects of sight, is—the directing of the attention to the action of those thoughts in our own mind which are not consciously distinguished. Every man may understand this, if he will but recall the state of his feelings in endeavoring to recollect a name, which he is quite sure that he remembers, though he can not force it back into consciousness. This region of unconscious thoughts, oftentimes the more working the more indistinct they are, may, in reference to this subject, be conceived as forming an ascending scale from the most universal associations of motion with the functions and passions of life,—as when, on passing out of a crowded city into the fields on a day in June, we describe the grass and king-cups as nodding their heads and dancing in the breeze,—up to the half-perceived, yet not fixable, resemblance of a form to some particular object of a diverse class, which resemblance we need only increase but a little, to destroy, or at least injure, its beauty-enhancing effect, and to make it a fantastic intrusion of the accidental and the arbitrary, and consequently a disturbance of the beautiful. This might be abundantly exemplified and illustrated from the paintings of Salvator Rosa.

I am now using the term beauty in its most comprehensive sense, as including expression and artistic interest,—that is, I consider not only the living balance, but likewise all the accompaniments that even by disturbing are necessary to the renewal and continuance of the balance. And in this sense I proceed to show, that the beautiful in the object may be referred to two elements,—lines and colors: the first belonging to the shapely (*forma*, *formalis*, *formosus*), and in this, to the law, and the reason; and the second, to the lively, the free, the spontaneous, and the self-justifying. As to lines, the rectilineal are in themselves the lifeless, the determined *ab extra*, but still in immediate union with the cycloidal, which are expressive of function. The curve line is a modification of the force from without by the force from within, or the spontaneous. These are not arbitrary symbols, but the language of nature, universal and intuitive, by virtue of the law by which man is impelled to explain visible motions by imaginary causative powers analogous to his own acts, as the Dryads, Hamadryads, Naiads, &c.

The better way of applying these principles will be by a brief and rapid sketch of the history of the fine arts,—in which it will be found, that the beautiful in nature has been appropriated to the works of man, just in proportion as the state of the mind in the artists themselves approached to the subjective beauty. Determine what predominance in the minds of the men is preventive of the living balance of excited faculties, and you will discover the exact counterpart in the outward products. Egypt is an illustration of this. Shapeliness is intellect without freedom ; but colors are significant. The introduction of the arch is not less an epoch in the fine than in the useful arts.

Order is beautiful arrangement without any purpose *ad extra ;* —therefore there is a beauty of order, or order may be contemplated exclusively as beauty.

The form given in every empirical intuition,—the stuff, that is, the quality of the stuff, determines the agreeable : but when a thing excites us to receive it in such and such a mould, so that its exact correspondence to that mould is what occupies the mind, —this is taste or the sense of beauty. Whether dishes full of painted wood or exquisite viands were laid out on a table in the same arrangement, would be indifferent to the taste, as in ladies' patterns ; but surely the one is far more agreeable than the other. Hence observe the disinterestedness of all taste ; and hence also a sensual perfection with intellect is occasionally possible without moral feeling. So it may be in music and painting, but not in poetry. How far it is a real preference of the refined to the gross pleasures, is another question, upon the supposition that pleasure, in some form or other, is that alone which determines men to the objects of the former ;—whether experience does not show that if the latter were equally in our power, occasioned no more trouble to enjoy, and caused no more exhaustion of the power of enjoying them by the enjoyment itself, we should in real practice prefer the grosser pleasure. It is not, therefore, any excellence in the quality of the refined pleasures themselves, but the advantages and facilities in the means of enjoying them, that give them the pre-eminence.

This is, of course, on the supposition of the absence of all moral feeling. Suppose its presence, and then there will accrue an excellence even to the quality of the pleasures themselves ; not only, however, of the refined, but also of the grosser kinds,—inasmuch as a larger sweep of thoughts will be associated with each enjoyment, and with each thought will be associated a number of sensations ; and so, consequently, each pleasure will become more the pleasure of the whole being. This is one of the earthly rewards of our being what we ought to be, but which would be annihilated if we attempted to be it for the sake of this increased enjoyment. Indeed it is a contradiction to suppose it. Yet this is the common *argumentum in circulo*, in which the eudæmonists flee and pursue.

* * * *

NOTES ON CHAPMAN'S HOMER.

*Extract of a Letter sent with the Volume.** 1807.

Chapman I have sent in order that you might read the Odyssey; the Iliad is fine, but less equal in the translation, as well as less interesting in itself. What is stupidly said of Shakspeare, is really true and appropriate of Chapman; mighty faults counterpoised by mighty beauties. Excepting his quaint epithets which he affects to render literally from the Greek, a language above all others blest in the "happy marriage of sweet words," and which in our language are mere printer's compound epithets—such as quaffed divine *joy-in-the-heart-of-man-infusing* wine (the undermarked is to be one word, because one sweet mellifluous word expresses it in Homer);—excepting this, it has no look, no air, of a translation. It is as truly an original poem as the Faery Queene;—it will give you small idea of Homer, though a far truer one than Pope's epigrams, or Cowper's cumbersome most anti-Homeric Miltonism. For Chapman writes and feels as a poet,—as Homer might have written had he lived in England in the reign of Queen Elizabeth. In short, it is an exquisite poem, in spite of its frequent and perverse quaintnesses and harshnesses, which are, however, amply repaid by almost unexampled sweetness and beauty of language, all over spirit and feeling. In the main it is an English heroic poem, the tale of which is borrowed from the Greek. The dedication to the Iliad is a noble copy of verses, especially those sublime lines beginning,—

O! 'tis wondrous much
(Through nothing prisde) that the right vertuous touch
Of a well written soule, to vertue moves.
Nor haue we soules to purpose, if their loves
Of fitting objects be not so inflam'd.
How much then, were this kingdome's maine soul maim'd,

* Communicated through Mr. Wordsworth.—*Ed.*

To want this great inflamer of all powers
That move in humane soules! All realmes but yours,
Are honor'd with him; and hold blest that state
That have his workes to reade and contemplate.
In which humanitie to her height is raisde;
Which all the world (yet, none enough) hath praisde.
Seas, earth, and heaven, he did in verse comprize;
Out sung the Muses, and did equalise
Their king Apollo; being so farre from cause
Of princes light thoughts, that their gravest lawes
May finde stuffe to be fashiond by his lines.
Through all the pompe of kingdomes still he shines
And graceth all his gracers. Then let lie
Your lutes, and viols, and more loftily
Make the heroiques of your Homer sung,
To drums and trumpets set his Angels tongue:
And with the princely sports of haukes you use,
Behold the kingly flight of his high Muse:
And see how like the Phœnix she renues
Her age, and starrie feathers in your sunne;
Thousands of yeares attending; everie one
Blowing the holy fire, and throwing in
Their seasons, kingdomes, nations that have bin
Subverted in them; lawes, religions, all
Offerd to change, and greedie funerall;
Yet still your Homer lasting, living, raigning.—

and likewise the 1st, the 11th, and last but one, of the prefatory sonnets to the Odyssey. Could I have foreseen any other speedy opportunity, I should have begged your acceptance of the volume in a somewhat handsomer coat; but as it is, it will better represent the sender,—to quote from myself—

A man disherited, in form and face,
By nature and mishap, of outward grace.

Dedication to Prince Henry.

Chapman in his moral heroic verse, as in this dedication and the prefatory sonnets to his Odyssey, stands above Ben Jonson; there is more dignity, more lustre, and equal strength; but not midway quite between him and the sonnets of Milton. I do not know whether I give him the higher praise, in that he reminds me of Ben Jonson with a sense of his superior excellence, or that he brings Milton to memory notwithstanding his inferiority. His moral poems are not quite out of books like Jonson's, nor yet do the sentiments so wholly grow up out of his own natural habit and grandeur of thought, as in Milton. The sentiments have been attracted to him by a natural affinity of his intellect, and so combined;—but Jonson has taken them by individual and successive acts of ch

Epistle Dedicatorie to the Odyssey.

All this and the preceding is well felt and vig... ously, though harshly, expressed, respecting sublime poetry *in genere;* but in reading Homer I look about me, and ask how does all this apply here? For surely never was there plainer writing; there are a thousand charms of sun and moonbeam, ripple, and wave, and stormy billow, but all on the surface. Had Chapman read Proclus and Porphyry?—and did he really believe them,—or even that they believed themselves? They felt the immense power of a Bible, a Shaster, a Koran. There was none in Greece or Rome, and they tried therefore by subtle allegorical accommodations to conjure the poem of Homer into the *βίβλιον θεοπαϱάδοτον* of Greek faith.

Epistle Dedicatorie to the Batrachomyomachia.

Chapman's identification of his fate with Homer's, and his complete forgetfulness of the distinction between Christianity and idolatry, under the general feeling of some religion, is very interesting. It is amusing to observe, how familiar Chapman's fancy has become with Homer, his life and its circumstances, though the very existence of any such individual, at least with regard to the Iliad and the Hymns, is more than problematic. N.B. The rude engraving in the page was designed by no vulgar hand. It is full of spirit and passion.

End of the Batrachomyomachia.

I am so dull, that neither in the original nor in any translation could I ever find any wit or wise purpose in this poem. The whole humor seems to lie in the names. The frogs and mice are not frogs or mice, but men, and yet they do nothing that conveys any satire. In the Greek there is much beauty of language, but the joke is very flat. This is always the case in rude ages;—their serious vein is inimitable,—their comic low, and low indeed. The psychological cause is easily stated, and copiously exemplifiable.

NOTE IN CASAUBON'S PERSIUS. 1807.

There are six hundred and sixteen pages in this volume, of which twenty-two are text; and five hundred and ninety-four commentary and introductory matter. Yet when I recollect, that I have the whole works of Cicero, Livy, and Quinctilian, with many others,—the whole works of each in a single volume, either thick quarto with thin paper and small yet distinct print, or thick octavo or duodecimo of the same character, and that they cost me in the proportion of a shilling to a guinea for the same quantity of worse matter in modern books, or editions,—I a poor man, yet one whom *βιβλίων κτήσεως ἐκ παιδαρίου δεινὸς ἐκράτησε πόθος*, feel the liveliest gratitude for the age which produced such editions, and for the education, which by enabling me to understand and taste the Greek and Latin writers, has thus put it in my power to collect on my own shelves, for my actual use, almost all the best books in spite of my small income. Somewhat too I am indebted to the ostentation of expense among the rich, which has occasioned these cheap editions to become so disproportionately cheap.

NOTES ON BARCLAY'S ARGENIS. 1803.*

Heaven forbid that this work should not exist in its present form and language! Yet I can not avoid the wish that it had, during the reign of James I., been moulded into an heroic poem in English octavo stanza, or epic blank verse;—which, however, at that time had not been invented, and which, alas! still remains the sole property of the inventor, as if the Muses had given him an unevadible patent for it. Of dramatic blank verse we have many and various specimens;—for example, Shakspeare's as compared with Massinger's, both excellent in their kind:—of lyric, and of what may be called Orphic, or philosophic, blank verse, perfect models may be found in Wordsworth:—of colloquial blank verse there are excellent, though not perfect, ex-

* Communicated by the Rev. Derwent Coleridge.

amples in Cowper;—but of epic blank verse, since Milton, there is not one.

It absolutely distresses me when I reflect that this work, admired as it has been by great men of all ages, and lately, I hear, by the poet Cowper, should be only not unknown to general readers. It has been translated into English two or three times —how, I know not, wretchedly, I doubt not. It affords matter for thought that the last translation (or rather, in all probability, miserable and faithless abridgment of some former one) was given under another name. What a mournful proof of the incelebrity of this great and amazing work among both the public and the people! For as Wordsworth, the greater of the two great men of this age,—(at least, except Davy and him, I have known, read of, heard of, no others)—for as Wordsworth did me the honor of once observing to me, the people and the public are two distinct classes, and, as things go, the former is likely to retain a better taste, the less it is acted on by the latter. Yet Telemachus is in every mouth, in every school-boy's and school-girl's hand! It is awful to say of a work, like the Argenis, the style and Latinity of which, judged (not according to classical pedantry, which pronounces every sentence right which can be found in any book prior to Boetius, however vicious the age, or affected the author, and every sentence wrong, however natural and beautiful, which has been of the author's own combination,—but) according to the universal logic of thought as modified by feeling, is equal to that of Tacitus in energy and genuine conciseness, and is as perspicuous as that of Livy, whilst it is free from the affectations, obscurities, and lust to surprise of the former, and seems a sort of antithesis to the slowness and prolixity of the latter—(this remark does not, however, impeach even the classicality of the language, which, when the freedom and originality, the easy motion and perfect command of the thoughts, are considered, is truly wonderful):—of such a work it is awful to say, that it would have been well if it had been written in English or Italian verse! Yet the event seems to justify the notion. Alas! it is now too late. What modern work, even of the size of the Paradise Lost —much less of the Faery Queene—would be read in the present day, or even bought, or be likely to be bought, unless it were an instructive work, as the phrase is, like Roscoe's quartos of Leo X., or entertaining like Boswell's three of Dr. Johnson's conversations. It may be fairly objected—what work of surpassing merit has given the proof?—Certainly, none. Yet still there are ominous facts, sufficient, I fear, to afford a certain prophecy of its reception, if such were produced.

NOTES ON CHALMERS'S LIFE OF SAMUEL DANIEL.

The justice of these remarks can not be disputed, though some of them are too figurative for sober criticism.

Most genuine! a figurative remark! If this strange writer had any meaning, it must be:—Headly's criticism is just throughout, but conveyed in a style too figurative for prose composition. Chalmers's own remarks are wholly mistaken; too silly for any criticism, drunk or sober, and in language too flat for any thing. In Daniel's Sonnets there is scarcely one good line; while his Hymen's Triumph, of which Chalmers says not one word, exhibits a continued series of first-rate beauties in thought, passion, and imagery, and in language and metre is so faultless, that the style of that poem may without extravagance be declared to be imperishable English. 1820.

BISHOP CORBET.

I almost wonder that the inimitable, humor and the rich sound and propulsive movement of the verse, have not rendered Corbet a popular poet. I am convinced that a reprint of his poems, with illustrative and chit-chat biographical notes, and cuts by Cruikshank, would take with the public uncommonly well. September, 1823.

NOTES ON SELDEN'S TABLE TALK.*

There is more weighty bullion sense in this book, than I ever found in the same number of pages of any uninspired writer.

OPINION.

Opinion and affection extremely differ. I may affect a woman best, but it does not follow I must think her the handsomest woman in the world.

* These remarks on Selden were communicated by Mr. Cary.—*Ed.*

* * * Opinion is something wherein I go about to give reason why all the world should think as I think. Affection is a thing wherein I look after the pleasing of myself.

Good! This is the true difference betwixt the beautiful and the agreeable, which Knight and the rest of that πλῆθος ἄθεον have so beneficially confounded, *meretricibus scilicet et Plutoni.*

O what an insight the whole of this article gives into a wise man's heart, who has been compelled to act with the many, as one of the many! It explains Sir Thomas More's zealous Romanism, &c.

PARLIAMENT.

Excellent! O! to have been with Selden over his glass of wine, making every accident an outlet and a vehicle of wisdom!

POETRY.

The old poets had no other reason but this, their verse was sung to music: otherwise it had been a senseless thing to have fettered up themselves.

No man can know all things: even Selden here talks ignorantly. Verse is in itself a music, and the natural symbol of that union of passion with thought and pleasure, which constitutes the essence of all poetry, as contra-distinguished from science, and distinguished from history civil or natural. To Pope's Essay on Man,—in short, to whatever is mere metrical good sense and wit, the remark applies.

Ib.

Verse proves nothing but the quantity of syllables; they are not meant for logic.

True; they, that is, verses, are not logic; but they are, or ought to be, the envoys and representatives of that vital passion, which is the practical cement of logic; and without which logic must remain inert.

NOTES ON TOM JONES.*

MANNERS change from generation to generation, and with manners morals appear to change,—actually change with some, but appear to change with all but the abandoned. A young man

* Communicated by Mr. Gillman.—*Ed.*

of the present day who should act as Tom Jones is supposed to act at Upton, with Lady Bellaston, &c. would not be a Tom Jones; and a Tom Jones of the present day, without perhaps being in the ground a better man, would have perished rather than submit to be kept by a harridan of fortune. Therefore this novel is, and, indeed, pretends to be, no exemplar of conduct. But, notwithstanding all this, I do loathe the cant which can recommend Pamela and Clarissa Harlowe as strictly moral, though they poison the imagination of the young with continued doses of *tinct. lyttæ*, while Tom Jones is prohibited as loose. I do not speak of young women;—but a young man whose heart or feelings can be injured, or even his passions excited, by aught in this novel, is already thoroughly corrupt. There is a cheerful, sunshiny, breezy spirit that prevails everywhere, strongly contrasted with the close, hot, day-dreamy continuity of Richardson. Every indiscretion, every immoral act, of Tom Jones (and it must be remembered that he is in every one taken by surprise—his inward principles remaining firm—) is so instantly punished by embarrassment and unanticipated evil consequences of his folly, that the reader's mind is not left for a moment to dwell or run riot on the criminal indulgence itself. In short, let the requisite allowance be made for the increased refinement of our manners,—and then I dare believe that no young man who consulted his heart and conscience only, without adverting to what the world would say—could rise from the perusal of Fielding's Tom Jones, Joseph Andrews, or Amelia, without feeling himself a better man;—at least, without an intense conviction that he could not be guilty of a base act.

If I want a servant or mechanic, I wish to know what he does:—but of a friend, I must know what he is. And in no writer is this momentous distinction so finely brought forward as by Fielding. We do not care what Blifil does;—the deed, as separate from the agent, may be good or ill; but Blifil is a villain;—and we feel him to be so from the very moment he, the boy Blifil, restores Sophia's poor captive bird to its native and rightful liberty.

Book xiv. ch. 8.

Notwithstanding the sentiment of the Roman satirist, which denies the divinity of fortune; and the opinion of Seneca to the same purpose; Cicero, who was, I believe, a wiser man than either of them, expressly holds the contrary; and certain it is there are some incidents in life so very strange and unaccountable, that it seems to require more than human skill and foresight in producing them.

Surely Juvenal, Seneca, and Cicero, all meant the same thing, namely, that there was no chance, but instead of it providence, either human or divine.

Book xv. ch. 9.

The rupture with Lady Bellaston.

Even in the most questionable part of Tom Jones, I can not but think, after frequent reflection, that an additional paragraph, more fully and forcibly unfolding Tom Jones's sense of self-degradation on the discovery of the true character of the relation in which he had stood to Lady Bellaston, and his awakened feeling of the dignity of manly chastity, would have removed in great measure any just objections,—at all events relatively to Fielding himself, and with regard to the state of manners in his time.

Book xvi. ch. 5.

That refined degree of Platonic affection which is absolutely detached from the flesh, and is indeed entirely and purely spiritual, is a gift confined to the female part of the creation; many of whom I have heard declare (and doubtless with great truth) that they would, with the utmost readiness, resign a lover to a rival, when such resignation was proved to be necessary for the temporal interest of such lover.

I firmly believe that there are men capable of such a sacrifice, and this, without pretending to, or even admiring or seeing any virtue in, this absolute detachment from the flesh.

ANOTHER SET OF NOTES ON TOM JONES.

Book i. ch. 4.

"Beyond this the country gradually rose into a ridge of wild mountains, the tops of which were above the clouds."

As this is laid in Somersetshire, the clouds must have been unusually low. One would be more apt to think of Skiddaw or Ben Nevis, than of Quantock or Mendip Hills.

Book xi. ch. 1.

"Nor can the Devil receive a guest more worthy of him, nor possibly more welcome to him than a slanderer."

The very word Devil, *Diabolus,* means a slanderer.

Book xii. ch. 12.

"And here we will make a concession, which would not perhaps have been expected from us; That no limited form of government is capable of rising to the same degree of perfection, or of producing the same benefits to society with this. Mankind has never been so happy, as when the greatest part of the then known world was under the dominion of a single master; and this state of their felicity continued under the reign of five successive Princes."

Strange that such a lover of political liberty as Fielding should have forgotten that the glaring infamy of the Roman morals and manners immediately on the ascent of Commodus prove, that even five excellent despots in succession were but a mere temporary palliative of the evils inherent in despotism and its causes. Think you that all the sub-despots were Trajans and Antonines? No! Rome was left as it was found by them, incapable of freedom.

Book xviii. ch. 4.

Plato himself concludes his Phædon with declaring, that his best argument amounts only to raise a probability; and Cicero himself seems rather to profess an inclination to believe, than any actual belief, in the doctrines of immortality.

No! Plato does not say so, but speaks as a philosophic Christian would do of the best arguments of the scientific intellect. The assurance is derived from a higher principle. If this be Methodism Plato and Socrates were arrant Methodists and New Light men; but I would ask Fielding what ratiocinations do more than raise a high degree of probability. But assuredly an historic belief is far different from Christian *faith.*

No greater proof can be conceived of the strength of the instinctive anticipation of a future state than that it was believed at all by the Greek Philosophers, with their vague and (Plato excepted) Pantheistic conception of the First Cause. S. T. C.

JONATHAN WILD.*

JONATHAN WILD is assuredly the best of all the fictions in which a villain is throughout the prominent character. But how impossible it is by any force of genius to create a sustained

* Communicated by Mr. Gillman.—*Ed.*

attractive interest for such a ground-work, and how the mind wearies of, and shrinks from, the more than painful interest, the μισητὸν, of utter depravity,—Fielding himself felt and endeavored to mitigate and remedy by the (on all other principles) far too large a proportion, and too quick recurrence, of the interposed chapters of moral reflection, like the chorus in the Greek tragedy, —admirable specimens as these chapters are of profound irony and philosophic satire. Chap. vi. Book 2, on Hats,*—brief as it is, exceeds any thing even in Swift's Lilliput, or Tale of the Tub. How forcibly it applies to the Whigs, Tories, and Radicals of our own times.

Whether the transposition of Fielding's scorching wit (as B. iii. c. xiv.) to the mouth of his hero be objectionable on the ground of *incredulus odi*, or is to be admired as answering the author's purpose by unrealizing the story, in order to give a deeper reality to the truths intended,—I must leave doubtful, yet myself inclining to the latter judgment. 27th Feb. 1832.

NOTES ON JUNIUS. 1807.

STAT NOMINIS UMBRA.

As he never dropped the mask, so he too often used the poisoned dagger of an assassin.

Dedication to the English nation.

The whole of this dedication reads like a string of aphorisms arranged in chapters, and classified by a resemblance of subject, or a cento of points.

Ib. If an honest, and I may truly affirm a laborious, zeal for the public service has given me any weight in your esteem, let me exhort and conjure you never to suffer an invasion of your political constitution, however minute the instance may appear, to pass by, without a determined, persevering resistance.

A longer sentence and proportionately inelegant.

Ib. If you reflect that in the changes of administration which have marked and disgraced the present reign, although your warmest patriots have, in

* 'In which our hero makes a speech well worthy to be celebrated; and the behavior of one of the gang, perhaps more unnatural than any other part of this history.'

their turn, been invested with the lawful and unlawful authority of the crown, and though other reliefs or improvements have been held forth to the people, yet that no one man in office has ever promoted or encouraged a bill for shortening the duration of parliaments, but that (whoever was minister) the opposition to this measure, ever since the septennial act passed, has been constant and uniform on the part of government.

Long, and as usual, inelegant. Junius can not manage a long sentence ; it has all the *ins* and *outs* of a snappish figure-dance.

PREFACE.

An excellent preface, and the sentences not so snipt as in the dedication. The paragraph near the conclusion beginning with "some opinion may now be expected," &c. and ending with "relation between guilt and punishment," deserves to be quoted as a master-piece of rhetorical ratiocination in a series of questions that permit no answer ; or (as Junius says) carry their own answer along with them. The great art of Junius is never to say too much, and to avoid with equal anxiety a common-place manner, and matter that is not common-place. If ever he deviates into any originality of thought, he takes care that it shall be such as excites surprise for its acuteness, rather than admiration for its profundity. He takes care? say rather that nature took care for him. It is impossible to detract from the merit of these Letters : they are suited to their purpose, and perfect in their kind. They impel to action, not thought. Had they been profound or subtle in thought, or majestic and sweeping in composition, they would have been adapted for the closet of a Sydney, or for a House of Lords such as it was in the time of Lord Bacon ; but they are plain and sensible whenever the author is in the right, and whether right or wrong, always shrewd and epigrammatic, and fitted for the coffee-house, the exchange, the lobby of the House of Commons, and to be read aloud at a public meeting. When connected, dropping the forms of connection, desultory without abruptness or appearance of disconnection, epigrammatic and antithetical to excess, sententious and personal, regardless of right or wrong, yet well-skilled to act the part of an honest warm-hearted man, and even when he is in the right, saying the truth but never proving it, much less attempting to bottom it,—this is the character of Junius ;—and on this character, and in the mould of these writings must every man cast himself, who would wish in factious times to be the important and long remembered agent of a faction. I believe that I could do all that Junius has done, and surpass him by doing many things which he has not done ; for example,—by an occasional induction of startling facts, in the manner of Tom Paine, and lively illustrations and witty applications of good stories and appropriate anecdotes in the manner of Horne Tooke. I believe I could do it if it were in my nature to aim at this sort of excellence, or to be enamored of the fame, and immediate influence, which would be its consequence and reward. But it is not in my nature. I not only love truth, but I have a passion for the legitimate investigation of truth. The love of truth conjoined with a keen delight in a strict and skilful yet impassioned argumentation, is my master-passion, and to it are subordinated even the love of liberty and all my public feelings—and to it whatever I labor under of vanity, ambition, and all my inward impulses.

Letter I. From this Letter all the faults and excellencies of Junius may be exemplified. The moral and political aphorisms are just and sensible, the irony in which his personal satire is conveyed is fine, yet always intelligible ; but it approaches too nearly to the nature of a sneer ; the sentences are cautiously constructed without the forms of connection ; the *he* and *it* everywhere substituted for the *who* and *which ;* the sentences are short, laboriously balanced, and the antitheses stand the test of analysis much better than Johnson's. These are all excellencies in their kind ; —where is the defect ? In this ;—there is too much of each, and there is a defect of many things, the presence of which would have been not only valuable for their own sakes, but for the relief and variety which they would have given. It is observable too that every Letter adds to the faults of these Letters, while it weakens the effect of their beauties.

L. III. A capital Letter, addressed to a private person, and intended as a sharp reproof for intrusion. Its short sentences, its witty perversions and deductions, its questions and omissions of connectives, all in their proper places are dramatically good.

L. V. For my own part, I willingly leave it to the public to determine whether your vindication of your friend has been as able and judicious as it was certainly well intended; and you, I think, may be satisfied with the warm acknowledgments he already owes you for making him the principal figure in a piece in which, but for your amicable assistamce, he might have passed without particular notice or distinction.

A long sentence and, as usual, inelegant and cumbrous. This Letter is a faultless composition with exception of the one long sentence.

L. VII. These are the gloomy companions of a disturbed *imagination;* the melancholy madness of poetry, without the *inspiration.*

The rhyme is a fault. 'Fancy' had been better; though but for the rhyme, imagination is the fitter word

Ib. Such a question might perhaps discompose the gravity of his muscles, but I believe it would little affect the tranquillity of his conscience.

A false antithesis, a mere verbal balance; there are far, far too many of these. However, with these few exceptions, this Letter is a blameless composition. Junius may be safely studied as a model for letters where he truly writes letters. Those to the Duke of Grafton and others, are small pamphlets in the form of letters.

L. VIII. To do justice to your Grace's humanity, you felt for Mac Quick as you ought to do; and, if you had been contented to assist him indirectly, without a notorious denial of justice, or openly insulting the sense of the nation, you might have satisfied every duty of political friendship, without committing the honor of your sovereign, or hazarding the reputation of his government.

An inelegant cluster of *withouts.* Junius asks questions incomparably well;—but *ne quid nimis.*

L. IX. Perhaps the fair way of considering these Letters would be as a kind of satirical poems; the short, and forever balanced, sentences constitute a true metre; and the connection is that of satiric poetry, a witty logic, an association of thoughts by amusing semblances of cause and effect, the sophistry of which the reader has an interest in not stopping to detect, for it flatters his love of mischief, and makes the sport.

L. XII. One of Junius's arts, and which gives me a high notion of his genius, as a poet and satirist, is this:—he takes for granted the existence of a character that never did and never can exist, and then employs his wit, and surprises and amuses his readers with analyzing its incompatibilities.

L. XIV. Continual sneer, continual irony, all excellent, if it were not for the 'all;'—but a countenance, with a malignant smile in statuary fixure on it, becomes at length an object of aversion, however beautiful the face, and however beautiful the smile. We are relieved, in some measure, from this by frequent just and well-expressed moral aphorisms; but then the preceding and following irony gives them the appearance of proceeding from the head, not from the heart. This objection would be less felt, when the Letters were first published at considerable intervals; but Junius wrote for posterity.

L. XXIII. Sneer and irony continued with such gross violation of good sense, as to be perfectly nonsense. The man who can address another on his most detestable vices in a strain of cold continual irony, is himself a wretch.

L. XXXV. To honor them with a determined predilection and confidence in exclusion of your English subjects, who placed your family, and, in spite of treachery and rebellion, have supported it upon the throne, is a mistake too gross even for the unsuspecting generosity of youth.

The words 'upon the throne,' stand unfortunately for the harmonious effect of the balance of 'placed' and 'supported.'

This address to the king is almost faultless in composition, and has been evidently tormented with the file. But it has fewer beauties than any other long letter of Junius; and it is utterly undramatic. There is nothing in the style, the transitions, or the sentiments, which represents the passions of a man emboldening himself to address his sovereign personally. Like a Presbyterian's prayer, you may substitute almost everywhere the third for the second person without injury. The newspaper, his closet, and his own person were alone present to the author's intention and imagination. This makes the composition vapid. It possesses an Isocratic correctness, when it should have had the force and drama of an oration of Demosthenes. From this, however, the paragraph beginning with the words 'As to the Scotch,' and also the last two paragraphs must be honorably excepted. They are, perhaps, the finest passages in the whole collection.

WONDERFULNESS OF PROSE.

It has just struck my feelings that the Pherecydean origin of prose being granted, prose must have struck men with greater admiration than poetry. In the latter it was the language of passion and emotion: it is what they themselves spoke and heard in moments of exultation, indignation, &c. But to hear an evolving roll, or a succession of leaves, talk continually the language of deliberate reason in a form of continued preconception, of a Z already possessed when A was being uttered—this must have appeared godlike. I feel myself in the same state, when in the perusal of a sober, yet elevated and harmonious succession of sentences and periods, I abstract my mind from the particular passage and sympathize with the wonder of the common people, who say of an eloquent man:—'He talks like a book!'

NOTES ON HERBERT'S TEMPLE AND HARVEY'S SYNAGOGUE.

G. HERBERT is a true poet, but a poet *sui generis*, the merits of whose poems will never be felt without a sympathy with the mind and character of the man. To appreciate this volume, it is not enough that the reader possesses a cultivated judgment, classical taste, or even poetic sensibility, unless he be likewise a *Christian*, and both a zealous and an orthodox, both a devout and a *devotional* Christian. But even this will not quite suffice. He must be an affectionate and dutiful child of the Church, and from habit, conviction, and a constitutional predisposition to ceremoniousness, in piety as in manners, find her forms and ordinances aids of religion, not sources of formality; for religion is the element in which he lives, and the region in which he moves.

The Church, say rather the Churchmen of England, under the two first Stuarts, has been charged with a yearning after the Romish fopperies, and even the papistic usurpations; but we shall decide more correctly, as well as more charitably, if for the Romish and papistic we substitute the patristic leaven. There even was (natural enough from their distinguished learning, and knowledge of ecclesiastical antiquities) an overrating of the Church and of the Fathers, for the first five or even six centuries; these lines on the Egyptian monks, "Holy Macarius and great Anthony" (p. 205) supply a striking instance and illustration of this.

P. 10.

> If thou be single, all thy goods and ground
> Submit to love; but yet not more than all.

Give one estate as one life. None is bound
To work for two, who brought himself to thrall.
God made me one man; love makes me no more,
Till labor come, and make my weakness score.

I do not understand this stanza.

P. 41.

My flesh *began unto my soul* in pain,
Sicknesses clave my bones, &c.

Either a misprint, or a noticeable idiom of the word 'began?' Yes! and a very beautiful idiom it is: the first colloquy or address of the flesh.

P. 46.

What though my body run to dust?
Faith cleaves unto it, counting every grain,
With an exact and most particular trust,
Reserving all for flesh again.

I find few historical facts so difficult of solution as the continuance, in Protestantism, of this anti-scriptural superstition.

P. 54. Second poem on *The Holy Scriptures.*

This verse marks that, and both do make a motion
Unto a third that ten leaves off doth lie.

The spiritual unity of the Bible = the order and connection of organic forms in which the unity of life is shown, though as widely dispersed in the world of sight as the text.

Ib.

Then as dispersed herbs do *watch* a potion,
These three make up some Christian's destiny.

Some misprint.

P. 87.

Sweet Spring, full of sweet days and roses,
A *box* where sweets compacted lie.

Nest.

P. 92. *Man.*

Each thing is full of duty:
Waters united are our navigation:
Distinguished, our habitation;
Below, our drink; above, our meat:
Both are our cleanliness. Hath one such beauty?
Then how are all things neat!

'Distinguished.' I understand this but imperfectly. Did they form an island? and the next lines refer perhaps to the then belief that all fruits grow and are nourished by water. But then how is the ascending sap 'our cleanliness?' Perhaps, therefore, the rains.

P. 140.

> But he doth bid us take his blood for wine.

Nay, the contrary; take wine to be blood, and *the* blood of a man who died 1800 years ago. This is the faith which even the Church of England demands;* for consubstantiation only *adds* a mystery to that of transubstantiation, which it implies.

P. 175. The Flower.

A delicious poem.

Ib.

> How fresh, O Lord, how sweet and clear
> Are thy returns! e'en as the flowers in spring;
> To which, besides their own demean,
> The late past frosts tributes of pleasure bring.
> Grief melts away
> Like snow in May,
> As if there were no such cold thing.

"The late past frosts tributes of pleasure bring."

υ — — — — υ υ — υ —

Epitritus primus + Dactyl + Trochee + a long word — syllable, which, together with the pause intervening between it and the word — trochee, equals υ υ υ – form a pleasing variety in the Pentameter Iambic with rhymes. Ex. gr.

* This is one of my Father's *marginalia*, which I can hardly persuade myself he would have re-written just as it stands. Where does the Church of England affirm that the wine *per se* literally *is* the blood shed 1800 years ago? The language of our Church is that "we receiving these creatures of bread and wine, &c. may be partakers of His most blessed body and blood:" that "to such as rightly receive the same, the cup of blessing is a partaking of the blood of Christ." Does not this language intimate, that the blood of Christ is spiritually produced in the soul through a faithful reception of the appointed symbols, rather than that the wine itself, apart from the soul, has become the blood? In one sense, indeed, it *is* the blood of Christ to the soul: it may be metaphorically called so, if, by means of it, the blood is *really*, though spiritually, partaken. More than this is surely not affirmed in our formularies, nor taught by our great divines in general. I do not write these words by way of *argument*, but because I can not re-print such a note of my Father's, which has excited surprise in some of his studious readers, without a protest.—S. C.

Thĕ lāte pāst frōsts | trībutĕs ŏf | plēāsūre | brīng.

N.B. First, the difference between – ᴗ | — and an amphimacer – ᴗ – | and this not always or necessarily arising out of the latter being one word. It may even consist of three words, yet the effect be the same. It is the pause that makes the difference. Secondly, the expediency, if not necessity, that the first syllable both of the Dactyl and the Trochee should be short by quantity, and only = – by force of accent or position — the Epitrite being true *lengths*.—Whether the last syllable be – or = – the force of the rhymes renders indifferent. Thus, ...

"As if there *were no such cold thing*." Had been no such thing.

P. 181.

Thou who condemnest Jewish hate, &c.
Call home thine eye (that busy wanderer),
That choice may be thy story.

Their choice.

P. 184.

Nay, thou dost make me sit and dine
E'en in my enemies' sight.

Foemen's.

P. 201. *Judgment.*

Almighty Judge, how shall poor wretches brook
Thy dreadful look, &c.

What others mean to do, I know not well;
Yet I here tell,
That some will turn thee to some leaves therein
So void of sin,
That they in merit shall excel.

I should not have expected from Herbert so open an avowal of Romanism in the article of *merit*. In the same spirit is "Holy Macarius, and great Anthony," p. 205.*

* Herbert, however, adds:

But I resolve, when thou shalt call for mine,
That to decline,
And thrust a Testament into thy hand:
Let that be scann'd;
There thou shalt find my faults are thine.

Martin Luther himself might have penned this concluding stanza.

Since I wrote the above, a note in Mr. Pickering's edition of Herbert has been pointed out to me:

P. 237. The *Communion Table.*

And for the matter whereof it is made,
The matter is not much,
Although it be of *tuch,*
Or wood, or metal, what will last, or fade;
So vanity
And superstition avoided be.

Tuch rhyming to *much*, from the German *tuch*, cloth, I never met with before, as an English word. So I find *platt* for *foliage* in Stanley's Hist. of Philosophy, p. 22.

P. 252. *The Synagogue*, by Christopher Harvey. *The Bishop.*

But who can show of old that ever any
Presbyteries without their bishops were:
Though bishops without presbyteries many, &c.

An instance of *proving too much.* If Bishop without Presb. B.=Presb. *i. e.* no Bishop.

P. 253. The *Bishop.*

To rule and to be ruled are distinct,
And several duties, severally belong
To several *persons.*

Functions of times, but not persons, of necessity? Ex. Bishop to Archbishop.

P. 255. *Church Festivals.*

Who loves not you, doth but in vain profess
That he loves God, or heaven, or happiness.

"The Rev. Dr. *Bliss* has kindly furnished the following judicious remark, and which is proved to be correct, as the word is printed 'heare' in the first edition (1633). He says: 'Let me take this opportunity of mentioning what a very learned and able friend pointed out on this note. The fact is, *Coleridge* has been misled by an error of the press.

What others mean to do, I know not well,
Yet I here tell, &c. &c.

should be *hear tell.* The sense is then obvious, and *Herbert* is not made to do that which he was the last man in the world to have done, namely, to avow 'Romanism in the article of merit.'"

This suggestion once occurred to myself, and appears to be right, as it is verified by the first edition: but at the time it seemed to me so obvious, that surely the correction would have been made before if there had not been some reason against it.—S. C.

Equally unthinking and uncharitable ;—I approve of them ;—but yet remember Roman Catholic idolatry, and that it originated in such high-flown metaphors as these.

P. 255. *The Sabbath, or Lord's Day.*

Hail	Vail
Holy	Wholly
King of days, &c.	To thy praise, &c.

Make it sense and lose the rhyme ; or make it rhyme and lose the sense.

P. 258. *The Nativity,* or *Christmas Day.*

Unfold thy face, unmask thy ray,
Shine forth, bright sun, double the day,
Let no malignant misty fume, &c.

The only poem in *The Synagogue* which possesses *poetic* merit ; with a few changes and additions this would be a striking poem.

Substitute the following for the fifth to the eighth line.

To sheath or blunt one happy ray,
That wins new splendor from the day.
This day that gives thee power to rise,
And shine on hearts as well as eyes:
This birth-day of all souls, when first
On eyes of flesh and blood did burst
That primal great lucific light,
That rays to thee, to us gave sight.

P. 267. *Whit-Sunday.*

Nay, startle not to hear that rushing wind,
  Wherewith this place is shaken, &c.

To hear at once so great variety
  Of language from them come, &c.

The spiritual miracle was the descent of the Holy Ghost: the outward the wind and the tongues: and so St. Peter himself explains it. That each individual obtained the power of speaking all languages, is neither contained in, nor fairly deducible from, St. Luke's account.

P. 269. *Trinity-Sunday.*

The Trinity
In Unity,
And Unity
In Trinity,
All reason doth *transcend.*

Most true, but not *contradict.* Reason is to faith, as the eye to the telescope.

EXTRACT FROM A LETTER

OF S. T. COLERIDGE TO W. COLLINS, R. A. PRINTED IN THE LIFE OF COLLINS BY HIS SON. VOL. I.

December, 1818.

To feel the full force of the Christian religion it is perhaps necessary, for many tempers, that they should first be made to feel, experimentally, the hollowness of human friendship, the presumptuous emptiness of human hopes. I find more substantial comfort now in pious George Herbert's Temple, which I used to read to amuse myself with his quaintness, in short, only to laugh at, than in all the poetry since the poems of Milton. If you have not read Herbert I can recommend the book to you confidently. The poem entitled " The Flower" is especially affecting, and to me such a phrase as " *and relish versing*" expresses a sincerity and reality, which I would unwillingly exchange for the more dignified " and once more love the Muse," &c. and so with many other of Herbert's homely phrases.

NOTES ON MATHIAS' EDITION OF GRAY.

ON A DISTANT PROSPECT OF ETON COLLEGE.

Vol. i. p. 9.

Wanders the hoary Thames along
His silver-winding way.—GRAY.

WE want, methinks, a little treatise from some man of flexible good sense, and well versed in the Greek poets, especially Homer, the choral, and other lyrics, containing first a history of compound epithets, and then the laws and licenses. I am not so much disposed as I used to be to quarrel with such an epithet as " silver-winding ;" ungrammatical as the hyphen is, it is not wholly *illogical*, for the phrase conveys more than silvery and winding. It gives, namely, the unity of the impression, the co-inherence of the brightness, the motion, and the line of motion.

P. 10.

> Say, Father Thames, for thou hast seen
>   Full many a sprightly race
> Disporting on thy margent green,
>   The paths of pleasure trace;
> Who foremost now delight to cleave,
> With pl[illegible]n, thy glassy wave?
>   The captive linnet which enthral?
> What idle progeny succeed
> To chase the rolling circle's speed,
>   Or urge the flying ball?—GRAY.

This is the only stanza that appears to me very objectionable in point of diction. This, I must confess, is not only *falsetto* throughout, but is at once harsh and feeble, and very far the worst ten lines in all the works of Mr. Gray, English or Latin, prose or verse.

P. 12.

> And envy wan, and faded care,[1]
> Grim-visaged comfortless despair,[2]
>   And sorrow's piercing dart.[3]

[1] Bad in the first, [2] in the second, [3] in the last degree.

P. 18.

> The proud are taught to *taste of pain.*—GRAY.

There is a want of dignity—a sort of irony in this phrase to my feeling that would be more proper in dramatic than in lyric composition.

On Gray's *Platonica*, vol. i. p. 299–547.

Whatever might be expected from a scholar, a gentleman, a man of exquisite taste, as the quintessence of sane and sound good sense, Mr. Gray appears to me to have performed. The poet Plato, the orator, Plato, Plato the exquisite dramatist of conversation, the seer and the painter of character, Plato the high-bred, highly-educated, aristocratic republican, the man and the gentleman of quality stands full before us from behind the curtain as Gray has drawn it back. Even so does Socrates, the social wise old man, the *practical* moralist. But Plato the philosopher, but the divine Plato, was not to be comprehended within the field of vision, or be commanded by the fixed immovable telescope of

Mr. Locke's human understanding. The whole sweep of the best philosophic reflections of French or English fabric in the age of our scholarly bard, was not commensurate with the mighty orb. The little, according to *my* convictions at least, the very little of proper Platonism contained in the *written* books of Plato, who himself, in an epistle, the authenticity of which there is no tenable ground for doubting, as I was rejoiced to find Mr. Gray acknowledge, has declared all he had written to be substantially Socratic, and not a fair exponent of his own tenets,* even this little, Mr. Gray has either misconceived or honestly confessed that, as he was not one of the initiated, it was utterly beyond his comprehension. Finally, to repeat the explanation with which I closed the last page of these notes and extracts,

> Volsimi ——— e vidi Plato
> (ma non quel Plato)
> Che'n quella schiera andò più presso al segno,
> Al qual' aggiunge, a chì dal Cielo è dato.†
>
> S. T. Coleridge, 1819.

P. 385. Hippias Major.

We learn from this dialogue in how poor a condition the art of reasoning on moral and abstracted subjects was before the time of Socrates: for it is impossible that Plato should introduce a sophist of the first reputation for eloquence and knowledge in several kinds, talking in a manner below the absurdity and weakness of a child; unless he had really drawn after the life. No less than twenty-four pages are here spent in vain, only to force it into the head of Hippias that there is such a thing as a general idea; and that, before we can dispute on any subject, we should give a definition of it.

Is not this, its improbability out of the question, contradicted by the Protagoras of Plato's own drawing? Are there no authors, no physicians in London at the present moment, of "the first reputation," *i. e.* whom a certain class cry up: for in no other sense is the phrase *historically* applicable to Hippias, whom a Sydenham redivivus or a new Stahl might not exhibit as pompous ignoramuses? no *one* Hippias amongst them? But we need not flee to conjectures. The ratiocination assigned by Aristotle and Plato himself to Gorgias and then to the Eleatic school, are posi-

* See Plato's second epistle φραστέον δή σοι δι' αἰνιγμῶν κ. τ. λ. and towards the end τὰ δε νῦν λεγόμενα Σωκρᾶτους ἐστὶ, κ. τ. λ. See also the 7th Epistle, p. 341.

† Petrarch's *Trionfo della Fama*, cap. terz. v. 4–6.

tive proofs that Mr. Gray has mistaken the satire of an individual for a characteristic of an age or class.

May I dare whisper to the reeds without proclaiming that I am in the state of Midas,—may I dare to hint that Mr. Gray himself had not, and through the spectacles of Mr. Locke and his followers, could not have seen the difficulties which Hippias found in a *general* idea, *secundum Platonem?*—S. T. C.

P. 386. Notes 289. Passages of Heraclitus.

> *Πιθηκῶν ὁ κάλλιστος αἰσχρὸς ἄλλῳ γένει συμβαλεῖν.—Ἀνθρώπων ὁ σοφώτατος πρὸς Θεὸν πιθηκὸς φανεῖται.*

This latter passage is undoubtedly the original of that famous thought in Pope's Essay on Man, b. ii. :—

> "And showed a Newton as we show an ape."

I remember to have met nearly the same words in one of our elder Poets.

Pp. 390–391.

> That a sophist was a kind of merchant, or rather a retailer of food for the soul, and, like other shopkeepers, would exert his eloquence to recommend his own goods. The misfortune was, we could not carry them off, like corporeal viands, set them by a while, and consider them at leisure, whether they were wholesome or not, before we tasted them: that in this case we have no vessel but the soul to receive them in, which will necessarily retain a tincture, and perhaps, much to its prejudice, of all which is instilled into it.

Query, if Socrates, himself a scholar of the sophists, is accurate, did not the change of *ὁ σοφός* into *ὁ Σοφιστής*, in the single case of Solon, refer to the wisdom-causing influences of his legislation? Mem. :—to examine whether *Φροντιστής* was, or was not, more generally used at first *in malum sensum*, or rather the proper force originally of the termination *ιστής*, *αστής*—whether (as it is evidently verbal) it imply a reflex or a transitive act.

P. 399. *Ὅτι Ἀμαθία.*

> This is the true key and great moral of the dialogue, that knowledge alone is the source of virtue, and ignorance the source of vice; it was Plato's own principle, see Plat. Epist. vii. p. 336. *Ἀμαθία, ἐξ ἧς πάντα κακὰ πᾶσιν ἐῤῥίζωται καὶ βλαστάνει καὶ εἰς ὕστερον ἀποτελεῖ καρπὸν τοῖς γεννήσασι πικρότατον.* See also *Sophist.* pp. 228 and 229, and *Euthydemus* from pp. 278 to 281, and *De Legib.* L. iii. p. 688, and probably it was also

the principle of Socrates: the consequence of it is, that virtue may be taught, and may be acquired: and that philosophy alone can point us out the way to it.

More than our word, Ignorance, is contained in the *'Αμαθία* of Plato. I, however, freely acknowledge, that this was the point of view, from which Socrates did *for the most part* contemplate moral good and evil. Now and then he seems to have taken a higher station, but soon quitted it for the lower, more generally intelligible. Hence the vacillation of Socrates himself; hence, too, the immediate opposition of his disciples, Antisthenes and Aristippus. But that this was Plato's own principle I exceedingly doubt. That it was not the principle of Platonism, as taught by the first Academy under Speusippus, I do *not* doubt at all. See the xivth Essay, pp. 96–102 of *The Friend.* In the sense in which *ἀμαθίας πάντα κακὰ ἐῤῥίζωται, κ. τ. λ.* is maintained in that Essay, so and no otherwise can it be truly asserted, and so and no otherwise did *ὥς εμοί γε δολεῖ*, Plato teach it.

BARRY CORNWALL.*

Barry Cornwall is a poet, *me saltem judice:* and in that sense of the term, in which I apply it to C. Lamb and W. Wordsworth. There are poems of great merit, the authors of which I should yet not feel impelled so to designate.

The faults of these poems are no less things of hope, than the beauties; both are just what they ought to be,—that is, new.

If B. C. be faithful to his genius, it in due time will warn him, that as poetry is the identity of all other knowledges, so a poet can not be a great poet, but as being likewise inclusively an historian and naturalist, in the light, as well as the life, of philosophy: all other men's worlds are his chaos.

Hints *obiter* are:—not to permit delicacy and exquisiteness to seduce into effeminacy. Not to permit beauties by repetition to become mannerisms. To be jealous of fragmentary composition,—as epicurism of genius, and apple-pie made all of quinces. *Item,* that dramatic poetry must be poetry hid in thought and passion,—not thought or passion disguised in the dress of poetry.

* Written in Mr. Lamb's copy of the 'Dramatic Scenes.'—*Ed.*

Lastly, to be economic and withholding in similes, figures, &c. They will all find their place, sooner or later, each as the luminary of a sphere of its own. There can be no galaxy in poetry, because it is language,—*ergo* processive,—*ergo* every the smallest star must be seen singly.

There are not five metrists in the kingdom, whose works are known by me, to whom I could have held myself allowed to have spoken so plainly. But B. C. is a man of genius, and it depends on himself—(competence protecting him from gnawing or distracting cares)—to become a rightful poet,—that is, a great man.

Oh! for such a man worldly prudence is transfigured into the highest spiritual duty! How generous is self-interest in him, whose true self is all that is good and hopeful in all ages, as far as the language of Spenser, Shakspeare, and Milton shall become the mother-tongue!

A map of the road to Paradise, drawn in purgatory, on the confines of Hell, by S. T. C. July 30, 1819.

ON THE MODE OF STUDYING KANT.

EXTRACT FROM A LETTER OF MR. COLERIDGE TO J. GOODEN, ESQ.*

ACCEPT my thanks for the rules of the harmony. I perceive that the members are chiefly merchants; but yet it were to be wished, that such an enlargement of the society could be brought about as, retaining all its present purposes, might add to them the ground-work of a library of northern literature, and by bringing together the many gentlemen who are attached to it to be the means of eventually making both countries better acquainted with the valuable part of each other; especially, the English with the German, for our most sensible men look at the German Muses through a film of prejudice and utter misconception.

With regard to philosophy, there are half a dozen things, good and bad, that in this country are so nicknamed, but in the only accurate sense of the term, there neither are, have been, or ever will be but two essentially different schools of philosophy, the Platonic, and the Aristotelian. To the latter but with a some-

* This letter and the following notes on Jean Paul were communicated by Mr. H. C. Robinson.—S. C.

what nearer approach to the Platonic, Emanuel Kant belonged; to the former Bacon and Leibnitz, and, in his riper and better years, Berkeley. And to this I profess myself an adherent—*nihil novum, vel inauditum audemus;* though, as every man has a face of his own, without being more or less than a man, so is every true philosopher an original, without ceasing to be an inmate of Academus or of the Lyceum. But as to caution, I will just tell you how I proceeded myself twenty years and more ago, when I first felt a curiosity about Kant, and was fully aware that to master his meaning, as a system, would be a work of great labor and long time. First, I asked myself, have I the labor and the time in my power? Secondly, if so, and if it would be of adequate importance to me if true, by what means can I arrive at a rational presumption for or against? I inquired after all the more popular writings of Kant—read them with delight. I then read the Prefaces of several of his systematic works, as the *Prolegomena*, &c. Here too every part, I understood, and that was nearly the whole, was replete with sound and plain, though bold and to me novel truths; and I followed Socrates' adage respecting Heraclitus: all I understand is excellent, and I am bound to presume that the rest is at least worth the trouble of trying whether it be not equally so. In other words, until I understand a writer's ignorance, I presume myself ignorant of his understanding. Permit me to refer you to a chapter on this subject in my Literary Life.*

Yet I by no means recommend to you an extension of your philosophic researches beyond Kant. In him is contained all that can be *learned*, and as to the results, you have a firm faith in God, the responsible Will of Man and Immortality; and Kant will demonstrate to you, that this faith is acquiesced in, indeed, nay, confirmed by the Reason and Understanding, but grounded on Postulates authorized and substantiated solely by the *Moral* Being. They are likewise *mine:* and whether the Ideas are regulative only, as Aristotle and Kant teach, or constitutive and actual, as Pythagoras and Plato, is of living interest to the philosopher by profession alone. Both systems are equally true, if only the former abstain from denying *universally* what is denied individually. He, for whom Ideas are constitutive, will in effect be a Platonist; and in those for whom they are regulative only,

* *Biographia Literaria*, chap. xii. p. 322.—S. C.

Platonism is but a hollow affectation. Dryden *could* not have been a Platonist: Shakspeare, Milton, Dante, Michel Angelo and Rafael could not have been other than Platonists. Lord Bacon, who never read Plato's works, taught pure Platonism in his *great* work, the *Novum Organum*, and abuses his divine predecessor for fantastic nonsense, which he had been the first to explode. Accept my best respects, &c.

S. T. COLERIDGE.

14 Jan. 1814. Highgate.

NOTES ON THE PALINGENESIEN OF JEAN PAUL.

WRITTEN IN THE BLANK LEAF AT THE BEGINNING.

——S ist zu merken, dass die Sprache in diesem Buch nicht sey wie, in gewöhnlich Bette, darin der Gedankenstrom ordentlich and ehrbar hinströmt, sondern wie ein Verwüstung in Damm and Deichen.*

Preface p. xxxi.

Two Revolutions, the Gallican, which sacrifices the individuals to the Idea or to the State, and in time of need, even the latter themselves;—and the Kantian-Moralist (Kantisch-Moralische), which abandons the affection of human Love altogether, because it can so little be described as merit; these draw and station us forlorn human creatures ever further and more lonesomely one from another, each on a frosty uninhabited island: nay, the Gallican, which excites and arms feelings against feelings, does it less than the Critical, which teaches us to disarm and to dispense with them altogether; and which neither allows Love to pass for the spring of virtue, nor virtue for the source of Love.†—*Transl.*

But surely Kant's aim was not to give a full *Sittenlehre*, or

* It is observable that the language in this book is not as in an ordinary channel, wherein the stream of thought flows on in a seemly and regular manner, but like a violent flood rushing against dyke and mole.

† Zwei Revoluzionen, diè gallische, welche der Idee oder dem Staate diè Individuen, and im Nothsal dièsen selber opfert, und die kantisch-moralische, welche den Affekt der Menschenliebe liegen lässet, weil er so wenig wie Verdienste geboten werden kan, diese ziehen und stellen uns verlassene Menschen immer weiter und einsamer aus cinander, jeden nur auf ein frostiges unbewohntes Eiland; ja die gallische, die nur Gefühle gegen Gefühle bewafnet und aufhezt, thut es weniger als die kritische, die sie entwafnen und entbehren lehrt, und die weder die Lièbe als Quelle der Tugend noch dièse als Quelle von jener gelten lassen kan.

system of practical material morality, but the *à priori* form—*Ethice formalis:* which was then a most necessary work, and the only mode of quelling at once both Necessitarians and Merit-mongers, and the idol common to both, Eudæmonism. If his followers have stood still in lazy adoration, instead of following up the road thus opened out to them, it is their fault, not Kant's.

S. T. C.

FROM BLACKWOOD'S EDINBURGH MAGAZINE, Oct. 1821.

LETTER FROM MR. COLERIDGE.

Dear Sir,—In the third letter (in the little parcel) which I have headed with your name, you will find my reasons for wishing these five letters, and a sixth, which will follow in my next, on the plan and code of a Magazine, which should unite the *utile* and *dulce*, to appear in the first instance. My next will consist of very different articles, apparently; namely, the First Book of my True History from Fairy Land, or the World Without, and the World Within. 2. The commencement of the Annals and Philosophy of Superstition; for the completion of which I am waiting only for a very curious folio, in Mr. **********'s possession. 3. The life of Holty, a German poet, of true genius, who died in early manhood; with specimens of his poems, translated, or freely imitated in English verse. It would have been more in the mode to have addressed myself to the Editor, but I could not give up this one opportunity of assuring you that I am, my dear Sir,

With every friendly wish, your obliged,

S. T. Coleridge.

Mr. Blackwood.

SELECTION FROM MR. COLERIDGE'S LITERARY CORRESPONDENCE WITH FRIENDS, AND MEN OF LETTERS.

No. I.

LETTER I. From a Professional Friend.

My Dear and Honored Sir,—I was much struck with your Excerpta from Porta, Eckartshausen, and others, as to the effect of the ceremonial drinks and unguents, on the (female) practitioners of the black arts, whose witchcraft you believe to have consisted in the unhappy craft of bewitching themselves. I. at least know of no reason, why to these *toxications* (especially when taken through the skin, and to the cataleptic state induced by them), we should not attribute the poor wretches' own belief of their guilt. I can conceive, indeed, of no other mode of accounting—I do not say for their suspicious last dying avowals at the stake; but—for their private and voluntary confessions on their death-beds, which made a convert of your old favorite, Sir T. Brown. Perhaps my professional pursuits, and medical studies, may have predisposed me to be interested; but my mind has been in an eddy ever since I left you. The connections of the subject with classical and with druidical superstitions, pointed out by you—the *Circeia pocula*—the herbal spells of the Haxæ, or Druidesses—the somniloquism of the prophetesses, under the coercion of the Scandinavian enchanters—the dependence of the Greek oracles on mineral waters, and stupefying vapors from the earth, as stated by Plutarch, and more than once alluded to by Euripides—the vast spread of the same, or similar usages, from Greenland even to the southernmost point of America;—you sent me home with enough to think of!—But, more than all, I was struck and interested with your concluding remark, that these, and most other superstitions, were, in your belief, but the CADAVER ET PUTRIMENTA OF A DEFUNCT NATURAL PHILOSOPHY.—Why not rather the imperfect rudiments? I asked. You promised me your reasons, and a fuller explanation. But let me speak out my whole wish; and call on you to redeem the pledges you gave, so long back as October, 1809, that you would devote a series of papers to the subject of Dreams, Visions, Presentations, Ghosts,

Witchcraft, Cures by sympathy, in which you would select and explain the most interesting and best attested facts that have come to your knowledge from books or personal testimony.

You can scarcely conceive how deep an interest I attach to this request; nor how many, beside myself, in the circle of my own acquaintance, have the same feeling. Indeed, my dear Sir! when I reflect, that there is scarcely a chapter of history in which superstition of some kind or other does not form or supply a portion of its contents, I look forward, with unquiet anticipation, to the power of explaining the more frequent and best attested narrations, at least without the necessity of having recourse to the supposition of downright tricks and lying, on one side, or to the Devil and his imps on the other. * * * *

Your obliged Pupil, and affectionate Friend,

J. L——.

P. S.—Dr. L. of the Museum, is quite of your opinion, that little or nothing of importance to the philosophic naturalist can result from Comparative Anatomy on Cuvier's plan; and that its best trophies will be but lifeless skeletons, till it is studied in combination with a Comparative Physiology. But you ought yourself to vindicate the priority of your claim. But I fear, dear C., that *Sic Vos, non Vobis* was made for your motto throughout life.

LETTER II. In answer to the above.

Well, my dear pupil and fellow-student! I am willing to make the attempt. If the majority of my readers had but the same personal knowledge of me as you have, I should sit down to the work with good cheer. But this is out of the question. Let me, however, suppose you for the moment, as an *average* reader—address you as such, and attribute to you feelings and language in character.—Do not mistake me, my dear L——. Not even for a moment, nor under the pretext of *mons a non movendo*, would I contemplate in connection with your name "id genus lectorum, qui meliores obtrectare malint quam imitari: et quorum *similitudinem* desperent, eorundem affectent *simultatem*—scilicet uti qui suo nomine obscuri sunt, meo innotescant."*

* The passage, which can not fail to remind you of H—— and his set, is from Apuleius's Lib. Floridorum—the two books of which, by the bye,

The readers I have in view, are of that class who with a sincere, though not very strong desire, of acquiring knowledge, have taken it for granted, that all knowledge of any value respecting the mind is either to be found in three or four books, the eldest not a hundred years old, or may be conveniently taught without any other terms or previous explanations than these works have already rendered familiar among men of education.

Well, friendly reader! as the problem of things little less (it seems to you) than impossible, yet strongly and numerously attested by evidence which it seems impossible to discredit, has interested you, I am willing to attempt the solution. But then it must be under certain *conditions.* I must be able to *hope*, I must have sufficient grounds for hoping, that I shall be understood, or rather that I shall be allowed to make myself understood. And as I am gifted with no magnetic power of throwing my reader into the state of *clear-seeing* (clairvoyance) or luminous vision; as I have not the secret of enabling him to read with the pit of his stomach, or with his finger-ends, nor of calling into act "the cuticular faculty," dormant at the tip of his nose; but must rely on WORDS—I can not form the hope rationally, unless the reader will have patience enough to master the sense in which I use them.

But why employ words that need explanation? And might I not ask in *my* turn, would you, gentle reader! put the same question to Sir Edward Smith, or any other member of the Linnæan Society, to whom you had applied for instruction in Botany? And yet he would require of you that you should attend to a score of technical terms, and make yourself master of the sense of each, in order to your understanding the distinctive characters of a grass, a mushroom, and a lichen! Now the psychologist, or speculative philosopher, will be content with you, if you will impose on yourself the trouble of understanding and remembering one of the number, in order to understand your own nature. But I will meet your question direct. You ask me, why I *use words that need explanation?* Because (I reply) on this subject there are no others! Because the darkness and the main difficulties that attend it, are owing to the vagueness and ambiguity of the

seem to have been transcribed from his common-place-book of *Good Things*, happy phrases, &c., that he had not had an opportunity of bringing *in* in his set writings.

words in common use; and which preclude all explanation for him who has resolved that none is required. Because there is already a falsity in the very phrases, "words in *common* use;" "the language of *common* sense." Words of most *frequent* use they may be, *common* they are not; but the language of the market, and as such, expressing *degrees* only, and therefore incompetent to the purpose wherever it becomes necessary to designate the *kind* independent of all degree. The philosopher may, and often does, employ the same words as in the market; but does this supersede the necessity of a previous explanation? As I referred you before to the botanist, so now to the chemist. Light, heat, charcoal, are every man's words. But *fixed* or *invisible* light? The *frozen* heat? Charcoal in its simplest form as *diamond*, or as black-lead? Will a stranger to chemistry be worse off, would the chemist's language be less likely to be understood by his using different words for distinct meanings, as carbon, caloric, and the like?

But the case is stronger. The chemist is compelled to make words, in order to prevent or remove some error connected with the common word; and this too an error, the continuance of which was incompatible with the first principles and elementary truths of the science he is to teach. You must submit to regard yourself ignorant even of the words, air and water; and will find, that they are not chemically intelligible without the terms, oxygen, nitrogen, hydrogen, or others equivalent. Now it is even so with the knowledge, which you would have *me* to communicate. There are certain prejudices of the common, *i. e.* of the *average* sense of men, the exposure of which is the first step, the indispensable preliminary, of all rational psychology: and these can not be exposed but by selecting and adhering to some one word, in which we may be able to trace the growth and modifications of the opinion or belief conveyed in this, or similar words, not by any revolution or positive *change* of the original sense, but by the transfer of this sense and the difference in the application.

Where there is but one word for two or more diverse or disparate meanings in a language (or though there should be several, yet if perfect synonymes, they count but for one word), the language is so far defective. And this is a defect of frequent occurrence in all languages, prior to the cultivation of science, logic, and philology, especially of the two latter: and among a free, lively, and ingenious people, such as the Greeks were, sophistry and the influence of sophists are the inevitable result. To check this evil by striking at its root in the ambiguity of words, Plato wrote the greater part of his published works, which do not so much contain his own system of philosophy, as the negative conditions of reasoning aright on *any* system. And yet more obviously is it the case with the Metaphysics, Analytics, &c. of Aristotle, which have been well described by Lambert as a dictionary of general terms, the process throughout being, first, to discover and establish definite meanings, and then to appropriate to each a several word. The sciences will take care, each of its own nomenclature; but the interests of the language at large fall under the special guardianship of logic and rational psychology. Where these have fallen into neglect or disrepute, from exclusive pursuit of wealth, excess of the commercial spirit, or whatever other cause disposes men in general to attach an exclusive value to immediate and palpable utility, the dictionary may swell, but the language will decline. Few are the books published within the last fifty years, that would not supply their quota of proofs, that so it is with our own mother English. The bricks and stones are in abundance, but the cement none or naught. That which is indeed the *common* language exists everywhere as the menstruum, and nowhere as the whole—See *Biographia Literaria**—while the language complimented with this name, is, as I have already said, in fact the language of the market. Every science, every trade, has its technical nomenclature; every folly has its *fancy-words;* every vice its own slang—and is the science of humanity to be the one exception? Is philosophy to work without tools? to have no straw wherewith to make the bricks for her mansion-house, but what she may pick up on the high-road, or steal, with all its impurities and sophistications, from the litter of the cattle-market?

For the present, however, my demands on your patience are very limited.—If as the price of much *entertainment* to follow, and I trust of something besides of less *transitory* interest, you will fairly attend to the history of *two* scholastic terms, OBJECT and SUBJECT, with their derivatives; you shall have my promise that I will not on any future occasion ask you to be attentive,

* P. 409.—S. C.

without trying not to be myself dull. That it may cost you no more trouble than necessary, I have brought it under the eye in numbered paragraphs, with *scholia* or commentary to such as seemed to require it.

Yours most affectionately,

S. T. COLERIDGE.

ON THE PHILOSOPHIC IMPORT OF THE WORDS, OBJECT AND SUBJECT.

§ 1.

Existence is a simple intuition, underived and indecomponible. It is no *idea*, no particular form, much less any determination or modification of the possible: it is nothing that can be educed from the logical conception of a thing, as its predicate: it is no *property* of a thing, but its reality itself; or, as the Latin would more conveniently express it—Nulla *rei* proprietas est, sed ipsa ejus *realitas*.

SCHOLIUM.

Herein lies the sophism in Des Cartes' celebrated demonstration of the existence of the Supreme Being from the idea. In the idea of God are contained *all* attributes that belong to the perfection of a being: but existence is such: therefore, God's existence is contained in the idea of God. To this it is a sufficient answer, that existence is not an attribute. It might be shown too, from the barrenness of the demonstration, by identifying the deduction with the premise, *i. e.* for reducing the minor or term *included* to a mere repetition of the major or term *including*. For in fact the syllogism ought to stand thus: the *idea* of God comprises the *idea* of all attributes that belong to perfection; but the *idea* of existence is such: therefore the idea of his existence is included in the idea of God.—Now, existence is no idea, but a *fact:* or, though we had an *idea* of existence, still the proof of a correspondence to a *reality* would be wanting, *i. e.* the very point would be wanting which it was the purpose of the demonstration to supply. Still the *idea* of the fact is not the fact itself. Besides, the term, idea, is here improperly substituted for the mere *supposition* of a *logical* subject, necessarily presumed in order to the conceivableness (*cogitabilitas*) of *any* qualities, properties, or attributes. But this is a mere *ens logicum* (vel etiam *grammaticum*), the result of the thinker's own unity of consciousness, and no less contained in the conception of a plant or of a chimera, than in the idea of the Supreme Being. If Des Cartes could have proved, that his idea of a Supreme Being is universal and necessary, and that the conviction of a reality perfectly coincident with the idea is equally universal and inevitable; and that these were in truth but one and the same act or intuition, unique, and without analogy, though, from the inadequateness of our minds, from the mechanism of thought, and the structure of language, we are compelled to express it dividually, as consisting of two correlative terms—this would have been something. But then it must be entitled a *statement*, not a demonstration—the necessity of which it would supersede. And something like this may perhaps be found true, where the reasoning powers are developed and duly exerted; but would, I fear, do little towards settling the dispute between the religious Theist, and the speculative Atheist or Pantheist, whether this be *all*, or whether it is even *what* we mean, and are bound to mean, by the word God. The old controversy would be started, what *are* the possible perfections of an Infinite Being—in other words, what the legitimate sense is of the term, infinite, as applied to Deity, and what is, or is not compatible with that sense.

§ 2.

I think, and while thinking, I am conscious of certain workings or movements, as acts or activities of my being, and feel myself as the power in which they originate. I feel myself *working;* and the sense or feeling of this *activity* constitutes the sense and feeling of EXISTENCE, *i. e.* of my actual being.

SCHOLIUM.

Movements, motions, taken metaphorically, without relation to space or place. *Κινήσεις μὴ κατὰ τόπον; αἱ ὥσπερ κινήσεις*, of Aristotle.

§ 3.

In these workings, however, I distinguish a difference. In some I feel myself as the cause and proper agent, and the movements themselves as the work of my own power. In others, I feel these movements as my own activity ; but not as my own acts. The first we call the active or positive state of our existence ; the second, the passive or negative state. The active power, nevertheless, is felt in both equally. But in the first I feel it as the *cause* acting, in the second, as the *condition*, without which I could not be acted on.

SCHOLIUM.

It is a truth of highest importance, that *agere et pati* are not different kinds, but the same kind in different relations. And this not only in consequence of an immediate re-action, but the act of *receiving* is no less truly an *act*, than the act of influencing. Thus, the lungs act in being stimulated by the air, as truly as in the act of breathing, to which they were stimulated. The Greek verbal termination, ω, happily illustrates this. Ποιῶ, πράττω, πάσχω, in philosophical grammar, are all three verbs active ; but the first is the active-*transitive*, in which the agency passes forth out of the agent into another. Τί ποιεῖς ; what are you doing? The second is the active-*intransitive*. Τί πράττεις ; *how* do you do ? or how *are* you ? The third is the active-*passive*, or more appropriately the active-*patient*, the verb *recipient* or *receptive*, τί πάσχεις ; what ails you ? Or, to take another idiom of our language, that most livelily expresses the co-presence of an agent, an agency distinct and alien from our own, What is the *matter with* you ? It would carry us too far to explain the nature of verbs *passive*, as so called in technical grammar. Suffice, that this class *originated* in the same causes, as led men to make the division of substances into living and dead—a division *psychologically* necessary, but of doubtful philosophical validity.

§ 4.

With the workings and movements, which I refer to myself and my own agency, there alternate—say rather, I find myself alternately conscious of, forms (= Impressions, images, or better or less figurative and hypothetical, *presences*, presentations), and of states or modes, which not feeling as the work or effect of my own power I refer to a power *other* than me, *i. e.* (in the language derived from my sense of sight) without me. And this is the feeling, I have, of the existence of outward things.

SCHOLIUM.

In this superinduction of the sense of *outness* on the feeling of the *actual* arises our notion of the *real* and reality. But as I can not but reflect, that as the other is to me, so I must be to the other, the terms real and actual, soon become confounded and interchangeable, or only discriminated in the gold scales of metaphysics.

§ 5.

Since both then, the feeling of my own existence and the feeling of the existence of things without, are but this sense of an acting and working—it is clear that to exist is the same as to act or work (*Quantum operor, tantum sum*); that whatever exists, works (= is *in action; actually* is; is *in deed*), that not to work, as agent or patient, is not to exist; and lastly, that patience (= *vis patiendi*) and the reaction that is its co-instantaneous consequent, is the same activity in opposite and alternating relations.

§ 6.

That which is *inferred* in those acts and workings, the feeling of which is one with the feeling of our own existence, or inferred *from* those which we refer to an agency distinct from our own, but in *both* instances is *inferred*, is the SUBJECT, *i. e.* that which does not appear, but *lies under* (quod *jacet subter*) the appearance.

§ 7.

But in the first instance, that namely which is inferred *in* its effects, and of course therefore *self*-inferred, the subject is a MIND, *i. e.* that which *knows* itself, and may be *inferred* by others; but which can not appear.

§ 8.

That, in or from which the subject is inferred, is the OBJECT, id quod *jacet ob* oculos, that which lies before us, that which lies straight opposite.

SCHOLIUM.

The terms used in psychology, logic, &c. even those of most frequent occurrence in common life, are, for the most part, of Latin derivation; and not only so, but the original words, such as quantity, quality, subject, object, &c. &c. were formed in the schools of philosophy for scholastic use, and in correspondence to Greek technical terms of the same meaning. Etymology, therefore, is little else than indispensable to an insight into the true force, and, as it were, freshness of the words in question, especially of those that have passed from the schools into the market-place, from the medals and tokens (σύμβολα) of the philosophers' guild or company into the current coin of the land. But the difference between a man, who understands them according to their first use, and seeks to restore the original impress and superscription, and the man who gives and takes them *in small change*, unweighed, and tried only by the *sound*, may be illustrated by imagining the different points of view in which the same *cowry* would appear to a scientific conchologist, and to a chaffering negro. This use of etymology may be exemplified in the present case. The immediate *object* of the mind is always and exclusively the *workings* or *makings* above stated and distinguished into two kinds, § 2, 3, and 4. Where the object consists of the first kind, in which the subject infers its own existence, and which it refers to its own agency, and identifies with itself (feels and contemplates as one with itself, and as itself), and yet without confounding the inherent distinction between subject and object, the subject witnesses to itself that it is a *mind*, *i. e.* a subject-object, or subject that becomes an object to itself.

But where the workings or makings of the second sort are the object, from objects of this sort we always infer the existence of a subject, as in the former case. But we infer it *from* them, rather than *in* them; or to express the point yet more clearly, we infer two subjects. *In* the object, we infer our own existence and *subjectivity; from* them the existence of a subject, not our own, and to this we refer the object, as to its proper cause and agent. Again, we always infer a correspondent *subject;* but not always a *mind*. Whether we consider this other subject as another mind, is determined by the more or less analogy of the objects or makings of the second class to those of the first, and not seldom depends on the varying degrees of our attention and previous knowledge.

Add to these differences the modifying influence of the senses, the sense of sight more particularly, in consequence of which this subject *other than* we, is presented as a subject *out of* us. With the sensuous vividness connected with, and which in part *consti-*

tutes, this outness or outwardness, contrast the exceeding obscurity and dimness in the conception of a subject, not a mind ; and reflect, too, that, to objects of the *first* kind, we can not attribute actual or separative outwardness ; while, in cases of the *second* kind, we are, after a shorter or longer time, compelled by the law of association to transfer this outness from the *inferred* subject to the *present* object. Lastly, reflect that, in the former instance, the object is identified with the subject, both positively by the act of the subject, and negatively by insusceptibility of outness in the object ; and that in the latter the very contrary takes place ; namely, instead of the object being identified with the subject, the subject is taken up and confounded in the object. In the ordinary and unreflecting states, therefore, of men's minds, it could not be otherwise, but that, in the one instance, the object must be lost, and indistinguishable in the subject ; and that, in the other, the subject is lost and forgotten in the object, to which a necessary illusion had already transferred that outness, which, in its origin, and in right of reason, belongs exclusively to the subject, *i. e.* the agent *ab extra* inferred from the object. For *outness* is but the feeling of otherness (alterity), rendered intuitive, or alterity visually represented. Hence, and also because we find this outness and the objects, to which, though they are, in fact, workings in our own being, we transfer it, independent of our will, and apparently common to other minds, we learn to connect therewith the feeling and sense of *reality ;* and the objective becomes synonymous first with *external*, then with *real*, and at length it was employed to express universal and permanent validity, free from the accidents and particular constitution of *individual* intellects ; nay, when taken in its highest and absolute sense, as free from the inherent limits, partial perspective, and refracting *media* of the human mind *in specie* (*idola tribûs* of Lord Bacon), as distinguished from mind *in toto genere*. In direct antithesis to these several senses of the term, objective, the subjective has been used as synonymous with, first, inward ; second, unreal ; and third, that the cause and seat of which are to be referred to the special or individual peculiarity of the percipients, mind, organs, or relative position. Of course, the meaning of the word in any one sentence can not be *definitely* ascertained but by aid of the context, and will vary with the immediate purposes, and previous views and persuasions of the writer. Thus, the egoist, or ultra-idealist, affirms all objects to be subjective; the disciple of Malbranche, or of Berkeley, that the objective subsists wholly and solely in the universal subject—God. A lady, otherwise of sound mind, was so affected by the reported death of her absent husband, that every night at the same hour she saw a figure at the foot of her bed, which she identified with him, and minutely described to the bystanders, during the continuance of the vision. The husband returned, and previous to the meeting, was advised to appear for the first time at the foot of the bed, at the precise instant that the spirit used to appear, and in the dress described, in the hope that the original might scare away the counterfeit; or, to speak more seriously, in the expectation that the impression on her senses from without would meet half-way, as it were, and repel, or take the place of the image from the brain. He followed the advice; but the moment he took his position, the lady shrieked out, "My God! there are *two!* and"—the story is an old one, and you may end it, happily or tragically, Tate's King Lear or Shakspeare's, according to your taste. I have brought it as a good instance of the force of the two words. You and I would hold the one for a *subjective* phenomenon, the other only for *objective*, and perhaps illustrate the fact, as I have already done elsewhere, by the case of two appearances seen in juxtaposition, the one by transmitted, and the other by reflected light. A believer, according to the old style, whose almanac of faith has the one trifling fault of being for the year of our Lord one thousand *four*, instead of one thousand *eight* hundred and twenty, would stickle for the *objectivity* of both.*

* Nay, and relate the circumstance for the very purpose of proving the reality or objective truth of ghosts. For the lady saw *both!* But if this were any proof at all, it would at best be a superfluous proof, and superseded by the bed-posts, &c. For if she saw the real posts at the same time with the ghost, that stood betwixt them, or rather if she continued to see the ghost, spite of the sight of these, how should she *not* see the *real* husband? What was to make the difference between the two solids, or intercept the rays from the husband's dressing-gown, while it allowed a free passage to those from the bed-curtain? And yet I first heard this story from one, who, though professedly an unbeliever in this branch of *ancient Pneumatics* (which stood, however, a niche higher, I suspect, in his good opinion, than Monboddo's *Ancient Metaphysics*), adduced it as a *something on the other side!*—A puzzling fact! and challenged me to answer it. And this too, was a man no less respectable for talents, education, and active

Andrew Baxter, again, would take a different road from either. He would agree with us in calling the apparition *subjective*, and the figure of the husband *objective*, so far as the *ubi* of the latter, and its position *extra cerebrum*, or in outward spaces, was in question. But he would differ from us in not identifying the agent or proper cause of the former—*i. e.* the apparition—with the subject beholding. The shape beheld he would grant to be *a making* in the beholder's own brain; but the *facient*, he would contend, was a several and *other* subject, an intrusive supernumerary or *squatter* in the same tenement or workshop, and working with the same tools (ὄργανα) as the *subject*, their rightful owner and original occupant. And verily, I could say something in favor of this theory, if only I might put my own interpretation on it—having been hugely pleased with the notion of that father of oddities, and oddest of the fathers, old TERTULLIAN, who considers these *soggetti cattivi* (that take possession of other folk's kitchens, pantries, sculleries, and water-closets, causing a sad *to-do* at *head* quarters) as creatures of the same order with the Tæniæ, Lumbrici, and Ascarides—*i. e.* the Round, Tape, and Thread-worms. Dæmones hæc sua corpora dilatant et contrahunt ut volunt, sicut *Lumbrici et alia quædam insecta*. Be this as it may, the difference between this last class of speculators and the common run of ghost-fanciers, will scarcely enable us to exhibit any essential change in the meaning of the terms. Both must be described as asserting the *objective* nature of the appearance, and in both the term contains the sense of real as opposed to imaginary, and of *out*ness no less than of *other*ness, the difference in the former being only, that, in the vulgar belief, the object is outward in relation to the whole circle, in Baxter's to the centre only. The

sound sense, than for birth, fortune, and official rank. So strangely are the healthiest judgments suspended by any out-of-the-way combinations, connected with obscure feelings and inferences, when they happen to have occurred within the narrator's own knowledge!—The pith of this argument in support of *ghost*-objects, stands thus: B = D: C = D: *ergo*, B = C. The D, in this instance, being the equal *visibility* of the figure, and of its *real* duplicate, a logic that would entitle the logician to dine off a leg of mutton in a looking-glass, and to set his little ones in downright earnest to hunt *the rabbits* on the wall by candle-light. Things, that fall under the same definition, belong to the same class; and visible, yet not tangible, is the generic character of reflections, shadows, and ghosts; and apparitions, their common, and most certainly their proper, *Christian* name.

one places the ghost without, the other within, the line of circumference.

I have only to add, that these different shades of meaning form no valid objection to the revival and readoption of these correlative terms in physiology* and mental analytics, as expressing the two poles of all consciousness, in their most general form and highest abstraction. For by the law of association, the same metaphorical changes, or shiftings and ingraftings of the primary sense, must inevitably take place in all terms of greatest comprehensiveness and simplicity. Instead of subject and object, put thought and thing. You will find these liable to the same inconveniences, with the additional one of having no adjectives or adverbs, as substitutes for objective, subjective, objectively, subjectively. It is sufficient that no heterogeneous senses are confounded under the same term, as was the case prior to Bishop Bramhall's controversy with Hobbes, who had availed himself of the (at that time, and in the common usage), equivalent words, *compel* and oblige, to confound the *thought* of moral obligation with that of compulsion and physical necessity. For the rest, the remedy must be provided by a dictionary, constructed on the one only philosophical principle, which, regarding words as living growths, offsets, and organs of the human soul, seeks to trace each historically, through all the periods of its natural growth, and accidental modifications—a work worthy of a Royal and Imperial confederacy, and which would indeed *hallow* the Alliance! A work which, executed for any one language, would yet be a benefaction to the world, and to the nation itself a source of immediate honor and of ultimate *weal*, beyond the power of victories to bestow, or the mines of Mexico to purchase. The realization of this scheme lies in the far distance; but in the meantime, it can not but beseem every individual competent to its furtherance, to contribute a small portion of the materials for the future temple—from a polished column to a hewn stone, or a plank for the scaffolding; and as they come in, to erect with them sheds

* "Physiology," according to present usage, treats of the laws, organs, functions, &c. of life; "Physics" not so. Now, *quære:* The etymological import of the two words being the same, is the difference in their application accidental and arbitrary, or a hidden irony at the assumption on which the division is grounded? *φύσις ἄνευ ζωῆς ἄνευ λόγȣ*, or *Λόγος περὶ φύσεως μὴ ζώσης ἐστὶ λόγος ἄλογος.*

for the workmen, and temporary structures for present use. The preceding analysis I would have you regard as my *first* contribution; and the first, because I have been long convinced that the want of it is a serious impediment—I will not say, to that self-*knowledge* which it concerns all men to attain, but—to that self-*understanding*, or *insight*, which it is all men's interest that *some* men should acquire; that the heaven-descended Γνῶθι Σεαυτόν," (Juv. Sat.) should exist not only as *a wisdom*, but as *a science*. But every science will have its rules of art, and with these its technical terms; and in this best of sciences, its elder nomenclature has fallen into disuse, and no other been put in its place. To bring these back into light, as so many delving-tools dug up from the rubbish of long-deserted mines, and at the same time to exemplify their use and handling, I have drawn your attention to the three questions:—What is the primary and proper sense of the words Subject and Object, in the technical language of philosophy? In what does *Objectivity* actually exist? —From what is all apparent or assumed Objectivity derived or transferred?

It is not the age, you have told me, to bring hard words into fashion. Are we to account for this *tender-mouthedness* on the ground assigned by your favorite, Persius (Sat. iii. 113):

> "Tentemus fauces: tenero latet ulcus in ore
> Putre, quod haud deceat crustosis radere verbis?"

But is the age so averse to hard words? Eidouranion; Phantasmagoria; Kaleidoscope; Marmorokainomenon (*for cleaning mantel-pieces*); Protoxides; Deutoxides; Tritoxides; and Dr. Thomson's Latin-greek-english Peroxides; not to mention the splashing shoals, that

> "——confound the language of the nation
> With long-tail'd words in *osity* and *ation*,"

(as our great living master of sweet and perfect English, Hook ham Frere, has it), would seem to argue the very contrary. In the train of these, methinks, object and subject, with the derivatives, look tame, and claim a place in the last, or, at most, in the humbler seats of the second species, in the *far-noised* classification—the long-tailed pigs, and the short-tailed pigs, and the pigs without a tail. *Aye, but not on such dry topics!*—I submit.

You have touched the vulnerable heel—'*Iis, quibus siccum lumen abest*," they must needs be *dry*. We have Lord Bacon's word for it. A topic that requires steadfast intuitions, clear conceptions, and ideas, as the source and substance of both, and that will admit of no substitute for these, in images, fictions, or factitious facts, must be *dry* as the broad-awake of sight and daylight, and desperately barren of all *that* interest which a busy yet sensual age requires and finds in the "*uda somnia*," and moist moonshine of an epicurean philosophy. For you, however, and for those who, like you, are not so satisfied with the present doctrines, but that you would fain try "another and an elder lore" (and such there are, I know, and that the number is on the increase), I hazard this assurance—That let what will come of the terms, yet without the *truths* conveyed in these terms, there can be no self-knowledge; and without THIS, no knowledge, of any kind. For the fragmentary recollections and recognitions of empiricism,* usurping the name of experience, can amount to opinion only, and that alone is knowledge which is at once real and systematic—or, in one word, *organic*. Let monk and pietist pervert the precept into sickly, brooding, and morbid introversions of consciousness—you have learnt, that, even under the wisest regulations, THINKING can go but *half* way toward this knowledge. To know the *whole* truth, we must likewise ACT: and he alone acts, who *makes*—and this can no man do, estranged from Nature. Learn to know thyself in Nature, that thou mayest understand Nature in thyself.

But I forget myself. My pledge and purpose was to help you over the threshold into the outer court; and here I stand, spelling the dim characters interwoven in the veil of Isis, in the recesses of the temple.

I must conclude, therefore, if only to begin again without too abrupt a *drop*, lest I should remind you of Mr. ——— in his Survey of Middlesex, who having digressed, for some half a score of pages, into the heights of cosmogony, the old planet between Jupiter and Mars, that *went off*, and split into the four new ones, besides the smaller rubbish for stone showers, the formation of

* Let y express the *conditions* under which E (that is, a series of forms, facts, circumstances, &c. presented to the senses of an individual) will become Experience—and we might, not unaptly, define the two words thus: $E + y =$ Experience; $E - y =$ Empiricism.

the galaxy, and the other world-worlds, on the same *principles*, and by similar accidents, superseding the *hypothesis* of a Creator, and demonstrating the superfluity of *church* tithes and country parsons, takes up the stitch again with—*But to return to the subject of dung*. God bless you and your

Affectionate Friend,

S. T. COLERIDGE.

LETTER III.—TO MR. BLACKWOOD.

DEAR SIR,—Here have I been sitting, this whole long-lagging, *muzzy*, mizzly morning, struggling without success against the insuperable disgust I feel to the task of explaining the abrupt chasm at the outset of our correspondence, and disposed to let your verdict take its course, rather than suffer over again by detailing the causes of the stoppage; though sure by so doing to acquit *my will* of all share in the result. Instead of myself, and of *you*, my dear sir, in relation to myself, I have been thinking, first, of the Edinburgh Magazine; then of the magazines generally and comparatively;—then of a magazine in the abstract; and lastly, of the immense importance and yet strange neglect of that prime dictate of prudence and common sense—DISTINCT MEANS TO DISTINCT ENDS.—But here I must put in one proviso, not in any relation though to the aphorism itself, which is of universal validity, but relatively to my intended application of it. I must assume—I mean, that the individuals disposed to grant me free access and fair audience for my remarks, have *a conscience*—such a portion at least, as being eked out with superstition and sense of character, will suffice to prevent them from seeking to realize the *ultimate* end (*i. e.* the maxim of profit) by base or disreputable means. This, therefore, may be left out of the present argument, an extensive sale being the common object of all publishers, of whatever kind the publications may be, morally considered. Nor do the means appropriate to this end differ. Be the work good or evil in its tendency, in both cases alike there is one question to be predetermined, viz. what class or classes of the reading world the work is intended for? I made the proviso, however, because I would not mislead any man even for an honest cause, and my experience will not allow me to promise an equal immediate circulation from a work addressed to the higher interests and blameless predilections of men, as from one constructed on the plan of flattering the envy and vanity of sciolism, and gratifying the cravings of vulgar curiosity. Such may be, and in some instances, I doubt not, has been, the result. But I dare not answer for it beforehand, even though both works should be equally well suited to their several purposes, which will not be thought a probable case, when it is considered, how much less talent, and of how much commoner kind, is required in the latter.

On the other hand, however, I am persuaded that a sufficient success, and less liable to drawbacks from competition, would not fail to attend a work on the former plan, if the scheme and execution of the contents were as appropriate to the object, which the purchasers must be supposed to have in view, as the means adopted for its outward attraction and its general circulation were to the interest of its proprietors.

During a long literary life, I have been no inattentive observer of periodical publications; and I can remember no failure, in any work deserving success, that might not have been anticipated from some error or deficiency in the means, either in regard to the mode of circulating the work (as for instance by the vain attempt to unite the characters of author, editor, and publisher), or to the typographical appearance; or else from its want of suitableness to the class of readers, on whom, it should have been foreseen, the remunerating sale must principally depend. It would be misanthropy to suppose that the seekers after truth, information, and innocent amusement, are not sufficiently numerous to support a work, in which these attractions are prominent, without the dishonest aid of personality, literary faction, or treacherous invasions of the sacred recesses of private life, without slanders, which both reason and duty command us to *disbelieve* as well as abhor; for what but falsehood, or that half truth, which is falsehood in its most malignant form, can or ought to be expected from a self-convicted traitor and ingrate?

If these remarks are well founded, we may narrow the problem to the few following terms,—it being understood, that the work now in question, is a monthly publication, not devoted to any *one* branch of knowledge or literature, but a magazine of whatever may be supposed to interest readers in general, not excluding the discoveries, or even the speculations of science, that are generally intelligible and interesting, so that the portion devoted to any one subject or department, shall be kept proportionate to the number of readers for whom it may be supposed to have a *particular* interest. Here, however, we must not forget, that however few the actual *dilettanti*, or men of the fancy may be, yet, as long as the articles remain generally intelligible (in *pugilism*, for instance), Variety and Novelty communicate attraction that interests all. *Homo sum, nihil humani a me alienum.* If to this we add the exclusion of theological controversy, which is endless, I shall have pretty accurately described the EDINBURGH MAGAZINE, as to its characteristic plan and purposes; which may, I think, be comprised in three terms, as a Philosophical, Philological, and *Æs-

* I wish I could find a more familiar word than æsthetic, for works of taste and criticism. It is, however, in all respects better, and of more reputable origin, than belletristic. To be sure, there is *tasty;* but that has been long ago emasculated for all unworthy uses by milliners, tailors, and the androgynous correlatives of both, formerly called *its*, and now yclept dandies. As our language, therefore, contains no other *usable* adjective, to express that coincidence of form, feeling, and intellect, that something which, confirming the inner and outward senses, becomes a new sense in itself, to be tried by laws of its own, and acknowledging the laws of the understanding so far only as not to contradict them; that faculty which, when possessed in a high degree, the Greeks termed *φιλοκαλία* but when spoken of generally, or in kind only, *τὸ αἰσθητικόν*; and for which even our substantive, Taste, is a—not inappropriate—but very inadequate metaphor; there is reason to hope, that the term *æsthetic*, will be brought into common use as soon as distinct thoughts and definite expressions shall once more become the requisite accomplishment of a gentleman. So it was in the energetic days, and in the starry court of our *English*-hearted Eliza; when trade, the nurse of freedom, was the enlivening counterpoise of agriculture, not its alien and usurping spirit; when commerce had all the enterprise, and more than the romance of war; when the precise yet pregnant terminology of the schools gave bone and muscle to the diction of poetry and eloquence, and received from them in return passion and harmony; but, above all, when from the self-evident truth, that what *in kind* constitutes the superiority of man to animal, the same *in degree* must constitute the superiority of men to each other, the practical inference was drawn, that every proof of these distinctive faculties being in a *tense* and *active* state, that even the sparks and crackling of mental electricity, in the sportive approaches and collisions of ordinary intercourse (such as we have in the wit-combats of Benedict and Beatrice, of Mercutio, and in the dialogues assigned to courtiers and gentlemen, by all the dramatic writers of that reign), are stronger indications of natural superiority, and, therefore, more becoming signs and accompaniments of *artificial* rank, than apathy, studied mediocrity, and the

thetic Miscellany. The word miscellany, however, must be taken as involving a predicate in itself, in addition to the three preceding epithets, comprehending, namely, all the ephemeral births of intellectual life, which add to the gaiety and variety of the work, without interfering with its express and regular objects.

Having thus a sufficiently definite notion of what your Maga zine is, and is intended to be, I proposed to myself, as a problem, to find out, *in detail*, what the *means* would be to the most perfect attainment of this end. In other words, what the *scheme*, and of what nature, and in what order and proportion, the *contents* should be of a monthly publication; in order for it to verify the title of a Philosophical, Philological, and Æsthetic Miscellany and Magazine. The result of my lucubrations I hope to forward in my next, under the title of "The Ideal of a Magazine;" and to mark those departments, in the filling up of which, I flatter myself with the prospect of being a fellow-laborer. But since I began this scrawl, a friend reminded me of a letter I wrote him many years ago, on the improvement of the mind, by the habit of commencing our inquiries with the attempt to construct the most absolute or perfect form of the object desiderated, leaving its practicability, in the first instance, undetermined. An essay, in short, *de emendatione intellectûs per ideas*—the beneficial influence of which, on his mind, he spoke of with warmth. The main contents of the letter, the effect of which, my friend appreciated so highly, were derived from conversation with a great man, now no more. And as I have reason to regard that conversation as an epoch in the history of my own mind, I feel myself encouraged to hope that its publication may not prove useless to some of your numerous readers, to whom Nature has given the stream, and nothing is wanting but to be led in the right channel. There is one other motive to which I must plead conscious, not only in the following, but in all of these, my *preliminary* contributions; viz. That by the reader's agreement with the principles, and sympathy with the general feelings,

ostentation of wealth. When I think of the vigor and felicity of style characteristic of the age, from Edward VI. to the restoration of Charles, and observable in the letters and family memoirs of noble families—take, for instance, the life of Colonel Hutchinson, written by his widow—I can not suppress the wish—O that the *habits* of those days could return, even though they should bring pedantry and Euphuism in their train!

which they are meant to impress, the interest of my future contributions, and still more, their permanent effect, will be heightened ; and most so in those, in which, as narrative and imaginative compositions, there is the least show of reflection, on my part, and the least necessity for it,—though I flatter myself not the least opportunity on the part of my readers.

It will be better too, if I mistake not, both for your purposes and mine, to have it said hereafter, that he dragged slow and stiff-knee'd up the first hill, but sprang forward as soon as the road was full before him, and *got in* fresh ; than that he set off in grand style—broke up midway, and came in broken-winded. *Finis coronat opus.* Yours, &c.

S. T. Coleridge.

LETTER IV. To a Junior Soph, at Cambridge.

Often, my dear young friend ! often, and bitterly, do I regret the stupid prejudice that made me neglect my mathematical studies at Jesus. There is something to me enigmatically attractive and imaginative in the generation of curves, and in the whole geometry of motion. I seldom look at a fine prospect or mountain landscape, or even at a grand picture, without abstracting the lines with a feeling similar to that with which I should contemplate the graven or painted walls of some temple or palace in Mid Africa,—doubtful whether it were mere Arabesque, or undeciphered characters of an unknown tongue, framed when the language of men was nearer to that of nature,—a language of symbols and correspondences. I am, therefore, far more disposed to envy, than join in the laugh against your fellow-collegiate, for amusing himself in the geometrical construction of leaves and flowers.

Since the receipt of your last, I never take a turn round the garden without thinking of his billow-lines and shell-lines, under the well-sounding names of Cumäids and Conchoids ; they have as much life and poetry for me, as their elder sisters, the Naiads, Nereids, and Hama-dryads. I pray you, present my best respects to him, and tell him, that he brought to my recollection the glorious passage in Plotinus, " Should any one interrogate Nature *how* she works ? if graciously she vouchsafes to answer, she will say, It behooves thee to understand me (*or better, and more literally*, to go along with me) in silence, even as I am silent, and work without words ;"—but you have a Plotinus, and may construe it for yourself.—(Ennead 3. l. 8, c. 3), attending particularly to the comparison of the process pursued by Nature, with that of the geometrician. And now for your questions respecting the moral influence of W.'s minor poems. Of course, this will be greatly modified by the character of the recipient. But that in the majority of instances it has been most salutary, I can not for a moment doubt. But it is another question whether verse is the best way of disciplining the mind to that spiritual alchemy, which communicates a sterling value to real or apparent trifles, by using them as moral diagrams, as your friend uses the oak and fig-leaves as geometrical ones. To have formed the habit of looking at every thing, not for what it is relative to the purposes and associations of men in general, but for the truths which it is suited to represent—to contemplate objects as *words* and pregnant symbols—the advantages of this, my dear D., are so many, and so important, so eminently calculated to excite and evolve the power of sound and connected reasoning, of distinct and clear conception, and of genial feeling, that there were few of W.'s finest passages—and who, of living poets, can lay claim to half the number ?—that I repeat so often, as that homely quatrain,

O reader ! had you in your mind
  Such stores as silent thought can bring ;
O gentle reader ! you would find
  A tale in every thing.

You did not know my revered friend and patron ; or rather, you do know the man, and mourn his loss, from the character I have* lately given of him.—The following supposed dialogue actually took place, in a conversation with him ; and as in part, an illustration of what I have already said, and in part as text and introduction to much I would wish to say, I entreat you to read it with patience, spite of the triviality of the subject, and mock-heroic of the title.

* In the 8th Number of The Friend, as first circulated by the post. I dare assert, that it is worthy of preservation, and will send a transcript in my next.

SUBSTANCE OF A DIALOGUE, WITH A COMMENTARY ON THE SAME.

A. I never found yet, an ink-stand that I was satisfied with.

B. What would you have an ink-stand to be? What qualities and properties would you wish to have combined in an ink-stand? Reflect! Consult your past experience; taking care, however, not to desire things demonstrably, or self-evidently incompatible with each other; and the union of these *desiderata* will be *your ideal* of an ink-stand. A friend, perhaps, suggests some additional excellence that might rationally be desired, till at length the catalogue may be considered as complete, when neither yourself, nor others, can think of any *desideratum* not anticipated or precluded by some one or more of the points already enumerated; and the conception of all these, as realized in one and the same artefact, may be fairly entitled, the

IDEAL *of an Ink-stand.*

That the pen should be allowed, without requiring any effort or interruptive act of attention from the writer, to dip sufficiently low, and yet be prevented, without injuring its nib, from dipping too low, or taking up too much ink: that the ink-stand should be of such materials as not to decompose the ink, or occasion a deposition or discoloration of its specific ingredients, as, from what cause I know not, is the fault of the black Wedgewood-ware ink-stands; that it should be so constructed, that on being overturned the ink can not escape; and so protected, or made of such stuff, that in case of a blow or a fall from any common height, the ink-stand itself will not be broken;—that from both these qualities, and from its shape, it may be safely and commodiously travelled with, and packed up with books, linen, or whatever else is likely to form the contents of the portmanteau, or travelling trunk;—that it should stand steadily and commodiously, and be of as pleasing a shape and appearance as is compatible with its more important uses;—and, lastly, though of minor regard, and non-essential, that it be capable of including other implements or requisites, always, or occasionally connected with the art of writing, as pen-knife, wafers, &c., without any addition to the size and weight, otherwise desirable, and without detriment to its more important and *proper* advantages.

Now (continued B.) that we have an adequate notion of what is to be wished, let us try what is to be done! And my friend actually succeeded in constructing an ink-stand, in which, during the twelve years that have elapsed since this conversation, alas! I might almost say since his death, I have never been able, though I have put my wits on the stretch, to detect any thing wanting that an ink-stand could be rationally desired to possess; or even to imagine any addition, detraction, or change, for use or appearance, that I could desire, without involving a contradiction.

HERE! (methinks I hear the reader exclaim) Here's a meditation on a broom-stick with a vengeance! Now, in the first place, I am, and I do not care who knows it, no enemy to meditations on broom-sticks; and though Boyle had been the real author of the article so waggishly passed off for his on poor Lady Berkley; and though that good man had written it in grave and good earnest, I am not certain that he would not have been employing his time as creditably to himself, and as profitably for a large class of readers, as the witty dean was while composing the Draper's Letters, though the Muses forbid that I should say the same of Mary Cooke's Petition, Hamilton's Bawn, or even the rhyming correspondence with Dr. Sheridan. In hazarding this confession, however, I beg leave to put in a *provided always*, that the said Meditation on Broom-stick, or *aliud quidlibet ejusdem farinæ*, shall be as truly a meditation as the broom-stick is verily a broom-stick—and that the name be not a misnomer of vanity, or fraudulently labelled on a mere compound of brain-dribble and printer's ink. For meditation, I presume, is that act of the mind, by which it seeks *within* either the *law* of the phenomena, which it had *contemplated* without (*meditatio scientifica*), or semblances, symbols, and analogies, corresponsive to the same (*meditatio ethica*). At all events, therefore, it implies *thinking*, and tends to make the reader *think;* and whatever does this, does what in the present over-excited state of society is most wanted, though perhaps least desired. Between the *thinking* of a Harvey or Quarles, and the thinking of a Bacon or a Fenelon, many are the degrees of difference, and many the differences in degree of depth and originality; but not such as to fill up the chasm *in genere* between thinking and no-thinking, or to render the discrimination difficult for a man of ordinary understanding, not under the same* contagion of vanity as the writer. Besides, there are shallows for the full-grown, that are the maxims of safe depth for the younglings. There are truths, quite *common-place* to you and me, that for the uninstructed many would be new and full of wonder, as the common daylight to the Lapland child at the re-ascension of its second summer. Thanks and honor in the highest to those stars of the first magnitude that shoot their beams downward, and while in their proper form they stir and invirtuate the sphere next below them, and natures pre-assimilated to their influence, yet call forth likewise, each after its own *form* or model, whatever is best in whatever is susceptible to each, even in the lowest. But, excepting these, I confess that I seldom look at Hervey's Meditations, or Quarles' Emblems,† without feeling that I would rather be the author of those books—of the innocent pleasure, the purifying emotions, and genial awakenings of the *humanity* through the whole man, which those books have given to thousands and tens of thousands—than shine the brightest in the constellation of fame among the heroes and *Dii minores* of literature. But I have a better excuse, and if not a better, yet a less general motive, for this solemn trifling, as it will seem, and one that will, I trust, rescue my ideal of an inkstand from being doomed to the same slut's corner with the *de tribus Capellis*, or *de umbra asini*, by virtue of the process which it exemplifies; though I should not quarrel with the allotment, if its risible merits allowed it to keep com-

* "Verily, to ask, what meaneth this? is no Herculean labor. And the reader languishes under the same vain-glory as his author, and hath laid his head on the other knee of Omphale, if he can mistake the thin vocables of incogitance for the consubstantial words which thought begetteth and goeth forth in."—*Sir T. Brown, MSS.*

† A full collection, a *Bibliotheca Specialis*, of the books of emblems and symbols, of all sects and parties, moral, theological, or political, including those in the Centenaries and Jubilee volumes published by the Jesuit and other religious orders, is a *desideratum* in our library literature that would well employ the talents of our ingenious masters in wood-engraving, etching, and lithography, under the superintendence of a Dibdin, and not unworthy of royal and noble patronage, or the attention of a Longman and his compeers. Singly or jointly undertaken, it would do honor to these princely merchants in the service of the muses. What stores might not a Southey contribute as notes or interspersed prefaces? I could dream away an hour on the subject.

pany with the ideal immortalized by Rabelais in his disquisition inquisitory *De Rebus optime abstergentibus*.

Dared I mention the name of *my Idealizer*, a name dear to science, and consecrated by discoveries of far-extending utility, it would at least give a *biographical* interest to this trifling anecdote, and perhaps entitle me to claim for it a yet higher, as a trait *in minimis*, characteristic of a class of powerful and most beneficent intellects. For to the same process of thought we owe whatever instruments of power have been bestowed on mankind by science and genius ; and only such deserve the name of inventions or discoveries. But even in those, which chance may seem to claim, "*quæ homini obvenisse* videantur potius quam homo *venire in* ea"—which come to us rather than we to them—this process will *most* often be found as the indispensable *antecedent* of the discovery—as the condition, without which the suggesting accident would have whispered to deaf ears, unnoticed ; or, like the faces in the fire, or the landscapes made by damp on a white-washed wall, noticed for their oddity alone. To the birth of the tree a prepared soil is as necessary as the falling seed. A Daniel was present ; or the fatal characters in the banquet-hall of Belshazzar might have struck more terror, but would have been of no more import than the trail of a luminous worm. In the far greater number, indeed, of these asserted boons of chance, it is the accident that should be called the *condition*—and often not so much, but merely the *occasion*—while the proper cause of the invention is to be sought for in the co-existing state and previous habit of the observer's mind. I can not bring myself to account for *respiration* from the stimulus of the *air*, without ascribing to the specific stimulability of the lungs a yet more important part in the joint product. To how many myriads of individuals had not the rise and fall of the lid in a boiling kettle been familiar, an appearance daily and hourly in sight ? But it was reserved for a mind that understood what was to be wished and knew what was wanted in order to its fulfilment—for an *armed* eye, which meditation had made contemplative, an eye armed from within, with an instrument of higher powers than glasses can give, with the logic of method, the only true *Organum Flevristicum* which possesses the former and better half of knowledge in itself as the science of wise questioning,* and the other half in

* "Prudens quæstio dimidium scientiæ," says our Verulam, the second

reversion,—it was reserved for the Marquis of Worcester to see and have given into his hands, from the alternation of expansion and vacuity, a power mightier than that of Vulcan and all his Cyclops: a power that found its practical limit only where nature could supply no limit strong enough to confine it. For the genial spirit, that *saw* what it had been *seeking*, and saw *because* it sought, was it reserved in the dancing lid of a kettle or coffee-urn, to behold the future *steam-engine*, the Talus, with whom the Britomart of science is now gone forth to subdue and *humanize* the planet! When the bodily organ, steadying itself on some chance thing, imitates, as it were, the fixture of "the inward eye" on its ideal shapings, then it is that Nature not seldom reveals her close affinity with mind, with that more than man which is one and the same in all men, and from which

"the soul receives
Reason: and reason is her *being!*"
Par. Lost.

Then it is, that Nature, like an individual spirit or fellow-soul, seems to think and hold commune with us. If, in the present contempt of all mental analysis not contained in Locke, Hartley, or Condillac, it were safe to borrow from "scholastic lore" a technical term or two, for which I have not yet found any substitute equally convenient and serviceable, I should say, that at such moments Nature, as another *subject* veiled behind the visible *object* without us, solicits the intelligible object hid, and yet struggling beneath the subject within us, and like a helping Lucina, brings it forth for us into distinct consciousness and common light. Who has not tried to get hold of some half-remembered name, mislaid as it were in the memory, and yet felt to be there? And who has not experienced, how at length it seems *given* to us, as if some other unperceived had been employed in the same search? And what are the objects last spoken of, which are *in* the subject (*i. e.* the individual mind), yet not *subjective*, but of universal validity, no *accidents* of a particular mind resulting from its individual structure, no, nor even of the *human* mind, as a particular class or rank of intelligencies, but of im-

founder of the science, and the first who *on principle* applied it to the *ideas* in nature, as his great compeer Plato had before dóne to the *laws* in the mind.

perishable subsistence; and though not *things* (*i. e.* shapes in outward space), yet equally independent of the beholder, and more than equally real—what, I say, are those but the *names* of nature? the *nomina quasi* *νόυμενα*, opposed by the wisest of the Greek schools to *phænomena*, as the intelligible correspondents or correlatives in the mind to the invisible supporters of the appearances in the world of the senses, the upholding powers that can not be seen, but the presence and actual being of which must be supposed—nay, *will be* supposed, in defiance of every attempt to the contrary by a crude materialism, so alien from humanity, that there does not exist a language on earth, in which it could be conveyed without a contradiction between the sense, and the words employed to express it!

Is this a mere random flight in etymology, hunting a bubble, and bringing back the film? I can not think so contemptuously of the attempt to fix and restore the true import of *any* word; but, in this instance, I should regard it as neither unprofitable, nor devoid of rational interest, were it only that the knowledge and reception of the import here given, as the etymon, or *genuine* sense of the word, would save Christianity from the reproach of containing a doctrine so repugnant to the best feelings of humanity, as is inculcated in the following passage, among a hundred others to the same purpose, in earlier, and in more recent works, sent forth by professed Christians. "Most of the men, who are now alive, or that have been living for many ages, are Jews, Heathens, or Mahometans, strangers and enemies to Christ, in whose *name* alone we can be saved. This consideration is extremely sad, when we remember how great an evil it is, that *so many millions of sons and daughters are born to enter into the possession of devils to eternal ages.*"—Taylor's Holy Dying, p. 28. Even Sir T. Brown, while his heart is evidently wrestling with the dogma grounded on the trivial interpretation of the word, nevertheless receives it in this sense, and expresses most gloomy apprehensions "of the ends of those honest worthies and philosophers," who died before the birth of our Saviour: "It is hard," says he, "to place those souls in hell, whose worthy lives did teach us virtue on earth. How strange to them will sound the history of Adam, when they shall suffer for him they never heard of!" Yet he concludes by condemning the insolence of reason in daring to doubt or controvert the verity of the doctrine, or "to question the justice of the proceeding," *which verity*, he fears, the woful lot of "*these great examples of virtue must confirm.*"

But here I must break off.

Yours most affectionately,
S. T. Coleridge.

LETTER V.—To the Same.

My dear D.—The philosophic poet, whom I quoted in my last, may here and there have stretched his prerogative in a war of offence on the general associations of his contemporaries. Here and there, though less than the least of what the Buffoons of parody, and the Zanies of anonymous criticism, would have us believe, he may be thought to betray a preference of mean or trivial instances for grand morals, a capricious predilection for incidents that contrast with the depth and novelty of the truths they are to exemplify. But still to the principle, to the habit of tracing the presence of the high in the humble, the mysterious Dii Cabiri, in the form of the dwarf Miner, with hammer and spade, and week-day apron, we must attribute Wordsworth's *peculiar* power, his *leavening* influence on the opinions, feelings, and pursuits of his admirers,—most on the young of most promise and highest acquirements; and that, while others are read with delight, his works are a *religion*. A case still more in point occurs to me, and for the truth of which I dare pledge myself. The art of printing alone seems to have been privileged with a Minerval birth, to have risen in its zenith; but next to this, perhaps, the rapid and almost instantaneous advancement of pottery from the state in which Mr. Wedgwood found the art, to its demonstrably highest practicable perfection, is the most striking fact in the history of modern improvements achieved by individual genius. In his early manhood, an obstinate and harassing complaint confined him to his room for more than two years; and to this apparent calamity Mr. Wedgwood was wont to attribute his after unprecedented success. For a while, as was natural, the sense of thus losing the prime and vigor of his life and faculties, preyed on his mind incessantly—aggravated, no doubt, by the thought of what he should have been doing this hour and this, had he not been thus severely visited. Then, what he should like to take in hand: and lastly, what it was desirable to do, and how far it might be done, till generalizing more and more, the mind began to feed on the thoughts, which, at their first evolution (in their *larva* state, may I say?), had preyed on the mind. We imagine the presence of what we desire in the very act of regretting its absence, nay, *in order* to regret it the more livelily; but while, with a strange wilfulness, we are thus engendering grief on grief, nature makes use of the product to cheat us into comfort and exertion. The positive shapings, though but of the fancy, will sooner or later displace the mere knowledge of the negative. All activity is in itself pleasure; and according to the nature, powers, and previous habits of the sufferer, the activity of the fancy will call the other faculties of the soul into action. The self-contemplative power becomes meditative, and the mind begins to play the geometrician with its own thoughts—abstracting from them the accidental and individual, till a new and unfailing source of employment, the best and surest nepenthe of solitary pain, is opened out in the habit of seeking the principle and ultimate aim in the most imperfect productions of art, in the least attractive products of nature; of beholding the possible in the real; of detecting the essential form in the intentional; above all, in the collation and constructive imagining of the outward shapes and material forces that shall best express the essential form, in its coincidence with the idea, or realize most adequately that power, which is one with its correspondent knowledge, as the revealing body with its indwelling soul.

Another motive will present itself, and one that comes nearer home, and is of more general application, if we reflect on the habit here recommended, as a source of support and consolation in circumstances under which we might otherwise sink back on ourselves, and for want of colloquy with our thoughts, with the objects and presentations of the *inner sense*, lie listening to the fretful *ticking* of our sensations. A resource of costless value has that man, who has brought himself to a habit of measuring the objects around him by their intended or possible ends, and the proportion in which this end is realized in each. It is the neglect of thus educating the senses, of thus disciplining, and, in the proper and primitive sense of the word, *informing* the fancy, that distinguishes at first sight the ruder states of society. Every mechanic tool, the commonest and most indispensable implements of agriculture, might remind one of the school-boy's second stage in metrical composition, in which his exercise is to contain *sense*, but he is allowed to eke out the scanning by the interposition, here and there, of an equal quantity of nonsense. And even in the existing height of national civilization, how many individuals may there not be found, for whose senses the non-essential so preponderates, that though they may have lived the greater part of their lives in the country, yet, with some exceptions for the products of their own flower and kitchen garden, all the names in the Index to Withering's Botany, are superseded for them by the one name, a *weed!* "*It is only a weed!*" And if this indifference stopt here, and this particular ignorance were regarded as the *disease*, it would be sickly to complain of it. But it is as a *symptom* that it excites regret—it is that, except only the pot-herbs of lucre, and the barren double-flowers of vanity, their own noblest faculties both of thought and action, are but weeds—in which, should sickness or misfortune wreck them on the desert island of their own mind, they would either not think of seeking, or be ignorant how to find, nourishment or medicine. As it is good to be provided with work for rainy days, Winter industry is the best cheerer of winter gloom, and fire-side contrivances for summer use, bring summer sunshine and a genial inner-warmth, which the friendly hearth-blaze may conspire with, but can not bestow or compensate.

A splenetic friend of mine, who was fond of *outraging* a truth by some whimsical hyperbole, in his way of expressing it, gravely gave it out as his opinion, that beauty and genius were but diseases of the consumptive and scrofulous order. He would not carry it further; but yet, he must say, that he *had* observed that very *good* people, persons of unusual virtue and benevolence, were in general afflicted with weak and restless nerves! After yielding him the expected laugh for the oddity of the remark, I reminded him, that if his position meant any thing, the converse must be true, and we ought to have Helens, Medicean Venuses, Shakspeares, Raphaels, Howards, Clarksons, and Wilberforces by thousands; and the assemblies and pump-rooms at Bath, Harrowgate, and Cheltenham, rival the *conversazioni* in the Elysian Fields. Since then, however, I have often recurred to the portion of truth, that lay at the bottom of my friend's conceit. It can not be denied, that ill health, in a degree below direct pain, yet distressfully affecting the sensations, and depressing the animal spirits, and thus leaving the nervous system too sensitive to pass into the ordinary state of feeling, and forcing us to live in alternating *positives*,* is a hot-bed for whatever germs, and tendencies, whether in head or heart, have been planted there independently.

Surely, there is nothing fanciful in considering this as a providential provision, and as one of the countless proofs, that we are most benignly, as well as wonderfully, constructed! The cutting and irritating grain of sand, which by accident or incaution has got within the shell, incites the living inmate to secrete from its own resources the means of coating the intrusive substance. And is it not, or may it not be, even so, with the irregularities and unevennesses of health and fortune in our own case? We, too, may turn diseases into pearls. The means and materials are within ourselves; and the process is easily understood. By a law common to all animal life, we are incapable of attending for any continuance to an object, the parts of which are indistinguishable from each other, or to a series, where the successive links are only numerically different. Nay, the more broken and irritating (as, for instance, the *fractious* noise of the dashing of a lake on its border, comparing with the swell of the sea on a calm evening), the more quickly does it exhaust our power of noticing it. The tooth-ache, where the suffering is not extreme, often finds its speediest cure in the silent pillow; and gradually destroys our attention to itself by preventing us from attending to any thing else.

* Perhaps it confirms while it limits this theory, that it is chiefly verified in men whose genius and pursuits are eminently *subjective*, where the mind is intensely watchful of its own acts and shapings, thinks, while it feels, in order to understand, and then to *generalize* that feeling; above all, where all the powers of the mind are called into action, simultaneously, and yet severally, while in men of equal, and perhaps deservedly equal celebrity, whose pursuits are objective and universal, demanding the energies of attention and abstraction, as in mechanics, mathematics, and all departments of physics and physiology, the very contrary would seem to be exemplified. Shakspeare died at 52, and probably of a decline; and in one of his sonnets he speaks of himself as gray and prematurely old: and Milton, who suffered from infancy those intense headaches which ended in blindness, insinuates that he was free from pain, or the anticipation of pain. On the other hand, the Newtons and Leibnitzes have, in general, been not only long-lived, but men of robust health.

From the same cause, many a lonely patient listens to his moans, till he forgets the pain that occasioned them. The attention attenuates, as its sphere contracts. But this it does even to a point, where the person's own state of feeling, or any particular set of bodily sensations, are the direct object. The slender thread winding in narrower and narrower circles round its source and centre, ends at length in a chrysalis, a dormitory within which the spinner undresses himself in his sleep, soon to come forth *quite a new creature.*

So it is in the slighter cases of suffering, where suspension is extinction, or followed by long intervals of ease. But where the unsubdued causes are ever on the watch to renew the pain, that thus forces our attention in upon ourselves, the same barrenness and monotony of the object that in minor grievances lulled the mind into oblivion, now goads it into action by the restlessness and natural impatience of vacancy. We can not perhaps divert the attention; our feelings will still form the main subject of our thoughts. But something is already gained, if, instead of attending to our sensations, we begin to *think* of them. But in order to this, we must reflect on these thoughts—or the same *sameness* will soon sink them down into mere feeling. And in order to sustain the act of reflection on our thoughts, we are obliged more and more to compare and generalize them, a process that to a certain extent implies, and in a still greater degree excites and introduces the act and power of abstracting the thoughts and images from their original cause, and of reflecting on them with less and less reference to the individual suffering that had been their first subject. The *vis medicatrix* of Nature is at work for us in all our faculties and habits, the associate, reproductive, comparative, and combinatory.

That this source of consolation and support may be equally in your power as in mine, but that you may never have occasion to *feel* equally grateful for it, as I have, and do in body and estate, is the fervent wish of

Your affectionate

S. T. Coleridge.

FROM BLACKWOOD'S EDINBURGH MAGAZINE, JAN. 1822.

Sundry
Select Chapters
From the Book of the
Two Worlds,
Translated from the Ori-
ginal ESOTERIC into the
Language of the
Border Land:
Comprising the *Historie* and *Gests*
of MAXILIAN, agnominated
COSMENCEPHALUS and a **Cousin-
German** of SATYRANE, the IDO-
LOCLAST —— a very true Novel
founded on Acts, aptly divided
and diversely digested into **Fyttes,
Flights, Stations** (or Landing-places)
Floors and **Stories** —— complete
in *Numeris*, more or less.

NOTA BENE.—By default of the decipherer, we are forced to leave the blank space before "Numeris" unfilled; a part of the work, we fear, still remaining in the **Oncephalic** character, a sort of SANS-SCRIPT, much used, we understand, by adepts in the occult sciences, as likewise for promissory notes. We should also apologize for the indiscretion of our author in his epistolary preface (seduced by the wish of killing two birds with one stone), in shutting up *vis à vis*, as it were, so respectable and comprehensive (not to say synodical,) a personage as THE READER with Dick Proof, corrector—of what press, we know not, unless, as we grievously suspect, he is in the employ of Messrs. Dash, Asterisk, Anon, and Company. Nor is this all; this impropriety being aggravated by sundry passages, exclusively relating and addressed to this Mr. Proof, which have an effect on the series of thoughts common to both the parties, not much unlike that, which a parenthesis or two of links, made of dandelion stems, might be supposed to produce in my Lord Mayor or Mr. Sheriff's gold chain. In one flagrant instance, with which the first paragraph in the

MSS. concluded, we have, by virtue of our editorial prerogative, degraded the passage to the place and condition of a *Note*.—EDITOR.

MOTTO.*

"How wishedly will some pity the case of ARGALUS and PARTHENIA, the patience of GRYSELD in Chaucer, the misery and troublesome adventures of the phanatic (*phrenetic?*) lovers in Cleopatra, Cassandra, Amadis de Gaul, Sidney, and such like! Yet all these are as mere romantic as Rabelais his Garagantua. And yet with an unmoved apprehension, can peruse the very dolorous and lamentable murder of MILCOLUMB the First, the cutting off the head of good KING ALPINUS, the poisoning of FERGUSIUS the Third by his own queen, and the throat-cutting of KING FETHELMACHUS by a fiddler! nay, and moreover, even the martyrdom of old QUEEN KETABAN in Persia, the stabbing of Henry Fourth in France, the sacrilegious poisoning of Emperor Henry Seventh in Italy, the miserable death of MAURICIUS the Emperor, with a wife and five children, by wicked PHOCAS,—can read, I say, these and the like fatal passages, recorded by holy fathers and grave chroniclers, with less pity and compassion than the shallow loves of Romeo for his Juliet in Shakspeare—his deplorable tragedies, or shun the pitiful wanderings of Lady Una in search of her stray Red-cross, in Master Spenser his quaint rhymes. Yea, the famous doings, and grievous sufferings of our own anointed kings, may be far outrivalled in some men's minds by the hardships of some enchanted innamorato in Ariosto, Parismus, or the two Palmerins."

FOULIS'S *History of the Wicked Plots and Conspiracies, &c.*

MOTTO II.

"Pray, why is it that people say that men are not such fools now-a-days as they were in the days of yore? I would fain know, whether you would have us understand by this same saying, as indeed you logically may, that formerly men were fools, and in this generation are grown wise. How many and what dispositions made them fools? How many, and what dispositions were wanting to make 'em wise? Why were those fools? How should these be wise? Pray, how came you to know that men were formerly fools? How did you find that they are now wise? Who made them fools? Who in Heaven's name made them wise? Who d'ye think are most, those that loved mankind foolish, or those that love it wise? How long has it been wise? How long otherwise? Whence proceeded the foregoing folly? Whence the following wisdom? Why did the old folly end now and no later? Why did the modern wisdom begin now and no sooner? What were we the worse for the former folly? What the better for the succeeding wisdom? How should the ancient folly have come to nothing? How should this same new wisdom be started up and established? Now answer me, an't please you." FRANCIS RABELAIS' *Preface to his Fifth Book.*

* Which *Posterity* is requested to reprint at the back of the title-page, for the present, Quo' North, quo' Blackwood quo' *concessēre Columnæ.*

EPISTLE PREMONITORY FOR THE READER;

BUT CONTRA-MONITORY AND IN REPLY TO DICK PROOF, CORRECTOR.

Of the sundry sorts of vice, Richard, that obtain in this sinful world, one of the most troublesome is *ad*vice, and no less an annoyance to my feelings, than a pun is to thine. "Lay your *scene* further off! !" Was ever historian before affronted by so wild a suggestion? If, indeed, the moods, measures, and events of the last six years, insular and continental, or the like of that, had been the title and subject-matter of the work; and you had then advised the transfer of the scene to Siam and Borneo, or to Abyssinia and the Isle of Ormus—there would be something to say for it, *verisimilitudinis causâ*, or on the ground of lessening the improbability of the narrative. But in the history of Maxilian!—Why, the locality, man, is an essential part of the *à priori* evidence of its truth!

In a biographical work,* the properties of place are indispensable, Dick. To prove this, you need only change the scene in the History of Rob Roy from the precipices of Ben Lomond, and the glens and inlets of the Trossacs (the Trossacs worthy to have made a W. S. but that a W. S. is only of God's making, "*nascitur non fit*") to Snow-hill, Breckneck Stairs, or Little Hell in Westminster—by going to which last-named place, Dick, when we were at the —— school, you evaded the guilt of forswearing for telling of me to our master, after you had sworn that you would go ——, if you did—well knowing where you meant me to understand you, and where in honor you ought to have gone—but this may be mended in time.

—— And lay the *time* further back! But why, Richard? I pray thee tell me why? *The present*, you reply, *is not the age of the supernatural.* Well, and if I admit, that the age at present is so fully attached to the unnatural in taste, the præternatural in life, and the contra-natural in philosophy,

* In biography, which, by the *bi-*, reminds me of a rejoinder made to me, nigh 30 years ago, by Parsons the Bookseller, on my objecting to sundry anecdotes in a MS. Life, that did more credit to the wit and invention of the author, than to his honesty and veracity. "*In a professed biography, Mr. P.*" quoth I, pleadingly, and somewhat syllabically.—"Biography, sir," interrupted he, "*Sell*ography is what *I* want."

as to have little room left for the supernatural—yet what is this to the purpose? I can not *antedate* the highly respectable personage, into whose company I have presumed to bring you—I may make THE READER sleep, but I can not make him one of the Seven Sleepers, to awake at my request for the first time since he fell into his long nap over the Golden Legend, or the Vision of Alberic! Or does the reader, thinkest thou, believe that witch and wizard, gnome, nymph, sylph, and salamander, *did* exist in those days; but that, like the mammoth and megatherim, the race is extinct? Will he accept as *fossils*, what he would reject as specimens fresh caught—herein differing widely from the old woman, who, as the things were said to have happened so far off and so long ago, hoped in God's mercy, there was not a word of truth in them? Thou mayest think this, Richard, but I will neither affront the reader by attributing to him a faith so dependent on dates, nor myself, whose history is a concave mirror, not a glass-case of mummies, stuffed skins of defunct monsters, and the anomalous accidents of nature.

Thus, Richard, might I multiply thy objection, but that I detest the *cui bono*, when it is to be a substitute for the *quid veri*. Nor will I stop at present to discuss thy insinuation against the comparative wisdom of the sires of our great-grandsires, though at some future time I would fain hear thy answers to the doubts and queries in my second motto, originally started by Master Rabelais, in that model of true and perpetual history, the Travels of Garagantua and his friends.

Without condescending to non-suit you by the *flaws* in your indictment, I assert the *peculiar* fitness of this age, in which, by way of compromising the claims of memory and hope, the rights both of its senior and of its junior members, I comprise the interval from 1770 to 1870.

An adventurous position, but for which the age, I trust, will be "my good masters"—the more so, that I must forego one main help towards establishing the characteristic epithets rightfully appertaining to its emblazonment—namely, an *exposé* of its own notions, of its own *morals* and *philosophy*. But Truth, I remember, is reported to have already lost her front teeth (*dentes incisores et prehensiles*) by barking too close at the heels of the restive fashion: a second blow might leave her blind as well as toothless. Besides, a word in your ear, Richard Proof, I do not half trust you. I mean, therefore, to follow Petrarch's* example, and confine my confidence on *these* points to a few dear friends and revered benefactors, to whom I am in the habit of opening out my inner man in the world of spirits—a world which the eyes of "the profane vulgar" would probably mistake for a garret floored and wainscoted with old books; tattered folios, to wit, and massive quartos in no better plight. For the due nutriment, however, of scorn and vanity—which are in fact much the same; for contempt is nothing but egotism *turned sour*—for the requisite supply, I say, of our social wants (Reviews, Anecdotes of Living Authors, Table-talk, and such-like provender), it will suffice if I hereby confess, that with rare exceptions these friends of mine were all born and bred before the birth of Common Sense by the obstetric skill of Mr. Locke, nay, prior to the first *creation* of intellectual Light in the person of Sir Isaac Newton —which latter event (we have Mr. Pope's positive assurance of the fact) may account for its universal and equable diffusion at present, the Light not having had time to collect itself into *individual* luminaries, the future suns, moons, and stars of the *mundus intelligibilis*. This, however, may be hoped for on or soon after the year 1870, which, if my memory does not fail me, is the date *apocalyptically* deduced by the Reverend G. S. Faber, for the commencement of the Millennium.

But though my prudential reserve on these points must subtract from my forces numerically, this does not abate my reliance on the sufficing strength of those that remain. No! with confidence and secular pride I affirm, there is no age you could suggest, the characteristic of which is not to be found in the present —that we are the quintessence of all past ages, rather than an age of our own. You recommend, you say, the Dark Ages; and

* The passage here alluded to, I should, as an elevated strain of eloquence warm from the heart of a great and good man, compare to any passage of equal length in Cicero. I have not the folio edition of Petrarch's works by me (by-the-bye, the worst printed book in respect of blunders I know of, not excepting even Anderson's British Poets) and can not therefore give any particular reference. But it is my purpose to offer you some remarks on the Latin Works of Petrarch, with a few selections, at a future opportunity. It is pleasing to contemplate in this illustrious man, at once the benefactor of his own times, and the delight of the succeeding, and working on his contemporaries most beneficially by that portion of his works, which is least in account with his posterity.—S. T. C.

that the present boasts to be the contrary. Indeed? I appeal then to the oracle that pronounces Socrates the most enlightened of men, because he *professed* himself to be in the dark. The converse, and the necessary truth of the converse, are alike obvious: besides, as already hinted, in time all light must needs be in the dark, as having neither reflection nor absorption; yet may, nevertheless, retain its prenomen without inconsistency, by a slight change in the last syllable, by a mere—for "*ed*" read "*ing*." For whatever scruples may arise as to its being an enlightened age, there can be no doubt that it is an enlightening one—an era of *enlighteners*, from the Gas Light Company to the dazzling Illuminati in the Temple of Reason—not forgetting the diffusers of light from the Penny-Tract-Pedlary, nor the numberless writers of the small, but luminous works on arts, trades, and sciences, natural history, and astronomy, *all* for the use of children from three years old to seven, interwoven with their own little biographies and nursery journals, to the exclusion of Goody Two Shoes, as favoring superstition, by one party; and of Jack the Giant-killer, as a suspicious parody on David and Goliah, by the other.

> Far, far around, where'er my eyeballs stray,
> By Lucifer! 'tis all *one milky-way!*

Or, as *Propria Quæ Maribus*, speaking (*more prophetico, et proleptice*) of the Irradiators of future (*i. e. our*) Times long ago observed, they are common, quite a *common* thing!

> Sunt *commune* Parens, Authorque; Infans, Adolescens;
> Dux; Exlex; bifrons; Bos, Fur, Sus atque Sacerdos.

So far, at least, you will allow me to have made out my position. But if by a dark age you mean an age concerning which we are altogether in the dark; and as, in applying this to our own, the Subject and Object, we and the age become identical and commutable terms; I bid adieu to all reasoning by implication, to all legerdemain of inferential logic, and at once bring notorious facts to bear out my assertion. Could Hecate herself, churning the night-damps for an eye-salve, wish for an age more in the dark respecting its own character, than we have seen exemplified in our next-door neighbor, the Great Nation, when, on the bloodless altar of Gallic freedom, she took the oath of peace and good-will to all mankind, and abjured all conquests but those of reason? Or in the millions throughout the continent, who believed her? Or than in the two component parties in our own illustrious isle, the one of whom hailed her revolution as "a stupendous monument of human wisdom and human happiness;" and the other calculated on its speedy overthrow by an act of bankruptcy, to be brought about or accelerated by a speculation in assignats, corn, and Peruvian bark? Or than in the more recent constitutional genius of the Peninsula—

> What time it rose, o'er-peering, from behind,
> The mountainous experience, high upheaped
> Of Gallic legislation—

and "taught by others' harms," a very *un*gallic respect for the more ancient code, vulgarly called the Ten Commandments, left the lands as it found them, content with excluding their owners —owners of four parts out of five, at least, the church and nobility—from all share in their representation? Or when the same genius, the emblem and vicegerent of the present age in Spain, poising the old indigenous loyalty with the newly-imported state-craft, secured to the monarch the revenue of a caliph, with the power of a constable? But Piedmont! but Naples—the Neapolitans! the age of patriotism, the firm, the disinterested—the age of good faith and hard fighting—of liberty or death!—yea, and the age of newspapers and speeches in Britain, France, and Germany—the *uncorrupted* I mean (and the rest, you know, as mere sloughs, rather than a living and component part, need not be taken into the calculation)—were of the same opinion! A dream for Momus to wake out of with laughing!

But enough! You are convinced on this point,—at least you retract your objection. And now what else? Does my history require, in the way of *correspondency*, a time of wonders, a revolutionary period? Does it demand *a nondescript age?* Should it, above all (as I myself admit that it should), be laid in an age "without a name," and which, therefore, it will be charity in me to christen by the name of the *Polypus?* An age, where the inmost may be turned outside—and "Inside out and outside in," I at one time intended for the title of my history—where the very tails, inspired by the spirit of independence, shoot out heads of their own? (Thanks, with three times three, to Ellis and Trembley, the first historiographers of the Polypus realm, for this beautiful emblem and natural sanction of the SOVEREIGNTY OF THE PEOPLE !) All, all are to be found in the age we live in—whose attributes to enumerate would exhaust the epithets of an Orphic hymn, and beggar the Gradus ad Parnassum !—All, all, and half besides—the feasibility of which I first learnt during the last war, at two public dinners severally given, one by Scottish, and the other by Irish patriots, where each assigned to their countrymen three fourths of our whole naval and military success. In each case, *à priori*, the thing was possible, nay, probable ; as each meeting the assertion passed *nem. con.* though there were eye-witnesses, if not pars-maximists present—and both were so much in earnest, that I could not find it in my heart to disbelieve either. But this is a digression. Or it may be printed as a parenthesis. All close thinkers, you know, are apt to be parenthetic.

One other point, and I conclude. You are a mighty man for parallel passages, Dick ! a very ferret for hunting out the pedigree and true parentage of a thought, phrase, or image. So far from believing in equivocal generation, or giving credit to any idea as an *Autochthon, i. e.* as self-sprung out of the individual brain, or *natale solum*, whence (like Battersea Cabbages, Durham mustard, Stilton cheese, &c.) it took its *market* name, I verily suspect you of the heresy of the Præ-Adamites ! Nay, I would lay a wager that the Thesis for your Doctor's Degree, should you ever descend from your correctorship of *typical* errata to that of misprints in the substance, would be : *quod fontes sint nullibi*. In self-defence, therefore, by *warrantable anticipation*,—a pregnant principle, Richard ! by virtue of which (as you yourself urged at the time) the demagogues that threw open the election of the Mayor of Garrett, hitherto vested in the blackguards of Brentford exclusively, to the blackguards of the country at large, exposed us to an invasion from the aristocracies of Tunis and Algiers ! N.B. Clarendon and the Quarterly are of the same opinion—prospectively, I say, for informers, and informatively for the reader, I make known the following :

Some ten or twelve years ago, as the Vassals of the Sun, *i. e.* the Bodies, count their time, being in the world of spirits, as above-mentioned, and in the Parnassian quarter, in literary chit-chat with Lucian, Aristophanes, Swift, Rabelais, and Molière, over a glass of green gooseberry wine (since the departure of the last-named spirit, articles of French produce have been declared contraband in the spiritual Parnassia)—I read them a rough *pre-existent*, or as we say here, copy, of Maxilian. When who should be standing behind my chair, and peeping over my shoulder (I had a glimpse of his face when it was too late, and I never saw a more Cervantic one), but a spirit from Thought-land (North Germany I should say), who, it seems, had taken a trip thither, during the furlough of a *magnetic crisis*, into which his Larva had been thrown by —— Nic, senior, M.D.* and a Mesmerist still in great practice. Well! there would have been no harm in this, for in such cases it was well known, that the spirit, on its return to the body, used to forget all that had happened to it during its absence, and became as ignorant of all the wondrous things it had seen, said, heard and done, as Balaam's ass. *Γίνεται δ' αὖ ὄνος ὁ ὄνος ἐξαγγελιζόμενος.* But unluckily, and only a few months before, Mr. Van Ghert (who, as *privy* counsellor to the King of the Netherlands, ought to have known better) had, by metaphysical skill, discovered the means of so softening the wax tablet in the patient's *cranium*, that it not only received, but retained, the impression from the movements of the soul, during her trance, re-suggesting them to the patient sooner or later, sometimes as dreams, and sometimes as original fancies. Thus it chanced, that the great idea, and too many of the sub-ideas, of my *ideal* work awoke, in the consciousness of this Prussian or Saxon,—— Frederic Miller is the name, he goes by——soon after the return of the spirit to its old chambers in his brain. Alas! my unfortunate intimacy with a certain well-known "Thief of Time," for which my originality had suffered on more than one former occasion, was part in fault! But, be this as it may, so it chanced, however, that before I had put a single line on paper (my time being, indeed, occupied in determining which of ten or twelve *pre-existents* I should transcribe first) out came the surreptitious duplicate, with such changes in names, scene of action, thought,

* See "Archiv des thierischen Magnetismus," edited by Professor Eschenmiayer and Co. I mentioned one of Dr. Nic's cases, with a few of Doctors Kieser's and Nasse's, and of Mr. Van Ghert's, to Lemuel Gulliver; but I found him strangely incredulous. *He* (he said) had never seen any thing like it. But what is that to the purpose? What does any one man's experience go for, in proving a negative at least? I could not even learn from him that he had ever met with a single Meteorolithe, or sky-stone, on its travels from the volcanoes of Jupiter, or the moon, to our earth.

images, and language, as the previous associations, and local impressions of the unweeting plagiarist had clothed my ideas in. But what I take most to heart, it so nearly concerning the credit of Great Britain, is, that it came out in *another* country, and in high Dutch! I foresee what my anticipator's compatriots will say —that *admitting* the facts as here related, yet the Anselmus is no mere transcript or version, but at the lowest *a free imitation* of the Maxilian: or rather that the English and German works are like two paintings by different masters from the same sketch, the credit of which sketch, *secundum leges et consuetudines mundi corpuscularis*, must be assigned to the said Frederic Miller by all incarnate spirits, held at this present time *in their senses*, and as long as they continue therein; but which I shall claim to myself, if ever I get *out of them.* And so farewell, dear Corrector! for I must now adjust myself to retire bowing, face or frontispiece, towards THE READER, with the respect due to so impartial and patient an Arbiter from the

AUTHOR.

MAXILIAN.

FLIGHT I.

IT was on a Whitsunday afternoon—the clocks striking five, and while the last stroke was echoing in the now empty churches —and just at the turn of one of the open streets in the outskirts of Dublin—that a young man, swinging himself round the corner, ran full butt on a basket of cakes and apples, which an old barrow-wife was offering for sale; and with such force, that the contents shot abroad, like the water-rays of a trundled mop, and furnished *extempore*—on the spur of the occasion, as we say—a glorious scramble to the suburban youngsters, that were there making or marring this double holiday. But what words can describe the desperate outburst, the *blaze* of sound, into which the beldam owner of the wares exploded! or the "boil and bubble" of abuse and imprecation, with which the neighbor gossips, starting from their gingerbread and whiskey stands, and clustering round him, astounded the ears and senses of the ill-starred aggressor! a tangle-knot of adders, with all its heads protruded towards him, would not have been more terrific. Reeling with surprise and shame, with the look and gesture of a child, that, having whirled till it was giddy-blind, is now trying to stop itself, he held out his purse, which the grinning scold with one snatch transferred to her own pocket. At the sight of this peace-offering, the circle opened and made way for the young man, who instantly pursued his course with as much celerity as the fulness of the street, and the dread of a second mishap, would permit. The flame of Irish wrath soon languishes and goes out, when it meets with no fuel from resistance. The rule holds true in general. But no rule is of universal application; and it was far from being verified by the offended principal in this affray. Unappeased, or calling in her fury only to send it out again condensed into hate, the implacable beldam hobbled after the youth, determined that though she herself could not keep up with him, yet that her curses should, as long at least as her throat and lungs could supply powder for their projection. Alternately pushing her limbs onward, and stopping not so much to pant as to gain a *fulcrum* for a more vehement scream, she continued to pursue her victim with "vocal shafts," as Pindar has it, or ὡς πϱῖνος ἐμπϱησθεὶς *i. e.* spitting fire like a wet candle-wick, as Aristophanes!

And well if this had been all—an intemperance, a gust of crazy cankered old age, not worth recording. But, alas! these jets and flashes of execration no sooner reached the ears of the fugitive, but they became articulate sentences, the fragments, it seemed, of some old spell, or wicked witch-rhyme:—

Ay! run, run, run,
Off flesh, off bone!
Thou Satan's son,
Thou Devil's own!
Into the glass
Pass
The glass! the glass,
The crystal glass!

Though there is reason to believe that this transformation of sound, like the burst of a bomb, did not take effect till it had reached its final destination, the youth's own *meatus auditorius;* and that for others, the scold's passionate outcry did not *verbally* differ from the usual outcries of a scold in a passion: yet there was a something in the yell and throttle of the basket-woman's voice so horrific, that the general laugh, which had spread round at the young man's expense, was suspended. The passengers halted, as wonder-struck; and when they moved on, there was a general murmur of disgust and aversion.

The student MAXILIAN—for he it was, and no other, who, following his nose, without taking counsel of his eyes, had thus plunged into conflict with the old woman's wares—though he could attach no sense or meaning to the words he heard, felt himself, nevertheless, seized with involuntary terror, and quickened his steps, to get as soon as possible out of the crowd, who were making their way to the pleasure-gardens, the Vauxhall of the Irish metropolis, and whose looks and curiosity converged towards him. His anxious zig-zag, however, marked the desire of haste, rather than its attainment: and still as he pushed and winded through the press of the various gay parties, all in holiday finery, he heard a whispering and murmuring, "The poor young man! Out on the frantic old hag!" The ominous voice and the wicked looks which the beldam seemed to project, together with the voice—and we are all, more or less, superstitious respecting *looks*—had given a sort of sentimental turn to this ludicrous incident. The females regarded the youth with increasing sympathy: and in his well-formed countenance (to which the expression of inward distress lent an additional interest), and his athletic growth, they found an apology, and, for the moment, a compensation, for the awkwardness of his gait, and the more than most unfashionable cut of his clothes.

It can never be proved, that no one of the Seven Sleepers was a tailor by trade; neither do I take on myself to demonstrate the affirmative. But this I will maintain, that a tailor, disenthralled from a trance of like duration, with confused and fragmentary recollections of the fashions at the time he fell asleep, blended with the images hastily abstracted from the dresses that passed before his eyes when he first reopened them, might, by dint of conjecture, have come as near to a modish suit, as the ambulatory artist had done, who made his circuit among the recesses of Macgillicuddy's Reeks, and for whose drapery the person of our luckless student did at this present time perform the office of *Layman*.* A pepper-and-salt frock, that might be taken for

* The jointed image, or articulated doll, as large, in some instances, as a full-grown man or woman, which artists employ for the arrangement and probation of the drapery and attitudes of the figures in their paintings, is called *Layman*. POSTSCRIPT. Previously to his perusal of the several par-

a greatcoat,—but whether docked, or only outgrown, was open to conjecture ; a black satin waistcoat, with deep and ample flaps, rimmed with rose-color embroidery ; green plush small-clothes, that on one limb formed a tight compress on the knee-joint, and on the other buttoned mid-way round the calf of a manly and well-proportioned leg. Round his neck a frilled or laced collar with a ribbon round it, sufficiently alien indeed from the costume below, yet the only article in the inventory and sum total of his attire that harmonized, or, as our painters say, was in some keeping—with the juvenile bloom, and [*mark, gentle Reader! I am going to raise my style an octave or more*]—and ardent simplicity of his face ; or with the auburn ringlets that tempered the lustre of his ample forehead ! like those fleecy cloudlets of amber, which no writer or lover of sonnets but must some time or other, in some sweet Midsummer Night's Dream of poetic or sentimental sky-gazing, have seen astray on the silver brow of the celestial Dian ! Or as I myself, once on a time, in a dell of lazy Sicily, down a stony side* of which a wild vine was creeping tortuous, saw the tendrils of the vine pencilling with delicate shadows the brow of a projecting rock of purest Alabaster, that *here* gleamed through from behind the tendrils, and *here* glittered as the interspace.

Yes, gentle Reader !—the diction, similes, and metaphors of

ticulars of the student's *tout-ensemble*,, I am anxious to inform the reader, that having looked somewhat more heedfully into my documents, I more than suspect that the piece, since it came from the hands of the Sartor of Macgillicuddy, had been most licentiously interpolated by genii of most mischievous propensities—the *boni socii* of the Etruscan and Samothracian breed ; the " Robin Good Fellows" of England ; the " Good Neighbors" of North Britain ; and the " Practical Jokers" of *all* places, but of special frequency in clubs, schools, and universities.

* The author asks credit for his having, here and elsewhere, resisted the temptation of substituting "*whose*" for "*of which*"—the misuse of the said pronoun relative " whose," where the antecedent neither is, nor is meant to be represented as, personal or even animal, he would brand, as one among the worst of those mimicries of poetic diction, by which imbecile writers fancy they elevate their prose—*would*, but that, to his vexation, he meets with it, of late, in the compositions of men that least of all need such artifices, and who ought to watch over the purity and privileges of their mother tongue with all the jealousy of high-priests set apart by nature for the pontificate. Poor as our language is, in terminations and inflections significant of the genders, to destroy the few it possesses is most wrongful.

the preceding paragraph, *are* somewhat motley and heterogene. I am myself aware of it. But such was the impression it was meant to leave. A harmony that neither existed in the original nor is to be found in any portraiture thereof, presents itself in the exact correspondence of the one to the other. My friend Panourgos, late of the Poultry Counter, but at present in the King's Bench, a descendant of the Rabelaisean Panurge, but with a trick of Friar John in his composition—acted on this principle. He sent an old coat to be dyed; the dyer brought it home blue and black: he beat the dyer black and blue: and this, he justly observed, produced a harmony. *Discordia concors!*—the motto, gentle Reader! prefixed by the masters of musical counterpoint, to the gnarled and quarrelsome notes which the potent fist of the Royal Amazon, our English Queen Bess, boxed into love and good neighborhood on her own virginals. Besides, I wished to leave your fancy a few seconds longer in the tiring-room. And here she comes! The whole figure of the student—She has *dressed* the character to a hair.—You have it now complete before your mind's eye, as if she had caught it *flying*.

And in fact, with something like the feeling of one flying in his sleep, the poor youth neither stopped nor stayed, till he had reached and passed into the shade of the alley of trees that leads to the gardens—his original destination, as he sallied forth from his own unlightsome rooms. And scarcely, even now, did he venture to look up, or around him. The eruption from the basket, the air-dance of cakes and apples, continued still before his eyes. In the sounds of distant glee he heard but a vibration of the inhuman multitudinous horse-laugh (ἀνάριθμον γέλασμα) at the street corner. Yea, the restrained smile, or the merry glance of pausing or passing damsel, were but a dimmer reflection of the beldam's *haggish* grin. He was now at the entrance gate. Group after group, all in holiday attire, streamed forward. The music of the wind instruments sounded from the gallery; and louder and thicker came the din of the merry-makers from the walks, alcoves, and saloon. At the very edge of the rippling tide, I once saw a bag-net lying, and a poor fascinated haddock with its neb through one of the meshes: and once from the garrison at Valette, I witnessed a bark of Greece, a goodly Idriote, tall, and lustily manned; its white dazzling cotton sails all filled out with the breeze, and even now gliding into the grand port

(*Porto Grande*), forced to turn about and beat round into the sullen harbor of quarantine.—Hapless Maxilian ! the havens of pleasure have *their* quarantine, and repel with no less aversion the plague of poverty. The *Prattique* boat hails, and where is his bill of health ? In the possession of the Corsair. Then first he recovered his thoughts and senses sufficiently to remember that he had given away—to comprehend and feel the whole weight of his loss. And if a bitter curse on his malignant star gave a wildness to the vexation, with which he looked upward,

> Let us not blame him : for against such chances
> The heartiest strife of manhood is scarce proof.
> We may read constancy and fortitude
> To other souls—but had ourselves been struck,
> Even in the height and heat of our keen wishing,
> It might have made our heart-strings jar, like his !
>
> *Old Play.*

Hapless Maxilian ! hard was the struggle between the tears that were swelling into his eyes and the manly shame that would fain restrain them. Whitsunday was the high holiday of the year for him, the family festival from which he had counted and chronicled his years from childhood upwards. With this vision before him, he had confined himself for the last four or five weeks to those feasts of hope and fancy, from which the guest is sure to rise with an improved appetite : and yet had put into his purse a larger proportion of his scanty allowance than was consistent with the humblest claims of the months ensuing. But the Whitsunday, the *alba dies*, comes but once a-year—to keep it, to give it honor due,—he had pinched close, and worked hard. Yes, he was resolved to make much of himself, to indulge his genius, even to a bottle of claret,—a plate of French olives,—or should he meet, as was not improbable, his friend, Hunshman, the Professor of Languages—*i. e.* a middle-aged German, who taught French and Italian : excellent, moreover, in pork, hams, and sausages, though the anti-judaic part of the concern, the pork shop, was ostensibly managed by Mrs. Hunshman, and since her decease, by Miss Lusatia, his daughter—or should he fall in with the Professor, and the fair Lusatia, why then, a bowl of Arrack punch (it is the ladies' *favorite*, he had heard the Professor say, adding with a smile, that the French called it *contradiction*),—Yes, a bowl of punch, a pipe—his friend, townsman and maternal descendant of the celebrated Jacob Behmen, had taught him to smoke, and was teaching him Theosophy—coffee, and a glass of Inniskillen to crown the solemnity. In this broken and parenthetic form did the bill of fare ferment in the anticipator's brain: and in the same form, with some little interpolation, by way of gloss, for the Reader's information, have we, sacrificing elegance of style to faith of History, delivered it.

Maxilian was no ready accountant; but he had acted over the whole expenditure, had rehearsed it in detail, from the admission to the concluding shilling and pence thrown down with an *uncounting* air for the waiter. Voluptuous Youth!

But, ah! that fatal incursion on the apple-basket—all was lost! The brimming cup had even touched his lips—it left its froth on them, when it was dashed down, untasted, from his hand. The music, the gay attires, the tripping step and friendly nod of woman, the volunteer service, the rewarding smile—perhaps, the permitted pressure of the hand felt warm and soft within the glove—all shattered, as so many bubbles, by that one malignant shock! In fits and irregular *pulses* of locomotion, hurrying yet lingering, he forced himself alongside the gate, and with many a turn, heedless whither he went, if only he left the haunts and houses of men behind him, he reached at length the solitary banks of the streamlet that pours itself into the bay south of the Liffey. Close by stood the rude and massy fragment of an inclosure, or rather the angle where the walls met that had once protected a now deserted garden,

"And still where many a garden-flower grew wild."

Here, beneath a bushy elder-tree, that had shot forth from the crumbling ruin, something higher than midway from the base, he found a grassy couch, a sofa or ottoman of sods, overcrept with wild-sage and camomile. Of all his proposed enjoyments, one only remained, the present of his friend, itself almost a friend—a Meerschaum pipe whose high and ample bole was filled and surmounted by tobacco of Lusatian growth, made more fragrant by folded leafits of spicy or balsamic plants. For a thing was dear to Maxilian, not for what it was, but for that which it represented or recalled to him: and often, while his eye was passing,

"O'er hill and dale, thro' CLOUDLAND, gorgeous land!"

had his spirit clomb the heights of Imaus, and descended into the vales of Iran, on a pilgrimage to the sepulchre of Hafiz, or the bowers of Mosellara. Close behind him plashed and murmured the companionable stream, beyond which the mountains of Wicklow hung floating in the dim horizon; while full before him rose the towers and pinnacles of the metropolis, now softened and airy-light, as though they had been the sportive architecture of air and sunshine. Yet Maxilian heard not, saw not—or, worse still,

> He saw them all, how excellently fair—
> He *saw*, not *felt*, how beautiful they were.

The pang was too recent, the blow too sudden. Fretfully striking the fire-spark into the nitred sponge, with glazed eye idly fixed, he transferred the kindled fragment to his pipe. True it is, and under the conjunction of friendlier orbs, when, like a captive king beside the throne of his youthful conqueror, Saturn had blended his sullen shine with the subduing influences of the star of Jove, often had Maxilian experienced its truth—that

> The poet in his lone yet genial hour
> Gives to his eye a magnifying power:
> Or rather he emancipates his eyes
> From the black shapeless accidents of size—
> In unctuous cones of kindling coal,
> Or smoke upwreathing from the pipe's trim bole,
> His gifted ken can see
> Phantoms of sublimity.

But the force and frequence with which our student now commingled its successive volumes, were better suited, in their effects, to exclude the actual landscape, than to furnish tint or canvas for ideal shapings. Like Discontent, from amid a cloudy shrine of her own outbreathing, he at length gave vent and utterance to his feelings in sounds more audible than articulate, and which at first resembled notes of passion more nearly than parts of speech, but gradually shaped themselves into words, in the following soliloquy:—

"Yes! I am born to all mishap and misery!—that is the truth of it!——Child and boy, when did it fall to my lot to draw king or bishop on Twelfth Night? Never! Jerry Sneak or Nincompoop, to a dead certainty! When did I ever drop my bread and butter—and it seldom got to my mouth without some such circuit—but it fell on the buttered side? When did I ever cry, Head! but it fell tail? Did I ever once ask, Even or odd, but I lost? And no wonder; for I was sure to hold the marbles so awkwardly, that the boy could count them between my fingers! But this is to laugh at! though in my life I could never descry much mirth in any laugh I ever set up at my own vexations, past or present. And that's another step-dame trick of Destiny! My shames are all immortal! I do believe, Nature stole me from my proper home, and made a blight of me, that I might not be owned again! For I never get older. Shut my eyes, and I can find no more difference between *eighteen* me and *eight* me, than between to-day and yesterday! But I will not remember the miseries that dogged my earlier years, from the day I was first breeched! (Nay, the casualties, tears, and disgraces of that day I never can forget.) Let them pass, however—school-tide and holiday-tide, school hours and play hours, griefs, blunders, and mischances. For all these I might pardon my persecuting Nemesis! Yea, I would have shaken hands with her, as forgivingly as I did with that sworn familiar of hers, and Usher of the Black Rod, my old schoolmaster, who used to read his newspaper, when I was horsed, and flog me between the paragraphs! I would forgive her, I say, if, like him, she would have taken leave of me at the School Gate. But now, *vir et togatus*, a seasoned academic—that now, that still, that evermore, I should be the whipping-stock of Destiny, the laughing-stock of Fortune." * *

* * * * * * *

N.B.—Of the "Selection from Mr. Coleridge's Literary Correspondence" the author said in a note to the *Aids to Reflection*, "which, however, should any of my readers take the trouble of consulting, he must be content with such parts as he finds intelligible at the first perusal. For from defects in the MS., and without any fault on the part of the Editor, too large a portion is so printed that the man must be equally bold and fortunate in his conjectural readings who can make out any meaning at all." —S. C.

NOTES.

(*a*) p. 17. It now seems clear to me, that my Father here alludes to a course of lectures delivered in 1808, and I think it most probable that, from some momentary confusion of mind, he wrote "sixteen or seventeen," instead of "ten or eleven;" unless his writing was wrongly copied. It does not appear that he lectured on Shakspeare in 1801 or 1802; but in March, April, and May of 1808, and I doubt not in February likewise, he lectured on Poetry at the Royal Institution. Schlegel's lectures, the substance of which we now have in the *Dramaturgische Vorlesungen*, were read at Vienna that same Spring; but they were not *published* till 1809, and it is mentioned in an Observation prefixed to part of the work printed in 1811, that the portion respecting Shakspeare and the English Theatre was re-cast after the oral delivery.

(*b*) p. 18. My Father appears to confound the date of publication with that of delivery, when he affirms that Schlegel's Dramatic Lectures were not *delivered* till two years after his on the same subjects: but the fact is, as has been mentioned in the last note, that those parts of Schlegel's *Dram. Vorlesung.* which contain the coincidences with my Father, in his view of Shakspeare, were not orally delivered at all—certainly not in the Spring of 1808, but added when the discourses were prepared for the press, at which time the part about Shakspeare was almost altogether re-written.

Few auditors of Mr. Coleridge's earliest Shaksperian lectures probably now survive. None of those who attended his lectures before April in 1808 have I been able to discover or communicate with. But I have found this record in Mr. Payne Collier's edition of Shakspeare, vol. vii. p. 193. "Coleridge, after vindicating himself from the accusation that he had derived his ideas of Hamlet from Schlegel (and we heard him broach them some years before the Lectures *Ueber Dramatische Kunst und Litteratur* were published) thus in a few sentences sums up the character of Hamlet. "In Hamlet," &c. *Introduction to Hamlet.*

(*c*) p. 22. It can hardly be necessary to remind any attentive reader, that my Father's declarations respecting independence of Schlegel relate to his view of the characteristic merits of Shakspeare, and to general principles of criticism, *established and applied by him in* 1808, and still earlier in conversation, not to his Lectures of 1818, fragments of which are contained in this volume. I think, however, that when in 1819 my Father wrote the record prefixed to the Notes on Hamlet (see p. 144) he could hardly have been aware how many of the German critic's sentences he had repeated in those latter lectures, how many of his illustrations had intertwined themselves with his own thoughts, especially in one part of his subject—the Greek Drama—by the time they were to be delivered in 1818. Had he been fully conscious of this, common caution would have induced him to acknowledge what he had obtained from a book which was in the hands of so many readers in England. I take this opportunity of giving notice that I shall make reference to Schlegel wherever I find thoughts or expressions of my Father's substantially the same as his, though I am by no means sure, that in all these passages there was a borrowing on the part of the former. Any one who has composed for the press, and has united with this practice habits of accurate revision and an anxiety to avoid both the reality and the appearance of plagiarism, will bear witness to the fact, that coincidences, both in the form and manner of thought, *especially in criticism*, are of the commonest occurrence. Several striking coincidences may be found between Schlegel in his Dramatic Lectures and Schelling's fine discourse *Ueber der bildenden Künste* (On the Imaging Arts). For example, Schelling observes respecting the Niobe of ancient sculpture, that "the expression is softened down by the very nature of the subject, since Sorrow, by transcending all expression, annuls itself, and thus that Beauty which could not have been *lifesomely* preserved, is saved from injury by the commencing torpor." Compare this with Schlegel's interesting criticism on the Niobe at the end of his third (now fifth) Lecture (vol. i. p. 90, 2d edit.). *Der Schmerz enstellt den überirdischen Adel der Züge üm so weniger da er durch die plötzliche Anhaufung der Schläge, der bedeutenden Fabel gemäss, in Erstarrung überzugehen scheint.* In proof of this also I would refer to Schelling's remarks on the difference between the nature and range of Sculpture and of Painting (*Phil. Schrift.* pp. 375–6), with those of Schlegel (vol. iii. p. 121), Lecture xii. (now xxii.) "Painting," says Schelling, "represents not by corporeal things, but by light and color,—through an incorporeal, and, in some measure, spiritual medium." "Its peculiar charm," says Schlegel of the same, "consists in this, that it makes visible in corporeal objects what is least corporeal, namely, light and air." Read also Schelling's parallel of the Ancient mode of thought with the Plastic Art, of the Modern with the Pictorial (*Phil. Schrift.*

pp. 346–7); and compare with Schlegel, Lecture i. (vol. i. p. 9) and Lect. ix.—now end of Lect. xvii.—(vol. ii. p. 172.) Read Schelling on Imitation of the Ancients, and on the Principle of Life as the source of essential character in Art (*Phil. Schrift.* pp. 347–8–9), and compare with the doctrine of Schlegel on the same points, Lect. i. (vol. i. pp. 6–7)—Lect. xii. (now xxii.) vol. iii. p. 146.

I make no doubt that these likenesses, or rather *samenesses*, of thought and language were matter of coincidence rather than adoption on the part of the latter promulgator, because, although the Oration was delivered at Munich, Oct. 12, 1807, half a year before Schlegel read his Lectures at Vienna, it was not published among the author's collected *Philosophical Writings* till 1809. I can not help here expressing my surprise at the unconscientious way in which positive charges of dishonest plagiarism are too often made and propagated. Not unfrequently such charges are brought forward on grounds which the accusers themselves have never properly examined, and of the true nature of which they are absolutely ignorant. Such inaccuracy in matters *nearly concerning the characters of men* indicates a want of truthfulness and consideration of what is due to others, far more reprehensible than any case of simple plagiarism, ever so clearly established.

GREEK DRAMA.

This Essay certainly contains a great deal which is to be found in Schlegel's *Dram. Vorlesungen.* The borrowed parts were probably taken from memory, for they seldom follow the order of composition in the original, and no one paragraph is wholly transferred from it. I must not omit, on this occasion, to acknowledge my obligations to Mr. Heath, formerly of Trinity College, Cambridge, who, in a letter to the late editor of Coleridge's *Remains*, dated April 26, 1838, pointed out, in a broad way, the parts of Schlegel's Lectures to which he considered Mr. C. to be indebted in this composition. His references are to the first edition, and for the sake of those who may possess that and not the second, to which my notes refer, I give them here. Vol. i. pp. 14, 15, 89; 97, 98; 103–4; 270, 272–3; 329, 30, et seq. —332; 334, 6, 7, 8.

(1) p. 23. For the following sentences to the end of the paragraph see Schlegel's vith (now xith) Lect. vol. ii. pp. 15, 16, 2d edit.

(2) p. 23. "The old comedy, however, is as independent and original a kind of poetry as tragedy; it stands on the same elevation with it; that is to say, it goes as far beyond a conditionate reality (*bedingte Wirklichkeit*) into the domain of free-creating fancy." Vol. ii. p. 17. "The comic Poet transports his personages into an ideal element as truly as the tragic." *Transl.* Ib. p. 21.

(3) p. 23. From "Tragedy is poetry," to the end of the following paragraph, is freely translated from Ib. pp. 17, 18, 19.

(4) p. 25. The reader may compare the last two paragraphs with Ib. pp. 19, 20: from *So wenig aber* to *in Freyheit setzt.*

(5) p. 26. Parts of the substance of this paragraph may be found in Lect. vii. (now xii.) pp. 59, 60, 61. The commencing sentences agree with Schlegel's remarks in Lect. vi. (now xii.) p. 26.—*Die alte Komödie hat mit der athenischen Freyheit zugleich geblühen*, &c. The observation that the moral law is the ground in tragedy, may be compared with Schlegel's teaching in Lect. vii. (now xiii.) vol. ii. p. 60. *Der höchste tragische Ernst*, &c.: and in Lect. ix. (now xvii.) vol. ii. p. 156. *Wir sehen hier eine neue Bestimmung*, &c. But neither thought nor language is identical in the two passages.

(6) p. 26. For great part of this paragraph see the same (viith now xiiith) Lecture, pp. 61, 2, 3, 4.

(7) p. 27. See Lect. iii. (now iv.) vol. i. p. 62, and p. 56.

(8) p. 28. "The Chorus," says Schlegel, "is the idealized spectator:" ii. 80, Lect. iii. (now v.) Compare also the next paragraph on the Chorus in connection with unity of place with remarks on the same subject in Lect. ix. (now xvii.) vol. ii. p. 165: and p. 168.

(9) p. 28. See Lect. iii. (now iv.) vol. i. pp. 90, 91–2.

(10) p. 29. Ib. 67–8.

(11) p. 29. "Rousseau," says Schlegel in his first Lecture, "recognized the contrast in Music, and showed that rhythm and melody was the ruling principle of ancient, as harmony is of modern music. On the imaging arts (*bildenden Künste*), Hemsterhuys made this ingenious remark, that the old painters are perhaps too much of sculptors, modern sculptors too much of painters. This touches the very point with which we are concerned: for, as I shall unfold more fully in the sequel, the spirit of collective ancient art and poetry is plastic, as that of the modern is picturesque."—*Tr.* vol. i. p. 9. On the same subject hear Schelling. "By this opposition not only may we explain the necessary predominance of Sculpture in Antiquity, of Painting in the modern world; the former being thoroughly plastic in its mode of thought, whilst the latter makes even the soul a passive organ of higher revelations; but this also may be inferred, that it is not enough to aim at the plastic in form and representation,—the prime requisite is to *think* plastically, that is to say, in the manner of the ancients. But if it is an injury to Art when Sculpture deviates into the sphere of painting, on the other hand, the restrictions of painting to plastic conditions, and form is a limitation arbitrarily imposed. For if the former, like gravity, operates on a single point, the latter, like light, may fill the whole world with its creations.—*Transl. Phil. Schrift.* pp. 376–7.

The reader may compare the first sentence of the Essay with Schlegel, vol. ii. pp. 15–16, for a general resemblance of thought.

(*d*) p. 35. This paragraph may be compared with Schlegel, Lect. xii. (now xvii.) vol. iii. pp. 116, 117; and p. 113:—*Es haben unter dem Menschengeschlecht, &c.* though there is no identity of expression.

(*e*) p. 35. Schlegel observes in his xiith (xxiind) Lecture, "We can readily admit that most dramatic works of English and Spanish poets are, according to the ancient sense, neither tragedies nor comedies; they are romantic entertainments—show-pieces (*schauspiele*). —*Transl.* vol. iii. p. 117.

(*f*) p. 36. Schlegel's opinion on stage-illusion, in reference to the old doctrine of the unity of time, is to be found in his ixth (now xviith) Lecture: see especially the paragraph *Corneille findet diese Regel*, &c. vol. ii. pp. 162, 3, 4; though there is no perfect coincidence with Mr. C.'s observations on the same subject anywhere, and for the most part none at all. Compare also Schlegel's remarks on stage-scenery and decorations in his xiiith (now xxviith) Lecture, pp. 74–77.

(*g*) p. 54. Most of the substance of the following paragraph may be found in the following of Schlegel's xiith (now xxiind) Lecture. "To be formless then is by no means permissible for works of genius; but of this there is no danger. In order to meet the objection of formlessness, we have but to understand properly *what Form is:* for this has been conceived by most men, and particularly by those critics who insist above all things on a strict regularity, in a mechanical sense, and not as it ought to be, organically. Form is mechanical when it is impressed upon any piece of matter by an outward operation, as a mere accidental ingredient, without regard to the nature of the thing, as for example, when we give any form at pleasure to a soft mass, to be retained after it has hardened. Organic form, on the contrary, is innate; it forms from within outward, and attains its determinate character together with the full development of the germ. Such forms are found in nature universally, wherever living powers are in action, from the crystallization of salts and minerals to plants and flowers, and from these again up to the human countenance. Even in fine art, as in the realm of that supreme artist, Nature, all genuine forms are organical, that is to say, they are determined by the nature and quality of the work. In a word, the form is no other than a significant exterior, the physiognomy of a thing,—when not defaced by disturbing accidents, a *speaking* physiognomy,—which bears true witness of its hidden essence.—The forms vary with the direction of the poetical sense."—*Transl.* vol. iii. pp. 115–16.

(*h*) p. 56. The doctrine of this section on Shakspeare's judgment may be compared with that of Schlegel laid down in Lect. xii. (now xxii.) vol. iii. pp. 126–30. *Nach alten stimmen zu urtheilen &c.* But such was Mr. Coleridge's doctrine before he had read Schlegel's *Dramatic Lectures;* and, as far as I have observed, there is no similarity of expression.

(*i*) p. 57. The leading thought in this simile is the same as in one of Schlegel's in his first Lecture, but the expression is different. "Many at first sight brilliant appearances in the domain of the fine Arts, &c. resemble the gardens which little children lay out; impatient to behold a creation of their hands complete on the instant, they break off twigs and flowers here and there, and plant them without more ado in the earth. At first the whole wears a goodly aspect; the childish gardener walks proudly up and down among his showy flower-beds, till all comes to a miserable conclusion, when the rootless plants hang down their withering leaves and blossoms, and only dry stalks remain; while the dark forest whereon the diligence of the artist was never bestowed, which rose up towards heaven before the memory of man, stands unshattered, and fills the solitary beholder with religious awe."

The same thought with its affecting images has been introduced by Mr. H. Taylor into his *Lay of Elena.*

"Then roamed she through the forest walks,
Cropping the wild flowers by their stalks,
And divers full-blown blossoms gay
She gathered, and in fair array
Disposed, and stuck them in the mound,
Which had been once her garden-ground.
They seemed to flourish for a while,
A moment's space she seemed to smile;
But brief the bloom and vain the toil,
They were not native to the soil."

Philip Van Artwelde, 3d edit.

(*j*) p. 58. See Schelling's Oration, pp. 376–7: and Schlegel, Lect. i. vol. i. p. 9, and Lect. ix. (now xvii.) vol. ii. p. 172.

(*k*) p. 58. "The Pantheon differs not more from Westminster Abbey or the Church of St. Stephen at Vienna, than the structure of a tragedy of Sophocles from that of a stage piece of Shakspeare."—*Transl.* Lect. i. vol. i. p. 10.

(*l*) p. 59. Ib. p. 9. See note 11 to Essay on the *Greek Drama.*

(*m*) p. 59. "We must conceive it (the Chorus) as the personified reflection on the action which is going on, &c. This is the general poetical import, which is no way affected by the fact, that the Chorus had a logical origin in the feasts of Bacchus, and ever retained among the Greeks a specially local signification."—*Transl.* Lect. iii. (now v.) vol. i. p. 79.

"It was intelligently remarked by the Sophist Gorgias, that Mars had inspired this last-named great drama (*The Seven before Thebes*) instead of Bacchus; for Bacchus, not Apollo, was the tutelary deity of tragic poets, which at first sight seems strange; but we must bear in mind, that the former was not the god of wine and joy alone, but of the higher inspirations."—*Transl.* Lect. iv. (now vi.) vol. i. p. 96.

(*n*) p. 60. Schlegel makes a remark in substance the same as this, Lect. iv. (now vi.) vol. i. p. 98: and again in Lect. ix. (now xvii.) vol. ii. pp. 165, 6. *Ferner lagen zwischen, &c.*

(*o*) p. 61. *Was der Duft eines südlichen Frühlings berauschendes, der Gesang der Nachtigall sehnsüchtiges, das erste Aufblühen der Rose wollüstiges hat, das athmet aus diesem Gedicht.* All that is intoxicating in the fragrance of a southern spring, all that is passionate in the song of the nightingale, all that is luxurious in the new-blown rose,—all alike breathe from this poem.—*Transl.*

Das Süsseste und das Herbeste, Liebe und Hass, &c. &c. "Whatever is sweetest and bitterest; Love and Hatred; glad festivities and gloomy resentments; tender embraces and vaults of the dead; fulness of life and self-destruction; here stand in thick array side by side; and in the harmonious miracle all these opposites are so molten into the unity of a compound impression, that the echo which the whole leaves upon the mind is like a single but endless sigh."—*Transl.* Lect. xii. (now xxv.) vol. iii. p. 207.

(*p*) p. 76. "In the zephyr-like Ariel the image of the air can not fail to be perceived; his very name expresses it, as on the other hand, Caliban signifies the hard earthly element." *Transl.* Lect. xii. (now xxiv.) vol. iii. p. 200. Schlegel's criticisms on *The Tempest* and on *The Midsummer Night's Dream* are especially genial and eloquent. The light rich works of fancy seem to have delighted him more, and are, perhaps, in general, more adequately characterized in his book, than those which contain more for the understanding. His view of Shakspeare, however, on the whole is most discriminating—and enhances our surprise at his partial injustice to Ben Jonson and Molière, whose faults he has noted acutely, but whose redeeming merits he does not seem to have beheld with an eye of equally fine discernment.

(*q*) p. 96. Mr. Collier thinks it very possible that the visions were parts of an older play. On the passage in Act i. sc. 5, he has this note. "The numbered beach" must be taken, as Johnson observes, for the *numerous* beach; and "twinned stones" of the preceding line refers to the likeness, as of twins, between the stones on the beach. Coleridge would read with Farmer "umbered" for "numbered;" but, if any change were required, we should be inclined to prefer that of Theobald, "Th' *unnumbered* beach." It seems to be intended to bring the multitude of similar stones on the beach into comparison with the multitude of similar stars in the sky, and this interpretation brings out "the rich *crop* of sea and land" into clear intelligibility. But is it meant that men's eyes can distinguish the stars above from the stones below, or the stars one from another and the stones likewise, though both are so numerous and so much alike? The grammar and construction seem to require the former sense, and yet the latter seems the best.

The passage of Act i. sc. 1, in Knight's edition stands thus:

> "You do not meet a man but frowns: our bloods
> No more obey the heavens, than our courtiers
> Still seem as does the king;"—

And is explained thus in a note: "As we have punctuated the passage, we think it presents no difficulty, *Blood* is used by Shakspeare for natural disposition, as in All's Well that ends Well—

> "Now his important blood will naught deny
> That she'll demand."

The meaning of the passage then is—You do not meet a man but frowns: our bloods do not more obey the heavens than our courtiers still seem as the king seems. As is afterwards expressed—

> —"They wear their faces to the bent
> Of the king's looks."

In Pisanio's speech (Act i. sc. 4) this edition has "*his* eye or ear." I would that my father could have seen Mr. Knight's *Shakspeare*, with its interesting illustrations, and its refined and genial criticism.

(*r*) 104. Mr. Payne Collier remarks on "path" in the present passage: "This verb was in use for *walk* by Drayton, one of the best writers of his time. All the old editions concur in 'path.'"

(*s*) p. 115. Schlegel says of Juliet in the *Charakteristiken und Kritiken*, "how thereupon her imagination falls into an uproar,—so many terrors bewilder the tender brain of the maiden,—and she drinks off the cup in the tumult, to drain which with composure would have evinced a too masculine resolvedness," p. 300. This is the only positive coincidence between my father's criticism on Romeo and Juliet with Schlegel's eloquent essay on the same play; but it is interesting to compare the two, especially when they speak of the family bonds that form the groundwork of the tale, of Romeo's first love, and of Mercutio. Those passages of Schlegel's critique are as follows: "The enmity of the two families is the hinge on which every thing turns: very appropriately therefore the representation commences with it. The spectator must have seen its outbreaks himself in order to know what an insuperable obstacle it is to the union of the lovers. The animosity of the masters has rather rude representatives; we see how far the matter must have gone when these foolish fellows can not meet without forthwith falling into a quarrel. Romeo's love to Rosalind makes up the other half of the argument. This has been to many a stumbling-block, and Garrick rejected it in his alteration of the play. To me it appears indispensable; it is like the overture to the musical sequence of moments, which all unfold themselves out of that first when Romeo beholds Juliet. Lyrically taken, though not in respect of the action,—(and its whole charm surely rests on the tender enthusiasm which it breathes,)—the piece would be imperfect if it did not contain within itself the rise of his passion. But ought we to see him at first in a state of indifference? How is his first appearance exalted through this, that, already removed from the circumstances of cold Reality, he walks on the consecrated ground of Fancy? The tender solicitude of his parents, his restless pinings, his determined melancholy, his fanatical inclination for loneliness, every thing in him announces the chosen one and the victim of Love. His youth is like a thunderous day in spring, when sultry air surrounds the loveliest, most voluptuous flowers. Shall his quick change of mind deprive him of sympathy?—or do we not argue from the instantaneous vanquishment of his first inclination, which in the beginning appeared so strong, the omnipotence of the new impression?" pp. 289, 290, 291. On the ancient feud of the two houses, Schlegel remarks in criticizing the concluding portion of the play, "Nay more: the reconciliation of the heads of the families over the dead bodies of their children, the only drop of balm left for the torn heart, is not possible except through their being informed as to the course of events. The unhappiness of the lovers is thus not wholly in vain; sprung out of the hatred, with which the piece begins, it turns, in the cycle of events, back towards its source and stops it up forever.

MERCUTIO.

"As it may be said of the whole piece, that it is one great antithesis, wherein love and hatred, what is sweetest and what is bitterest &c. &c. are closely intermingled, so likewise the jocund levity of Mercutio is associated with, and opposed to, the melancholy enthusiasm of Romeo. Mercutio's wit is not the cold offspring of intellectual effort, but flows spontaneously out of his incessant vivacity of temper. That same rich measure of fancy, which, in Romeo, joined with deep feeling, engenders an inclination to romance, in Mercutio, amid the influences of a clear head, takes a turn toward pleasure. In both the very highest point of life's fulness is visible; in both appears also the swift transiency of whatever is most exquisite, the perishable nature of all blossoms, over which the whole drama is one tender strain of lamentation. Mercutio, as well as Romeo, is doomed to early death. He deals with his life as with a sparkling wine, which men drink off hastily ere its lively spirit evaporates."

I ADD THIS CHARACTER OF PARIS.

"The well-meaning bridegroom, who thinks that he has loved Juliet right tenderly, must do something out of the common way: his sensibility ventures out of its every-day circle, though fearfully, even to the very borders of the romantic. And yet how far different are his death-rites from those of the Beloved! How quietly he scatters his flowers! Hence I can not ask, "Was it necessary, that this honest soul too should be sacrificed? Must Romeo a second time shed blood against his will? Paris belongs to those persons whom we commend in life, but do not immoderately lament in death; at his last moments he interests us especially by the request to be laid in Juliet's grave. Here Romeo's generosity breaks forth, like a flash of light from darksome clouds, when he utters the last words of blessing over one that has become his brother by misfortune."

(*t*) p. 133. "In the progress of the action this piece (*Macbeth*) is quite the reverse of *Hamlet;* it strides forward with astounding rapidity from the first catastrophe (for so may Duncan's murder be named) to the last, 'Thought and done!' is the general motto, for, as Macbeth says:—

"'The flighty purpose never is o'ertook,
Unless the deed go with it.'"—*Transl.*

Lect. ii. (now xxv.) vol. iv. pp. 9, 10. "If *Romeo and Juliet* shines in the colors of the dawn, but a dawn whose purple clouds already announce the thunder of a sultry day, Othello, on the other hand, is a picture with strong shadows: one may name it a tragical Rembrandt." Lect. xii. (now xxv.) vol. iii. p. 208.

(*u*) p. 135. "It is wonderful," says Weber, "to find Mr. Steevens join with the last editors of Beaumont and Fletcher in accusing them of having sneered at Shakspeare, when they assumed the very innocent and common privilege of parody." The passages in which their great master is sportively imitated are in the mock heroical vein,* and

* The instances are these, *Woman-Hater*, Act iii. sc. 1, a parody on Hamlet:—*The Knight of the Burning Pestle*, first a parody on Macbeth, followed by "Sooth, George, his

as my Father has himself elsewhere observed, "to parody is not to satirize." Why should it be thought that B. and F. meant to detract from the great man by such mimicries, any more than to disparage Spenser, whose *Faery Queen* is so freely parodied in *The Knight of the Burning Pestle?* I would not urge against this notion how little cause the younger dramatists had, *in their day*, to envy Shakspeare; or that they appear to have been amiable and kindly persons, because the human heart has many folds and windings, and the hearts of men that lived three hundred years ago are not easily perused *throughout;* but it seems to me, that the passages themselves refute the charge of malicious intention. Would the gall of enmity and poison of envy have thus been poured forth in the form of festive lemonade and rum-punch? can we imagine that it would have been exhaled in a spirit of innocuous fun and jollity? There is always something piquant in the allusion to well-known impressive tragic passages in the midst of comedy. Shakspeare himself puts an expression of Marlowe's into the mouth of Pistol in mimicry of

"Holla, ye pamper'd jades of Asia!"
Tamburlaine, Part ii. Act iv. sc. 4.

---

very ghost would have folks beaten." Act v. sc. 1. Secondly, in the Prologue, a repetition nearly *verbatim* of Hotspur's bravura speech, "By Heaven! methinks, it were an easy leap;" and thirdly, what none of the editors, as far as I know, have noticed, a parody on an incident in *Romeo and Juliet*—when Luce feigns death and is conveyed out of her father's house in a coffin.—In *The Scornful Lady*, Act ii. sc. 1, Sir Roger says, in allusion to Hamlet's famous soliloquy:—

'To sleep, to die; to die, to sleep; a very figure, Sir.'

The same play contains a reference, as has been supposed, to Lear:—

"This fellow, *with his bluntness*, hopes to do
More than the long suits of a thousand could."

In *The Noble Gentlemen*, Act iii. sc. 4, is what Theobald calls *a flirt* on *Henry the Fifth*, Act iii. sc. 1.—Weber an "innocent parody." In *The Woman's Prize*, Act v. sc. 14, "Let's remove our places" has been said to be plainly a sneer at *Hamlet:* and Petruchio's declaration,

"Something I'll do; but what it is I know not." Act ii. sc. 4.

ditto at *Lear;* a suggestion which Mr. Dyce rebuts by "Nonsense; there is more of compliment than 'sneer' in these recollections of Shakspeare." Besides these there may be others, but I have not observed any, except a sentence at the end of *The Beggar's Bush*, which none of the editors seem to understand: Mr. Dyce thinks that Steevens has not hit the meaning by any of his conjectures. Higgen winds up a swaggering, canting speech with the words 'the spirit of Bottom is grown bottomless.' He has just declared that he will not 'turn the wheel for Crab the rope-maker,' but have a free course and go seek his fortune in England. Perhaps therefore his words mean only this: "Though I am but a clown, like Bottom, my spirit is not to be confined: the resources of my courage and ingenuity are endless." In Act ii. sc. 1 of this play there is another good-natured parody on *Henry the Eighth*. Mason remarks on the absurdity of the supposition, that such allusions were meant for serious sarcasm: but so far was the notion carried, that Meed even found ridicule of Ophelia's catastrophe in Savil's speech at the end of Act iii. of *The Scornful Lady:*

'I will run mad first; if that get not pity,
I'll drown myself to a most dismal ditty.'

—a line parodied by many of our early dramatists. If the author of *Tamburlaine* had been the lesser play-wright, and the author of Henry IV. the greater, commentators would perhaps have exclaimed, "What an envious ill-conditioned slave was that Shakspeare to *sneer* at the divine Marlowe!"

(*v*) p. 144. Sir H. Davy made his great discovery, the decomposition of the fixed alkalies and detection of their metallic bases, in October of 1807. In March, 1808, Mr. C. was in the midst of that course of Lectures to which, in my belief, he refers in this record, as appears from a letter of Sir Humphrey Davy to Mr. Poole of Nether Stowey, published in the life of that distinguished philosopher by Dr. Paris, vol. i. p. 224. It seems to have been mainly through Davy's advice and intervention, that my father was induced to give this course of Lectures. In August, 1807, he wrote thus to Mr. Poole: "If Coleridge is still with you, be kind enough to let him know, that I wrote nearly a week ago two letters about Lectures, &c. &c. The Managers of the Royal Institution are very anxious to engage him; and I think he might be of material service to the public and benefit to his own mind, to say nothing of the benefit his purse might also receive. In the present condition of society his opinions in matters of taste, literature and metaphysics, must have a healthy influence; and unless he soon becomes an actual member of the living world, he must expect to be hereafter brought to judgment for hiding his light."—Vol. i. p. 262.

These feelings of affectionate interest were reciprocated by my father, who followed Sir Humphry's brilliant career in a triumphant and gratulant spirit. "I rejoice," said he, in a letter to Mr. Purkis. "in Davy's progress. There are three suns recorded in Scripture:—Joshua's that stood still; Hezekiah's that went backward; and David's that went forth and hastened on his course, like a bridegroom from his chamber. May our friend's prove the latter! It is a melancholy thing to see a man like the sun in the close of the Lapland summer, meridional in his horizon; or like wheat in a rainy season, that shoots up well in the stalk but does not *kern*. As I have hoped, and do hope more proudly of Davy than of any other man, &c., my disappointment would be proportionally severe."

Dr. Paris tells the following anecdote in proof of "the fascinations of Davy's style." "A person having observed the constancy with which Mr. Coleridge attended these lectures, was induced to ask the poet, what attractions he could find in a study so unconnected with his known pursuits. 'I attend Davy's lectures,' he said, 'to increase my stock of metaphors.'"* I doubt not the charms of Sir Humphry's style or my father's delight in it—a poetical turn of thought and tem-

* Vol. i. p. 128

perament was plainly the cement, which united the poetic philosopher and the philosophic poet—or philosopher and poet—in such special sympathy: but that the latter sought to enrich his metaphoric storehouse by borrowing ready-made tropes and figurative expressions from his friend, if so the story is to be understood, I doubt exceedingly. My father was fond of illustrating mental facts by physical analogies, of explaining and adorning metaphysical subjects by images obtained from the Realm of Nature at the hands of the physical Sciences, especially chemistry;—I believe it was the mere *material* for metaphoric language that he sought to gather from the lips of his friend. Even this, however, could have been but a secondary inducement to my father to attend the discourses of the great philosophic genius of the day: he loved knowledge for its own sake too well to seek it principally for any but its own sake alone.

(*w*) p. 146. See note *s*.

(*x*) p. 146. Mr. Strachey, in a recently published *Essay on Hamlet*, wherein he maintains that "Coleridge is our true guide in the study of Shakspeare," and observes how "immeasurably more profound his criticisms are than those of Schlegel or Goethe," extracts the two foregoing paragraphs, prints the last sentence, "He mistakes the seeing his chains, &c." in italics, and proceeds to say:—"This masterly view of Hamlet's character needs no recommendation of mine; it is, I suppose, universally recognized by all students of Shakspeare in the present day as *the* criticism. But I would call attention to the passages of it, which I have marked with italics. Though Coleridge is supported by Goethe, Schlegel, and all the commentators I know of in the present and previous centuries, in his assertion that Hamlet delays action till action is of no use, and dies the victim of mere circumstance and accident, I must hesitate to agree to his conclusion. Nay, presumptuous as I feel it to be, to set myself against such an array of authorities, I must believe that Hamlet, being exactly the character that Coleridge describes him, does yet end by mastering that characteristic defect, and that he dies not a victim, but a martyr,—winning, not losing, the *cause* for which he dies." Mr. Strachey endeavors to show that this was Shakspeare's direct intention, in reference to which the whole plot of the drama is constructed—that he meant to represent Hamlet as doubly a conqueror in death,—not only as an avenger and punisher of another's crime, but as a victor over his own besetting sin of irresolution. Analyzing the conclusion of the play he alleges, that "Hamlet has come once more into the king's presence, not with any plan for the execution of his just vengeance, but with, what is much better, the faith that an opportunity will present itself, and the resolution to seize it instantly." "Nothing but the knowledge that he was dying, that now or never must the blow be struck, could have sufficiently spurred Hamlet to do a deed so utterly repugnant to his over-wrought sensibilities, as the killing with his own hand his uncle, his mother's husband, and his king. He had shrunk from the task again and again, though he knew it was his appointed duty; but he had resigned himself to Heaven, and looked for strength to be sent him thence, in Heaven's own way." These remarks are very interesting, as indeed is the whole essay of which they form a part; but whether they establish the point that Hamlet in death is more than a vanquisher of his father's assassin,—that while he strikes the fatal blow at him, he overcomes his own native vice of irresolution,—may be questioned. At no time, during the period represented in the drama, would Hamlet have wanted power to execute his appointed task on the application of an extraordinary stimulus goading him at once to performance without allowing opportunity for that refined meditation on the nature of the thing proposed and that nice calculation of consequences, which is apt to suspend, if not to paralyze, the hand of action. When he killed Polonius intending to kill the king, Hamlet displayed the same power to do the work on a sudden impulse that he shows in the catastrophe, when he knows that now the blow must be struck or never. It is indeed a notion most unworthy of Hamlet, that he strikes at last to avenge *himself*, not his father; he avenges his father, his mother, and himself all at once, and punishes at the same time that one spirit of evil, from which all the crimes of the "murderous damned Dane" had proceeded. But this sudden vengeance is yet no proof that he had subdued the *propensity* to "delay action till action was of no use." It does not appear that he enters the king's presence with any determinate intention of despatching him on that occasion: just before the fencing-match was proposed to him he resolves to "quit him with his arm," in a certain "interim;"—the time that should elapse before the report of his practices arrived from England; but had he not been both incited and capacitated to the final act by means which he had not himself either foreseen or provided, he might again have out-staid his opportunity and thought too precisely on the event for execution. It may be remarked also, that by the Queen's death, one great source of Hamlet's vacillating reluctance to despatch her husband was removed: he could *now* say: "Follow my mother." "So shall you hear," says Horatio,

> "Of carnal, bloody, and unnatural acts;
> Of *accidental judgments*, casual slaughters;
> Of deaths put on by cunning and forc'd cause;—
> And in this upshot, purposes mistook
> Fall'n on the inventors' heads."—

The king's death by the hand of Hamlet must come under the head of "accidental judgments" as well as that of Laertes; otherwise it is not referred to at all in this summary. Goethe, with his usual point and impressiveness, observes that the catastrophe is so contrived as to appear a fulfilment of destiny rather than the result of human acts, and thus to approve the common saw, "Man proposes but God disposes." "Purgatory fire sends forth its spirit to demand vengeance, but in vain; conspiring circumstances incite to vengeance, but in vain. Neither powers of the earth nor powers under the earth are able to achieve that work which it is reserved for Fate to accomplish. The judgment hour arrives. The wicked man falls with the good. One generation is mown down and another springs up to succeed it."*

"Goethe," says the author of the essay before quoted, "as his wont is, describes with exquisite transparency of thought and word all that meets his piercing, passionless, comprehensive gaze, as he looks on Hamlet *from without;* Coleridge, in *his* way, contemplates his subject *from within*, and the result shows the superiority of his method."† I should say indeed that the criticism on Hamlet, in *Wilhelm Meister* taken at large, rather exhibits the genius of Goethe than illustrates that of Shakspeare, or breathes the spirit of his wide-souled drama. It was like him who imagined a Werter and a Mignon to suppose the import of the whole to be this:—"a great deed imposed on a soul not framed and fitted for any such enterprise: as if an oak-tree were planted in a costly vase, that should have received none but exquisite flowers into its bosom; the roots extend and the vessel is shivered to pieces."‡ Consider too the plot which he so calmly proposes to substitute for that of our immortal bard!—a neat compact single little plot, which keeps the eyes of spectators within due compass instead of driving their imaginations abroad into all the ends of the earth."§ *Anstatt dass sonst seine Einbildungskraft in der ganzen Welt herumgejagt wurde!*—This was a plot indeed to delight a Serlo, the manager of a little theatre, and flatterer of little narrow-thoughted audiences! But with Goethe's leave we will keep "the troubles in Norway, the battle with young Fortinbras, the embassy to the old Uncle, Horatio's return from Wittenberg, the journey of Laertes to France, the sending of Hamlet to England."—*We* can not dispense with these things, these "thin loose threads which run through the whole piece"—if Serlo could. Such remarks to the worshippers of Goethe would perhaps appear as over bold as his on Shakspeare's drama appears to the writer of them. Schlegel's critique on Hamlet is found in his xiith (now xxvth) Lecture. "The general aim of the work," he says, is to show that a reflectiveness which pursues all the

* *Wilhelm Meister.*—Book iv. chap. 15.

† Shakspeare's Hamlet; an attempt to find the Key to a great moral Problem by Methodical Analysis of the Play.

‡ *Hier wird ein Eichbaum in ein köstliches Gefäss gepflanzt, das nur liebliche Blumen in seinen Schoos hätte aufnehmen sollen; die Wurzeln dehnen sich aus, das Gefäss wird zernichtet.*—Book v. chap. 13.

§ Book v. chap. 4.

relations and possible consequences of an action even to the last limits of human foresight, paralyzes the power of performance, as Hamlet himself expresses it:—

> " And thus the native hue of resolution
> Is sicklied o'er with the pale cast of thought;
> And enterprises of great pith and moment
> With this regard their currents turn away
> And lose the name of action."

Schlegel says of Hamlet, that chance and necessity alone excite him to bold strokes and sharp measures, and he describes the catastrophe of the play as brought about by accident. He takes a less favorable view of the Prince of Denmark's character than either Goethe or my Father, for he thinks him not only wanting in practical energy and resolvedness, but naturally addicted to artifice and dissimulation, fond of the round-about path for its own sake; a hypocrite toward himself, and of so skeptical a temper, that he can not retain a firm hold of any belief, and even begins to look on his father's ghost as an illusion when it is no longer present to his sight. " He goes so far as to aver that nothing is either good or evil, but as thinking makes it; the poet loses himself with his hero, in a maze of meditation, where neither end nor beginning is to be found."

(*y*) p. 158. " In corroboration of this criticism," says Mr. Strachey (in which perhaps we have an instance of that intuitive power, which Coleridge possessed so remarkably, of anticipating *à priori* the evidence of facts which he happened to be unaware of), it is worth while to notice the Play by Marlowe and Nash, with the title of the *Tragedie of Dido, Queen of Carthage*, published in 1594, which Steevens discovered, and has given an extract from. This extract is (in Hamlet's words) " Æneas' tale to Dido; and thereabout of it especially, where he speaks of Priam's slaughter;—" and though there is not a line, hardly a thought of it, the same as the passage which the player recites, and which is of course Shakspeare's own, still the style is so like, that the audience would probably have been reminded of Marlowe's play, and so have experienced the sensation of hearing real men quoting a real play; nay, if they retained only a general recollection of the original, might have supposed that the quotation was actually from Marlowe's " Tragedie of Dido, Queen of Carthage." The first and last lines of Steevens' extract, give a sufficient notion of it.

> " At last came Pirrhus fell, and full of ire,
> His harnesse dropping bloud ; and on his speare,
> The mangled head of Priam's yongest sonne ;
> And after him his band of Mirmidons,
> With balles of wildfire in their murdering pawes,
> Which made the funerall flame that burnt faire Troy;
> All which hem'd me about, crying, this is he.
>
> *   *   *   *

Jove's marble statue 'gan to bend the brow,
As lothing Pirrhus for this wicked act;
Yet he undaunted tooke his father's flagge,
And dipt it in the old king's chill cold bloud,
And then in triumph ran into the streetes,
Through which he could not pass for slaughtered men:
So leaning on his sword, he stood stone still,
Viewing the fire wherewith rich Ilion burnt."

Schlegel says of the player's speech about Hecuba that it must be judged not in itself but by the place which it occupies. In order that it may appear as a dramatic fiction relatively to the play at large, it must be distinguished from the loftier poetry of the latter as theatrical elevation is from simple nature. On this account Shakspeare composed the play in *Hamlet* throughout in sententious rhymes full of antitheses. But this solemn measured tone would not suit a discourse in which strong emotion ought to prevail, and thus the poet had no other expedient left him than that which he adopted,—exaggeration of the pathos. The speech, no doubt, is falsely emphatical, but this is so combined with true grandeur, that an actor practised in artificially exciting within himself the emotions he imitates, may really be carried away by it." Lecture xiith (now xxvth) pp. 215, 216.

(*z*) p. 164. "The speech of the Porter," says Mr. P. Collier in his introduction to *Macbeth*, p. 96, "is exactly of the kind which the performer of the part might be inclined to enlarge, and so strongly was Coleridge convinced that it was an interpolation by the player, that he boldly "pledged himself to demonstrate it." This notion was not new to him in 1818; for three years earlier he had publicly declared it in a lecture devoted to *Macbeth*, although he admitted that there was something of Shakspeare in "the primrose way to the everlasting bonfire." It may be doubted whether he would have made this concession, if he had not recollected "the primrose path of dalliance" in *Hamlet*. My father seemed inclined to reject as not genuine in Shakspeare whatever was not worthy of Shakspeare: but there are parts of his works not with any show of probability to be rejected, which are discreditable to his taste and judgment, as much, perhaps, and in the same way, as the sentences he wished to discard. If the Porter's "soliloquy and his few speeches afterwards" are interpolations, the play, as it proceeded from his hands, must have wanted that comic ingredient, which is found in all his other tragic productions. Mr. Coleridge, as we have seen, can hardly believe the genuineness of two vile punning lines in a speech of Mark Antony in *Julius Cæsar:*

"O world! thou wast the forest to this hart,
And this, indeed, O world! the heart of thee."
Act iii. sc. 1.

Considerable inroads must be made into the text of Shakspeare, if it is to be weeded of all such coarse flowers as these;—even in passages of deep interest the great man has sometimes flawed his goodly work by the introduction of a worthless play on words. To the instances of this adduced by Mr. Hallam, others might be added out of *Romeo and Juliet:* some of Romeo's conceits,—as when in Act iv. sc. 3, he compares the grave that holds his dead fair one to a *lantern*, would be generally condemned, I think, as frigidly fantastic, but for the predominance of beauty and passion in the drama, assimilating and fusing into the harmony of one golden glow the grotesque and the graceful. My Father admits that "the subterraneous speeches of the Ghost" in *Hamlet* "are hardly defensible;" to me they seem as low a bathos, after the awful and affecting representations that precede them, as can easily be imagined. The arguments of Schlegel, Mr. Knight, and others, for the genuineness of *Titus Andronicus*, even from the internal evidence, appear to me very strong. The faults and the deficiencies of that drama are precisely such as the immature Shakspeare might—probably would—be guilty of; and faulty and defective as the piece may be, in comparison with the great man's later performances, it is yet at once—as it seems to me—too vigorous and too poetical to be assigned to any other writer of Shakspeare's age except Jonson, or Beaumont and Fletcher, and that it is none of theirs we know both from the style, and from outward proof in abundance.

(*aa*) p. 164. "That Shakspeare has any such invincible and inordinate passion for playing with words and syllables I can not myself perceive. It is true he often makes a lavish use of this figure; in other pieces he has but sparingly interspersed verbal witticisms; nay in some, Macbeth for instance, not a single pun is to be found."—Transl. Lect. xii. (now xxiii.) Vol. iii. p. 157.

(*bb*) p. 173. "It is a far graver objection that Shakspeare wounds our feelings by exhibiting unveiled the most loathsome moral hatefulness; that he remorselessly harrows up the mind, and even shocks the eye by spectacles of insufferable horror. But in truth he has never arrayed the fierce blood-thirsty passions in an attractive exterior, never adorned wickedness with a false show of magnanimity; and he is, on that account, every way deserving of praise. Twice he has portrayed absolute villains; but in how masterly a way, even here, he has avoided impressions of too painful a nature may be seen in Iago and in Richard the Third." Transl. Lect. xii. (now xxiii.) vol. iii. p. 157. Shakspeare's works contain a triumvirate of thoroughly evil men; for Edmund might have been named with the bloody tyrant Richard, and the "demi-devil" Iago; to *him* we might apply Hamlet's character of his Uncle—and call him a "remorseless, treacherous, *kindless* villain."

(*cc*) p. 203. Mr. Dyce in his excellent edition of Beaumont and Fletcher notices almost all these remarks on his authors. Of the present one he says—"A note unworthy of this great writer; for 'quires' is fully as absurd a conjecture as 'carcass.' Mason rightly observes that to call a man's body his *four quarters* is a vulgar phrase at this day. Theobald *did* give the speech as blank verse (—this play was not edited by Seward—) but with an arrangement in the earlier part different from that which (though not altogether satisfactory) I have thought it better to adopt." Vol. iii. p. 28.

(*dd*) p. 204. Mr. Dyce calls this also an unfortunate conjecture: seeing that "Drayton (whose *Heroical Epistles* and *Owl* are spoken of in the earlier part of this passage), though a voluminous author, was not the writer of a vast number of popular tracts, which, according to Sir Roger, were consumed in cellars and tobacco shops." Former editors, he tells us, maintained the reading "Nich. Broughton," a blunder rendered ludicrous by the simple fact that the name of the mystical divine in question was not *Nicholas* but *Hugh*. In short "Ni. Br." in his opinion is undoubtedly put for Nicholas Breton, of whose pieces in verse and prose a catalogue may be found in Lowndes's Bibliog. Manual,—but who is now remembered only as the writer of the pretty ballad of *Phillida and Corydon*. See Dyce's Beaumont and Fletcher, vol. iii. p. 28.

(*ee*) p. 206. Mr. Dyce puts double notes of admiration at this proposal of "Astræa": and explains thus: "The old text is doubtless right—meaning—she has a face which looks like a book; the book of the heavens looks very like her (the heavens, astrologically speaking, being one great book in which the deity has written the history of the world, and in which men may read their fortunes, &c.)" Vol. x. p. 241.

Perhaps the poet had a more simple, sensuous, and impassioned meaning,—referred less to *astrology* than to the splendor of the heavens' outward face which is ever telling the glory of God.

(*ff*) p. 206. "Mr. Theobald," says Mr. Dyce, "totally misunderstood this passage, and therefore pointed it thus:

> "And lets the serious part of life run by
> As thin neglected sand, whiteness of name
> You must be mine," &c.

To my surprise Coleridge defends Theobald's punctuation, which was introduced into the text in direct opposition to all the old editions." Vol. x. p. 263.

Another passage in this play has greatly puzzled successive editors and been set down as corrupt by all but the last—Mr. Dyce. Charles, *entering from his study*, exclaims:

> "What a noise is in this house! My head is broken
> *Within a parenthesis*; in every corner,
> As if the earth were shaken with some strange colic,
> There are stirs and motions." Act iii. sc. 3.

This was altered by Cibber (in *Love Makes a Man*) into "My head is broken with a parenthesis in every corner." And Weber thought the words in italics (which he conjectured to be a printer's direction taken up into the text) "as ridiculous a blunder as ever passed the press." Mr. Dyce only holds himself not at liberty to reject them, and explains them as follows: "Charles (who is always thinking of books) seems to mean that his head is broken by the noise pressing upon it as a sentence is inclosed within the marks called parentheses." Ib. p. 38. It seems to me that Charles is not likening the noise pressing upon him to the hooks of the parenthesis, but intimating that, in his study, from which he has just impatiently issued, he is surrounded by noises, many and various, as an inclosed sentence by the main text with its multitude of words, the parenthetical marks representing the walls of his apartment. He was in a *parenthesis* in his study and the noises were all around. Any one who has had restless fellow-lodgers in the rooms above and below those which he occupies, or musical neighbors on each side of him in a thin-walled tenement, may understand what it is to have one's *head broken within a parenthesis.*

(*gg*) p. 211. Mr. Dyce speaks of these emendations as "not worth citing;" and indeed they are among the remarks which my father himself, I believe, would not have reprinted. His verbal criticism is curiously characteristic; but is often too far-fetched and fantastic to be adopted.

(*hh*) p. 220. Mr. Dyce says, surely the verse recommences at "Fill me this day," &c. Vol. i.

I venture to add from myself a few suggestions in regard to the text of B. and F. The first respects the sense of a passage in *The Two Noble Kinsmen:*

Theseus speaks thus of Palamon and Arcite:

> "Bear them speedily
> From our kind air (to them unkind) and minister
> What man to man may do; *for my sake, more;*
> Since I have known fights' fury, friends' behests,
> Love's provocations, zeal in a mistress' task,
> Desire of liberty, a fever, madness,
> 'T hath *set a mark which Nature could not reach to*
> Without some imposition, sickness in will,

Or wrestling strength in reason. For our love,
And great Apollo's mercy, all our best
Their best skill tender." Act i. sc. 4.

Dyce's edit. vol. xi. pp. 351-2.

Mr. Dyce thinks "the explanations which have been offered of this very difficult passage so unsatisfactory," that he omits them. Seward's and Weber's interpretations seem to me clearly wrong, because they both suppose that "set a mark" refers to an impression *made on the heart and mind* of the speaker;—that by "imposition" *special personal experience* is signified; and that Theseus means to say of these excitements, that they have produced an effect on the spirits of men, which Nature could not attain to without some influence of events or circumstances out of the ordinary course.—Should we not rather read it thus?—Extraordinary excitements have appointed and rendered possible a *higher degree of achievement* than man's natural strength could enable him to perform without something *put on*, or added to, his original powers, either by the morbid force of a disordered will,—a frenzied vehemence of action,—or, on the other hand, by some special exertion and remarkable vigor of the higher faculties of the soul; for, as we sometimes have *de una causa dos efectos*, so from two opposite causes—disease of will and strength of reason—one and the same effect may proceed. "Set a mark" may contain an allusion to archery, and refer to a certain extent or quantity of achievement. The sentiment is perhaps rather affectedly expressed, because here as elsewhere in this drama the author seems to have been imitating the pointedness, pregnancy and consequently partial obscurity of the Shaksperian style. Few writers have a clearer, easier one than Fletcher, when he is not reaching after that of another man and a greater man than himself, like Mercury seeking to bend the bow of Apollo or wield the club of Hercules.

In *The Maid's Tragedy:* Act i. sc. 1, "Who hath he taken then?" says Melantius of Amintor, on hearing that he has forsaken Aspatia. Lysippus, according to Mr. Dyce, replies,—

"A lady, sir,
That bears the light *above her*, and strikes dead
With flashes of her eye."—Vol. i. p. 324.

Weber adopted the reading of 4to. 1622, "about her." Mason could find no sense in the passage standing thus, and would substitute,

That bears the *lightning's power* and strikes dead—"

for which B. and F. are greatly obliged to him! It seems to me, that Weber's reading is the best; and that "bears the light above her" would but indistinctly express "is very superior to her:" while "bears the light *about* her" may perhaps mean, that she is surrounded with a halo or glory, as divine or super-excellent persons are commonly represented. Mr. Dyce compares the passage with what Amintor says afterwards:

> "thy sister
> Accompanied with graces *above her*:"

but in this line the metre allows us to emphasize *her*: to do so in the other injures the harmony.

Again in Act iii. sc. 1. Mr. Dyce points the conclusion of Amintor's speech thus:

> "Stay, stay, my friend;
> I fear this sound will not become our loves;
> No more embrace me!"—p. 362.

The other editors, except Theobald, point it thus:

> "No more; embrace me!"

which appears to me from the context, to be right: for Amintor had *not* been embracing him before, but holding him off sadly and suspiciously, to gaze upon him, when the other would have flown into his arms. Because he had found Evadne, after all the promise of her luminous brow and stately presence, base, false, degraded; he feels as if the brother was to prove the same, spite of his 'noble looks.'

> "Now I will outbrave all, make all my servants (drunk)
> And my brave deed shall be writ in wine for virtuous."
> *The False One*, Act ii. sc. 3.

Mr. Dyce thinks that Septimius, to whom these words belong, would hardly go so far as to talk of making all *men* his servants, and therefore adds "drunk," which gives the line a totally different sense. But the assassin has been setting forth in lofty style the force of gold:

> "This God creates new tongues and new affections,
> And, though I had killed my father, give me gold,
> I'll make men swear I have done a pious sacrifice."

After this flight to say he would *make all* (men) *his servants* was but one waft higher than he had flown before. On the other hand, not to mention the metrical awkwardness, would it not be too sudden a descent to declare, that he would make all his *servants drunk* in order that in their tipsiness they might exalt his brave deed—a fellow too like Septimius with few servants if any? Mr. Dyce is of opinion that the second line, on the common reading of the first, is nonsense. "Why should his brave deed be *writ in wine* for virtuous?" "Writ in wine" is obviously opposed to "writ in water," which occurs in *Henry VIII.** and in *Philaster.*† May we not suppose that the villain winds up his vain speech by anticipating that in every jovial

* Act iv. sc. 2.
† Act v. sc. 9. See the original in *Catull. Carm.* lxx.

banquet in the land his act shall be extolled amid flowing cups and become the theme of vinous eloquence?

(*ii*) p. 220. The two letters by Mr. Robinson from which these extracts are taken, were preserved by Mrs. Clarkson to whom they were addressed and restored by her to the writer, who, at my entreaty, placed them in my hands. I must apologize to him for preferring my judgment to his in thinking that they will interest the affectionate readers of my father's writings, who are thankful for any portion of light, that is cast upon his views and intellectual movements. In the same note in which my friend, Mr. Robinson, expresses the opinion to which I have just adverted, he relates of my father:—"I can testify to his saying on one occasion, but which I do not know, 'If all the comments that have been written on Shakspeare by his editors could have been collected into a pile and set on fire, that by the blaze Schlegel might have written his lectures, the world would have been equally a gainer by the books destroyed and the book written.' A better proof could not be afforded that he did not mean to gain credit by pilfering thoughts out of a magazine, which he invited his hearers to explore." I regret that Mr. Robinson did not attend and report of all the discourses delivered by Mr. Coleridge in the Spring of 1808; but he first became acquainted with my father, and obtained admission to his lectures in May of that year.

"I am very anxious to see Schlegel's book (the *Dram. Vorlesungen*) before the lectures commence," says my father in a letter to Mr. Robinson written at the back of a copy of the prospectus of his lectures in 1811, now printed in this volume. This shows that he first became acquainted with his fellow-lecturer's general views of Shakspeare three years after he had put forth his own in 1808; and after the time when he had prepared himself again to speak of his "judgment in the construction of his dramas, in short of all that belongs to him as a Poet, and as a dramatic Poet, &c." See the Prospectus.

(*kk*) p. 223. If Dr. Bell was over-praised, over-preferred in his lifetime, he has surely been too much disparaged and undervalued since his departure. The plan of mutual tuition, which he brought into use, was no refined instrument for the production of moral or intellectual effects, but it was a machinery for the saving of adult labor, by means of which some portion of useful knowledge was imparted to numbers, who would otherwise have had none at all. He alone at one period represented the cause of national education in connection with the church: his system kept the place, and in some degree prepared the way, for all the better educational schemes which are at this time in actual operation or contemplated. No man, could have done the work which Dr. Bell performed without some remarkable endowments; and I must ever think that, though not of fine intellect or enlarged capacity, he yet possessed, on his one great theme, the nature of the human mind in childhood and the best way of bringing it happily into action, some tincture of sound philosophy. He constantly enforced and drew attention to the principle (not then so generally admitted as now), that Education is to be speeded forward by Encouragement, beckoning on from before, rather than by Fear urging from behind; because he saw that the former gives power, while it inspires desire, to advance; the latter with its envenomed goad, stupefies in attempting to stimulate. He was always insisting on the maxim that dulness, inattention and obstinacy in the taught, generally arises from want of sense, temper and honest diligence on the part of teachers.

Dr. Bell was an enthusiast of philanthropy as truly, I believe, if not as nobly as Clarkson, Howard, or John Wesley, and had within him at least a certain quantity of precious fire to burn up somewhat of the ignorance, and consequent misery, of this world.* It is often observed that such enthusiasm may be neither the result nor the accompaniment of true Christian charity; that a man may bestow strength, time, and money, on the public, whilst, in his private sphere, he is selfish and exacting, or sensual and corrupt; that he may be raising a temple to the honor of his own inventions, while he thinks himself a model of self-devotedness. So far as these remarks are true (and perhaps it is *not* the truth, that any man who makes it the business of his life to promote the general good, and habitually spends and is spent in that cause, has been from the first wholly uninspired with a pure and genuine zeal), they apply to all the public agents of philanthropy. No faults or failings that can be imputed to Dr. Bell disprove his title to be enrolled in that band; nor ought he to be denied the credit due to those whose aims in life are of the higher sort. Mr. Carlyle insists, that "the professional self-conscious friends of humanity are the fatalest kind of persons to be met with in our day;" but this can be affirmed of those alone whose schemes are conceived unwisely or without any real regard to the good of the classes to be affected by them; surely it is not "benevolence prepense" or the *conscious deliberate* endeavor to be *fellow-workers with God*, that causes such failures. Of Dr. Bell it should be remembered that at Swanage he showed the same activity in promoting the welfare of others in obscure and unobserved ways, which he afterwards displayed in more noticeable enterprises;—that he established the straw-plait manufactory and the practice of vaccination in a corner of the land before he undertook to re-model all the schools of the kingdom on the Madras

* "Brother Ringletub, the Missionary, inquired of Ram-Dass, a Hindoo man-god, who had set up for godhead lately, what he meant to do, then, with the sins of mankind? To which Ram-Dass at once answered, he had *fire enough* in him to burn up all the sins in the world.—Surely it is the test of every divine man, that he *have* fire in him to burn up somewhat of the sins of the world, of tho miseries and errors of the world: why else is he there?" Carlyle's *Miscellanies*, vol. iv. pp. 290–91.

system.* As Master of Sherborne Hospital, he continued the old system in the mode of dealing with ecclesiastical revenues a little after the time when it began to strike against the consciences of many; *his* conscience was not sensitive on the side of church interests, and his public spirit was all flowing away in another channel. If his marriage was not happy, here too, among men of mark, he has had too many partners in misconduct or misfortune; persons who devote themselves to the public are apt to bestow too little thought or pains on their own private affairs; what wonder if the fruit prove blighted or bitter, when there has been such carelessness in choosing the seed and in attending to its germination? That in youth Dr. Bell must have possessed considerable personal attractions, and shown marks of worth, is evident from the warm and worthy friends he acquired by personal qualities alone. His conduct during the earlier part of his career was distinguished by industry and earnestness; nor was it wanting in private liberality and family affection. During his employment at Madras he gathered golden opinions, and, had he died at the end of it, would have been remembered, while memory of him remained, as a zealous and disinterested, as well as an able and ingenious man. Throughout the latter half of a long life his character seems to have deteriorated; so it will ever be with men who, by a successful course of exertion, acquire power and importance, their intellectual not being on a par with their other personal endowments,—men in whom a vigorous body supports a resolute will, and gives effect to the suggestions of a quick and lively though not enlarged mind, while clearness and depth of insight, freedom and foresight of thought are not among the gifts assigned them at their birth. Such a piece of mental mechanism, wherein the practical faculty so predominates over the reflective—energy and perseverance in action so exceed the power of duly determining action—is sure to get wrong in the working, and lose its internal balance more and more. Success, long continued, corrupts the heart; opposition, which often comes in full tide at last when little experienced at first, exacerbates the temper; and meantime the ventilation of abstract or imaginative thought, refreshing and renovating, like a breeze that has swept the plain of ocean, and comes charged with the salubrious particles which it bears within its bosom, is wanting to the engrossed and over-busy mortal, who, in the last stages of his life's journey, while he draws nearer to the other world, is ever receding further and further from it in mental preparedness, and goes on perpetually increasing his burden as he "crawls toward death." All this which I have said would be brought before the reader's mind more effectually, were he to peruse the present Mr. Southey's Life of Dr. Bell,—a faithful and feeling record, which must ever have a place, I think, in the great store-house of

* See the *Life of Dr. Bell*, vol. ii. chap. xix.

British Biography. Two paragraphs of the *Statesman's Manual* are devoted by my Father to Bell and Lancaster :* in one of them he says: "But take even Dr. Bell's original and unsophisticated plan, which I myself regard as an especial gift of Providence to the human race; and suppose this incomparable machine, this vast moral steam-engine, to have been adopted and in free motion throughout the Empire; it would yet appear to me a most dangerous delusion to rely on it as if this of itself formed an efficient national education."

NOTES TO LECTURE XIII.

ON POESY OR ART.

(*ll*) p. 328. It has been stated elsewhere (*Biographia Literaria* Introd. p. 33), that for many positions of this Lecture the author was indebted to Schelling's admirable Oration—*Ueber das Verhältniss der Bildenden Künste zu der Natur : Philosophische Schriften*, pp. 341–96. Here, as well as in his Lecture on the Greek Drama, Mr. Coleridge seems to have borrowed from memory. A few short sentences are taken almost *verbatim;* but for the most part the thoughts of Schelling are mixed up with those of the borrower, and I think that, on a careful comparison of the Lecture with the oration, any fair reader will admit that, if it be Schelling's—and that the leading thought of the whole is his, I freely own,—it is Coleridge's also. But this question every student will be able to decide for himself even without going beyond the present volume.

N.B. The title of Schelling's Discourse has been commonly translated, *On the Relation between the* Plastic *Arts and Nature;* yet the term *Plastic* refers to Sculpture exclusively, and is never applied either by Schelling or Schlegel to Painting: and Schelling's discourse treats *der Bildenden Künste*, of the figuring or imaging Arts, in their relationship to Nature.† *Bild* is a picture, a print, as well as a graven image. The verb πλάσσω is "strictly used of the artist who works in soft substances, such as earth, clay, wax." Liddell and Scott. Still *die Plastik* is generally applied to carving or sculpture; but never, I believe, to the mere expression of shape and visual appearance by painting, drawing, or printing.

* Works. I. p. 460.

† He says of Raphael, p. 379. "The bloom of the most cultivated life, the perfume of fancy, together with the aroma of the spirit breathe forth unitedly from his works;" and his criticism on Correggio, pp. 378–9, is remarkably genial and beautiful.

(*mm*) p. 328. See the next note.

(*nn*) p. 330. *Phil. Schrift.* pp. 344–5. "For the imaging art (*die bildenden Künst*), in the oldest form of expression, is styled *a dumb poetry*. The author of this definition doubtless meant to intimate thereby that, like Poetry, it is intended to express intellectual thoughts, conceptions, which the soul originates, not, however, by means of speech, but as silent Nature does, through form, through sensuous works independent of herself. Thus the imaging or figuring art stands evidently as an active bond betwixt the Soul and Nature, and can be conceived only in the vital mean—*in der lebendigen Mitte*,—between both. Yea, since its relationship with the *Soul* it has in common with every other art, and with Poetry in particular, that (relation) whereby it is connected with Nature, and becomes, like Nature, a productive power, remains as the only one that is peculiar to it: and to this alone can we refer a theory which shall be satisfactory to the understanding, as well as furthering and beneficial to art." *Transl.* Compare also with a passage, which will be presently quoted, in p. 352.

(*oo*) p. 230. See the last note.

(*pp*) p. 230. Ib. pp. 345–6. "But has not Science, then, always recognized this relationship? Has not every theory of later times even set out from the fixed principle, that Art should be the imitatress of Nature? It has so: but what did this broad general principle avail the artist, amid the various significations (*Vieldeutigheit*) of the conception of Nature, and when there were almost as many representations of this Nature as different modes of existence?"

(*qq*) p. 331. Compare with the following passage, *Phil. Schrift.* p. 356. "How comes it that, to every cultivated sense, imitations of the so named real, carried even to illusion, appear in the highest degree untruthful,—even convey the impression of spectres; whereas a work, in which the idea is dominant, seizes us with the full force of truth,—nay, transports us for the first time into the genuine world of reality? Whence does this arise, save from the more or less obscure perception, which proclaims, that the idea is that alone which lives (*das allein Lebendige*) in Things:—that all else is beingless and empty shadow?"—*Tr.*

(*rr*) p. 331. Ib. p. 347. "Should then the disciple of Nature imitate every thing in her without distinction, and in every thing all that belongs to it, *und von jedem jedes?* Only beautiful objects, and even of these only the beautiful and perfect should he repeat."—*Tr.*

(*ss*) p. 331. Compare with the following. Ib. p. 351. "We must depart from the form in order to win it back again, to win back *itself*, perceived as true, livingly and in the light of understanding. Consider the most beautiful forms, what remains, when in thought you have abstracted from them the operative principle? Nothing but bare unessential properties, such as extension and space-relationship. * * * * * *Nicht das Nebeneinanderseyn macht die Form*,—it is not the contiguity or mutual nearness of parts that constitutes form, but the manner thereof (the mode in which it takes place). But this can only be determined through a positive power, *dem Aussereinander vielmehr entgegenwirkende* —opposed even to that condition of space whereby things are perceived as without one another, which subjects the variety (or manifoldness) of parts to the unity of an idea (*Begriff*): from the power which works in the crystal even to that which, like a soft magnetic stream, gives to the parts of matter in human frames a disposition and situation relative to one another, whereby the conception,—the essential unity and beauty—can become visible."—*Tr.* Compare with this passage the last sentence of the first paragraph of Mr. C.'s Lecture.

(*tt*) p. 332. Ib. p. 353. "This effective science is the bond in Nature and Art between the conception and form; between body and soul."—*Tr.*

(*uu*) p. 332. Ib. p. 352. "The science, through which Nature works, is indeed like to no human science, which is united with self-reflection: *mit der Reflexion ihrer selbst.* In it conception is not distinct from art, nor design separate from execution."—*Tr.*

(*vv*) p. 332. Compare with this passage: *Ph. Schrift.* p. 353. "If that artist is to be accounted fortunate and praiseworthy beyond all others, on whom the Gods have bestowed this creative spirit, so will the work of art appear excellent in that proportion wherein it shows us, as in outline, this uncounterfeited power of creation and effectivity."—*Tr.*

(*ww*) p. 332. Ib. pp. 353–4. "It has long been perceived that, in Art, not every thing is performed with consciousness: that with the conscious activity an unconscious power must be united, and that the perfect union and interpenetration of these two accomplishes that which is highest in Art. Works that want this seal of conscious science are recognized through the sensible deficiency of a self-subsistent life independent of the life which produces them: while, on the other hand, where this operates, Art imparts to its work, together with the highest clearness of the understanding, that inscrutable reality, through which it appears like to a work of Nature."

"The attitude of the Artist toward Nature should frequently be explained by the maxim, that Art in order to be such, must, in the first instance, depart from Nature, and only return to her in the last fulfilment. The true sense of this appears to be no other than what follows. In all natural existences the living idea appears only as a blind agent; were this true of the Artist, he would not be distinguishable from Nature in general. Were he to subordinate himself consciously and altogether to the actual, and repeat that which exists with servile fidelity, he would bring forth masks (*Larven*), but no works of Art. For this cause he must remove himself from the product or creature, but only for the sake of raising himself up to the creative power, and seizing that intellectually or spiritually. Hereby he rises into the domain of pure ideas; he forsakes the creature in order to win it back again with a thousandfold profit, and in this way he will come back to Nature indeed."—*Tr.*

(*xx*) p. 333. Ib. p. 354. (*Next Sentence.*) "The Artist should by all means strive after that spirit of Nature which operates in the inner being of things through form and visual appearance no otherwise than as through speaking symbols,—(*jenem im Innern der Dinge wirksamen durch Form und Gestalt nur wie durch Sinnbilder redenden Naturgeist soll der Künstler allerdings nacheifern*): and only in so far as, in his imitation, he livingly seizes this, has he himself produced any thing of truth."—*Tr.*

Compare also with this passage, Ib. p. 348. "The *object* of imitation was altered—imitation went on as before. In the place of Nature came the sublime works of Antiquity, from which the scholar was occupied in taking the outward form, but without the spirit that filled it."—*Tr.*

(*yy*) p. 333. Ib. p. 347. "When we view things not in respect to their essence, but to the empty abstract form, then they speak not at all to the inward being in ourselves—(*so sagen sie auch unserm Innern nichts*): we must put into them our own mind (*Gemüth*), our own spirit, if they are to respond to us."—*Tr.*

(*zz*) p. 333. Ib. p. 355. "For works which should be the result of a combination of forms in themselves even beautiful, *einer Zusammensetzung auch übrigens schöner Formen*, would yet be devoid of beauty, inasmuch as that whereby peculiarly the work or the whole is beautiful can not be mere form,—*nicht mehr Form seyn kann.* It is above Form,—is Being—the Universal—the look and expression of the indwelling Spirit of Nature.—*Es ist über die Form, ist Wesen, Allgemeines, ist Blick und Ausdruck des inwohnenden Naturgeistes.*"

(*aaa*) p. 334. Ib. pp. 356–7. "By the same principle (that the conception (*Begriff*) is the sole life of things—*das allein Lebendige in den Dingen*), we may explain all the opposed cases which are adduced as examples of the surpassing of Nature by Art. When it arrests the swift course of human years, when it unites the vigor of full-blown manhood with the soft charm of early youth, or presents a mother of grown-up sons and daughters in the perfect condition of powerful beauty, what does it but remove that which is non-essential—Time. If according to the remark of the distinguished critic (*Kenner*), each growth of Nature has but a single moment of true perfect beauty, we may also say that it has but one moment of full existence. In this moment it is what it is in all eternity: beside this there pertains to it only a becoming and a ceasing to be. Art, in representing that moment, lifts it out of time; makes it appear in its true essence, in the eternity of its life."—*Tr.*

(*bbb*) p. 334. Ib. pp. 375–6. "But the case appears to be very different with Painting and with Sculpture. For the former represents, not like the latter, through corporeal things, but through light and color, thus even through an incorporeal and in some measure spiritual medium."—*Tr.*

(*ccc*) p. 335. Ib. p. 348. "But they (the lofty works of antiquity) are just as unapproachable; nay, they are more unapproachable than the works of Nature; they leave us colder even than those do; unless we bring with us the spiritual eye to pierce through the husk or veil, and perceive the operative energy within them."—*Tr.*

(*ddd*) p. 336. Ib. p. 357. "When once we have abstracted from form all the Positive and Essential, it can not but appear restrictive, and, as it were, hostile in respect of the Essence; and the same theory, which called forth the false ineffective Idealistic, must, at the same time, tend to the formless in Art. Form would indeed circumscribe the Essence, if it were independent of it. But, if it exists with and through the Essence, how should it feel itself restricted through that which itself creates? Violence might be done it by a form forced on it from without, but never by that which flows from itself. On the contrary it will rest satisfied in this, and find therein its existence as self-subsistent and self-included."—*Tr.*

(*eee*) p. 336. Ib. pp. 361–2. "Winkelmann compares Beauty to water, which, drawn from the bosom of the spring, is held the purer the less taste it has. It is true that the highest Beauty is characterless; just as we say also that the Universe has no determinate dimension, neither length, nor breadth, nor depth, because it contains them all in a like infinitude; or that the Art of creative Nature is formless, because itself is subjected to no form."—*Tr.*

I have now brought forward not only every sentence in Schelling's Oration which has been adopted in the Lecture, but also, to the best of my ability, every passage to which the author can be conjectured to have *possibly* owed a suggestion. I have translated the extracts very literally with more regard to exact fidelity than to idiomatic elegance: and I am not without a hope that these specimens may induce some readers to study Schelling's refined treatise at length in the original. An English translation of it is named as one of the "Catholic Series," published by Mr. Chapman, 142, Strand. Translations are useful as aids to a rapid perusal of the originals; taken as substitutes for them they are apt in some measure, to mislead, and give a partially false coloring to that which they aim to represent.

ERRATA.

NOTES OMITTED.

pp. 105–6. "The art displayed in the character of Cleopatra is profound," and Schlegel says of this heroine: "The coquettish arts of Cleopatra are displayed without reserve: she is an equivocal creature, made up of regal pride, womanish vanity, voluptuousness, fickleness, and true attachment. Although the passion she feels and inspires is devoid of moral dignity, it yet excites interest as an invincible fascination. The lovers seem formed for each other, Cleopatra being as singular in her seductive charms as Antony in the splendor of his achievements." Vol. iv. p. 20, edit. 2. Lecture xii. now xxvi.

p. 118. "—glorious subjects; especially Henry I. &c. &c., and Henry VII." "This has been already done by Ford" a reviewer suggested, in his fine Tragedy of *Perkin Warbeck*, brought upon the stage by Macklin in a modernized form."

Of Macklin's performance this anecdote is told by Badeley, the Actor:—"I was sitting one evening at the Cider Cellar with Macklin, and incidentally observed (for I was not very deeply read in theatrical history), that I wondered there had not been a play written on the story of Perkin Warbeck. 'There has, sir,' gruffly replied Macklin. 'Indeed! and how did it succeed?' 'It was damned, sir.' 'Bless me! it must have been very ill written then—such a story! Pray, Mr. Macklin, who was the stupid author?' 'I, sir!' roared the veteran, in a tone that took away, continued Badeley, all desire to renew the conversation." Gifford's edition of Ford, vol. ii. *Introduction to Perkin Warbeck.* In the *MS. Notes to Langbaine, by Oldys*, quoted by Gifford, Macklin's "silly performance" is spoken of, as if it were no revival of Ford's play, but an original composition. It was produced in December, 1745, on occasion of the rebellion under the Pretender's eldest son; and another drama on the same story was brought out at the same time by Joseph Elderton, a young Attorney.

p. 178.—" seeming justification of our blackamoor or negro Othello." "I believe," says an anonymous critic, "in one edition of *Coryatt's Crudities* there is a drawing of the Venetian General, Othello, representing him *tawny*. Schlegel's reasons for Othello's blackness might be compared with Coleridge's against it." Schlegel's view of the subject is as follows: "What a happy mistake it was that led Shakspeare to convert 'the Moor,' under which name, in the original story, a baptized Saracen of the Northern coast of Africa was unquestionably meant, into a proper negro! We recognize in Othello the wild nature of that burning zone, which produces the most violent beasts of prey, and the deadliest poisons, subdued in appearance only by love of fame, by foreign laws of honor, and by nobler and milder manners. His jealousy is not that jealousy of the heart which is compatible with the tenderest sensibility and devotedness toward the beloved object; it is that sensual frenzy, which in torrid climes has produced the unworthy confinement of women and other unnatural usages. A drop of this poison shed in his veins sets his whole blood in a ferment. The Moor appears noble, open, confiding, grateful for the love shown him;—and he *is* all this; and, furthermore, he is a hero, who despises danger, a worthy commander of armies, a true servant of the state; but in a moment the mere physical force of passion overthrows all his acquired and habitual virtues, and gives the upper hand to the savage over the cultivated man in his nature. Even in the expression of his rage to revenge himself on Cassio, the despotism of the blood over the will betrays itself. At last, in his repentance, a genuine tenderness for his murdered wife and anguish from the sense of honor destroyed speak out of him in presence of the witnesses of his deed: and in the midst of all this he falls upon himself with the fury with which a tyrant tortures a rebellious slave. He suffers, like a double man, at once in the higher and the lower sphere into which his being is divided." Vol. iii. pp. 288, 9. Lecture xii. (xxv.)

p. 291.—" the crusading armaments." There must have been some mistake in the report of this passage, if not in the original conception of it; for the last crusades were undertaken in the earlier part of the thirteenth century; Dante's poetry was not produced till the beginning of the fourteenth. The error was noted in a critique on the *Lit. Rem.*

The Signature S. C. has been omitted by mistake in two or three Notes at the foot of the page.

END OF VOL. IV.

www.ingramcontent.com/pod-product-compliance
Lightning Source LLC
LaVergne TN
LVHW020921110826
845150LV00004B/733

* 9 7 8 1 4 2 5 5 5 4 9 9 6 *